The Chinese Dreamscape

300 BCE–800 CE

Harvard-Yenching Institute Monographs 122

The Chinese Dreamscape

300 BCE–800 CE

Robert Ford Campany

Published by the Harvard University Asia Center
Distributed by Harvard University Press
Cambridge (Massachusetts) and London 2020

Printed in the United States of America

The Harvard-Yenching Institute, founded in 1928, is an independent foundation dedicated to the advancement of higher education in the humanities and social sciences in Asia. Headquartered on the campus of Harvard University, the Institute provides fellowships for advanced research, training, and graduate studies at Harvard by competitively selected faculty and graduate students from Asia. The Institute also supports a range of academic activities at its fifty partner universities and research institutes across Asia. At Harvard, the Institute promotes East Asian studies through annual contributions to the Harvard-Yenching Library and publication of the *Harvard Journal of Asiatic Studies* and the Harvard-Yenching Institute Monograph Series.

The Harvard University Asia Center publishes a monograph series and, in coordination with the Fairbank Center for Chinese Studies, the Korea Institute, the Reischauer Institute of Japanese Studies, and other faculties and institutes, administers research projects designed to further scholarly understanding of China, Japan, Vietnam, Korea, and other Asian countries. The Center also sponsors projects addressing multidisciplinary and regional issues in Asia.

Library of Congress Cataloging-in-Publication Data

Names: Campany, Robert Ford, 1959– author.
Title: The Chinese dreamscape, 300 BCE–800 CE / Robert Ford Campany.
Description: First. | Cambridge : Harvard University Asia Center, 2020. | Series: Harvard-Yenching Institute monographs ; 122 | Includes bibliographical references and index. |
Identifiers: LCCN 2020016040 | ISBN 9780674247796 (hardcover : acid-free paper) | ISBN 9780674247802 (paperback : acid-free paper)
Subjects: LCSH: Dreams--China--History. | Dream interpretation--China--History--To 1500.
Classification: LCC BF1078 .C279 2020 | DDC 154.6/30931--dc23
LC record available at https://lccn.loc.gov/2020016040

Index by Mary Mortensen

♾ Printed on acid-free paper

Last figure below indicates year of this printing
29 28 27 26 25 24 23 22 21 20

for Sue

When there is nothing to be grasped, a man, free of mind and breath and endowed with steadfast knowledge, becomes dissolved in the pure and supreme reality, as a lump of salt in water. He has torn asunder the web of delusion, and he sees everything as if it were a dream.

—*Laghu-Avadhūta Upaniṣad*
Translation by Patrick Olivelle

Dreaming is a longer and more lucid wakefulness. Dreaming is knowing. In addition to diurnal learning arises another, necessarily rebellious form of learning, beyond the law.

—Octavio Paz, *The Siren and the Seashell*

You and I are both things. What nonsense,
that one of us should think it is the other which is the thing!
若與予也皆物也，奈何哉其相物也！

—A certain old oak tree,
addressing a carpenter in a dream

Chinese. Chinese people or objects observed in a dream signify a satisfactory solution to all your problems. However, if the objects were damaged or the people seemed unfriendly, you may expect to make (or receive surprise guests from) a long journey.

—Robinson and Corbett, *The Dreamer's Dictionary from A to Z*

Contents

Tables

Preface

When I was a boy, on my family's bookshelves there sat a dictionary of dream symbols. It was a slender, tattered mass-market paperback. Opening it, one found single words in boldface, alphabetically arranged, each followed by a terse indication of what one's dream portended.[1] I have long since forgotten what any of its entries had to say. But I do remember the mixture of fascination, skepticism, and unease I felt each time I consulted it. The very idea that dreaming of, say, a staircase indicated some specific fortune was captivating. It meant that much of what I dreamed, rather than being the haphazard jumble it seemed, was actually a code concealing a message about what the future held in store. And it meant that the code was not peculiar to me, but transpersonal. The meanings the book assigned to dream elements were quite specific yet seemingly arbitrary, as if there were some arcane system behind them. Yet I could discern no logic or pattern in the correlations, and if they had been generated by a system, it not only went unexplained—it went unmentioned. I was left to ponder the idea that dreams are symbolic messages whose meanings are utterly non-intuitive, to put it mildly, and whose sender, if any, remained a mystery. Long after I stopped consulting the little book, its baleful-seeming blue spine continued to haunt me from among the many others on the shelf in the living room behind the piano, reminding me constantly of a strange, wonderful, spooky fact of life: that the meaning of one third of our experience as humans must remain opaque to us.

Many years later I set out to write a book about dreams and dreaming in early medieval China. The longer I worked on it, the more it became clear that there was too much rich material, and that the topic had too many facets, to be treated adequately in a single volume. So the one book became two. The one you now hold is the first. The second, titled *Dreaming and Self-Cultivation in China, 300 BCE–800 CE*, deals with the many relationships between dreams and various projects of self-cultivation. It dovetails at certain points with this one, and I refer to it now and then throughout these pages.

Acknowledgments

I am profoundly grateful to the Chiang Ching-kuo Foundation for International Scholarly Exchange for a generous Scholar Grant that sustained a semester of research leave in the spring of 2017. It is only thanks to such support that humanistic scholarship remains possible.

I thank the patient souls who turned out to hear me speak on this topic over more than a decade, at meetings of the American Academy of Religion and the Association for Asian Studies, as well as at Belmont University, the Buddhist Academy of Shanghai, Charles University (Prague), Columbia University, l'École Pratique des Hautes Études (Paris), the University of Kentucky, the Universität Leipzig, the Medieval Chinese Studies Workshop at Rutgers University organized by Wendy Swartz, Penn State University, the University of Michigan, New York University, the University of California at Berkeley, the University of California at Santa Barbara, the University of Southern California (which generously sponsored a 2009 workshop, Visions of the Night, looking cross-culturally at dreams), the University of Tennessee at Knoxville, Princeton University, Washington University in St. Louis, and Yale University.

Several colleagues have contributed encouragement, suggestions, bibliographic tips, and provocative questions. A partial list (with apologies to anyone I may have omitted) includes Robert Ashmore, Mark Csikszentmihalyi, Mick Hunter, Ed Shaughnessy, and Mayfair Yang. Anna-Alexander Fodde-Reguer, Kevin Groark, Christopher Jensen, and Brigid E. Vance kindly shared their doctoral dissertations with me. Steve Bokenkamp, Erica Fox Brindley, Anna-Alexander Fodde-Reguer, Christopher Jensen, Brigid Vance, and an anonymous reader took time away from their own writing to comment on mine.

Bob Graham and Kristen Wanner at the Publications Program of Harvard University Asia Center were lovely to work with (even through the pandemic!). Special thanks to Linda Campany, Chris Campany, Peter Haskins, Maggie Higgins, Michael Higgins, †Tovi the four-legged assistant, and especially Sue Higgins. Their unfailing love, support, and good humor have meant more to me than I can say.

RFC

Note to the Reader

Chinese characters are given where the wording is important to my argument, or where the person mentioned is an important or recurring figure. When quoting Western-language publications, romanizations of Chinese are silently converted to the Hanyu Pinyin system (except for the publications' titles). All chronological dates fall in the common era (CE) unless noted. Translations are my own except where indicated.

When referring to specific passages in Chinese texts, I follow these conventions:

- a colon (:) separates a physical volume in a set from a page number in that volume
- a period (.) separates a chapter or scroll 卷 number from a page number, even when (as is often the case) the volume in question is continuously paginated
- a slash (/) separates a chapter or scroll number from the ordinal position of the item in question in the chapter or scroll in question
- lowercase letters following page numbers indicate recto (a) and verso (b) pages or (in the case of the Taishō canon) horizontal registers (a, b, or c)
- the > sign indicates that instead of the character before the sign I am following the alternate reading given after it

Reconstructed pronunciations are usually based on Kroll, *Student's Dictionary of Classical and Medieval Chinese*, and translations of office titles are usually based on Hucker, *Dictionary of Official Titles*.

CHAPTER ONE

Mapping the Dreamscape

This is a book about dreams and dreaming in China from the end of the Warring States period to the late Tang—roughly speaking from 300 BCE to 800 CE. It does not attempt to answer the question "What did Chinese people dream about?" so much as it excavates and ponders what people thought dreaming was and, even more, what they did with and about dreams, or what roles dreams played in their lives, as reflected in texts that have come down to us.

Any such project must at once confront the question of method. How should such a topic be "mapped"? Indeed, can it be? This is not an idle question. It matters how we frame things, how we specify in words what it is we seek to know. For example, scholars often treat cultures as smoothly integrated wholes. The following formulation from Catherine Gallagher and Stephen Greenblatt would seem innocuous enough:

> We are intensely interested in tracking the social energies that circulate very broadly through a culture, flowing back and forth between margins and center, passing from zones designated as art to zones apparently indifferent or hostile to art, pressing up from below to transform exalted spheres and down from on high to colonize the low. . . . [This approach grows out of] a fascination with the entire range of diverse expressions by which a culture makes itself manifest.[1]

But, as Caroline Levine responds,

> That "a culture" should have a "center" and an "entire range of diverse expressions" implies a wholeness, a unity; that it is crisscrossed by "social energies" that "circulate" and "flow" suggests that there can be no apprehension of culture without networked movement. The "culture" that is

the focus of historicist cultural studies emerges here as precisely a harmonious cooperation of network and whole.[2]

And so let me begin by laying this card on the table: When it comes to thinking and writing about the history of religions and cultures, by default I reject the assumption that there was only one system-like theory or account of anything—especially anything as nebulous as dreams. Anthropologists have found that conflicting theories of dreaming flourish side by side even in small-scale communities,[3] and historians have shown how noted intellectuals' accounts of dreaming vary according to context.[4] Perhaps this will surprise only system-seeking academics. In China (as in any other society) we find no single, universally assumed theory of dreams, but rather a hodgepodge of disparate, even conflicting theories (and plenty of vague ideas that don't even rise to the level of theories)—sometimes in the same text—just as we find diverse notions of the afterlife, or views on the existence and nature of spirits, or theories about the efficacy of sacrificial offerings, or *arguments* about many other things besides. This messiness, rather than posing a problem to be overcome or explained away, constitutes an aspect of what we seek to understand.

It's well known that China has been home to a small set of "traditions" or "isms." Perhaps, then, surveying their respective canons for relevant passages would yield up the Buddhist, the Daoist, the Confucian, and the "folk" view of dreaming. These could then be set side by side and compared.[5] The problem with proceeding in this way isn't just that there was never one single, standard Buddhist or Daoist attitude toward something as ubiquitous as dreams, though that is certainly and quite obviously true, as we will see. Nor is it just that, say, Daoists' fixed set of "beliefs" about dreaming can't be assumed to have been completely and straightforwardly reported in the texts chosen for inclusion in this or that compendium.[6] The baseline problem is the unconsidered use of a particular model for conceiving of individuals' relationships to "traditions." It will not do to assume a syllogism along the lines of "Buddhists believed X about dreams. P 'was a Buddhist.' Therefore P believed X about dreams." "Buddhists," say, were not Buddhists only. Their Buddhism was not an identity-dye that indelibly colored every fiber of their being and every facet of their experience, least of all their dream lives and their waking approaches to them. Rather, people who were engaging with the repertoire of ideas and practices we call "Buddhism" were living alongside others in far-flung land areas now known as China.[7] From Jiaozhou to Dunhuang, they shared with other people of many persuasions what we might think of as *a Sino-cosmopolis*, or, to use Alexander Beecroft's term, a Panhuaxia, entailing, at a minimum, a shared writing system, a common if loose and variegated set of old and revered texts, and the many key terms, values, genres, macronarratives, writing practices, and personages that were baked into that writing system and those texts.[8]

Surveying the works produced over several centuries in that cosmopolis, we find multiple understandings regarding dreams. Yet if we read across those texts with our own questions in mind (more on these questions in a moment), a certain shape emerges: the Chinese might have called it an implicit patterning (*li* 理, the veins visible in translucent stone). The understandings of dreams that we find in the archive are not as numerous as the passages in which they are reflected.[9] And—here is the important point—that patterning cuts across and underlies all the familiar "isms." It has its seams and fissures, but they do not correspond at all to the container-like "isms" that run rampant in academic textbooks and curricula. The situation resembles the one described by Jonathan Z. Smith as bedeviling the study of the religions of the Late Antique Mediterranean:

> Much will depend on the framing of the issue. The traditional vague terminology of "Early Christianity," "Jewish," "Gentile," "Pagan," "Greco-Oriental," etc. will not suffice. Each of these generic terms denote[s] complex plural phenomena. For purposes of comparison, they must be disaggregated and *each component compared with respect to some larger topic of scholarly interest*. That is to say, *with respect to this or that feature, modes of Christianity may differ more significantly between themselves than between some mode of one or another Late Antique religion*. The presupposition of "holism" is not "phenomenological," it is a major, conservative, theoretical presupposition which has done much mischief in the study of religious materials, nowhere more so than in the question of Christian "origins."[10]

My approach has therefore been to select a "larger topic of scholarly interest"—dreams and dreaming—and to develop a small set of questions that get at "this or that feature" by allowing us to pinpoint non-obvious differences and similarities. This takes us behind the surfaces of what texts say to see how aspects of dream-related thought or practice *worked* and *what work* they allowed to be done with dreams.

The patterning that is made evident in this way I call a *dreamscape*. This is hardly a household word, so I had better say something about how I intend it, especially since it seems to have propagated its way through a surprising range of contexts in recent decades.[11] It is the title, for example, of not one but two sci-fi cinematic thrillers, a play, several recorded musical albums and songs, and a foundation dedicated to making the world accessible to people with disabilities. It figures in the titles of more than a dozen books, as well as in the names of a series of virtual-reality immersive experiences available at theaters, an online gaming platform, a record label, and a German progressive metal band, and is sometimes used as a general term for dream scenes in cinema. In her elegant study of the role of dreams in Ottoman biographies, Asli Niyazioğlu seems to mean by dreamscape the total array of things dreams were about in Ottoman society—their *contents*—although the reader is left to infer this from her passing uses.[12] Ling Hon Lam centrally positions "dreamscape" in his study of the emergence of what he terms "theatricality" in late imperial China, although I confess I am unable to discern what he means by it.[13]

In any event, here is what I do *not* mean by dreamscape: I do not mean the imaginary topography or landscape experienced, seen, or traversed within some dreamer's dream (or an aggregate of such landscapes garnered from multiple dream accounts).[14] Nor do I mean merely the *contents* of dreams reported in extant records. Rather, by dreamscape I mean the shape or structure of the things extant texts had to say about dreams over the centuries in question—a sort of *imaginaire* of dreams, the total array of the types of things dreams were thought to be, whether and how they carried significance, what was made of them, what they were used for, how they were responded to. I think of this book as a *mapping* of the dreamscape of China in the period indicated, and what I mean by mapping is a sketching of the shape of the topic, that is, a laying out of the array of ideas and practices involving dreams, heuristically imagined as if it were a geographic terrain with a variegated set of features and topoi.

Before we proceed, it bears emphasizing that this dreamscape both was and is a *made* and not a *found* thing; it is not something that enjoys "own being," as Buddhists might say. This is true in two senses. First, like any other big bundle of ideas and practices—notions of the afterlife, say—the dreamscape was a made thing in that it was constructed gradually by innumerable hands over centuries as people (many of whom will forever remain unknown to us individually) dreamed, thought and talked and wrote and read about dreams, used dreams and dreaming for various practical and rhetorical purposes, and ultimately collected, edited, repurposed, and disseminated written texts having to do with dreams. Second, the dreamscape is a made thing in that this mapping is my creation based on what I have found in the archive of extant texts. It is a product, that is, of my interaction with the sources. How well it is made, how useful it is, must depend, of course, on the extent to which readers deem it to have illuminated the topic and the source texts. But I can plead that while discerning a set of patterns running through the texts, I have nevertheless stressed variety, complexity, indeterminacy, and ambiguity in order to avoid the essentialist trap of "treating sources separated by hundreds or even thousands of years of history as complementary pieces" fitting ever so smoothly "in the great pattern of Chinese civilization," as Haun Saussy rightly charges the brilliant sinologist Marcel Granet (1884–1940) with having done.[15]

Here, then, are the questions I have borne in mind when reading through the archive. In any given text or group of texts, what is imagined to happen in dreaming? What was done with dreams? How were they responded to? What were they used for? What other elements of life were they set in relation to? In short, what, in any given case, was made of dreams, as a function of what they were thought to be?

I have found there to be at least five clusters of answers to these questions, each of them discernible in a wide swath of materials produced in multiple communities, traditions, centuries, and genres. For convenience, I will term these clusters *paradigms*. Although they exhibit a bit more looseness than that word might suggest to some readers, each cluster does have a logic that helps bind its parts into a stable formation.

The exorcistic paradigm: The dream is an assault, an incursion, by an exogenous being. The frequent response involves ritual action, embedded in a semiotic process, through which the dream agent is driven off and in theory prevented from returning, often by appeal to a third party. This ritual response has a performative character, in several senses: it includes "performative utterances"[16] designed to effect (not just describe) what is spoken; the speaker wielding the ritual assumes a distinctive role, performing the identity of someone empowered to issue commands to intruding spirits; and the ritual changes, or claims to change, a state of affairs in the world.

The prospective paradigm: What appears in dreams is a code, meaning that dreams aren't really about what they appear to be about. The signs comprised in dreams must be interpreted by someone. When interpreted, only selected aspects of the dream count. The yield is almost always a prediction. Dream interpretation is thus a class of divination. Neither the dream nor the interpretation is performative in nature. (What this means will become clearer by contrast with some other paradigms.)

The visitation paradigm: Dreams are face-to-face encounters with other beings across some ontological, spatial, or taxonomic gap. The encounter is direct, not in code. Some message is delivered; something changes as a result of the dream. Often a transfer of gifts, or else retribution for wrongs, takes place through the dream. The dream is a real event in the world, not a meta-statement about the world. It is performative in this sense.

The diagnostic paradigm: The dream concerns aspects of the dreamer. It indicates the nature and origin of a problem (medical or otherwise) within the dreamer. Dreams thus open access to an otherwise hidden domain within the dreaming subject. The dream is usually in code, not direct. Interpretation is thus required, and the work done by texts of this paradigm is primarily to provide keys for such interpretation.

The spillover paradigm: The dreamer is a self-cultivator of some sort, and the dream is understood from that point of view. The dream itself is a continuation of waking cultivational activity. The dream is almost always a direct encounter, not coded. The dream has a performative character, in more than one sense: the dreamer through the dream performs the new identity being shaped by his self-cultivational practice; the dream advances the practice; the dreamer is not simply a passive witness to the dream. Dreams may be actively sought through practices of incubation.[17]

I stress that these paradigms were not thought up independently of the texts and then imposed on them. Rather, they emerged from the process of pondering the questions above in relation to the texts. They may fit some particular cases rather loosely, and there may be mentions of dreams that do not fit any of them. But each paradigm seems to cohere rather well. And I think this array of paradigms helps us make sense of the massive jumble of relevant material preserved in the archive.[18]

"We"

Dreaming has been a difficult topic to write about, for several reasons. Most obviously, there is the inherent elusiveness, strangeness, and ephemerality of dreaming itself. (I am intentionally not adopting as my own, or for purposes of this study, any one of the "modern" or "scientific" views of dreaming or its evolutionary function. If pressed, I would say simply that it's a type of imagination during sleep.)[19] It would be hard enough to write something cogent about one's own dreams; writing about dreaming in a distant land two millennia ago is something else again. Then there is the overwhelming quantity of relevant Chinese material, combined with its often fragmentary, partial nature. In the archive we find innumerable mentions of dreams but surprisingly few sustained discussions of the topic. But there is also the question of a researcher's own stance toward the topic and the material; that is, there is a question of authorial voice. The way I approach the subject, the bits of evidence I've selected, and what I say about them all inevitably reflect not only the limits of my own knowledge—that much is true of any scholarly project—but also my own initial assumptions about the phenomenon of dreaming itself. For it was these assumptions that largely determined what struck me as notable or trivial, surprising or commonplace, in the Chinese archive. And yet the process of researching and writing this book has also changed my own view of dreaming, just as several other researchers have written of having their views on dreaming changed by their experiences in the field.[20] Inescapably, then, I find I am a character in the story this book tells. Let me explain.

When one is writing about another culture and time, one finds many things that seem unremarkable, but one is also struck by things that seem unfamiliar or surprising. For one is always implicitly (or explicitly) comparing one's own assumptions to those found in the other culture's archive. One may be surprised not only at how certain questions were answered but also at questions that didn't get asked at all, dogs that didn't bark in the night. This sort of outsider's surprise is an indispensable research tool. Surprise occasions thought. It points to places where one might usefully sink a shovel and dig further, deepening one's understanding of the other culture while revising one's own starting assumptions.[21] As Marshall Sahlins has put it, "Like ethnography itself, an anthropology of history requires that one get outside the culture at issue, the better to know it."[22] He elaborates on the point by quoting a passage from Mikhail Bakhtin to this effect:

> There is an enduring image, that is partial, and therefore false, according to which to better understand a foreign culture one should live in it, and, forgetting one's own, look at the world through the eyes of this culture. . . . To be sure, to enter in some measure into an alien culture and look at the world through its eyes, is a necessary moment in the process of its understanding; but if understanding were exhausted at this moment, it would have been no more than a single duplication, and would have brought nothing new or enriching. *Creative understanding* does not renounce its self, its place in time, its culture; it does not forget anything. The chief matter of understanding is the *exotopy* of the one who does the understanding—in time, space, and culture—in relation to that which he wants to understand creatively. Even his own external aspect is not really accessible to [a] man, and he cannot interpret it as a whole; mirrors and photographs prove of no help; a man's external aspect can be seen and understood only by other persons, thanks to their spatial exotopy, and thanks to the fact that they are *other*.
>
> In the realm of culture, exotopy is the most powerful lever of understanding. It is only to the eyes of an *other* culture that the alien culture reveals itself more completely and more deeply (but never exhaustively, because there will come other cultures, that will see and understand even more).[23]

In other words, as Sahlins sums up the point, "It takes another culture to know another culture."[24]

So far so good, for our present purposes. But midway through the process of making this book I realized that a fly had landed in the exotopy ointment. The more I found myself characterizing aspects of the Chinese dreamscape as "liable to surprise us" or "different from what we are accustomed to," and the more I attributed views of dreaming to "modern dreamers" or simply to "us," the more uneasy I became. Who was the "we" whose reactions I assumed would resemble my own? What was "our" view of dreaming, a view that would stand in illuminating contrast to the ones I was writing about? It takes another culture to know another culture, but here what was happening was that another culture was revealing to me my ignorance about my own culture. Having started out unconsciously assuming that most of my readers thought about dreams more or less the way I did, I came to realize that although I had learned something about old Chinese views of dreaming, I was still abysmally ignorant of contemporary North American, European, and for that matter Asian views.[25] A "rhetoric of common sense"[26] about what dreaming is or why (and whether) it matters, I realized, was not viable. The problem, therefore, was not simply that "we [historians] must . . . prepare ourselves for the possibility that these people whose lives we are sharing for the moment are not necessarily earlier versions of ourselves whom we can know just by knowing ourselves."[27] It was also that I couldn't assume my contemporary readers were other versions of me, either, when it came to their dream lives and to their views on what dreaming is, and whether and how dreams matter.

My first attempts to remedy my ignorance of my audience took the form of several unscientific polls of friends on social media. From these I was quite surprised to learn that although I myself couldn't recall ever having had a dream that later turned out to have precisely foretold a future event, many friends had. Although I had never in a dream experienced myself as being another person, or a member of another species, some friends had. Although I had never dreamed of being spoken to in human speech by an animal, some friends had.[28] Gradually I realized that although some writers have generalized my own rather impoverished assumptions across the entirety of "the West" or "modernity"—in statements such as "Western culture deems dreams as meaningless"[29] or "Culturally we are a dream deprived society"[30]—there actually exists a much more variegated set of attitudes toward, and experiences of, dreaming even among people I know personally. So I cast about for studies of these attitudes and experiences—studies, that is, of the views of dreaming held by contemporary, ordinary North Americans or

Europeans, not by professional psychologists or neuroscientists. Frustrated by the apparent lack of any engaging, large-scale monograph on this unexpectedly rich topic,[31] I nonetheless stumbled across a wealth of smaller social scientific studies. These confirmed that my own (since partially abandoned) view of dreams as primarily having to do with myself, my own anxieties and memories and hopes, and as insignificant to anyone but me, are not necessarily representative of my own culture or of members of other contemporary cultures in the developed world.

For example, one survey of attitudes toward dreams held by students from the United States, South Korea, and India found that a majority of subjects treat the content of their dreams as more meaningful than the content of waking thoughts. This same study noted that many respondents think some of their dreams provide insight into future events. Yet it is telling that the study's authors, unable to square this belief with their own assumptions (which more closely resemble the ones I started with), were quite confident in writing it off: "Horrible dreams about plane crashes might be evidence that someone is anxious about a meeting they are scheduled to attend, but such dreams are certainly not evidence that a plane crash is imminent."[32] (Dreams can't be taken as predicting future events, after all, if their only possible topic is the dreamer herself—postcards from the dreamer to the dreamer about the dreamer. Deena Newman has pointed out that although divination thrives in the contemporary West, "anthropologists have failed to write about diviners' experience because their own beliefs have prevented them from recognizing any such thing as that experience.")[33]

Over half the subjects surveyed in another study believe that the dead "can actually visit us in dreams."[34] More than half the subjects of a study based in modern Tehran indicated they believe dreams carry important messages.[35] Upwards of 80 percent of respondents in another study saw dreams as containing important information.[36] One study turned up more than one hundred cases of mutual dreams (two or more persons having the same dream at the same time) reported by speakers of English.[37] Several surveys point to a gender difference across multiple cultures: contemporary women are more likely than men to recall and share their dreams, and to attribute significance to them or seek to interpret them.[38] Taken together, these survey-based studies were of course partial, based on an aggregate of perhaps no more than seven thousand subjects in several contemporary cultures,[39] but they sufficed to indicate this much with certainty: that my own view of dreaming, limited and impoverished as it was, could in no way serve as a gauge of what my readers might find surprising in the Chinese archive.

But there was more. I realized I had ensnared myself in a familiar trap: the myth of disenchantment, partly rooted in Max Weber's ambivalent and complex notion of *Entzauberung*, which is synonymous neither with secularization nor with rationalization.[40] That is, having imagined that "our" entire modernity shared my own narrow and impoverished view of dreaming, I slipped into thinking in all too contrastive, binary terms about the premodern, non-Western Other that is ancient and medieval China.[41] Charles Taylor has captured some of the myth's key elements, though he himself doesn't seem to view it as myth but rather as fact:

> Everyone can agree that one of the big differences between us and our ancestors of 500 years ago is that they lived in an "enchanted" world and we do not. We might think of this as our having "lost" a number of beliefs and the practices they made possible. Essentially, we become modern by breaking out of "superstition" and becoming more scientific and technological in our stance toward our world. But I want to accentuate something different. The "enchanted" world was one in which spirits and forces defined by their meanings (the kinds of forces possessed by love potions or relics) played a big role. But more, the enchanted world was one in which these forces could shape our lives, both psychical and physical. One of the big differences between our forerunners and us is that we live with a much firmer sense of the boundary between self and other. We are "buffered" selves. *We* have changed.[42]

Palliatives have been offered to this macronarrative of modernity's disenchantment. Jane Bennett, to mention a single writer, has pointed to "survivals," as it were (not her term), of enchantment on this side of the supposed gulf between our era and all that went before.[43] Her project is, I take it, meant to comfort us in our arid modernity. But others have rejected the entire disenchantment trope as a strange modern myth, a story we tell ourselves about ourselves that is massively belied by evidence. As Bruno Latour puts it, "Haven't we shed enough tears over the disenchantment of the world? Haven't we frightened ourselves enough with the poor European who is thrust into a cold soulless cosmos, wandering on an inert planet in a world devoid of meaning?"[44] Jason Josephson-Storm has compiled an impressive dossier of counter-evidence, arguing that "these new philosophers [such as Bennett], like the poststructuralists they seek to replace, are rebelling against a hegemon that never achieved full mastery. The enchanted ontologies and spiritualized orientations to nature they describe as missing have been available all along."[45] It turns out that my own society and the others to which most of my readers belong have a much more vibrant set of ideas about dreaming than I had realized. I was the one who was disenchanted.

And so I was at grave risk of treating Chinese views of dreaming as an "own Other," a reversed image of my own views on the subject. As Haun Saussy has pungently asked, "Is the point of the Chinese case to furnish the counterfactual to a story made and told elsewhere?"[46] "China," he observes, "most often enters discourse as the countercase to an essentialized West, the West being the one possible source of those magnificent burdens or crippling illusions to which the vision of China puts an end. (For 'the West,' we may read 'modernity'—and deal with the essentialism all over again.)"[47] In the course of writing this book I have accordingly tried to de-essentialize my views of modern Western views of dreams, as well as coming to have different views of my own on the nature of dreaming.[48] I have also avoided treating all of the Chinese materials examined here as uniformly indicative of one single "Chinese" view of dreaming, instead emphasizing their variety. And I've avoided lumping "modern/Western" and "Chinese" views respectively into one big dyad, in part by mentioning along the way textual, historical, and anthropological examples from other societies and cultures, so as to situate both sets of views into a much larger field of possibilities. But at the end of the day one must write from some particular perspective; one must write as someone in particular at some particular time. And perhaps some, at least, of my readers will open this book with the same assumptions I myself initially had, that dreaming is rather isolated from the rest of our lives, that it's a merely mental event, something confined to the dreamer's own head and involving no one else, usually of little real significance to anyone (even ourselves) and unlikely to be shared except as a mere curiosity among a small circle of intimates. So I have purposely left intact some of the initial framing and some of my expressions of wonder and surprise. With Saussy I plead, "in mitigation for my own indulgences, that each chapter has been written with a built-in record of its own process of construction, in the belief than an artefact duly signed and dated has nothing to apologize for. (I follow astronomers in using 'artefact' to mean a distortion of representation caused by the means of representation.)"[49]

At a workshop where I compared the category "religious" to certain indigenous Chinese concepts, I was once issued a challenge: Could my paper be rendered into Chinese? The point, as I understood it, was either that my argument was too enmeshed in Western categories and terminology to even be translated intelligibly, or that if it were translated, it would have lost its point. If we imagine the same question transposed to this book you are holding, my answer would be this: yes, the work could be translated into Chinese, and what would be translated is not a set of assertions made from no particular point of view but rather the record of the *process* of making sense of certain material by a person with certain particular presuppositions, starting points, blind spots, capacities, and incapacities. Readers of the translation might in turn be surprised at what I'm surprised at. Or they might share my surprise—perhaps for the same reasons I had, or for different ones. In any case, there is no eye in the sky through which we serenely and neutrally contemplate the history below on earth. Each of us who write writes as someone, from some place and some time in particular. The idea that any conceivable scholar should or could note the same things of any set of data is positivist nonsense. But the data are there to check our work against, and there are scholarly communities to do the checking.

Dreams and Alterity

At the heart of this book is the difficult question of how we are to understand the relationship between dreams and culture. Are dreams always only "expressions" of the culture and society to which their dreamers belong? For us as historians, is culture the limit of what dreams must be about? Are they "cultural" all the way down? Are they reducible to reflections of social processes? Or are we to allow dreams a certain force of their own, not limited to the cultural—a certain alterity, a surplus, something not always fully assimilable?

As a way into the problem, consider some ruminations on visual artifacts by anthropologist Christopher Pinney, who observes that for sociology as conceived in the tradition of Emile Durkheim, "the artifact becomes an empty space, of interest only because of the 'meanings' that invest it with significance. In the battle between the object world and the world of human relations, it is the latter which (through a circular procedure) inevitably triumphs. [As Bruno Latour writes]: 'To become a social scientist is to realize that the inner properties of objects do not count, that they are mere receptacles for human categories.'"[50] Pinney continues, "The fate of objects in the [Arjun] Appadurai and [Nicholas] Thomas accounts is always to live out the social life of men, or to become entangled in the webs of culture whose ability to refigure the object simultaneously inscribes culture's ability to translate things into signs and the object's powerlessness as an artifactual trace."[51] In other words,

> Because it has [been] decided in advance that these images are a visual manifestation of an ideological force,[52] [textual historiography] is unable to catch hold of the ways in which *the materiality of representation creates its own force field.* Consequently, a very straightforward Durkheimianism emerges in which the image somehow draws together and exemplifies . . . everything which can be identified as potentially determining it, and which the historian wishes to have deposited in the image as the validation of his or her supposition.[53]

By contrast, Pinney "refuses to use images as illustrations of something already established elsewhere and asks whether it is possible to envisage history as in part determined by struggles occurring at the level of the visual."[54] To this end he introduces the concept of *torque*, by which he means an object's resistance to being simply a blank screen onto which social meanings can be projected:

> If the understanding of images' "social life" stresses their malleability, their suppleness in the face of changing time and place, I would like to reintroduce the presence, "tension" (as a limit to tensility), or "torque" of the image and explore the ways in which its time is never necessarily that of the audience. . . . Clearly there is a dialectical process of (what

> heuristically we might term) subjects making objects making subjects. But to stress the smoothness of this dialectical process is to take us back to the "national (or cultural) time-space" of eighteenth-century Germany.[55] I would rather stress instead the disjunctures and fractures in this process and the likelihood of uncontemporaneous practices in which . . . there are . . . objects never fully assimilable to any "context."[56]

What Pinney says about artifacts (minus its exclusive focus on temporality) I venture to say about dreams. It would be too easy, I think, to see dreams as just more manifestations of the culture of their time, a culture we feel we have already come to grips with by other means. It would be too simple to see them as mere reflections of social structures or tensions, as if society were all dreams had to be about. I think it is important to respect them (at least sometimes) as stubbornly unassimilable, intrinsically strange, resistant to digestion, a persistently pinging reminder of alterity.[57] Like Lucretius' figure of the *clinamen* or the unpredictable swerve taken by falling particles, dreams swoop into waking life at an angle, potentially introducing turbulence.[58] This, I think, is why some languages feature special grammatical markers or "domain-specific dream language[s]" or "dream tongues"[59] used only when narrating dreams: they occupy a zone that is epistemologically and ontologically distinct.[60] Dreams bring alterity into human subjectivity.[61] As Douglas Hollan has observed, "Dreams are not rigidly determined by cultural processes. People do not merely register or reproduce cultural meanings and beliefs in their dreams; they use, manipulate, and transform these . . . resources in . . . creative . . . ways."[62] "Anthropologists have often concentrated on how dreams are culturally patterned and socially interpreted. . . . The . . . tendency has been to treat dreams as social facts and cultural texts. . . . The only danger here is that we may become so comfortable with the idea of dreams as cultural constructions that . . . we disregard dreams as experiences," warns Charles Stewart.[63] And as Waud Kracke writes, "Dreams are the most obstinate stumbling block to our secure knowledge that we 'know' the world around us, that we all share the same experience of it and of each other."[64] One author even compares the challenges in reporting on our own dreams to those facing anthropologists trying to make sense of other cultures.[65] While it may be true that some dream reports culled from any given time and place will "conform to the dream genres of the day,"[66] and that there are such things as "typical" dreams,[67] not all dreams conform and not all are typical, whether measured against each other or against waking life. David Linden points out that

> The most useful thing about the *experience* of dreaming . . . is not the detailed content of dreams. It's not so crucial that you dream of a cigar rather than a shoe, or of your father rather than your mother. What's most important about dreaming is that it allows you to experience a world where the normal waking rules don't apply, where causality and rational thought and our core cognitive schemas . . . melt away in the face of bizarre and illogical stories. And, while you dream, you accept these stories as they unfold. Essentially, the experience of narrative dreams[68] allows you to imagine explanations and structures that exist outside of your waking perception of the natural world. In your waking life you may embrace the distorted structures of the dream world or you may be a hard-headed rationalist, or you may blend the two (as most of us do), but in all cases the experience of dreaming has thrown back the curtain and allowed you to imagine a world where fundamentally different rules apply.[69]

Dreams have anomalousness built into them, in several ways: we have experiences of the sort we have while awake, yet we are asleep, our bodies more or less immobile. We interact with familiar people and animals who are no longer alive. We see people now old as young. In fact, time is obliterated.[70] All sorts of things deemed impossible in waking life occur regularly in dreams. Sometimes while having these experiences we realize we are dreaming. And even when a dream is mundane, there is the jarring experience of waking up to find we were "only" dreaming, and when we tell of our dreams we are acutely aware that our words cannot do them justice. "Dreams have an aspect that is in principle ineffable. . . . Dreams are always groomed to be tellable at the expense of their original, often chafingly mysterious, atmosphere."[71] Even the most quotidian dreams therefore have a touch of the uncanny about them. And we are not the only species who dream, as anyone who has ever spent time with a dog or a cat well knows.

One thing this book is about, then, is people's attempts to wrestle with the alterity of dreams, their striving to see them instead as comprehensible signs. Taken raw, dreams can act as menacing things with teeth. The response, whatever it is, often seems like an attempt to defang dreams. We see this most clearly in those texts where the dream is configured as an exogenous agent presumed to be up to no good (at least not *our* good). If the dream was an Other, the responder's first instinct was to name it and drive it off. But schemes of interpretation, too, were a way to cool down the hot alterity of dreams by means of semiosis. Dream semiotics was a locative enterprise. (What's meant by "locative" is explained a few pages below.) Seen in this light, the archive amounts in part to a record of many people's attempts to smooth over, semiologize, incorporate, and render meaningful and/or non-threatening the strangeness that is dreams. But meanwhile others wanted to accentuate that strangeness to wage certain kinds of arguments, as we will see, and their efforts, too, made it into the archive.

Of course, we do not have direct access to other people's dreams. (We don't even have direct access to our own dreams except while we are dreaming them.) It is not dreams themselves we study, but the written traces of representations of dreams that have survived down to our time.[72] We study accounts of dreams that were couched and framed as they were for certain persuasive purposes. But there is more. Each and every dream account or dream-related text that we have, we have because it was shared with other people and because it was received, taken up, and transmitted in turn by yet other people. It is not simply written accounts of dreams we study, but written accounts of dreams that were deemed worthy by people other than the dreamer of being preserved. We study the records and results of the *responses* to dreams—oneiric reception history. The history of dreams is, and can only be, the history of the reception of particular dreams or of reflections about dreams in general and what we might do with them. Some of this archive of reception can be seen as attempts to tamp down the alterity of dreams, other parts of it as attempts to highlight that alterity.

And so however mysterious dreams themselves might be, and however solitary dreaming itself might be (although, as we'll see, many Chinese views of dreaming didn't portray it as solitary at all), telling and interpreting dreams were acts situated very much in this world, in one's social circles, by means of narrative and language. The processes by which meaning was created from dreaming were social processes. They were interlocutory, intersubjective, and interactive. Dreams are intrinsically strange, but they are not an idiolect. They are built out of imagery and language drawn from the shared world of society, because humans are social beings. They are also built out of bits of the physical environment, because humans are embodied beings who live in constant interaction with their surroundings. In dreaming, or at least in telling our dreams to ourselves and to others once we're awake, we don't reinvent the wheel: we fabricate new scenes in which wheels figure. Our dreams might impact the shared waking world in tiny or large ways. Their significance might be assessed by us or by others in communities of discourse according to shared means of interpretation. And finally, for the historian or even for the anthropologist, others' dreams are only accessible through their public accounts of them. I will return to questions of reception and social memory toward the end of chapter 4.

Dreaming and Animism Revisited

From the inception of modern theorizing about religion, dreaming has held a key place in it. Indeed, for Edward Burnett Tylor dreaming was one of only two phenomena (the other being death) that sparked the very origin of religion. Tylor's theory is well known, but I want to revisit the famous passage in which he draws his connections, not to beat the dead horse of nineteenth-century "evolutionary" anthropology and comparative religion but to illuminate, from a somewhat oblique angle, one of the things my own book is about.

The passage, published in 1871:

> It seems as though thinking men, as yet at a low level of culture, were deeply impressed by two groups of biological problems. In the first place, what is it that makes the difference between a living body and a dead one; what causes waking, sleep, trance, disease, death? In the second place, what are those human shapes which appear in dreams and visions? Looking at these two groups of phenomena, the ancient savage philosophers probably made their first step by the obvious inference that every man has two things belonging to him, namely, a life and a phantom. These two are evidently in close connexion with the body, the life as

> enabling it to think and feel and act, the phantom as being its image or second self; both, also, are perceived to be things separable from the body, the life as able to go away and leave it insensible or dead, the phantom as appearing to people at a distance from it. The second step would seem also easy for savages to make, seeing how extremely difficult civilized men have found it to unmake. It is merely to combine the life and the phantom. As both belong to the body, why should they not also belong to one another, and be manifestations of one and the same soul? Let them then be considered as united, and the result is that well-known conception which may be described as an apparitional-soul, a ghost-soul. This, at any rate, corresponds with the actual conception of the personal soul or spirit among the lower races, which may be defined as follows: It is a thin unsubstantial human image, in its nature a sort of vapour, film, or shadow; the cause of life and thought in the individual it animates, independently possessing the personal consciousness and volition of its corporeal owner, past or present; capable of leaving the body far behind, to flash swiftly from place to place; mostly impalpable and invisible, yet also manifesting physical power, and especially appearing to men waking or asleep as a phantasm separate from the body of which it bears the likeness; continuing to exist and appear to men after the death of that body; able to enter into, possess, and act in the bodies of other men, of animals, and even of things.[73]

These are, he goes on to write, "doctrines answering in the most forcible way to the plain evidence of men's senses, as interpreted by a fairly consistent and rational primitive philosophy. So well, indeed, does primitive animism account for the facts of nature, that it has held its place into the higher levels of education."[74]

The first thing to note about this passage is that it emerged not just from Tylor's reading of accounts by missionaries and colonial administrators, but also from his attendance at London spiritualist séances, as evidenced in a diary he kept that was discovered only in 1969.[75] For Tylor, spiritualism represented the *survival* of this low level of culture into his own day and his own society; "the received spiritualistic theory of the alleged phenomena belongs to the philosophy of savages."[76] Yet in his diary he wrote, of one display of spirit writing he witnessed, "I think it was genuine, & afterwards, I myself became drowsy & seemed to the others about to go off likewise. To myself I seemed partly under a drowsy influence, and partly consciously shamming, a curious state of mind which I have felt before & which is very likely the incipient stage of hysterical simulation."[77] Tylor came close to succumbing to enchantment by what he saw as the vestiges of an earlier stage of culture still very much alive in his own time and place, vestiges he saw it as the duty of his "science of culture" to "mark . . . out for destruction."[78]

The second thing to note is the implications of the explanatory trope Tylor uses. Lacking information about how the idea of "souls" actually originated in the prehistory of humans, Tylor resorts to a thought experiment of the sort dubbed by E. E. Evans-Pritchard the "if I were a horse fallacy."[79] Significant for our purposes is the specific nature of this thought experiment. Tylor posits animism as the result of a rational deduction. The deduction is made from very limited sensory evidence, notably including the evidence of dreaming. He imaginatively places primordial humans into a sort of Rawlsian "original position" behind a "veil of ignorance"[80] in which they are stripped of language and culture (crucially, culture not as Tylor understands it but as subsequent anthropologists and others have understood it)[81] yet expected to produce the same ontological inferences from their limited experience of dreaming and death as would David Hume or any other sensible British empiricist. What sort of entity must exist to render these experiences possible? Why, of course "a thin unsubstantial human image, in its nature a sort of vapour, film, or shadow," and so on.

This way of thinking did not end with Tylor. When the great Dutch sinologist Jan Jakob Maria de Groot set himself the monumental task of coming to grips with "the religious system of China," it was under the aegis of Tylorian "animism" that he did so, in volumes published from 1892 to 1910.[82] Roger Lohmann can write, "Ethnographers do repeatedly find that many peoples understand what they see on dream travels as evidence for the existence of spirits,"[83] as if the idea of spirits were only newly suggested to them by the "evidence" of their dreams, or as if they waffled on the question of whether spirits actually exist but were then persuaded by oneiric evidence. Yang Jianmin and Fu Zhenggu, both quoting a passage from Friedrich Engels' *Ludwig Feuerbach und der Ausgang der klassischen deutschen Philosophie* (1886), make the same move.[84] Marshall Sahlins has criticized Gananath Obeyesekere's reading of the Hawaiian reception of Captain Cook along similar lines. The "condition of an objectified nature," he writes, "is not the ontology of

Hawaiian *relations* to the world. This does not mean that Hawaiians are unempirical—let alone that they privilege the 'ideal' over the 'real'—but it does mean that they draw conclusions of their own from their empirical experiences."[85] "The bodies of the god represent its *relationship* to human activities."[86] Or again:

> Because these empirical judgments . . . are mediated by a distinct way of life, they cannot be determined from naïve sensory perceptions. . . . Things are known by their relationships to a system of local knowledge, not simply as objective intuitions. . . . "Objectivity" is culturally constituted. It is always a distinctive ontology. Nor is it then some sort of hypothesis or "belief" that is likely to be shaken by this or that person's skepticism or experimental attitude. It is not a simple sensory epistemology but a total cultural cosmology that is precipitated in Hawaiian empirical judgments of divinity.[87]

Waud Kracke makes the same point: the frequency with which people contact spirits in their dreams seems to support Tylor's view, he writes, but in fact they support its converse. It's not that people who begin without the idea of spirits or souls end up creating it to explain the experience of dreaming, but rather that "dreams are a way in which the adept, whether priest or lay person, can realize in his or her personal experience the presence of the beings that, *according to the communal religion*, inhabit the cosmos. . . . [It's a matter of] how individuals make spiritual entities real for themselves in their dreams."[88]

In other words, it is not the case that people dream in an ontological and epistemological vacuum, then newly arrive at the very idea of spirits to explain their dream experience. Instead, in dreams they meet beings the idea of whom (and *relationships* with whom) already exist in their community, however much those relationships might be newly initiated, or furthered or changed, in and through dreams. Likewise, when we "moderns" "animate the computers we use, the plants we grow, and the cars we drive," to use examples discussed by Stewart Guthrie, we do not do so because of "wrong perceptual guesses"; instead, "we relationally frame them. We learn what they do in relation to what we do, how they respond to our behavior, how they act towards us, what their situational and emergent behavior (rather than their constitutive matter) is."[89] In other words, animism is actually a *relational epistemology*,[90] or "the attribution by humans to nonhumans of an interiority identical to one's own,"[91] or the recognition "that the world is full of persons, only some of whom are human, and life is always lived in relationship with others."[92] In such epistemologies, dreams play important roles in affording face-to-face encounters and other intensifications of relationships with a big range of Others. This aspect of dreaming is taken up in chapter 5.

Concepts; Roads Taken and Not Taken

Before moving into an analysis of Chinese texts I will briefly explain a few concepts that will prove useful, as well as mention a few things this book does and doesn't attempt to do, and why.

Locative vs. Utopian

Responding to Mircea Eliade's one-size-fits-all concept of the function of cosmogonic myth, Jonathan Z. Smith developed a binary typology of styles of religion. He did not propose to characterize all religions in essentialist terms but merely to delineate two contrastive tendencies that may be seen at work in some religions and cultures sometimes. His typology plays a key role (if not always a plainly visible one) in this book, so let me briefly explain it here.[93]

Without yet naming it locative/utopian, Smith first enunciated the typology in the following terms: "One finds in many archaic cultures a profound faith in the cosmos as ordered in the beginning and a joyous celebration of the primordial act of ordering as well as a deep sense of responsibility for the maintenance of that order through repetition of the [cosmogonic] myth, through ritual, through norms of conduct, or through taxonomy." (This describes what he would later term the locative style.) However, "in some cultures the structure of order, the gods that won or ordained it, creation itself, are discovered to be evil and oppressive. In such circumstances, one will rebel against the paradigms and seek to reverse their power, frequently employing . . . the very same ritual techniques which had maintained the original order." As examples of this style, which he would later term utopian, he offers yogic escape from Brahmanic ritual order and Hellenistic gnosticism's rejection of the inherited gods and cosmology. With such rejection, "liminality becomes the supreme goal rather than a moment in a rite of passage."[94]

Smith further articulated the locative type using as examples the figure of the hero-that-failed, as seen in Gilgamesh and Orpheus. In the locative type, the world is a bounded environment; "order is produced by walling, channeling, and confining" the vastness of waters or deserts. By contrast, in the utopian type,

> the structures of order are perceived to have been reversed. Rather than the positive limits they were meant to be, they have become oppressive. Man is no longer defined by the degree to which he harmonizes himself and his society to the cosmic patterns of order; but rather by the degree to which he can escape the patterns. Rather than the hero-that-failed of the locative world-view, the paradigm here is the hero-that-succeeded . . . in escaping the tyrannical order. . . . The man of wisdom is no longer the sage but the savior—he who knows the escape routes.[95]

Smith warned against reading the typology in developmental or sequential terms, with the locative always preceding the utopian.

Finally, Smith introduced "social situation" into the model—a further departure from Eliade. He warned that the very success of modern scholarship in limning locative worldviews should give us pause, because such studies often represent hierarchical societies whose "most persuasive witnesses" are the views produced by "organized, self-conscious scribal elites who had a deep vested interest in restricting mobility and valuing place." Such views, he cautioned, "ought not to be generalized into the universal pattern of religious experience and expression."[96]

I find Smith's typology useful for three reasons. First, it focuses on how people situate their own traditions vis-à-vis those of others, rather than seeing them as isolated, self-contained units that somehow develop on their own. We understand texts and practices better when we consider the things they constituted alternatives to. Second, the typology focuses on an often unremarked aspect of traditions, namely, people's stances toward order, showing us (against the commonplace structuralist and functionalist notion that religions are always essentially about maintaining order) that there are moments when rebellion against or escape from order becomes religiously valued.[97] And third, like the notion of dreamscape, it cuts across traditional isms.

Emergent Forms, Affordance, and Umwelt

Especially in chapter 5 I use "form" (and sometimes "pattern") in ways that may be unfamiliar, as well as "affordance" and *Umwelt*, likely even less familiar. All these concepts were first developed in work on semiotics.

Form always indicates, of course, "an arrangement of elements—an ordering, patterning, or shaping."[98] We often think of form as something humans uniquely impose as if from above, through their "cultures" and by intention, on "nature," a world otherwise formless. By contrast, from recent work in biosemiotics, information theory, and anthropology I draw the notion that some forms are *emergent* in the world, meaning that rather than being imposed by humans on unpatterned material, they arise from interactions among things and beings (including human beings)—they arise immanently, without there being any "director" behind or above the process. Emergent forms in this broader sense are constraints on possibility that arise from dynamic interplay among the several properties of things. They are "unprecedented relational properties, which are not reducible to any of the more basic component parts that give rise to them"[99] and which are not imposed from outside the interaction.

As an example, take Eduardo Kohn's elucidation of how, in Amazonian forests, "rubber falls into a form."[100] What does this mean? Due to specific properties of rubber trees (their need for water, their susceptibility to parasites), a set of constraints governs their possible distribution on the land: they end up widely and evenly spaced, not clumped together. The distribution of water also falls into a form: due to climatic and geographic factors water in the Amazon basin is plentiful and only flows in one direction, downhill. Thus small creeks flow into streams, which flow into smaller rivers, which flow into larger ones, and this pattern repeats itself until the Amazon empties into the Atlantic. "For largely unrelated reasons there exist, then, two patterns or forms: the distribution of rubber throughout the landscape and the distribution of waterways. . . . Therefore, wherever there is a rubber tree it is likely that nearby there will be a stream that leads to a river."

The Amazon rubber economy was essentially a massive exploitation of these interlinked patterns. Humans navigated up the river network to find rubber, then floated the trees downstream, linking physical and biological domains into an economic system. This network exhibited another regularity that was key to the form into which rubber fell: "self-similarity across scale," meaning that "a pattern at one level is nested within the same pattern at a higher more inclusive one." This network's self-similarity is unidirectional: smaller rivers flow into larger ones, not vice versa. Both the network and its unidirectionality were mirrored in the self-similar repeating pattern of creditor-debt relations that emerged during the rubber boom. "A rubber merchant located at one confluence of rivers extended credit upriver and was in turn in debt to the more powerful merchant located downriver at the next confluence. This nested pattern linked indigenous communities in the deepest forests to rubber barons at the mouth of the Amazon and even in Europe."[101]

Humans were not the only beings who harnessed this unidirectionally nested pattern linking water and plant life. Amazon river dolphins congregate at the mouths of rivers, like traders, feeding on the fish that gather there due to the nested nature of the river network. All of this patterning occurred because of the properties of the several components (rubber trees needing water and distance from other rubber trees, water branching and flowing downhill, humans seeking economic resources to exploit and amassing capital with which to do so) and their interactions and relations to one another. It *emerged* from those properties and interactions and relations, without need of any embedded homunculi directing the process from within or any agent imposing pattern from without.

J. J. Gibson introduced the concept of *affordance* in his *Ecological Approach to Visual Perception* in the 1970s. As Nurit Bird-David summarizes it, "Things are perceived in terms of what they afford the actor-perceiver because of what they are for him. Their 'affordance,' as Gibson calls it, 'cuts across the dichotomy of subjective-objective. . . . It is equally a fact of the environment as a fact of behavior. . . . An affordance points both ways, to the environment and to the observer.'"[102] For our purposes, affordance proves to be a useful concept because it cuts across the subject/object dichotomy. The view of dreaming as nothing but a mental event in the dreamer—a view I tend to bring to this subject despite my efforts to bracket it—would leave little but the dreamer for dreams to be about. To think of dreaming as an affordance is to open oneself to thinking of it differently, as a mode or vehicle of relationship between the dreamer and the dreamed, *leaving open* the question of the ultimate ontological status of what is dreamed. As we'll see in chapter 5, the ways in which dreaming was construed in many Chinese texts meant that it afforded a surprisingly wide array of possibilities.

Finally, the concept of *Umwelt* was introduced early in the twentieth century by the Estonian-born German biologist Jakob von Uexküll. A creature's *Umwelt* is "the ecological niche as *the animal itself* apprehends it."[103] In a classic and beautifully rendered passage, von Uexküll describes how the *Umwelt* of a tick consists of—and *only* of—the presence or absence of butryic acid (secreted by all mammals).[104] Counterintuitively, it is this severe *constraint* on the tick's sensitivity to its environment that allows it to function superbly as a tick. Using this notion, we can read narratives of human encounters with spirit-foxes, for example, as partial sketches of what the world is like to a spirit-fox. Every extra-human self who visited people in dreams had its *Umwelt*, whose nature was at least partially revealed through the dream encounter.

These ideas become useful for thinking about the interactions that occur in and through dreams between living human beings and other kinds of selves—deceased human beings, animals, insects, trees, and "spirits" of various sorts. One thing the concepts have in common, other than their roots in semiotic theory, is this: they insist on seeing individual beings in relation to other beings and to their environments. They emphasize that all life is semiosis, that all living things are fundamentally grounded in semiotic processes, that to engage in semiosis is to be a self (not necessarily a human self) with aims, and that "to exist as a body is to exist neither as a pure subject nor as a pure object but rather . . . in a manner that overcomes this opposition."[105] "We humans, then, are not the only ones who interpret the world. 'Aboutness'—representation, intention, and purpose in their most basic forms—is an intrinsic structuring feature of living dynamics in the biological world. Life is inherently semiotic."[106] For our purposes, these concepts will prove useful in offering ways of thinking and speaking about the dreamer *in relation to* the various other beings with whom he or she interacts in dreams—and vice versa. Where most of us are used to thinking of humans as the imposers of pattern on the neutral, formless blank slate of "nature," these concepts enable us to see the patterning of interactions among beings as something that arises between them in the context of their specific situation together in the world. Dreaming, as we'll see, played a key role in such interactions.

Some Roads Not Taken

It's easy to imagine some of the materials introduced below being plugged into a universalizing theory or interpretation mill, perhaps that of Jung or, especially, Freud. After all, we've seen the dreams of some Amazonian people unabashedly analyzed in Freudian terms, with the anthropologist gliding easily into the role of psychotherapist to his subjects;[107] the recorded dreams of Aelius Aristides (d. 181) "decoded" to reveal their "latent unconscious meaning";[108] Alexander the Great diagnosed based on his dreams as Oedipal, having a mother complex, and therefore overly driven to succeed, then criticized for being unable to recognize his dreams as warnings from his own unconscious because this "modern" view was "inaccessible" to him;[109] and an Indonesian dreamer chided for not "recogniz[ing] the manifest content of [a] dream as a product of his own imagination," as a good Freudian subject would.[110] Such universalizing theories of something as fundamental to human experience as dreams, however brilliantly conceived, are, in my view, monuments to intellectual arrogance (not to mention artefacts and tools of colonial power). They deserve to be historicized in their turn, and they have been. I occasionally mention them as examples of particular ways people have analyzed dreams, but I do not use them as vehicles for analyzing anything.[111]

Some scholars have tried to decide whether or not this or that specific dream account from ancient or medieval times represents an "actual, authentic dream experience."[112] So, for example, we find the fascinating dream record of Aelius Aristides combed through to separate his "genuine dreams" from instances of mere "literary invention," with "stereotypical religious motifs and imagery" counted as evidence of "inauthenticity."[113] There have been attempts to develop exportable criteria for judging which ancient records of dreams were actually dreamt and which were not.[114] I find this to be a fruitless path of inquiry. We cannot usefully get a handle on whether this or that dream actually occurred as reported, but we can know what work the dream record was designed to do in its own time and place, and how it was received by others. When relating specific Chinese dream accounts, therefore, I make no assertions about whether the dream was actually dreamt. Instead I am interested in how this or that dream was asserted, in a piece of writing that has survived, to have been dreamt by someone in particular.

Why did I choose the time period of the late Warring States through the end of the late Tang? To some extent the choice is arbitrary, based on nothing more than the limits of my expertise. It is also partly based on the dating of some manuscript material that I wanted to include; that material is clustered near both ends of this time span. Beyond this, I would wager that most of the important topoi on the Chinese dreamscape as it can be glimpsed through later sources had already been formed during the long time span treated here. Nevertheless, I do not argue that any big change in understandings of dreaming or in uses of dreams occurred during the span treated here, nor do I assert that nothing important changed after it. Any such change would in any case be impossible to demonstrate conclusively, given the partial quality of available evidence.[115]

I have surely scanted here the political uses of dreams—something I mention now and then but do not isolate as a topic of analysis.[116] Lucid dreaming (a widespread and fascinating phenomenon in which the dreamer is aware, as the dream is occurring, that it's a dream) gets short shrift because, with the possible exception of a few Daoist texts,[117] I have found few readily recognizable mentions of it in the archive treated here. I have paid insufficient attention to notions of sleep, although fortunately this is a topic on which Antje Richter has worked extensively.[118] I have probably also failed to do justice to the gendered aspects of dreams and dream discourse, and to other facets of the topic that might be of keen interest to readers. There is ample material for others to push further with, and I only hope my book will prove useful to them.

I must caution that this book is not intended as a *survey* of anything. I do not claim to give an exhaustive account of what was thought and written about dreams during the long period in question, or even in any given century. I do not comprehensively cover any particular genre of writing, or focus on any given text. Indeed, I'm not sure what an exhaustive account of this topic would look like. There is no shortage of texts that might have been commented on but that go unmentioned on these pages. My organization of material is driven by a set of questions, and my discussions were chosen with those questions in mind. What I hope to have provided isn't a comprehensive treatment of the dreamscape but a foray around and across it. The texts are drawn from several genres: scriptures, classics, biographies, essays, anecdotes, histories, treatises, anthologies, and poems, as well as dream interpretation manuals and other manuscripts found at Shuihudi, Dunhuang, Wangjiatai, and elsewhere. Some might object that the Chinese record regarding dreams during this period is much too fragmentary and partial to allow for any comprehensive treatment. But this is in fact something that recommends the topic to me. All records of the ancient and medieval past are fragmentary and partial: it's just that, in this case, the fact is so glaring that it can't be ignored. Like dreams themselves, the record is disjointed and multivalent. Systematicity in the material, and the hope of exhaustive "coverage" of it, are twin chimeras. Better, then, to approach the subject admitting this frankly from the start, and let the questions guide us.

There is nothing about the questions I will ask that makes them uniquely pertinent to Chinese culture. That is by design. And the reader will note that studies of other cultures are cited throughout this book, sometimes as examples paralleling (or posing useful contrasts to) Chinese passages, sometimes for the illuminating questions, categories, or phrasings used by their authors. Some might wonder why this is necessary. My answer is twofold. On the one hand, our thinking about the China case only stands to be enriched by considering what scholars of other cultures have made of dream-related materials. That is, it stands to be enriched by considering China precisely *as a case* alongside others rather than being treated, as it often has been, in isolation or as a mere Other to "the West," even if the comparisons are left implicit or undeveloped. On the other hand, the cross-cultural study of dreaming ought to be perfumed, as Buddhists might say, by the thinking, writing, and practice involving dreams in a civilization as old as that of China. It is vital that we place Chinese materials in conversation with questions, issues, and problems pertinent to the study of culture and religion broadly conceived. Both sides of the conversation have only to gain thereby.

Why This Topic

So, why write a book on this topic? In brief:

- Studying writings about dreams and dreaming allows us to glimpse some of the processes—not necessarily smooth or easy processes—by which people made meaning from their own and others' experiences.
- Views of dreaming, and records of dreams alleged to have occurred, reveal much about notions of the self and of nonhuman beings and the cosmos. Most especially they reveal ideas about the *relations* between humans and various Others. Dreaming was a zone of encounter with Others.
- Dream interpretation is a mode of divination, and divination is an important aspect of thought and practice in any society.
- Many aspects of Chinese religions and culture are shot through with bureaucratic metaphors, but dreaming is one area where this is not the case. None of the major theories or metaphors for dreaming involve what we might term a bureaucratic idiom, although much recorded dream content does have to do with bureaucracies of this world and the next.
- As a topic, dreaming sits at the crossroads of cultural semiotics, healing traditions, concepts of the self, ontology, epistemology, rhetoric, disciplines of self-cultivation, and modes of legitimation. It lives at the seam where individuals and culture meet. This makes it a rich and endlessly fruitful topic for reflection.
- Dreaming is very widely distributed among living beings—dogs, cats, horses, some birds, perhaps octopuses, fish, eels, and platypuses dream[119]—yet what people have made of dreams is beautifully variegated. This book is a mapping of some of the things Chinese people made of dreams.

The plan of the book is straightforward. Chapter 2 looks at what sort of process or event dreaming was imagined to be. Chapters 3 and 4 address "indirect" dreams that were seen as requiring some sort of interpretation; they deal mostly with the prospective paradigm. Chapter 5 addresses "direct" dreams that did not require interpretation; it deals mostly with the visitation paradigm. An epilogue reflects on the limits within which any study like this must work.

CHAPTER TWO

The Elusive Nature of Dreaming

What, for Chinese writers and readers, *were* dreams, and what models of the human self were implicated in particular notions of dreaming? Having surveyed the extant archive with these questions in mind, I want to sketch a map of this aspect of the dreamscape, using selected texts as examples.[1] We here open up the black box of dreaming itself, seen as a process or event. What was its actual mechanism thought to be? This chapter first sets the problem, "In the world imagined in, or glimpsed through, this or that document, dreaming is what happens when (X)," and then it solves for X.

Mumbles and Metaphors

I will issue two initial caveats. First, we will see a welter of notions of what dreaming is—sometimes in the same work. This should not surprise us. It tends to be the norm in most cultures and periods, and given the inherent mysteriousness of dreams it could hardly be otherwise.[2] (On top of that, cultures are messy repertoires, not tightly integrated systems.)[3] Second, the passages constituting evidence on this topic are mostly under-theorized and merely suggestive. They often flash by as authors hurry on to make points about other topics. Seldom is the nature of dreaming as a process taken up in its own right. We therefore find ourselves having to infer models of dreaming from passages where they are only implicit—at least if we want to know what was thought about the genesis of dreams, matters that have been justly observed to hold more interest for us than for authors and readers from previous eras.[4] Perhaps this is inevitable when it comes to something as nebulous as dreams, where almost everyone has had the experience but no one quite knows why it happens. As Barbara Tedlock writes of notions of dreaming in Amerindian nations,

> These diverse theories are not static, internally consistent grammars or sets of ideas disconnected from the activities of everyday life. Rather, they are linked to social action and interpreted, manipulated, and employed in distinct ways in various contexts by individuals. Dream communication involves a convergence in the passing theories of individuals who embrace ad hoc strategies to make sense of a particular utterance. As Richard Rorty put it, "a theory is 'passing' because it must constantly be corrected to allow for mumbles, stumbles, malapropisms, metaphors, tics, seizures, psychotic symptoms, egregious stupidity, strokes of genius, and the like."[5]

As a convenient shorthand I will refer to these theories or bundles of notions as "models," with the caveats noted. Along the way we will glimpse models not only of the process or event of dreaming but also of the self who dreams, or to whom dreams happen, the dreamer not necessarily seen as the agent of the process.[6] On, then, to the mumbles and metaphors.

Contact by Exogenous Spirits

One common model, and the earliest documented,[7] has three working parts. Some outside entity contacts the dreamer during sleep. That entity is an extra-human being of some kind—an individualized agent, often with an agenda, whether clear or not. And the contact is not solicited or triggered in any evident way by the dreamer's actions—at least not within the frame of the passage in question.[8] Whether the exogenous agent has been prompted to appear due to some off-camera deed by the dreamer remains a question in some cases.

At this model's simplest level, some entity *appears* to the dreamer during sleep, and any mechanism, any epistemological or ontological framework making this possible, goes unaddressed. In Shang oracle inscriptions we find records of divinations regarding personages seen in dreams by royals. The divinations are meant to determine the identities of these personages so that appropriate ritual action might be taken.[9] In several cases the divinatory charge takes the form 王夢隹X, where X is the name of a deceased person and the graph *wei* 隹 is a copula bearing the sense of "due to, because of, caused by": thus "The king's dream was due to X" or "As for the king's dream, it was X." (Sometimes the charge is paired with a negative version, the spirits addressed being invited to choose: 王夢隹X / 王夢不隹X, "The king's dream was due/was not due to X.")[10] It is not entirely clear (at least to me) whether what is being sought in such charges is the identity of the deceased individual *seen* in the dream,[11] the agent responsible for producing the dream, or both. At least one inscription implies that some sort of spirit-entity directly caused the king's dream and should therefore be exorcised.[12]

We see a similar model at work in two daybooks (*rishu* 日書) on bamboo strips, buried in 217 BCE and recovered at Shuihudi 睡虎地 in Hubei Province in 1975. And the same idea informs a passage in a Dunhuang manuscript dating from the late Tang or earlier.[13] The Shuihudi A passage reads:

> When a person has foul dreams, on wakening then unbind the hair, sit facing the northwest and chant this prayer: "Heigh! I dare to declare you to Qinqi. So-and-so[14] has had foul dreams. Flee back home to the place of Qinqi. Qinqi, drink heartily, eat heartily. Grant so-and-so great broadcloth.[15] If not coins, then cloth. If not cocoons, then silkstuff." Then it will stop.[16]

Comparing this, the other Shuihudi daybook passage, and the Dunhuang manuscript we find remarkable consistency, despite minor differences in wording. To readers who have had a nightmare each text prescribes a ritual that includes unbinding the hair, facing northwest (northeast in the Dunhuang text), and voicing an invocation (*zhu* 祝 in Shuihudi B, *zhou* 呪 in the Dunhuang text) or prayer (*dao* 禱 in Shuihudi A) to a being named Qinqi (Shuihudi A), Wanqi (Shuihudi B), or Boqi (Dunhuang),[17] who oversees the spirits responsible for causing bad dreams. With the incantation the speaker urges this divine overseer to enjoy the proferred food and, in return, to prevent recurrence of nightmares. He also commands the dream-causing spirits to return to their overseer. The formula closes with the request, for good measure, that Qinqi/Wanqi/Boqi bestow material blessings in exchange for the offerings. All three incantations imply what the Dunhuang one states explicitly: "May crushing dreams cease, giving rise to great blessings" 厭夢息興大福. These texts are among the many participating in what I call the *exorcistic paradigm*.

Built on the same model of dreaming, and likewise constituting an incantatory mode of writing, is Wang Yanshou's 王延壽 "Rhapsody on Dreams" ("Meng fu" 夢賦, mid-2nd century), which Donald Harper has shown to be "both a poem about a nightmare and an incantation to expel nightmare demons."[18] The wakened dreamer summons spiritual aid or declares his own empowered spiritual status, vocalizes demons' names, threatens them, and performatively narrates their expulsion.[19]

Introducing the poem is a short prose preface in which Wang Yanshou says he had the nightmare in question while still a boy. He obtained "demon-cursing writings" 罵鬼之書 created by the noted author, poet, courtier, and master of esoterica Dongfang Shuo 東方朔, he says, and then wrote the rhapsody. "When people later on have dreams, chant it aloud to drive off the demons. Time and again it will prove effective" 後人夢者讀誦以却鬼, 數數有驗. The reader is thus primed to read the text not just as a poetic narrative of one person's experience—though it is that—but also as incantatory performative speech, speech that effects the results it describes. The line "This vassal does not presume to conceal it" 臣不敢蔽, paired with the crediting of the verses to Dongfang Shuo, implies that the poet is here making available magical words that had previously been transmitted only esoterically.[20]

The rhapsody itself contains fifty-eight lines. The first three introduce the dream. In lines 50 to 52 the speaker awakens and describes the dream's aftermath. Lines 53 to 58 are an epilogue listing five previous, well-known instances in which apparent losses (including initially baleful-seeming dreams) were converted to gains, ending with a final invocation: "Turn misfortune to fortune, that I might be forever without grief" 轉禍爲福永無恙兮. This closing formula anticipates the Dunhuang incantation mentioned above.[21] As we will see later in this chapter, it was echoed by other writers but in a very different register, that of moral self-cultivation.

Lines 4 through 49 relate the dream itself. Here we find two alternating types of lines and registers of speech. Some, of varying length, provide descriptive narrative. Others, of three words each, contain a strong verb of action ("smite," "stun," "cleave," "beat," "flog," "bind," etc.) followed by the binomic name of a type of demon, for example: "Backhand Ogre Fiend. Hack Goblin Blighter. Behead Earth Bogy. Batter Ditch Dweller." The poem's main body is thus at once a catalog of demons and a repertoire of exorcistic commands.[22] At two points (lines 8 and 49) the speaker declares himself to be a culminant person (*zhenren* 真人) "harboring the pure harmony of Heaven and Earth" 含天地之淳和. These self-characterizations, too, come off as performative claims to authority, challenging any power the demons might have thought they had to assault him in his sleep. He positions himself as one entitled to express outrage that demons dare attack someone of his status.

The result is thus at once a narrative of a nightmare, a performative utterance effecting its dissipation, and the script for an incantation to be recited by other dreamers to ward off their own nightmares.[23] Harper explains, "The persona of the poet in the dream is not only a dreamer, but simultaneously an incantor and exorcist. The vivid language of the demonic battle is effective not only because of its verbal ingenuity, but [also] because it is in fact incantatory language."[24]

This conception of the causes of (bad) dreams, and the complex of other elements making up the exorcistic paradigm, persisted through medieval times. The paradigm shows up in numerous methods recommended to practitioners of various self-cultivational regimens.[25] In this model, dreamers are not the agents of dreaming at all. They are its passive subjects. Its agents are exogenous beings, and dreaming is a frightening and inherently dangerous experience those Others subject us to.[26] As portrayed in these texts, our best response to a nightmare is to ascertain the identity of the agent so as to exorcise it. The ontological or epistemological mechanism by which demonic Others are able to cause such visions during sleep is not broached. More surprisingly, these agents' motives for making us dream remain murky. What do they hope to gain? What is clear is that imagery of foulness, violence, and pollution predominates: nightmares are above all a breaching of boundaries. The ritual response restores order by expelling the responsible agents and policing the bounds of the sleep-vulnerable self.

Before moving on, we should note an unusual alternative strategy that works from the same platform: launching a mission to destroy dream-agents at their source, a counter-oneiric preemptive strike. This was the extreme measure taken by Yangcheng Zhaoxin, consort of Liu Qu 劉去 (d. 71 BCE), king of Guangchuan. After the couple had executed Wang Zhaoping and another of his consorts along with their women slaves, Zhaoxin fell ill and dreamed that the women were denouncing Qu in the afterlife courts. Qu responded, "How dare they reappear and frighten me! Let them be burned!" He had their corpses disinterred and immolated. Later Zhaoxin, out of jealousy, ordered another of Qu's consorts (named Tao Wangqing) killed, but she escaped and threw herself into a well. Zhaoxin declared to the king, "Formerly, when we killed Zhaoping, she returned [in a dream] to frighten me. I want to have Wangqing ground up and burned so that she cannot become a spirit" 使不能神. So her body was extracted from the well, mutilated, dismembered, burned with poisons in a cauldron, and reduced to ashes.[27]

We have many stories from medieval times in which a living person, often a traveler, dreams of a deceased person announcing that their nearby tomb is compromised and requesting assistance. Often the dreamer responds by first confirming, in waking life, the facts announced in the dream, then taking measures to repair the tomb. The ghost may reappear in a subsequent dream (or waking vision) to thank the living party.[28] (Examples are discussed in chapter 5.) In some ways such stories convey a different worldview: the interaction seems to be regarded as non-threatening, and is based on—or is an argument for—cooperation between the two parties. The focus is not on the dreamer, nor the impact the dream has on him, but on the relationship between the dreamer and the Other who makes contact. But the core model of what dreaming is—a channel of unsolicited contact with a spirit-agent who arrives with an agenda—remains the same.

Response to Valorized Action

In the biography of one Liu Yin 劉殷, we read that while still a young boy, he dreamed of a person informing him of grain buried under the western fence of his property. The next day he dug and found it. The container bore an inscription: "Seven years' worth of grain, [measuring] one hundred stones,[29] is bestowed on filial son Liu Yin." He and his family lived on it for seven years.[30]

In this model, too, to dream is to be contacted by exogenous agents. But here the dreamer triggers the contact. How? We quickly learn to search earlier in the story for the clue. In this case, the vessel inscription holds the answer: Liu is a filial son, and the grain is the response—by heaven, the cosmos, something or someone Out There—to his virtue. How did the cosmos detect Liu's filiality? Again the earlier part of the story supplies the mechanism. Liu was orphaned quite young. His paternal great-grandmother is living in his home, and she is not eating well, distraught because she craves violets to eat but it's winter. So Liu, having gone to the marshes to search for violets anyhow, tearfully bewails his inability to supply what his elder wants, voicing the prayer 願 that "august heaven and sovereign earth" 皇天后土 take pity on him. He keeps it up until he hears a voice urge him to stop crying, whereupon he notices a large patch of violets growing nearby and harvests some to take home. Then comes the dream subnarrative.

Dreams like this are a channel of contact with other beings, and the contact is unambiguously a *response* to something the dreamer did in waking life. This stimulus—the dreamer's action—may be valorized positively or negatively, but in all cases it is something *marked* in whatever discourse is at play. In Liu Yin's case the stimulus is filial piety, performed in an uninhabited area in an emotional declaration amounting to a speech act. Elsewhere it might be ritual acts of devotion, as in this story from Wang Yan's 王琰 collection of tales intended to promulgate Buddhist piety, *Records of Signs from the Unseen Realm* (*Mingxiang ji* 冥祥記, ca. 490):

> During the Jin Xingning period [363–65] there lived the monk Zhu Fayi. He dwelled in the mountains and was an avid practitioner. . . . He was well versed in numerous scriptures and had especially good command of the *Lotus Sutra*. . . .
>
> In the second year of the Xian'an period [372], he suddenly felt a strange sensation in his heart. Afterwards he was acutely ill for a protracted time. He tried various cures but none helped. . . . He gave up trying to effect a cure but instead entrusted himself with utmost sincerity

> to [the bodhisattva] Sound Observer. He kept it up for several days. One day he fell asleep and dreamed he saw a monk arrive to see about his illness. The monk set about curing it, cutting him open and pulling out his bowels and liver, washing them clean of filth. Fayi saw that many impure things had collected and concentrated in them. Once the washing was complete, the monk returned the organs to Fayi's body and said to him, "Your illness is now cured." When he awoke, his symptoms had dissipated, and soon he had recovered fully. Considering that the *Lotus Sutra* says that "sometimes [Sound Observer] appears in the image of a monk or brahman,"[31] one suspects that the monk seen in Fayi's dream may have been such an instance.[32]

Fayi's dream has striking effects in his body, emphasizing that the dream visitor and the surgical procedure were quite real. Again, here the dream is directly triggered by the dreamer's prior actions, actions that are positively valorized in the religious habitus in question. The dream is a bodhisattva's response (*ying* 應) to the stimulus (*gan* 感) of the dreamer's intense devotional concentration. This record makes the additional point that such striking responses are fulfillments of promises made in a famous sutra chapter. The sutra provided a warrant for undertaking specific devotional actions with an expectation of divine response in the form of dreams or visions. Reports of events deemed to be such responses were then circulated to confirm the sutra's claims and prove the efficacy of the actions it prescribed.[33]

Negatively valorized acts could also trigger dream responses, and by nearly the same basic mechanism—with the exception that in positive instances such as those we've just glimpsed there is often a pronounced element of emotional concentration, or tightly focused attention, on the part of the dreaming protagonist. This element isn't seen in many narratives of dreams that are responses to wrongs, unless we count the dreamer's sense of dread. A classic story type here is that of the vengeful ghost. Another features animals returning for vengeance when people have broken pacts with them or gratuitously harmed them. We will see examples of both types in chapter 5.

Finally, there were what were known in Buddhist discourse as acts of truth. These were declarations of fact or resolve, a type of speech act conceived as having the power to elicit striking responses from the cosmos in confirmation of their truth. They combined elements, then, of divination and epistemological confirmation.[34] Responses triggered by such utterances could include dreams, as for example in a story involving the well-known scholar-monk Dao'an 道安 (312–85):

> An frequently annotated the sutras, but he feared that [his interpretations] did not harmonize with their principles, so he pronounced the following vow [*praṇidhāna* / *shi* 誓]: "If what I have explained is not too far from the principles, may I behold an auspicious sign." He then dreamed that he saw an Indian monk with white hair and long eyebrows, who told him, "Your annotations to the sutras, sir, are quite in harmony with their principles. As for me, I have not obtained nirvāṇa and I live in the Western regions. I will help you to spread the teaching. From time to time you may set out food for me." Later, when the [vinaya collection] *Shisong lü* 十誦律 arrived [in China], Huiyuan 慧遠 realized that the one Dao'an had dreamed of was Piṇḍola. Thenceforth they established a seat to make food offerings to him, and everywhere this became the rule.[35]

All of the examples in this section share a fundamental structure of ideas, the standard term for which was *ganying* 感應, or "stimulus and response," and a common set of working parts. The cosmos, or some agent operating in it, is exquisitely sensitive to what the dreamer has intended and done. The dream is, or is part of, the finely tuned response evoked by the dreamer's thoughts, words, or deeds. Such responses are so attuned to their stimuli that the Western Han author Lu Jia 陸賈 (d. ca. 178 BCE) characterized their relationship using the metaphor of two perfectly fitting tallies, or *fu* 符.[36] In any given instance, this responsiveness plays out on a spectrum of characteristics running from personal and intentional at one end to mechanical and automatic at the other. In other words, the response may take the form of a particular being who shows up, speaks, and acts, or it may take the form of an impersonal, seemingly automatic event. But in every case, it's an action by the dreamer (or, more abstractly, the action's moral quality or truth) that triggers the resonant dream response. Dreaming thus operates like a membrane sensitive to pressure from either side.

This model of dreaming is also central to what I call the *spillover paradigm*, in which dreams become extensions of the self-cultivational projects that occupy waking life.[37]

The Wandering of Souls

In another early model, dreams occur when one of our multiple souls—cloudsouls (*hun* 魂), whitesouls (*po* 魄), or simply the dreamer's "spirit" (*shen* 神)—wanders outside the body during sleep. The view that we have multiple souls is attested to as early as the *Zuo Tradition* (largely formed by the end of the 4th century BCE).[38] So far as I am aware, the earliest extant passage to unequivocally characterize soul-wandering as something that happens during sleep, thus implying that it accounts for dreaming, occurs in the *Qiwu lun* 齊物論 chapter of *Zhuangzi* 莊子 (ca. 320 BCE?).[39] That the idea is mentioned without elaboration suggests it already had some currency:

> While it [the heart-mind 心] sleeps, the cloudsouls contact [things] 其寐也魂交
> When it wakes, the bodily form opens up [to sensory input] 其覺也形開
> Whatever we come in contact with entangles it 與接爲搆
> Each day we use that heart-mind of ours for strife 日以心鬬.[40]

Asleep or awake, whether through our cloudsouls or our bodies, the passage argues, we have the unfortunate tendency to become entangled 搆 with things we come into contact with (交 and 接).

Similarly, in the "Essence and Spirit" (*Jingshen* 精神) chapter of *Huainanzi* (139 BCE) we find it said of the culminant persons "whose natures are merged with the Way" that

> They take life and death to be a single transformation 以死生爲一化
> And the myriad things to be a single whole 以萬物爲一方
> They merge their essence with the root of Grand Purity[41] 同精於太清之本
> And roam freely beyond the boundless 而游於忽區之旁
> They have vital essence but do not expend it 有精而不使
> They have spirit but do not set it into motion 有神而不行
> They match the artlessness of the great unhewn 契大渾之樸

And take their stand amid the supremely pure 而立至清之中
Thus their sleep is dreamless 是故其寢不夢
Their wisdom is traceless 其智不萌
Their whitesouls do not sink 其魄不抑
Their cloudsouls do not ascend 其魂不騰.[42]

I reserve comment on this positive valuation of dreamlessness for another occasion.[43] Here what is important is that this Western Han passage understands non-dreaming as the non-journeying of the souls. In the same vein we find Ban Gu writing in a rhapsody, "Communicating with the Hidden" ("Youtong fu" 幽通賦), in 54 or 55 CE:

My cloudsoul, solitary and alone, contacted the spirits 魂煢煢與神交兮
True feelings came forth during night sleep 精誠發於宵寐
I dreamed of climbing a mountain and, gazing afar, 夢登山而迥眺兮
Glimpsed the semblance of a hidden man 覿幽人之髣髴.[44]

And, as a plank in an argument to the effect that the "soul" is distinct from the body and survives its death, we find dreaming enlisted in an important early sixth-century debate in which Liang emperor Wu became personally involved: "I now adduce dreaming to prove that the body and the soul are not mutually inextricable. While someone is sleeping, their body is an unconscious thing, and yet they see things in that state. What they see is what their soul has met up with in its wanderings."[45]

This same ancient model was taken up and elaborated in the various Daoisms that began sprouting from the first century CE onward. The ante was typically upped, so that nocturnal soul-wandering was now portrayed as dangerous or even catastrophic. One of the most explicit and elaborate examples may be found in a Shangqing scripture known for short as the *Purple Texts*, in passages counseling the reader-practitioner to take specified measures to anchor his cloudsouls and whitesouls within the body during sleep, lest they roam and get into trouble. The three cloudsouls 三魂 are described as naïve youths liable to being taken advantage of by the rougher sorts they might run into Out There beyond the borders of the body. On certain nights of the month

> They depart the body to roam afar, fleeing the chamber like whirlwinds. Sometimes they are forcibly detained by others' cloudsouls or by outside demons. Sometimes the sprites capture and enregister them as one of their own. Sometimes they are unable to find their way back and are thenceforth separated from the body. Sometimes they are attacked by outside cloudsouls, and the two *qi* fight one another. In all such cases, the Ruddy Infant will be driven by anxiety. Its concentration will be focused on other things, and it will lack form as it moves about. Your heart will be grieved and your thoughts constricted.

The Ruddy Infant 赤子 referred to here is the embryonic self the adept is supposed to be gestating within through various self-cultivational practices. The cloudsouls' nocturnal roamings thus compromise the very heart of Shangqing practice. When the seven whitesouls 七魄 become ummoored, things are even more dire:

> When the seven whitesouls wander free, [they] roam into all sorts of corruption and filth. Sometimes they have intercourse with blood-eaters, those demons and sprites who wander to and fro. Sometimes they enter into sexual relations with corpses. Sometimes they corrupt and delude the Ruddy Infant, joining together in lasciviousness to attack their own residence. Sometimes they visit the Three Offices or the River Sire to tell of your transgressions.[46] Sometimes they are transformed into *wangliang* 魍魎 demons to bewitch you. Sometimes they lead demons into the body or call perverse forces to destroy you. All [these] injuries and illnesses are caused by the transgressions of the whitesouls. The whitesouls' nature is to delight in your death; their most ardent desire, to destroy you.[47]

This model of the wandering of souls perdured for centuries. At the outset of the most complete Dunhuang manuscript addressing dreams, there is a short passage that mentions the constitution of the human person as based on the four elements (*sida* 四大), the three cloudsouls, and the six (not, in this case, seven) whitesouls. Then this statement appears: "Dreams are the vague-seeming results of the spirit [or spirits] traveling about and getting attached to things" 夢是神遊依附髣髴.[48]

This view of dreaming presumes a self that is *dividual*, multipartite, and fissiparous.[49] Among our several elements and multiple souls there are some particularly volatile ones, and it is their activity that accounts for dreaming. Sleep is a relaxation of self-control and enables these wanderings; as such it is inherently dangerous.[50] Sleep thus resembles death, which was also imagined as the escape of souls from the body and, for some of them, a long journey outward, upward, or downward.[51] These metaphorical models had real implications in thought, practice, and narrative: some return-from-death anecdotes vividly recount the soul's sometimes reluctant return to the body following its temporary sojourn to the land of the dead. Such views of dreaming are widely attested in other societies.[52]

But even our small sampling of passages suffices to show that soul sojourns by themselves are not necessarily enough to generate a dream. Rather, dreams arise from encounters or contacts with 交 or attachments to 依附 other beings or agents during soul journeys. Underneath such words there perhaps lurks a hint of sexual contact. Dreaming is therefore a volatile soul's temporary escape during sleep, but it is also already an interaction even before the dreamer wakes and tells others of the dream.

Response to Energetic and Bodily Stimuli

A passage in *Liezi* 列子 (formed ca. 300–330)[53] explains how dreams are connected to the experiences and sensations a person comes into contact with during the day:

> A body's becoming full or empty, diminishing or growing, in every case is due to its connection with heaven and earth and its responses to things by their kinds. So when the Yin energy is strong, in dreams you grow frightened while walking through great waters. When the Yang energy is strong, in dreams you burn up while walking through great fires. When the Yin and Yang are both strong, you dream of sparing or killing. When you overeat, you dream of giving presents; when you starve, of receiving them. For the same reason, when you suffer from giddiness, you dream of floating in the air; when you suffer from a sinking, congested feeling,

> you dream of drowning. When you fall asleep lying on your belt, you dream of snakes; when a flying bird pecks your hair, you dream of flying. As it turns dark you dream of fire, falling ill you dream of eating; after drinking wine you are anxious [in your dream], after singing and dancing you weep.
>
> Liezi says: "The spirit chances on it, and we dream; the body encounters it, and it happens. Hence by day we imagine and by night dream what the spirit and the body each chances upon" 神遇爲夢,形接爲事. 故晝想夜夢,神形所遇.[54]

For the writer of this text, the content of dreams varies according to the body's "connection with heaven and earth and its responses to things by their kinds" 皆通於天地, 應於物類. This is a facet of dreaming mentioned by other authors (e.g., Wang Fu, as we'll see below) when making the point that dreams are sometimes *not* a good basis for augury, for, in such cases, all they reflect is environmental or somatic stimuli. Judging from its other discussions of dreams, the *Liezi* also consistently rejects dreams as a basis for divination (and, in fact, rejects any divination at all, viewing it as proceeding from a flawed approach to life). What the phenomenon of dreaming *is* useful for, in that text as well as in *Zhuangzi*, is making arguments about the limits of human knowledge.[55] The wise person realizes that this is all there is to dreams—that dreams, like waking experiences, are simply the products of what we happen to have chanced upon. Dreams' contents are simply not important.

Manifestation of Inner Struggle

Some Daoists developed a theory that elaborated on the archaic view seen in Wang Yanshou's poem, formalizing and upgrading it into an esoteric teaching vouchsafed by gods to select humans. Here, however, the agents involved in producing certain dreams in us are congenital parts of multipartite human selves—Others within. They are endogenous but alien parts that the practitioner strives to banish from the embattled Daoist self, which is the federation of human and divine agencies dwelling within the landscape of the body.

An early example comes in the account of the transcendent Liu Gen 劉根 in Ge Hong's 葛洪 *Traditions of Divine Transcendents* (*Shenxian zhuan* 神仙傳, ca. 317). In the passage, Liu Gen is recounting to a disciple how he had earlier received personal instruction from a famed transcendent of old, Han Zhong 韓眾.[56]

> The divine personage [Han Zhong] said, "If you desire long life, the first thing you must do is to expel the three corpses 三尸. Once the three corpses are expelled, you must fix your aim and your thought, eliminating sensual desires." I then received from him [the scripture] *Divine Methods in Five Sections* (*Shenfang wupian* 神方五篇) [for this purpose].[57] It says:
>
> "The ambushing corpses 伏尸 always ascend to Heaven to report on people's sins on the first, fifteenth, and last days of each month. The Director of Allotted Lifespans [Siming 司命][58] deducts from people's ledger accounts and shortens their lifespans accordingly. The gods within people's bodies want to make people live, but the corpses want to make them die. When people die, their gods disperse. The corpses, once in this bodiless state, become ghosts 鬼, and when people sacrifice to [the dead] these ghosts obtain the offering foods. This is why the corpses want people to die. When you dream of fighting with an evil person, this is [caused by] the corpses and the gods at war [inside you] 夢與惡人鬬爭此乃尸與神相戰也."[59]

Here, it's not quite true that the corpses themselves are the agents responsible for dreams. Rather, combat between them and the dreamer's own spirits is what triggers the dream—not all dreams, it seems, but specifically those in which one is fighting another person. Both sets of parties to this struggle are agents with clear aims; they are, in fact, selves. (More of this to come in chapter 5.) There is a quasi-direct relationship between the dream's cause and its content: direct in the sense that a fight going on within manifests as a dream in which one is fighting, quasi- in the sense that in the dream the real identities of the fighters are transposed—a Daoist *Traumwerk*. There is a strong aesthetic component to this body of lore. Throughout the Daoist discourse on these indwelling "corpses" or "worms" there runs a strong theme of disgust, which plays out in the sorts of dreams attributed to their activities. "Corpses" and dreams caused by them pose a constant threat to the purity carefully maintained in waking life by the practitioner.[60]

Although the three corpses are malevolent when seen from our human viewpoint, they perform a legitimate function in the spirit-world administrative system that is responsible for monitoring lifespan and morality. Their motives, as the passage explains, are clear, unlike those of the demonic attackers envisioned in the more archaic model we saw above with Wang Yanshou's rhapsody. Expelling them allows for peaceful sleep untroubled by nightmares. Early medieval Daoist texts specified various methods for this.[61]

Like some other theories we will survey, this one attributed dreams—at least dreams of certain specific content—to otherwise imperceptible processes going on *inside* the dreamer. For that reason it held that such dreams were diagnostic of a particular inner process occurring at the time of the dream. It is thus an example of the *diagnostic paradigm*, many more examples of which are discussed in *Dreaming and Self-Cultivation*.

Manifestation of Inner Imbalance

Models of the causes of dreams sometimes show up in surprising places—in a discourse on acupuncture, for instance. The earliest extant, lengthy discussion of needle therapy, dating perhaps to the second century, appears in *The Yellow Thearch's Classic on the Numinous Pivot* (*Huangdi neijing lingshu* 黄帝内經靈樞). A section titled "Excess Pathogenic [*Qi*] Produces Dreams" ("Yinxie fameng" 淫邪發夢) links dreaming to the status and location of *qi* in the body.[62] The discussion first asserts that "regular pathogenic *qi*" (*zheng xie* 正邪, with the *qi* implied)[63] originate from outside the body and attack within, moving about and flying into the air together with the cloudsouls and whitesouls, disturbing sleep and causing dreams. Here, then, is a hybrid explanation of dreaming: it results from the wandering of our souls, and, furthermore, either this wandering is caused, or its effects are enhanced, by the activity of pathogenic *qi*, an exogenous force. Exactly how this works is left unexplained.

But the real point of the text is to offer a diagnostic tool, and so it quickly moves from this general assertion about the origins of *qi* to a series of specific ones about the locations and states of *qi* within. The rest of the chapter takes the form of a list of dream contents correlated with specific types of *qi*—an oneiric iatromancy, or the use of divination to diagnose and treat illness.[64] It can be summarized in two tables (see tables 1–2). First:

Table 1. Dreams associated with abundant *qi* in *Huangdi neijing lingshu*

In this state of *qi*:	One dreams of:
Yin *qi* 陰氣 abounds	wading through a big water, and is fearful
Yang *qi* 陽氣 abounds	a big fire, and of being burned
both Yin and Yang *qi* abound	mutual killing 相殺*
qi abounds above [in the body]	flying
qi abounds below [in the body]	falling
one is hungry	taking something
one has eaten much	giving away
liver *qi* abounds	being enraged
lung *qi* abounds	being in fear and weeping, and of rising into the air
heart *qi* abounds	laughing while being fearful at the same time
spleen *qi* abounds	singing and being joyful; a heavy body
kidneys *qi* abounds	the lower back and spine being disconnected

*相殺 can also be understood as "killing someone."

The treatment in every case of overabundant *qi* 盛氣, we are told, is to apply acupuncture to the relevant point and drain off 瀉 the excess *qi* there. The text then moves on to list oneiric signs of receding *qi* 厥氣, which settle where there is an insufficiency of proper *qi*. In this case the treatment is to apply acupuncture to the relevant point and supplement 補 the *qi* there. The correlations are:

Table 2. Dreams associated with insufficient *qi* in *Huangdi neijing lingshu*

When receding *qi* settle here:	One dreams of:
heart-mind	smoking fires on hills and mountains
lungs	rising into the air, seeing unusual gold and iron items
liver	mountain forests with trees
spleen	hills and large swamps
kidneys	standing at an abyss, or drowning
bladder	making a journey
stomach	eating and drinking
large intestine	fields and wilderness
small intestine	crowded streets in cities
gall bladder	fighting, court appearances, cutting oneself
genitalia	sexual intercourse
neck	decapitation
lower leg	being unable to walk, mired in soil
thighs and arms	participating in a ritual
bladder and colon	urination and defecation

The text offers no rationales for any of these specific correlations, although commentators have speculated about some of them, and some seem intuitive (stomach/eating, genitalia/intercourse). In any case, these lists amount to both a theory of the causes of certain dream contents and a guide to interpreting dreams as diagnostic of specific pathological dispositions of *qi* in the inner landscape of the body. Here, as in some texts considered in the next chapter, etiology and interpretation are two sides of the same coin. Causation is implied, but the passage is not primarily concerned with etiology, offering no details as to how or why *qi* phenomena produce these specific dream contents.[65] What is clear is that the reason for discussing dreams at all is a therapeutic one. And again we find an implication that shows up in other texts (with other agendas): any dreaming is a disturbance. A person with properly distributed *qi* would perhaps, by these lights, not dream at all.

The distinct models of dreaming that I have separated out in this chapter for purposes of analysis are sometimes found combined. This one, for example, is linked to the model of contact with indigenous spirits in medical texts such as *On the Origins and Symptoms of Disease* (*Zhubing yuanhou lun* 諸病源候論) by Chao Yuanfang 巢元方 (fl. ca. 605–16). There, women whose inner organs are depleted of *qi* are said to be prone to dream of intercourse with ghosts or demons 與鬼交通 because their weakened condition leaves them vulnerable to being violated by these "ghostly pathogens" 邪鬼魅. In addition to experiencing these dreams, women in this condition would exhibit symptoms such as "not wanting to see anyone . . . laughing while alone, and weeping without reason." This heavily gendered linkage of (men's fears around) women's wayward emotions, sexual frustration, erotic dreams, demonic violation, and *qi* depletion persisted for centuries.[66]

Result of Mental Activity

Wang Chong 王充 (27–ca. 100), in his *Assay of Arguments* (*Lun heng* 論衡) as it has come down to us, does not devote a discrete chapter to dreams. But he does touch on the topic at several points.[67]

One of these comes in the chapter "Inquiry into Spirits" ("Ding gui" 訂鬼).[68] Wang Chong begins by arguing that ghosts or spirits in the world are not formed from "the essence or spirit of deceased persons" 人死精神 but are instead engendered by "people's thoughts and imaginings" 人思念存想. When sick, people grow fearful and anxious. In that state they tend to "imagine things" 存想, "their eyes seeing things that aren't there" 目虛見.[69] So, people when ill and in pain say that they see spirits beating them with rods. These visions are "the imagination of unreal things" 存想虛致, not "reality" 實. An excess concentration of vital essence 精 leaks into the sense organs, causing a person to see, hear, and otherwise sense what's not real. Similarly, Wang says, if a person who's sleeping is anxious or afraid, he will dream of being struck or pressed upon all over. So, whether seen while awake or sensed 聞 while asleep, apparitions of ghosts and spirits disturb our essence and spirits 精神.

So far we can tease out two theories of what dreams are and why they occur. In one, the metaphoric register is mentalist: fear and anxiety lead to the imagining of things not actually there. The other is *qi*-based: an excess of vital essence produced by mental concentration seeps into the sense organs and causes them to perceive things that aren't really there. In both cases, Wang draws on terminology familiar from discourses on self-cultivation involving the processing of vital essence and the visualization or actualization of scenes.

Then comes a third theory. While asleep, having been fatigued by the day's activities, we look inward—"the light of the eyes reverses" 目光反. When this occurs "our essence and spirits see the simulacra of people and other creatures" 精神見人物之象矣. (*Xiang* 象 or "simulacra" figures importantly in oneiric discourse; I discuss it further in chapters 3 and 4.) Sick people, too, have fatigued *qi* and depleted essence, so even when they aren't asleep, the light of the eyes is disturbed as if they were, causing them to see the simulacra of creatures. In this they are like someone dreaming. In both cases, when such a vision forms they don't know whether they are awake or dreaming/imagining, so they can't tell whether what they are seeing is real. This is caused by the depletion of their essence and *qi*. Madmen and people approaching death similarly suffer from disoriented essence. Sleep, illness, and madness, then, are all characterized by a depletion of the light of the eyes, and this is why people in these conditions all see the simulacra of things that are not actually there.

In the "Ordering the Anomalous" ("Ji yao" 紀妖) chapter[70] Wang turns to a common theory of dreaming, one he attributes (interestingly) to diviners although it was much more widely held: that it results from the wandering of cloudsouls. On this account, he says, if you see the celestial god Di 帝 in a dream, it's because your cloudsoul ascended to heaven. Wang objects: to ascend to heaven would be like climbing a mountain. When we dream of climbing a mountain, our feet (in the dream) climb it, and with our hands we use a walking staff. Only thus can we climb. But there is no stairway to heaven. How could our cloudsoul travel so fast? It is, after all, composed of vital essence and *qi*. How could our essence and breath move so rapidly, when their motion is like that of clouds and fog? And even if the cloudsoul could move as swiftly as a flying bird, it still wouldn't be able to ascend so far and return in the time it takes to have a dream. Wang concludes that what we see in dreams is not real 非實事, and what he means by this is that it is not the experience of our cloudsoul's literal activities outside our bodies during the dream. Instead, what we see in dreams are simulacra—things that are, by definition, not the things they represent, even if they *are* accurately interpretable by skilled diviners.

Finally, in the "Disputation on Death" ("Lun si" 論死) chapter Wang Chong compares dreamers to dead persons. The comparison serves his argument that spirits of the dead lack the capacity to survive apart from the body, or at least that they lack the ability to harm living people.

> The real nature of dreams is doubtful. Some say they occur when the essence and spirits, remaining inside the body, form auspicious or inauspicious simulacra 惑言夢者，精神自止身中，為吉凶之象. Others say the essence and spirits travel about [outside the body], encountering people and things 或言精神行，與人物相更. Now if the essence and spirits really remain in the body [during dreaming], then those of deceased persons should do likewise. If it were the case that they really travel about, then, if a person dreamed of harming or killing another person or being harmed or killed, upon inspection the next day the other person's body or their own [ought to bear marks and wounds], but there is in fact no such verification. If dreams happen because of the essence and spirits, then those are the same essence and spirits dead persons have. So if the essence and

spirits of dream[er]s cannot hurt people, how could the essence and spirits of the dead hurt people?[71]

Consistent with his other discussions, Wang thus opts for the first theory and debunks the second. So he rejects any theory of dreams that explains them as the wandering of souls, on the grounds that such theories require impossible feats. Note that in making this argument he presumes, as do most other early texts, that the soul is not an immaterial entity but is something gaseous and subtle.

Taking these passages as a group, we might say that Wang Chong articulates the most *internalist* of early medieval views of dreaming. He grants that at least some dreams may be effectively divined[72] and that some are "direct." But he disavows both spirit travel and actual contact by exogenous spirits as the cause of dreams. Indeed, he sees nothing "real" about dreams, even "direct" ones.[73] Rather, what we see or experience in dreams is only simulacra, *xiang* 象. These are produced strictly internally, in a way he describes either mentalistically, in terms of the mind imagining things, or pneumatically, as an excess or disturbance of essence and spirit. There is no question of real beings visiting us in our sleep, nor of one of our souls wandering outside the body at night and having real encounters in the world. There does not seem to be any external influence on our dreams whatsoever, whether atmospheric, sensory, or otherwise.

Before leaving Wang Chong, we should pause to note that he introduced a concept that would later prove momentous in Chinese dream discourse: the dyad of real and false, or actual and fictive, *shi* 實 versus *xu* 虛. For Wang Chong, some dreams may carry meaning and be successfully divined, but not because what we see in dreams is real. What we see are simulacra, which may be interpreted to yield indications of actual events to come, just like cracks opened in a tortoise shell by the diviner's rod. It remains a question specifically how and why, for him, this is possible.

Wang Chong's was not the only text that approached some dreams simply as thoughts in the mind. We will see several examples below.

Categorizations

Taxonomies represent attempts to bring order to unruly, confused, messy areas of life, and dreams are certainly one such area. When we come upon lists of distinct dream symbols and their meanings, or categorizations of dreams into types, we are looking at the results of people's efforts to bring the indeterminacy of the oneiric realm under some sort of order. At those moments, dreams and dreaming have become recognized as intellectual problems with real consequences, and so we humans have attempted to sort them. Ancient and medieval cultures produced not only catalogs of the meanings of dream elements but also taxonomies of types of dreams, such as those of Artemidorus and Macrobius, as well as explicit theories of the causes of dreams, some of them naturalistic, a tradition in Western antiquity that extends from the pseudo-Hippocrates through Aristotle and Lucretius to Cicero and Artemidorus.[74] Not all such enterprises are scholastic in nature. Even small-scale communities settle onto informal taxonomies of dreams and standardize the meanings attached to specific contents.[75]

As early as the pre-Han *Zhou Rites* (*Zhou li* 周禮)[76] one such taxonomy was articulated in China. And already in it we see a pronounced tendency shared by most Chinese taxonomies of dreaming: to distinguish types of dreams based, in part, on what was understood to cause them. In a list—itself an attempt to impose order on a murky past—of officers at an imagined Zhou court, appearing in a section on various kinds of diviners, we find a diviner of dreams. The brief passage lists six standard dream types: ordinary, or emotionally neutral (or perhaps what later authors would mean by direct or non-symbolic [*zheng* 正]);[77] horrific or odious (*e* 噩); yearning (*si* 思); diurnal (*wu* 寤);[78] happy (*xi* 喜); and fearful (*ju* 懼).[79] This typology largely keys on emotional tone, although "yearning" and "diurnal" hint at a causal theory, namely that such dreams are simply carryovers from waking experience. The context perhaps implies that the seasonal cycles of *qi* were thought to influence dream content, but this is not articulated. In all cases the dreamer whose dreams are divined (and, in the case of foul dreams, ritually expunged)[80] is the ruler. From this passage alone we would not assume that anyone else's dreams were thought to warrant interpretation—not surprising in a text imagining the workings of the Zhou polity.[81]

Wang Fu's Taxonomy

Wang Fu's 王符 (ca. 90–165) second-century *Discourses of a Recluse* (*Qianfu lun* 潛夫論) sketches one of the most ambitious theories-cum-taxonomies of dreams in the early medieval period.[82] He lays out ten categories. On analysis they seem driven by two criteria: dreams' causes, and ways of interpreting them. His typology thus diverges significantly from the much more laconic one in the *Zhou Rites*. I will first summarize his categories,[83] synthesizing what he writes about each (the text as it has come down to us is in some disarray),[84] then discuss how his taxonomy bears on the causes and nature of dreams.

1. Dreams that are literal or direct (keyword: *zhi* 直). The example given is drawn from the *Zuo Tradition*: Yi Jiang 邑姜, the wife of King Wu, had conceived a child when she dreamed that the god Di told her two things: that her son would be called Yu 虞 and that Di would give him the principality of Tang. When the child was born, his hand was indeed found to bear the character *yu*, and later he was indeed invested with Tang.[85] I have more to say about this category further on in this chapter; records of dreams of this sort form the primary topic of chapter 5.
2. Dreams that are indirect or imagistic (keyword: *xiang* 象). The example is drawn from a line in the *Odes*: Bears are the oneiric signs or indicators (*xiang* 祥) that a son will be born; snakes are the signs of daughters. I take up this category in chapters 3 and 4.
3. Dreams caused by distilled thought and produced by concentration (key phrase: *yi jing* 意精). Example: Confucius, in a time of disorder, thought so much on the Duke of Zhou that at night he dreamed of him. (The allusion is to *Analects* 7.5.) This seems to be only a theory of the cause of certain dreams, not a guide to interpretation. Comparing it to the next category suggests that Wang did not regard this type as good material for prognostication.
4. Dreams caused by longing or recalled thought (keywords: *xiang* 想; *si* 思). "Whatever the mind dwells upon can appear

in a dream. If someone is worried about something, that person will dream about it" 人有所思, 即夢其到; 有憂即夢其事. 此謂記想之夢也. "When one thinks about something during the day and then dreams about it at night, one moment it may appear auspicious and the next moment it may seem inauspicious. The good or bad presage of such a dream is not to be relied upon. This is called a dream that recalls one's thoughts" 晝有所思, 夜夢其事, 乍吉乍凶, 善惡不信者, 謂之想.[86] Wang rejected these dreams for purposes of augury because all they really indicate is the dreamer's own state of mind, not influences from an Elsewhere.

5. Status-dependent dreams (keywords: *ren* 人, *wei* 位). If a nobleman dreams about a certain incident, it might be interpreted as auspicious, but if a common person dreams about it, it might be inauspicious. "Noble and base, wise and foolish, male and female, old and young are what is meant by 'status.'"
6. Dreams produced by sensations (keyword: *gan* 感). "If it is cool and rainy when one dreams, it will cause dreams marked by oppressed and confused sensations. If it is hot and dry, one will feel unsettled and restless while dreaming. In the case of great chill, the dreamer will feel sorrow. A gusty wind will make the dreamer feel as though he is drifting away. These are dreams produced by sensations of *qi*."
7. Dreams conditioned by the season (keyword: *shi* 時). "In spring one dreams of issuance and growth, in summer of height and brightness. In autumn and winter, one dreams of maturity and storing up. This is known as dreaming in accordance with the seasons."
8. Oppositional or antithetical dreams (keyword: *fan* 反). Wang gives a famous example from the *Zuo Tradition*: "When Duke Wen of Jin 晉文公 waged battle at Chengpu, he dreamt that Chuzi 楚子 bent over him and sucked out his brains. As bad as this may seem, when they came to battle, it was Duke Wen who was victorious. This is called an antithetical dream."[87] "The good fortune of Yin at its height and the misfortune of Yang at its zenith are what is known as 'antithetical.'"

9. Dreams caused by illness (keyword: *bing* 病). "If someone has an Yin disorder, he will dream of chill. If the malady is Yang, the dream will be of heat. Internally induced disorders produce dreams of confusion. Externally induced disorders cause dreams of issue. There are dreams associated with all manner of diseases that produce the sensation of disintegration at certain times and of congestion on other occasions. These are called illness dreams."[88]
10. Temperament-dependent dreams (keywords: *qing* 情, *xing* 性). "People's temperaments and hearts differ, and they vary in their likes and dislikes. Some consider one thing auspicious, others consider it ominous. One must examine each case for oneself, and constantly divine in accordance with the nature of the individual. These are called temperament-dependent dreams."

This is a complex, multi-vectored taxonomy, if not quite as complex and multi-vectored as that "certain Chinese encyclopedia" imagined by Borges and since traded upon as an emblem of Oriental alterity in the pages of Foucault and beyond.[89] Initially it might seem that we could separate the categories into two main groups: those primarily involving a theory about the causes and conditions of dreams (types 3, 4, 6, 7, 9, and 10), and those mostly concerned with how the dream is to be interpreted (types 1, 2, 5, and 8). But things are not so neat. Sometimes a cause of a dream is also, or implies, a factor to consider when interpreting it.[90] Take temperament-dependent dreams (category 10), for example. What Wang says here can be read both as a theory about what shapes dreams' content and as a consideration to apply when interpreting dreams. The same is true of pathological dreams (category 9) and, even more evidently, status-dependent dreams (5). Wang's initial characterization of antithetical dreams (8) contains not a whiff about causes and treats only interpretation—but his final characterization opens the possibility that the Yin/Yang cycle causes this type. And in the case of dreams produced by sensation (6) and by the season (7), Wang articulates only theories of causes, giving no instruction on interpretation. Perhaps these are suggestions of variables to consider, to the effect of "Don't forget that the season or atmospheric stimuli may be responsible for certain dream elements. Ignore these when divining."

Still, we can glean some theories of the causes of dreams—with the caveat that some of these categories are probably best seen not as theories of why we dream at all, but of why we dream of certain things and not others on particular occasions, with implications for such dreams' suitability for prognostication. They fall into five sorts. One (comprising categories 3 and 4) is mentalist in nature, having to do with the mind's preoccupations. Tellingly, as we saw in Wang Chong's vocabulary, the language used to characterize these mentalist categories (dreams caused by distilled mentation [*yi jing* 意精] and by longing or mental absorption [*xiang* 想 and *si* 思]) overlaps with contemporary regimens of mental, biospiritual, and religious self-cultivation. His language also evokes a contemporary story type in which someone thinks so intently of a distant loved one, longing for their return, that their body transforms into stone, forever frozen in a posture of scanning the horizon.[91]

A second causal theory might be implied in category 5, status-dependent dreams. (But this category probably should be read as concerning only interpretation, not causes. Such is certainly supported by Wang's brief comments on it.) A third is implied in category 10, temperament-dependent dreams (*qing* 情 and *xing* 性): that what people dream is a function of their dispositions or character—what we might term their personality. Categories 6 (dreams produced by sensations [*gan* 感]) and 7 (dreams produced by the season [*shi* 時]) posit a fourth cause—atmospherics, climate, time of year. And category 9, pathological dreams (*bing* 病), attributes certain dreams to illness. Some of the causal factors Wang Fu lists are environmental—atmospherics (temperature, humidity, wind) or seasonal—but most apply to aspects of the dreamer's own person. Category 5, suggesting that dreams are caused by or should be interpreted according to the dreamer's social status, contrasts strongly with portrayals both in China and elsewhere of dreams as social levelers.[92] Another way to parse the list would be to divide the causes into two large groups, ones having to do with the dreamer's mind (*xin* 心) and the rest. Only two of them involve the mind and its activities of thinking and longing, and Wang rejects these as unsuitable for prognostication, a point to which I return in the next chapter.

An unexpected omission is the wandering-soul theory. It could be that Wang intended his list not as an exhaustive inventory of dreams' causes but simply as a notation of factors affecting the specific content of what we dream on this or that occasion—factors that should be considered when prognosticating. In other words, Wang might have presupposed the wandering-soul model and created this typology as an overlay. Another seeming omission is dreams of epiphany or visitation, in which a god, ghost, or other spirit appears and delivers a message. But Wang does adduce one such example from the *Zuo Tradition* to illustrate direct 直 dreams: a deity appears and makes literal (not coded) predictions, which later pan out. Perhaps for Wang Fu, "direct" dreams *just were* ones in which such a divine visitation occurred. Even if so, we find no theology, no theorization of how, metaphysically speaking, spirits appear to us while we are sleeping. The category of "direct" dreams, like that of "indirect" dreams—and indeed probably the entire discussion—is oriented toward the task of prognostication, not the question of cause.

Why does Wang Fu discuss dreams at all? In light of where his discussion ends, this is not an idle question. After laying out the categories and mentioning other aspects of dream interpretation (addressed in the next chapter), he reframes the entire topic as it relates to moral self-cultivation. When given an auspicious omen, he writes, if a person cultivates virtue, good fortune will come to fruition—but if the same person behaves badly while in possession of the auspicious omen, "good fortune will be transformed into bad" 福轉爲禍. Similarly, when given a bad omen, if a person behaves badly, bad fortune will result—but, if the same person demonstrates moral conduct while in possession of the bad omen, it will cause "bad fortune to be transformed into good" 禍轉爲福.[93] This last phrase echoes one found in Wang Yanshou's rhapsody and anticipates one found in a Dunhuang demonological manuscript, but those texts, as we saw above, contain an incantatory formula. Here, by contrast, the only relevant mechanism is moral self-cultivation; the only relevant agency, the dreamer's. For Wang Fu, dreaming is one of the many topics a gentleman must understand. But the most important thing he must understand about it is that dreams, even those that can be interpreted to yield accurate predictions of fortune or misfortune, are at best warnings. Fortune is not irrevocable. It is shaped by moral conduct.

Buddhist Classifications

Several vinaya passages (that is, passages in texts giving rules for Buddhist monks) classify dreams. Often this topic is introduced in the context of assessing whether karma is generated by actions performed while dreaming.

A passage in a late fifth-century Chinese translation of a vinaya commentary titled *Shanjianlü piposha* 善見律毘婆沙,[94] for example, takes up dreams because of an exception: monks incur demerit for masturbating to ejaculation, the text notes, except while dreaming. The commentary first explains the exception in a surprising way, by saying that the Buddha ruled on bodily activity 身業, not mental activity 意業, despite the fact that the emission being discussed is physical, albeit caused by a dream. But the passage goes on to clarify that what is regulated in the vinaya is intentional, deliberate action. Action carried out while dreaming is not an offense because it's involuntary.

The text proceeds to taxonomize dreams into four types, the first two being of little interest to the authors.[95] First we have dreams caused by disharmony among the four constituent elements of the person 四大不和, these being earth, water, fire, and air. Some examples are dreams of sliding down a mountain, flying, seeing a predator, or being chased by a bandit. Next come dreams caused by "things previously seen," meaning dreams of things experienced the previous day.

The other two categories receive more attention. The third is dreams caused by *devas* or divine persons 天人. "There are some divine persons who are good acquaintances 善知識天人 [that is, who wish us well and help us to do good], others who are evil acquaintances. If they are good acquaintances, they display good dreams 現善夢 in which people are enabled to do good things. If they are evil acquaintances, they cause people to harbor evil thoughts and they display evil dreams" 令人得惡想現惡夢. And the fourth category is dreams "based on thought" 想夢.[96] Of this category the *Shanjianlü piposha* explains: "In the case of such dreams, the person in previous lives has accumulated fortune and merit, or else demerit 想夢者, 此人前身, 或有福德或有罪. If he has accumulated fortune and merit, then a good dream is displayed" 若福德者現善夢; "if demerit, then an evil dream is displayed" 罪者現惡夢. The example given is perhaps the best-known Buddhist dream narrative, which tells of how, when the future Buddha was about to enter his mother's womb, she dreamed a white elephant descended from heaven and entered her right side. The text continues: "If one dreams that one is worshiping the Buddha, reciting sutras, upholding the precepts, performing donations, or doing other meritorious actions, these are all dreams based on thought."

The two pairs of types are then distinguished in a surprising way. The first two are dismissed as "empty, not real" 虛不實. The second two, those caused by divine persons and those due to previous-life karmic seeds, are characterized as "real" 眞實.[97] The criterion seems to be whether a dream figures in the production of karmic merit or sin. In the characterization of these "real" types of dreams a noteworthy locution is used: "dreams are displayed" 現夢 to us. The agents handling this display in the first case are the visiting beings; in the second, presumably our own karma.[98]

The discussion closes by returning to the question of intention and culpability. Whether one dreams of doing good or evil, one "does not reap the fruit of retribution" 不受果報 "because the mental actions are faint and feeble" 以心業羸弱故. "They cannot trigger a karmic fruit" 不能感果報. Here the factor of intention is given a materialistic explanation: one's thoughts during dreams *are* actions 業, but they are too faint to generate karmic residue.[99]

A second Buddhist typology similarly arises in a vinaya discussion of whether ejaculating while dreaming generates karma—a persistent problem for monks, it seems, in medieval times in several traditions and lands. (Here, too, monks must have been relieved to read that the answer was no.)[100] In this case the text in question is the Mahāsāṅghika vinaya, *Mohesengqi lü* 摩訶僧祇律, brought from India by Faxian 法顯 and translated by Buddhabhadra in 418.[101] It distinguishes five categories of dreams: (1) "Actual" 實, "as when the Tathāgata was still a bodhisattva and saw five sorts of dreams no differently than if they were actual" 所謂如來爲菩薩時. 見五種夢如實不異. (2) "Non-actual" 不實, "as when someone sees a dream and then wakes to find that [what was dreamed of] did not actually occur" 若人見夢覺不實. (3) "Unclear" 不明了, "as when someone dreams something and then cannot recall the order of events in it" 如其夢不記前後中間. (4) "Dream within a dream" 夢中夢, "as when one dreams that one is telling others about a dream" 如見夢即於夢中爲人說夢. (5) "First think, then dream" 先想後夢, "as when one dreams at night about what one thought about during the day" 如晝所作想夜便輒夢.[102]

A third taxonomy is found in the *Mahāvibhāṣā[śāstra?]* 阿毘達磨大毘婆沙論, a Sarvāstivāda commentary on an Abhidharma text, compiled in Kashmir in the second century[103] and translated by Xuanzang 玄奘 between 645 and 664. Here we find five reasons for what is seen in dreams: (1) Dreams are "induced by other [beings or entities]" 他引, such as gods, transcendents, spirits, or sages, or by invocations or drugs. (2) Dreams are caused by past events: one sees what one previously thought about, or what one habitually did. (3) Dreams show what will come to pass: one sees signs 相 of auspicious or inauspicious things that will occur. (4) Dreams are based on discrimination: one dreams of what one is longing for or worrying about. (5) Dreams are caused by illness: if the elements are disharmonious one will have a corresponding dream.[104] The first, second, and fifth of these largely overlap with *Shanjianlü piposha* categories, while the third and fourth do not. (The fourth is reminiscent of one of Wang Fu's.) All but the third category offer theories as to the causes of certain dreams. The third, that of predictive dreams, asserts that some dreams do prefigure the future, but like many other texts leaves unanswered the questions of why and how.

Like the *Zhou Rites* and Wang Fu taxonomies, these and similar Buddhist ones combine multiple notions of why we dream and what dreams are.

The Implications of Narratives

We now come to narratives that imply certain causes of dreams without spelling these out. Such stories are often, among other things, arguments about what dreams essentially are and how we should regard them. And here again the metaphysics usually remain murky. It is up to the inquirer to infer whatever can be inferred from any given narrative.

Nevertheless, I begin with a story that is unusual for explicitly taking up the nature of dreams as an intellectual problem.[105] It features Yue Guang 樂廣 (252–304), who served as president of the imperial secretariat and was remembered as a brilliant conversationalist and skilled writer. The slightly more substantial of the two surviving versions[106] is preserved in *Traditional Tales and Recent Accounts* (*Shishuo xinyu* 世說新語, ca. 430).[107] Yue's interlocutor in the anecdote is a youth named Wei Jie 衛玠, who would later become his son-in-law. Jie asked Guang about dreams. "They're thoughts" (*xiang* 想, perhaps "imaginings" comes closer), Guang offered. Jie pushed further: "But dreams occur when body and spirit(s) aren't in contact. How can they be thoughts?" 形神所不接而夢, 豈是想邪. Yue elaborated: "They're the result of causes" (*yin* 因). He continued: "No one's ever dreamed of entering a rat hole riding in a carriage, or of eating an iron pestle after pulverizing it, because in both cases there have never been any such thoughts or causes."[108]

Guang's initial take may strike us as unremarkable, resembling as it does some modern accounts of what dreaming is, i.e., mentation without sensation.[109] But it confounds young Wei Jie, who is working from the wandering-soul theory. Jie sees no way to reconcile this theory with Guang's notion that dreams are the "thoughts" of the sleeper. For Wei Jie, dreams are liminal, Other. Yue Guang's theory seems to reduce dreaming to ordinary mentation, a mere recombining of thoughts and experiences from everyday waking life—a jumble of memories.[110]

The story then takes a surprising turn. Wei Jie "pondered over what was meant by 'causes' for days without coming to any understanding, and eventually became ill." Implied is that the boy's intense but fruitless reflection on Yue Guang's theory caused his illness. (Later in life he would be known for being sickly.)[111] Yue Guang, hearing of this, at once called for his carriage and went to see the lad, making a detailed explanation for his benefit. (Would that we were privy to it!) Wei Jie began to recover at once. Such, the story suggests, is the mysteriousness of the origins and causes of dreams.

But, characteristically for *Traditional Tales and Recent Accounts*, the narrative twists once more before closing. "Sighing, Yue Guang remarked, 'In this lad's breast there will never be any incurable sickness.'" Learned contemporaries would have recognized the allusion to a story in the *Zuo Tradition*—a story about a dream. Duke Jing of Jin (r. 599–581 BCE) was ill and sought a physician in Jin. The earl of Jin sent a physician named Huan to cure him. Before Huan arrived, the duke dreamed his illness took the form of two boys. One said, "That's a good physician. I fear he'll hurt us." The other replied, "If we stay above the diaphragm and below the heart, what can he do to us?" When the physician arrived, he announced, "Your illness is incurable. It's above the diaphragm and below the heart. If I attack it directly I can't touch it; if I puncture, I can't reach it. Drugs won't get to it either." The duke replied, "You're a good physician."[112]

In the *Zuo Tradition* substory, the cause of an illness is both personified and specified in a dream, even if the resulting knowledge affords no cure. The physician's diagnostic skill is confirmed by the oneiric and narrative form taken by the disease. Dreams themselves are not explained. Rather, a dream is used to explain, by personifying and narrativizing, the intractability of an illness. In the outer story of Wei Jie and Yue Guang, the point seems to be that young Jie, now equipped with a superior understanding of dreams, will be able to avoid such an outcome. With the allusion, Yue also invites a parallel between himself and the physician in the old tale: just as Huan visited the duke to try to cure him, correctly diagnosing his inability to do so in correspondence with the patient's dream, so Yue has cured Wei Jie, by explaining dreams and thus solving the puzzle that absorbed the young man to the point of sickening him.

Knowing the cause of a dream is therapeutic, then. As was the case for Wang Fu and for the acupuncture text and the Buddhist vinayas, so here, assigning causes to dreams was not idle theory-making: it bore ameliorative purpose. In Wang Fu's case it was part of a program of educational formation and moral self-cultivation. For young Wei Jie, knowing why dreams occur relieved both cognitive and physical suffering.

But when it comes to narratives involving dreams, sometimes the apparently simplest are the most perplexing. Consider this story from Gan Bao's 干寶 early fourth-century *Records of an Inquest into the Spirit Realm* (*Soushen ji* 搜神記):

> During the Wu period, Xu Boshi fell ill. He had master of the Dao Lü Shi set up an altar for him. Shi had two disciples, Dai Ben and Wang Si. All three of them lived in Haiyan. Boshi invited the disciples to assist Shi. During a nap, however, Shi dreamed that he ascended to the Northern Dipper in the heavens,[113] where he saw attendants saddling three horses outside, saying, "Tomorrow we'll use one of these to welcome Shi, one for Ben, and one for Si." When Shi woke from his dream, he said to Ben and Si, "Since the time of our deaths has arrived, go home quickly and

> take leave of your families!" They all dropped what they were doing and departed. Boshi thought it strange and tried to detain them, but [Shi] said, "I fear we will not be able to see our families!" Within the space of one day, all three men died at the same time.[114]

Lü needs no divination to understand the meaning of his dream. It is not a coded message. His dream has afforded him a direct glimpse of something unfolding at a very distant locale, as if a scout had stumbled upon an unexpected enemy troop movement on the eve of battle. Not only that, but the story anticipates doubt of the truth of what he saw, only to head it off: the three men's simultaneous deaths the next day *confirm* it. The implicit argument, then, is that at least some dreams are real encounters yielding direct insight into what is to come. But exactly *how* does it come to pass that Lü, while asleep here, sees what is happening there, so far away? Perhaps some medieval readers would have surmised that a journey by one of Lü's cloudsouls was responsible (though, as we've seen, Wang Chong would have rejected this as impossible). The story does not so much as hint at any specific mechanism. There does not seem to have been a theory of dreaming in the available repertoire to readily account for these events. Yet the story insists that the events really happened.

Then there are narratives that, far from taking a stance on or implying a theory about the nature of dreams, seem to arise from dreaming's very indeterminacy. For example: "Liu Ya 劉雅, a clerk in Huainan, dreamed a black lizard dropped from the ceiling into his belly. Because of this he suffered from a painful stomach illness."[115] Are we to see the dream-lizard as an external thing, however insubstantial, that entered Liu's body via the dream (the way the future Buddha entered his mother's side in the form of her dream of an elephant) and so caused his malady? Or were the stomach cramps psychosomatically induced, as we are prone to phrase it, by the fear occasioned by his dream? The Wu minister Sun Jun 孫峻 (219–56) is said to have fallen ill and died at the age of thirty-eight as a direct result of having dreamed of being struck by Zhuge Ke (203–53).[116] Again, should we read this as the report of a ghost's unusually effective assault on a living party through a dream, or as an unusually severe case of what in our era might be called psychosomatic effects of dreaming? Or was this a distinction without a difference? A final instance:

Han emperor Ling dreamed of the previous emperor Huan angrily upbraiding him for two unjust executions and warning that the victims were filing plaints 訴 with heaven against him, and "when he awoke he was terrified, and soon died" 既覺而恐，尋亦崩.[117]

We will see similar cases in subsequent chapters. But we have now moved imperceptibly from dreams' causes to their effects, so it is time to bring this chapter to a close.

Only Connect

Looking back at what has been surveyed here, three points stand out.

The first is that although there were exceptions and although the details varied, the default view was that dreaming *connects* the dreamer with other beings or entities. Around 500 BCE Heraclitus reportedly observed that "for those who are awake there is a single, common universe, whereas in sleep each person turns away into his own, private one."[118] For him, the true and the good are located in the common, while the merely private is of little significance.[119] The notion that while awake we participate in a common world whereas when asleep we each withdraw into an idiosyncratic, solipsistic cocoon, would likely strike many readers today as common sense.[120] But it seems to run against the grain of much of Chinese thought about dreaming, just as Heraclitus was likely speaking against the grain of his own social world. In China, dreaming in most cases entangled the dreamer with others. It embedded the dreamer in matrices of other beings or forces. Dreaming connects us; it's an encounter. Parts of us flow out and bump into things, or things flow or bump into us, and one of the purposes of this chapter has been to show that in China *that is predominantly what dreaming consisted of*. The point is not that the self was seen as lacking boundedness[121] but that something we tend to understand as private and merely subjective was instead mostly seen as relational and intersubjective.

The inner conflict theory might count as an exception. There, if the dream results from an encounter, it's an encounter among indwelling components of human selves. But some of those components are alien—Others within. The dream itself is a symptom of conflict between the alien and the proper parts of us, like the distorted sounds of a distant battle carried to us on the wind, while we strive to expel them out beyond the bounds of the self. The theory that dreams indicate specific imbalances of "pathogenic *qi*" in us might appear to be another exception. But the passage articulating this theory pictures the wandering of our souls as part of the mechanism of dreaming, and this theory involves the activity of exogenous, hostile forces. Yet another seeming exception are Buddhist theories that dreams were caused by disharmony among the four elements, or by karma. But those same passages picture other beings as "displaying" some dreams to us. And even when a dream is due to a factor from one of our own previous lives, the self who dreams is, in effect, dividual—but now dividual in being distributed over rebirth-time rather than across internal bodily space.

The theories of Wang Chong and Yue Guang—that dreaming is simply mental activity—seem to have been minority reports against the background of the larger dreamscape. Yet even for Wang the tie-in between the self and the energies of the cosmos is essential, even if dreams turn out to be nothing but the mind's imaginings: it's because of the condition of one's *qi* that one dreams, and that condition depends upon one's relationship to the larger environment. Perhaps Yue Guang's theory is the most internalist of all—and the closest to some recent neuroscientific models: dreams are reshuffled thoughts, recombined bits of memory. But even there we see posited a surprising continuity with waking experience, in that we dream only about types of situations we have experienced in life. Yue's reported statement obliquely and partially anticipates a position in modern dream theories known as the continuity hypothesis.[122]

A second point relates closely to the first. Of any depiction of the process of dreaming we may ask: Who (or what) makes dreams? Who (or what) is the doer of whatever action results in a dream? Many views of dreaming assume that the dreamer herself is the agent. Freud's theory springs to mind, as do all neuroscientific theories of dreaming of which I'm aware. Some ancient and medieval thinkers shared this identification of the agent of dreaming with the person having the dream—though often with different implications and for different reasons. Thus, for example, the *Bṛihad-Āraṇyaka Upaniṣad*:

> When one goes to sleep, he takes along the material of this all-containing world, himself tears it apart, himself builds it up, and dreams by his own brightness, by his own light. Then this person becomes self-illuminated.
>
> There are no chariots there, no spans, no roads. But he projects from himself chariots, spans, roads. There are no blisses there, no pleasures, no delights. But he projects from himself blisses, pleasures, delights. There are no tanks there, no lotus-pools, no streams. But he projects from himself tanks, lotus-pools, streams. For he is a creator.[123]

Again, what is striking about the Chinese dreamscape is that only relatively seldom is the dreamer herself assumed to be the maker of her dream. More often than not, the one who "has" the dream takes the position of its passive subject, witness, or even victim, and the agent is someone or something else.

A third point that stands out when we look back over these texts is that none of them broaches dreaming as a topic of interest in its own right. Usually dreams mattered and were discussed *for therapeutic reasons*. One needed to know what dreams were in order to live a certain kind of life, be a certain kind of person, understand what is to be done, avoid being deluded. Wang Chong compares dreaming with dying, and we sense that the topics were never very far apart: both were seen as liminal, dangerous, likely to trigger perturbation. The Buddhist classifications sometimes take up the question of what dreaming is in order to address concern about the karmic consequences of ejaculation during sleep. Discussing them was ameliorative. This is true even for a text such as the *Liezi*, which doesn't take dreams very seriously except as reminders not to take any changes too seriously. Its teaching on dreams is a kind of therapy, meant to take the sting out of dreams. Yue Guang, too, is shown doing this in the story about him.

This is also why it proves hard to disentangle theories of what dreaming is from notions about how (or whether) to interpret dreams. The discourse on dreams was largely a practical, not a theoretical or disinterested, discourse. Thinking and writing and reading and talking about dreams, like most everything else in ancient and medieval societies that appears to us to be "philosophy," was a technique of life.[124] Questions about dreaming were inextricably bound up with questions about how best to live.

I close this chapter with a reminder about the myth of disenchantment. It would be easy to slip under the spell of the idea that the sorts of under-theorized notions we have seen here have now happily been replaced, thanks to modern, Western science, by the truth about dreaming, and that therefore these quaint, enchantment-tinged folk notions have only Chinese culture to illuminate for us. I want to resist this. It is true that thanks to functional magnetic resonance imaging, sleep laboratories, and the rest, we now have tools for peering inside the neurology of dreaming (and new ideas about what constitutes peering inside). But the inherent mysteriousness of dreaming hasn't been (dis)solved. It has merely receded a farther interval from our grasp. It's clearly important and useful, for all sorts of reasons, to know that neurons fire in these and these ways during sleep. But the firings are not the dream. And they do not fully account for how the dream feels and seems to us, both while we're dreaming and after we've awakened. Even less do they account for what we make of our dreams once we pause to recount the experience. As another writer put it: "We can certainly say that the pattern of brain activity during narrative dreaming can explain many of the usual features of dream content. This level of explanation does not, however, address either the purpose of dreams or the question of whether dream content is meaningful. So, why do we dream? The short answer, sadly, is that we don't really know."[125]

We now close up the black box of dreaming, moving on to examine some of the things people did with dreams and made from dreams.

CHAPTER THREE

Interpretations and Interpreters, Part I

Do dreams mean things?

Not all texts in early and medieval China answered in the affirmative. As we saw in discussing the *Zhou Rites*, dream interpretation was classed as a kind of divination—the highest kind, according to some authorities.[1] Divination usually presupposes a locative worldview privileging the maintenance of order and boundaries, in which signs may be reliably read according to some correlative logic. And to inquire into a dream's meaning is to worry about the future, about outcomes. Dreams are divined because dreamers fear what may happen and want to gain advantage by peering into the unknown— and this was even more so when dreaming itself was often regarded as a perturbation.

Dreams, Divination, and Delusion

Dream divination can be seen as a strategy for managing anxiety, including the anxiety of having dreamed.[2] Sarah Iles Johnston has aptly characterized divination in general as playing

> the role of a buffer. It stands between the world as humans experience it on an everyday basis, and other worlds which they can only imagine but which threaten to impinge upon their everyday world in deleterious ways: the world of the dead, the world of the gods, the world of the past and the world of the future. Divination is not only . . . a way of *solving* a particular problem in and of itself, but [is also] a way of *redirecting* the problem out of one of these other worlds, in which it seems to be rooted, and into the everyday world, where one is better able to solve it with human skills.[3]

Divination works by crossing "the boundary between our world and another one . . . and return[s] with information that, by limiting the bewildering array of potential futures, however vaguely, . . . lessens our anxiety."[4] For our purposes, then, three elements of divination, including the interpretation of dreams, are crucial. Divination "provides a feeling of control within chaotic circumstances"[5] by narrowing the field of possibilities and promising insight into what lies ahead. It does so by moving across a cosmic, ontological, or epistemological boundary, bringing information into human space where it can be used to advantage. And it wields some sort of semiotic system in which signs, although obtained by a partially random process (in the case of dreams, their seeming spontaneity and even their very strangeness), reassuringly end up making sense.

But all three of these components come in for constant criticism in the inner chapters of *Zhuangzi* and in the *Liezi*, for example.[6] Although dreams are mentioned prominently in both texts, they do not figure as the basis for divinations. They serve either as convenient rhetorical devices or as planks in arguments about other matters. In a divination-heavy society this was not a neutral stance but was taken in full awareness that it was a minority report. What purpose could divining the future serve, after all, for a man who describes himself as unperturbed by the vicissitudes of life?

> I do not think it an honor if the whole district praises me, nor a disgrace if the whole state reviles me; I have no joy when I win, no anxiety when I lose; I look in the same way at life and death, riches and poverty, other men and pigs, myself and other men; I dwell in my own house as though lodging in an inn, look out at my own neighborhood as though it were a foreign and barbarous country. Having all these ailments, titles and rewards cannot induce me, punishments and fines cannot awe me, prosperity and decline and benefit and harm cannot change me, joy and sorrow cannot influence me.[7]

For this gentleman, divination has no importance; but divination's being beside the point is something the *Liezi* wishes to argue. In the same vein, both *Zhuangzi* and *Liezi* record a story about a shaman named Ji Xian and his encounter with Liezi's teacher, Huzi 壺子, the

Gourd Master. Although it does not involve dreams, this parable may illuminate what happens when a locative divination technique meets an anti-locative worldview. Ji Xian's art is that of physiognomy (*xiang* 相), scanning the face, head, palms, and other surfaces of the body (of humans, horses, or other creatures) for signs of fortune.[8] Impressed by Ji Xian's abilities, Liezi brings him in to physiognomize his teacher. Over a series of four encounters Huzi shows the shaman different configurations of his inner energies. Each is described in figurative, deliberately opaque language that evokes Daoist cosmogonic narratives of the emergence of things from original Nothing and their gradual divergence into specificity. The series begins with mentions of earth and soil, then moves upward toward heaven and beyond as it also rewinds time toward primordial non-differentiation. At the final stage, "I have just shown him," says Huzi,

> Myself before we first came out of our Ancestor 未始出吾宗
> With him I dissolved, and drifted winding in and out of things
> 吾與之虛而猗移
> Unknowing who and what we were 不知其誰何
> To him it seemed we had floundered 因以爲茅靡
> It seemed that the waves had swept us away 因以爲波流.[9]

At each meeting the shaman imagines he has a handle on Huzi's prognosis but grows increasingly befuddled until, at the last, he panics and flees. This is because his physiognomic art deals in form. Huzi shows him formlessness, something for which he is so unprepared that one glimpse unhinges him. The shaman's method works like a sprocket wheel, but Huzi has no chain for the sprocket's teeth to bite into. Liezi, for his part, henceforth "treated all things as equally his kin," stood "detached from all things," and "from the carved jade returned to the unhewn block," a Daoist figure for non-differentiation. The parable vividly captures the incongruity between the locative domain of divination and the anti-locative stance of Daoist texts such as these. It is therefore unsurprising that these texts eschew any discussion of interpreting dreams and in fact maintain that it's best not to dream at all.[10]

Nor was there much room or rationale for divination in Buddhist texts privileging emptiness and non-duality. Such texts usually associate dreams not with knowledge but with delusion, cognitive error, and ephemerality. Many Buddhist sutras (Mahāyāna and otherwise) invoke a standard list of similes meant to image the illusory or dependent nature of phenomena: "like a magical illusion 幻, a dream 夢, an echo 響, a reflection 光, a shadow 影, a metamorphosis 化, a bubble 水中泡, an image in a mirror 鏡中像, a mirage 熱時炎, the moon reflected in water 水中月," for example, in the larger *Prajñāpāramitā sutra* 放光般若經, translated by the Khotanese monk Mokṣala 無叉羅 and others in 291.[11] Similarly, the *Vimalakīrti Sutra* 維摩詰所説經 in Kumārajīva's translation (completed in 406) tells us that "this body is like a bit of foam that cannot be grasped. This body is like bubbles that do not last very long. This body is like a mirage, generated from thirst. This body is like a banana tree, with nothing solid within. This body is like a magical illusion, arising from confusion. This body is like a dream, an illusory view," and so on.[12] Texts—of which there were many—emphasizing the mind's role in creating phenomena often likened its activity (even while awake) to dreaming: the default stance is to take external phenomena as real, but, like dreams, they have no being apart from the mind's activity. Yu Fakai 于法開 (ca. 310–70) is reported by Ji Zang 吉藏 (549–623) to have gone further, likening this realm of saṃsāra and rebirth to a long night and all our thoughts and ideas in it to a dream, from which we may awaken by following the Buddhist path. The world is like a mere dream, with sentient beings as its protagonists, and the dream is produced by their deluded consciousness.[13] In texts like these, dreams were nothing other than delusion, or evidence of the mind's tendency to attribute external reality to things that exist only in the mind. But this was hardly the only Buddhist view of dreams, as we will see.

Direct Versus Indirect Meanings: A Fissure in the Dreamscape

Such texts as the ones just discussed represent a minority view. Since antiquity, as evidenced already in oracle bone inscriptions and other early texts,[14] the default stance was that dreams—at least some of them—*do* mean things. They *portend*. And whatever they were deemed to mean, it was often a matter of lives and fortunes, and the recording of these dreams was important work in society.

An enormous question now arises. *How* were dreams' meanings ascertained? Here the Chinese dreamscape cleaves into two great realms or modes—modes that might sometimes appear in the same text (as, for example, in the Xun Maoyuan story discussed below, in the Wordplay section) but that constitute irreducibly distinct understandings of how dreams signify. Some dreams were taken to be of great importance, but their meaning lay on the surface. No interpretation was called for. Neither the characters in the stories relating such dreams nor the stories' compilers pause to wonder whether the dreams can be taken at face value. A message is conveyed, but straightforwardly, not in code. Emphasis falls on who appeared, what the message was, and what resulted from the encounter. These are presumably what Wang Fu (but not, quite, Wang Chong) meant by *direct* 直 dreams, as seen in the previous chapter.[15] I will take up such texts in chapter 5.[16]

The other great mode of dream culture saw dreams as signifying *indirectly*, presenting a hermeneutical challenge. Dreams speak, but they speak in code. They must be deciphered for their meaning to be revealed. This chapter and the next take up texts that approach dreams in this way.

Initial Observations on Dream Interpretation

To begin, I will outline six general points.

First, seeing dreams as code created work for something (manuals and methods of interpretation) or someone (the dreamer, family members and friends, professional diviners) to do. If dreams' meanings were non-obvious, then someone had to arrive at them somehow. Someone had to have invented the method of decoding, and someone had to use it to interpret dreams. Thus was opened a cultural niche, one that was filled over the centuries by many texts and persons. And since dreams' meanings are often, to understate the case, non-obvious, it was a big niche.

Second, in every act of interpretation of which we have record, and indeed in any hypothetical case we might imagine, there is the question of who interprets.[17] There are only three basic possibilities, and I will track and sometimes comment upon these throughout this and the next chapter. The dream was either interpreted by the dreamer himself, by a family member or other acquaintance, or by a specialist. The first two scenarios suggest that dream interpretation was an activity in which many people took interest and cultivated skill. The third points to a social role documented from ancient times forward. Toward the end of the next chapter I discuss a handful of named interpreters who appear multiple times in early medieval writings.

Third, every dream interpretation of which we have record proves not only that someone saw fit to write an account of the dream and its meaning, but also that someone told of their dream to someone else prior to the writing. Anecdotes of dream interpretation always include scenes of telling, and these afford us glimpses of the social networks in which dreams were initially divulged and discussed. Recounting a dream was a type of cultural performance.[18] So was the process of interpreting a dream. It could occur in a private conversation, a chance encounter, an institutional setting such as a court or temple, or in a group of friends. It could be informal, ad hoc, or highly ritualized.[19] Both of these processes, the telling and the interpreting, were distinct from dreaming itself. However nebulous and fleeting dreams themselves might be, telling and interpreting dreams were acts situated very much in this world, in social circles, narrative, and language. Telling about and interpreting dreams with friends was a form of gossip.[20] Interpreting dreams in a court or official setting was a more formal exercise, often with more at stake, but was no less social in nature. The exchange of anecdotes of strikingly clever and successful interpretations was itself an important aspect of dream culture, one that generated and preserved many of the texts we now have. I will return to this important aspect of dream interpretation toward the end of chapter 4.

Fourth, most recorded interpretations that have survived involve either predicting the future or penetrating the fog of contemporary events to uncover latent truths. And in most recorded cases the prediction or diagnosis is borne out by subsequent happenings. There was little point in recording a prediction that later proved false, unless one wanted to argue the futility of dream interpretation or the dishonesty of one of its practitioners. (In the section on Named Professional Interpreters in chapter 4 I briefly discuss reports of faked dreams.) But this aspect of dream interpretation was, we might say, a key cultural scenario[21] reperformed in every instance and in every record of successful divination, one that repeatedly argued, in the face of apparent disorder, that the cosmos is actually an ordered matrix. I return to this point in the conclusion to chapter 4.

Fifth, specific modalities for interpreting dreams perhaps helped shape, and were shaped by, ways of interpreting discrete passages in classical and scriptural texts, particularly those such as the *Book of Odes* that were either seen as both authoritative and opaque in content, or else viewed as having no obvious relevance to the situation to which one wished to apply them.[22] In both arenas, interpretation often proceeded from single bits of input extracted from larger settings: single words, in textual hermeneutics, or single images, in dream hermeneutics. More broadly, modalities of dream interpretation could be fruitfully compared with specific ways of decoding omens or other anomalies, or the surface appearance of the face or body (in physiognomy), or even the inner character of persons based on their behaviors.[23] These are topics deserving of more sustained treatment than is possible here.[24]

Sixth, as we saw in the previous chapter both Wang Fu and Wang Chong use the same key term when discussing dreams that are not "direct" but that instead require interpretation: *xiang* 象. We must pause to consider its implications.

Dreams as Comprising xiang 象

Many texts use *xiang* to name the specific contents of dreams that mean what the interpretation says the dream means.[25] For example, a passage in *Hou Han shu* (26.908) has a man dreaming of being in a large hall. The interpreter of his dream predicts he will obtain office, based on the claim that dreaming of being in a large hall is "a form and *xiang* of palaces and bureaus" 宮府之形象. By the Han period *xiang* was a decidedly loaded term with an august pedigree. Western scholars have often translated it as "image" or "symbol," but others have questioned these equivalences.[26] The difficulty of capturing its sense is illustrated by James Legge's translation of the *Xi ci* 繫辭 (a text on which I will elaborate below), where *xiang* is variously rendered as "figure," "emblem," "indication," "semblance (shadowy form of things)," "represent," "symbolize," "visible figure," "emblematic interpretations," and "symbolic figure." Schafer proposes "effigy, simulacrum . . . analogue, counterpart, equivalent, other-identity." He explains: "Celestial events are the 'counterparts' or 'simulacra' [*xiang*] of terrestrial events; sky things have doppelgängers below, with which they are closely attuned."[27] Peterson, Rutt, and Cheng use "figure,"[28] and Lewis, "correlate,"[29] both of which have the advantage of functioning as both noun and verb, as does *xiang*.

Since the *Dao de jing* 道德經 features the Dao 道, which is similar to dreams in being ineffable, its usages are of some value here. "This [either the Dao itself or the "thread 紀 of the Dao"] is called the formless form, the thingless *xiang*" 是謂无狀之狀无物之象 (chapter 14). Conceived as a thing 物, the Dao is shapeless and formless, but "inside there are *xiang*" (chapter 21). "The great *xiang* has no shape" 大象無形 (chapter 41). "Hold on to the great *xiang* and the whole world will come to you" (chapter 35).[30] These are not the clearest of phrasings. Fortunately the earliest extant, partial commentary on the *Dao de jing*, in *Han Fei zi* 韓非子 (ca. 240 BCE)[31], glosses the chapter 14 passage thus:

> People rarely see a living elephant [*xiang* 象], but if they chance upon the bones of a dead elephant, then, going by this configuration 案其圖, they imagine 想 what it was in life. Therefore the means by which people are able to have an idea of or imagine something are all called "elephants/correlates" [*xiang*象]. Similarly here, although the Dao cannot be heard or seen, the sage takes hold of its visible accomplishments to localize and make visible its form 聖人執其見功以處見其形. Therefore the text says "the formless form, the thingless *xiang*."[32]

This creative gloss suggests that the point of having *xiang* is to provide a pathway to an otherwise unavailable counterpart. There is a non-arbitrary linkage between *xiang* and their absent correlates, a linkage gestured at by the noun *tu* 圖, but the elephant's bones are not a mimetic representation, much less an icon, of the now-vanished animal: rather, their configuration merely suggests what the creature once looked like. It is up to human observers to imagine (*xiang* 想) the absent creature based on the visible correlate. Just so, sages seize upon concrete, visible examples of the Dao's "accomplishments" to serve as correlates to the formless Dao, which though not distant or dead is, like the vanished elephant, not directly observable. It is up to us to imagine what the Dao is like based on these correlates. Passages in the *Huainanzi* 淮南子 and Guo Pu's 郭璞 preface to the *Classic of Mountains and Waterways* (*Shanhai jing* 山海經) say that sages uniquely have the ability to discern *xiang* for strange or uncannily morphing creatures—deducing their whole form and thus their true categorical identity—and so are able to remain unperturbed in their presence.[33]

Returning to matters oneiric, an unsettling question arises. If the *xiang* of which dreams are made are the counterparts of other things, what and where are those other things? Of what are dream-*xiang* the correlates or analogues? If they have been fashioned as a basis upon which we might imagine their counterparts, who or what did the fashioning? Seeing the bones, we imagine the living elephant. Seeing the accomplishments, we imagine the Dao. Seeing dreams, we imagine—what? The expected answer would seem to be that we imagine a future course of events. But, as seen in the previous chapter, the mechanism for this is decidedly unclear. We understand the process that leads from a living elephant to an arrangement of bones. We don't quite understand the process involving the Dao, but we can accept that at least metaphorically there is a thingless thing called the Dao that effects results in the world (such as when water cuts a path through rock—one of the Dao's figures mentioned in *Dao de jing*) and we can imagine what it is like by seeing those results. But how does it happen that when a person dreams of X, it means Y will likely occur? Most of the texts sampled below simply do not pause to consider this question. Neither the mental or cosmic mechanisms that produce dreams in us nor their ontological status are taken up for reflection. Instead, the focus rests on how, having dreamed, we may extract what the dream has to say.

Aside from the *Dao de jing*, the other early *loci classici* for *xiang* are two: the "Xi ci" 繫辭, or "Commentary on the Appended Phrases," a fragmentary discourse attached to the *Classic of Changes* (*Yi jing* 易經) sometime before the mid-second century BCE,[34] and Wang Bi's 王弼 (226–49) glosses on the "Xi ci" along with his discourse "Clarifying the *Xiang*" 明象, both included in his commentary on the *Classic of Changes*.[35] Of the many "Xi ci" passages on *xiang*, two are of particular interest here.

> Sages could see all the mysteries under heaven, and, following their form and appearance, made fitting *xiang* [Rutt has "representations," Lynn "images"] of them, which are therefore called *xiang*.[36]
>
> 聖人有以見天下之賾,而擬諸其形容,象其物宜,是故謂之象.
>
> The Master said: "Writing does not fully convey speech. Speech does not fully convey meaning." Can we then not know the sages' meaning? The Master said: "The sages established *xiang* to convey all meanings, invented hexagrams to convey the innate tendencies of things and their deviations, and attached phrases [to the hexagrams] to convey all in words, [so that] the transformations and flow [from one hexagram to another] would convey all benefits and drumming and dancing [the Changes] would convey their numinous power."[37]
>
> 子曰,書不盡言,言不盡意.然則聖人之意,其不可見乎.子曰:聖人立象以盡意,設卦以盡情偽,繫辭以盡其言,變而通之以盡利,鼓之舞之以盡神.

The main argument of these not entirely clear statements is that the *xiang* of the *Changes* embody mysteries otherwise inaccessible to us and fully convey meanings that cannot be expressed in speech or in writing—a rather odd claim to find in a verbal divination manual.[38] Again, as seen in the *Dao de jing* passages and the *Han Fei zi* gloss, the reason for having *xiang* is to convey more completely something that cannot otherwise be adequately articulated or grasped. And this text supplies a word for what is conveyed by *xiang*: *yi* 意, "meanings" or "ideas."

Because the meaningful things seen in dreams were termed *xiang*, we are invited once again to transfer these notions about *xiang* in divination generally and in the *Changes* more specifically into the oneiric realm. And when we do, questions again arise. If, in the case of the *Changes*, the sages created *xiang* to transmit ideas and mysteries otherwise hard to grasp, who fashions the *xiang* seen in our dreams? Why do we dream in *xiang* at all—why not simply and always dream in *yi* 意, meanings or ideas, directly? Most seriously, the commentary's claims for *xiang* create problems for those who would divine dreams, because they circumscribe the effectiveness of any verbal interpretation. From the point of view of the "Xi ci," there is a plenitude to the *xiang* that cannot be fully captured in words. Any verbal conveyance of a dream's meaning will leave something out. Whatever meaningful content went into dreams (by whatever mysterious agency or process) to end up fully expressed in their *xiang*, no oral or written characterization can exhaustively extract it. We thus end up with a picture rather like that sketched by Moulay Abedsalem, an illiterate Moroccan pallbearer and shroud maker befriended by the anthropologist Vincent Crapanzano: "What one dreams is what the soul has witnessed. Dream distortion results, he said, from the mind's . . . inability to translate accurately what the soul has experienced. Insofar as mind has to make use of words to convey dreams, it is words that distort them. [But] how else, [he] asked with terrible irony, would we know our dreams" at all?[39]

But Wang Bi's comments on this last notion have the effect of walking it back. For him, both the *xiang* of the *Changes* and any attached verbal explanations are mere expedients designed to get across the meaning (*yi* 意). Once the reader has gotten the meaning, the words and the *xiang* may be abandoned, like *Zhuangzi*'s fish bait and rabbit snare after getting the fish and rabbit.[40] As Ronald Egan notes, "It is not just that 'images' may be dispensed with once the idea has been grasped, but also that keeping an 'image' in mind . . . ensures that the idea will *not* be grasped. . . . Consequently, Wang Bi arrives at his conclusion that 'getting the ideas is in fact a matter of forgetting the images' (得意在忘象)."[41] In the oneiric realm, Wang Bi's stance on the mere expediency—yet communicative adequacy—of *xiang* allows for confidence in the verbal interpretation of *xiang* in dreams.

In any event, seeing dreams as consisting of *xiang* opens up certain ways of responding to them and closes off other possible ways. If dreams comprise *xiang*, and if *xiang* are semiotic signs, then dreams cannot be taken at face value; if they mean something, their meaning is not what appears on the surface. The images seen in dreams then become instances of something more general. As a communicative event, the dream is thus ratcheted up a level, and its components can be read in light of some general divination system (*langue*) of which any particular dream component is merely an instance (*parole*).[42] This is what I mean when I say that in the prospective paradigm, dreams occupy a meta-level with respect to the world of events, whereas in the visitation paradigm dreams are themselves events in the world.

On now to the texts.

Dreambooks

We have many texts attesting to how dreams were interpreted, but they are of only two basic types. On the one hand we have *lists of dream indications* paired with what they generally portend; on the other, *narratives* of specific situations in which a dream is related and then interpreted by someone. These two types of texts contain very different sorts of information about how and by whom meaning was attached to dreams, and they document very different modes of interpretation.

I will refer to the first sort of text as *dreambooks*. Probably every culture has at some point developed standardized lists of dream signs: "The list is, perhaps, the most archaic and pervasive of genres,"[43] as Jonathan Z. Smith observed. Its prime function is information retrieval. Ancient and medieval cultures developed forms of *Listenwissenschaft*, "a science which takes as its prime intellectual activity the production and reflection on lists, catalogs, and classifications, which progresses by establishing precedents, by observing patterns, similarities, and conjunctions, by noting repetitions. Such a science is particularly noticeable in omen and legal materials."[44] Dreambooks are *Listenwissenschaft* applied to dreams. Such lists are one way in which societies have sought to bring some degree of order and regularity into the intrinsically strange oneiric realm.[45] They do not necessarily depend on writing: oral cultures have often developed standardized arrays of dream signs as well.[46]

We know that written keys to dream signs existed in China from early times, although to my knowledge no pre-Qin examples have been transmitted. In his *Penetrating Account of Customs* (*Fengsu tongyi* 風俗通義), Ying Shao 應劭 (140–206) quotes from the *Yanzi chunqiu* 晏子春秋 (pre-2nd century BCE)[47] an anecdote in which a man suffering from illness has a dream divined and the diviner asks permission to consult his manual before proceeding.[48] Ban Gu's 班固 (32–92) bibliographic catalog in the *History of the Han* lists two dreambooks totaling thirty-one rolls.[49] At least eight dreambooks are listed in the *History of the Sui* catalog (completed in 656).[50] In a passage in the *History of the Jin* (completed 646–48[51]) narrating events dating to the end of the third century, a governor, impressed by a dream diviner's accuracy, asks to see the manual he used—his *zhan shu* 占書 or "divination book."[52] Written keys to dream

Table 3. Common dream figures and their meanings in Wang Fu's *Discourses of a Recluse*

Figures	Meaning
1. Clarity, purity; luxuriant groves and forests; palaces, implements, things newly completed.	Plans will be brought to completion; happiness.
2. Things foul, filthy, rotten, broken, withered, dark; tottering, instability; obstruction; loosening, sinking, falling.	Plans impeded, not brought to fruition.
3. Monstrous beasts or plants; odious things.	Trouble [lacuna].
4. Charts, paintings; things before they have taken shape; false inscriptions, empty vessels.	Pretense and deception.
5. Actors, singers, dancers; children's games and toys.	Joy and laughter.

signs were thus fairly commonplace, if not ubiquitous, throughout the Han and early medieval periods.[53]

Wang Fu, in his second-century discussion, gives a list of common dream signs and their general meanings. He was perhaps generalizing over various manuals or else bits of folk practice known to him. In his list he mentions five clusters of common dream figures (*xiang* 象) and their associated meanings (see table 3).[54]

We have some manuscript material as well. Hunan University's Yuelu Academy in 2007 purchased a batch of roughly two thousand ancient bamboo and wood slips from a Hong Kong antiquities dealer. The cache was later enlarged by a private donation to 2,174 slips. The slips, which had clearly been looted from a tomb, were of unknown provenance, but scholars have determined that the calligraphy dates to the Qin period (221–206 BCE) and that, based on some of the administrative details mentioned in them, they were probably buried with an official in what is now Hubei.[55] This corpus comprises texts dealing with local administration, law, music, and mathematics. One of them was a manual of dream interpretation.

This untitled manual, insofar as it can be reconstructed,[56] follows three main interpretive principles. One group of passages assigns meaning to dreams based solely on the day or time of day when the dream occurred. For example, one slip reads in part: "*Wu* or *ji* dreams [i.e., dreams occurring at these times in the temporal cycle of hours or days] [foretell] conversations. *Geng* or *xin* dreams [foretell] happiness. *Ren* or *gui* dreams [foretell] disturbances."[57] As another slip in the series[58] explains, "Each day is divided into five [segments], each night into three: auspicious and inauspicious have their segments, good and odious their causes."[59] Other passages key on a combination of when the dreams occurred and what they contained. For instance: "If on a *jia* or *yi* day one dreams of felling trees: auspicious. If on a *bing* or *ding* day one dreams of wildfire on a sunny elevation: auspicious. If on an *wu* or *ji* day one [dreams of] official business:[60] auspicious. If on a *geng* or *xin* day one dreams of [1-character lacuna] on a mountain and casting [?] bells: auspicious."[61] The third and commonest type of entry assigns a meaning to dream content without regard to when the dream took place. But here the interpretations go far beyond "auspicious" or "inauspicious," offering much more specific predictions. For example: "[If one dreams of] wading across a stream, [it means] a noted person will arrive. If one dreams of a well or canal, [it means] one will lose wealth."[62] And in some of these entries the prediction is further specified according to whether the dreamer is a man or a woman: "If one dreams of grain being produced from the [lacuna], if a man, one will acquire capital, if a woman, one will acquire iron vessels."[63]

A slightly more complex dreambook-style hemerological guide also appears in one of the two bamboo-strip daybooks (*rishu* 日書) excavated from the tomb at Shuihudi 睡虎地, dating to 217 BCE.[64] This guide to dream meanings involves four vectors: the day on which the dream occurs, according to the "heaven stems" (*tiangan* 天干) system of the sexagenary day-counting cycle; the predominant color of imagery (black, green, or blue) seen in the dream; the particular categories of phenomena (clothing, the sun) seen in the dream; and the five phases.[65] The meanings are prognostic and uniformly auspicious.

Twelve manuscripts of dreambooks (plus a handful of smaller fragments) dating from the ninth and tenth centuries were recovered at Dunhuang.[66] These texts are quite similar in genre and format to the Qin-period slips acquired by the Yuelu Academy. Taken together, this whole corpus of bamboo and paper manuscripts probably represents fairly adequately the dreambook genre as it existed from the late classical to the medieval period. Some of the Dunhuang texts are on rolls, others in codex form.[67] In some cases the same text is represented by more than one manuscript, with variations that sometimes appear to be copyists' errors but other times seem to indicate divergent interpretive traditions. Overall, most dream signs tagged as auspicious in one text are similarly tagged in the others, indicating a degree of uniformity in the basic interpretation.

There is likewise uniformity in format. With very few exceptions, these texts take the form of lists of dream signs, each introduced by the phrase "if you see in a dream" (*meng jian* 夢見), followed by what they portend. Here are just a few examples from the only complete text among them, *New Collection of the Duke of Zhou's Book for Interpreting Dreams* (*Xinji Zhougong jiemeng shu* 新集周公解夢書):[68] To dream of ascending into the sky means one will have a noble child. To dream of seeing a clear sky means concord and great joy. To dream of looking up at the sky presages long life. To dream of seeing the sun and moon means a great amnesty is coming. To dream of being illuminated by the sun and moon means great honors. To dream of the sun and moon disappearing is greatly inauspicious. And so on.

The Dunhuang manuals typically divide signs and their meanings according to topical categories[69] for ease of consultation, much in the way contemporaneous "category books" (*leishu* 類書) covering wide ranges of topics were organized.[70] This is a level of organization not seen in the sole pre-Han dreambook so far recovered. Drège and Drettas identify thirteen such categories that recur in these works: the heavens; the earth; vegetation; habitations; familial and marital matters; official affairs; religious institutions, roles, and rites; agriculture; the body and familiar objects; beverages and foods; vehicles, travel, and commerce; animals wild and domestic; water and fire.[71]

It is unclear whether the Dunhuang manuals were meant for, and owned and used by, professional dream diviners or non-specialists.[72] The Yuelu Academy slips seem to have been buried with an official unlikely to have been an oneiromancy specialist. Either way, the process would presumably have gone something like this: Someone had a dream and then recollected it. They, or the party interpreting the dream on their behalf (a diviner, family member, or friend), selected an image from it that seemed especially important. The person doing the interpreting opened the manual, located the relevant section, and checked whether the image was listed there—and, if so, the interpreter derived a prognosis. If my own experience is any guide (and it may well not be), almost any dream that can be recalled upon waking contains more than one image, but the manuals give no guidance on how to choose the most important one for divining. However the choice was made, reducing an entire dream narrative to a single element is one of the most striking things about this mode of interpretation. It sits at the opposite end of a spectrum from some twentieth-century methods in which every last detail in a dream, however apparently trivial, is held to be meaningful.[73]

In addition to giving lists of signs and their meanings, two of the Dunhuang manuscripts, including *New Collection of the Duke of Zhou's Book for Interpreting Dreams* as attested in P3908, provide an alternate, purely hemerological way to interpret dreams: by the day, or the hour of the day, in which the dream occurred.[74] In one manuscript, for example, to dream—of anything—on a day designated *mao* 卯 in the cycle of twelve branches (*shi er zhi* 十二支) is inauspicious and means that there will be quarrels. In another manuscript, to dream on that day means that a visitor will arrive and that administrative affairs are to be avoided.[75]

Interpreting solely based of the timing of the dream, entirely ignoring its content, seems to have been relatively unusual, and is seldom mentioned in dreambooks or narrative texts. (As we have seen, however, examples occur in the Qin-period strips discussed above. An early precedent in transmitted texts comes in the *Zuo Tradition*, when Zhao Yang 趙鞅 [d. 496 BCE] dreams of a naked boy whirling and singing—seemingly a vivid dream image, though perhaps less so in the early China cultural context than in ours—and his dream is interpreted solely in terms of its timing relative to a solar eclipse, while its content is completely ignored.)[76] Such a practice finds parallels in the hemerological diagnostic systems recovered from some excavated medical manuscripts, in which illnesses are identified solely by the days in the cycle on which they began.[77]

The dreambooks' most notable rhetorical feature is that they provide no rationale for assigning specific meanings to dream content. The meanings are simply stated as givens—though not as self-evident, since in that case there would be no need for dreambooks. One way to understand this is as a function of the intended practicality of these manuals:

theoretical discussions are dispensed with so that the user can get right down to business.[78] Another is to see it as a considered persuasive strategy, one that is arguably similar to that evidenced in exorcism manuals from earlier times.[79] Perhaps the very strangeness or seeming arbitrariness of these keys to dreams' secret meanings were meant to enhance their perceived authority. The texts partially display what purports to be an insider's knowledge of dreams' mysterious symbolic code, while concealing the supposed logic of how it was first arrived at and by whom—except insofar as the titles of some of these works associate them with an authoritative, ancient cultural figure, the Duke of Zhou of whom Confucius had famously lamented his failure to dream.[80] This simultaneous display of arcane knowledge (or its effects) and concealment of how it was derived is common in texts conveying esoterica as well as stories of the exploits of masters of esoterica.[81]

Hermeneutically, the dreambook mode is most striking for two things: its stripped-down simplicity, achieved by reducing an entire dream sequence to a single image and by excluding everything else from consideration; and its assigning of a single, fixed meaning to that image. Whatever else may have appeared in the dream, and whatever circumstances might pertain in the dreamer's life situation, all these are bracketed. The complexity and ambiguity of dreams, and the jumble of circumstances attending them, are determinedly ignored. Instead we find a plotting of one-to-one correspondences between single images (or times of dreaming) and their purported significations—a grid of settled correlations, reducing the muddle, mutability, affective tone, and bizarreness of dreams to a locative scheme of semiotic order. And yet the interpretive output provided by the book, although in some cases only general ("auspicious" or "inauspicious"), was sometimes quite specific ("the ancestors wish to eat," "a traveler will arrive," "your wife is having an affair"). Of course, the relative simplicity of dreambooks' interpretive grids is merely an aspect of the texts themselves. In terms of how their prognostic output may have been used by people in negotiating their lives, there was much room—indeed, much need—for creativity. The manuals provide a rough idea of only one thing to expect. It was up to users to decide how, or whether, to apply it to their lives.[82]

In his *Discourses of a Recluse*, Wang Fu reflects on why dream divinations can sometimes be inaccurate. What he says yields insight into some of the many factors people saw as relevant when using dreambooks in actual life situations. He asks why clear dreams often foretell nothing while murky ones sometimes give true augury. The reason: "Those who discuss their dreams are hindered by the fact that they do not understand analytic terminology; they can only attach names to things in an ignorant and confused manner" 本所謂之夢者, 困不了[> 憭] 察之稱, 而懵憒冒名也.[83] A bit further on he observes: "In the case of dreams on a given night, numberless transformations may occur. The dreamer may see a succession of hundreds of different things, and so it is difficult for him to examine and tell of it. This is why diviners are not always accurate. It is not the fault of the divination [method or book] but of the dreamer" 今一寢之夢, 或屢遷化, 百物代至, 而其主不能究道之, 故占者有不中也. 此非占之罪也, 乃夢者過也.[84] Wang Fu recognizes that how the dreamer narrates the dream to an interpreter will necessarily shape its interpretation—an insight developed, in ways he could never have imagined, by Sigmund Freud.[85] When predictions based on dream interpretations failed to come true, many clients of diviners or users of dreambooks probably faulted the diviner or the book, whereas Wang redistributes much of the blame to dreamers themselves. But he goes on to recognize that "some people do tell of their dreams in great detail, yet the diviner may fail to assign things [in the dream] to the proper categories or correctly gloss its scenes, and so his predictions of good or bad may not pan out. This is not because the books are deceptive but because the interpreter has erred. Thus the hardest thing in oneiromancy is understanding the manuals used" 或言夢審矣, 而說者不能連類傳觀, 故其善惡有不驗也. 此非書之罔, 乃說之過也. 是故占夢之難者, 讀其書爲難也.[86] The one part of the process Wang Fu does not fault is the dreambooks themselves. If the dreamer tells of the dream adequately and the interpreter applies the book skillfully, considering both the dreamer's feelings and temperament and the timing of the dream[87]—phrasing that encompasses several of the categories of dreams he articulates earlier in the same discourse—then an apt interpretation, while never guaranteed, is likely.

In dreambooks, then, in terms of content and method of interpretation, we might say that the messiness of the oneiric realm was at least apparently brought under a sort of order. But much of the necessary reductive work took place off-page, as the user decided which dream image to look up. And the simplicity of the meanings supplied in the books, lending a false appearance of orderliness to the dream world, allowed for—indeed required—much pliability in application, so much so that the guidance given in the books amounts to very little. Coupled with the fact that the majority of meanings given in the Dunhuang manuals are auspicious rather than inauspicious,[88] it seems that what the dreambooks provided their users was, as in any other method of divination, "a feeling of control within chaotic circumstances,"[89] a bolstering against uncertainty that was only as potent as the client's confidence in the manuals and the diviners. It might be that for an ordinary person, simply having such a book, even if it was seldom consulted, was itself reassuring. And for a professional diviner, possessing such a manual was an important badge of authority. For both sorts of users, owning this sort of mapping of the oneiric realm must have functioned almost talismanically.[90]

One other rhetorical feature of dreambooks bears mentioning. It is possible that, for some readers, such lists also functioned prescriptively. It is as if they said, regarding inauspicious figures, "These are the bad figures—avoid dreaming them!" and, regarding auspicious ones, "These are the best dreams to have—dream them!"[91] Yet these imagined injunctions assume dreamers have some control over what they dream, which is not the case outside of techniques of lucid dreaming (of which I have yet to find many clear examples). Perhaps it would be better to say that for most users the dreambook lists sometimes functioned aspirationally.

Interlude: A Buddhist Dreambook

I know of at least one extensive Buddhist dreambook.[92] While reserving a more in-depth discussion of it for elsewhere, I want to compare it briefly to the texts described above.

In 713 the southern Indian monk Bodhiruci 菩提流支, who had arrived in Chang'an and Luoyang in 693,[93] completed his supervision of the translation and assemblage of forty-nine separate sutras into a collection known as *Heap of Jewels* (*Da baoji jing* 大寶積經, *Ratnakūṭa*), devoted to aspects of the bodhisattva path.[94] One of them was *Sutra on the Explication of Dreams for Bodhisattvas* or *Pusa shuomeng jing* 菩薩說夢經 (*Svapnanirdeśa*[?], in T 310, 11:80c–91b, also titled *Jingju tianzi* 淨居天子會, taking up *juan* 15–16 of *Da baoji jing*). Its translation is attributed to Dharmarakṣa (fl. ca. 266–308), probably falsely, but in any case it is known to have existed in Chinese by 598.[95]

What this text contains is an extensive system for dream-based self-diagnosis by Buddhist practitioners who understood themselves to be progressing on the bodhisattva path toward Buddhahood. The text lists 108 dream signs (*xiang* 相, *lakṣaṇa*) and their meanings.[96] After the standard sort of sutra introduction, the text opens by simply listing the 108 signs. Then follows the main body, in which each sign is decoded to indicate the particular point on the ten-stage bodhisattva path the dreamer has reached. Following each diagnosis (in most cases) comes a prescription of practices to remove whatever karmic blockage is evidenced by the dream so that the dreamer can advance on the path.

The text reproduced in the Taishō Sino-Japanese canon is in some disarray but is coherent enough to allow its working principles to be discerned.[97] Many of the dream signs have to do with Buddhist practice and concerns, but some do not. The sutra's main functions are diagnostic and therapeutic. The key information included in each of the 108 diagnoses is which stage of the (standard ten-stage) bodhisattva path the dreamer has reached. Most diagnoses allow that the dreamer may be at any of several stages, up to all ten of them.[98] In such cases, further details are added to fine-tune the diagnosis according to what was dreamed. For example, for one who dreams of being a king (sign 90), if he is frightened in the dream, this indicates he is at the first stage of the path; if he is visiting a monastery in the dream, the second stage; if sightseeing in a park, the third stage; if making offerings to gods, the fourth stage; if in a large city, the fifth stage; and so on.[99]

The interest of the text does not stop at diagnosis, however, and extends to etiology and the prescription of therapies. Explanations are provided of how the practitioner came to have a particular karmic obstruction, hindrance, or blockage (*ye zhang* 業障, *karmāvaraṇa* or *nīvaraṇa*) due to particular types of failings in previous lives.[100] To dream of sitting atop Mount Sumeru, for example (sign 68, 87a22), indicates an insufficiency of karmic merit due to having befriended evil persons, cultivated wickedness, and ignored the advice of good friends in past lives. To see oneself at the top of a mountain (sign 69, 87a29) indicates one has disrespected preachers of Dharma. To dream of seeing oneself smeared with filth, a particularly inauspicious sign (number 89, 88c25), indicates one has maligned the Buddha and habitually practiced evil deeds. These past-life karmic etiologies are familiar from other Buddhist texts, including ones outlining divination procedures not based on dreams, such as the *Consecration Sutra* (*Guanding jing* 灌頂經), composed in China in the fifth century, and the sixth-century *Sutra for Divining Retribution for Good and Bad Karma* (*Zhancha shan'e yebao jing* 占察善惡業報經).[101] On the other hand, some karmic obstructions are attributed not to one's own misdeeds in past lives—at least not directly—but to the activity of demons who throw karmic obstacles in the practitioner's path.

The text recommends specific actions to remove the blockages revealed by each type of dream. Sign 73 (87b24), for example, in which one has dreamed of mounting a dragon or elephant, specifies that the bodhisattva should cultivate reverence and generosity and avoid delusion and falsehood. The listing under sign 99 (89c15), in which the dream is of seeing lightning issuing from a thundercloud, prescribes cultivating thoughts of goodness, relinquishing attachments, and gathering more spells (*tuoluoni* 陀羅尼; *dhāraṇī*). The recommended practices are standard bits of the bodhisattva's repertoire, but the advice varies across the 108 dream signs, implying that the specific practices linked to each dream sign are especially good for removing the particular obstruction indicated. And some of the prescribed practices are unusually rigorous, such as the three years of continuous, day and night confession after dreaming of being smeared in filth (sign 89).

How does this text compare to the dreambooks discussed above? In the *Pusa shuomeng jing*, as in the other dreambooks, dreams signify indirectly; their surface content is not what they are really about. Here, too, the manual for decoding them takes the form of a list of signs paired with their meanings—although it is made suppler and more complex by the inclusion of numerous sub-rubrics under each main sign. But in this case the meanings are in some ways much more specific than those seen in the Yuelu Academy and Dunhuang manuals. And this text, unlike the other dreambooks we've discussed, has pronounced etiological and prescriptive elements: it not only provides the meaning of dream signs but also tells the reader *why* (though not *how*) he or she has seen this image in a dream and what to do in response. The sutra is in a position to prescribe specific courses of action because it can assume its reader is operating in a circumscribed matrix of practice governed by known assumptions and rules. This text, unlike the dreambooks surveyed above, is diagnostic, not predictive—it is inward or backwards looking, not prospective. The hidden information it brings across is not a likely future course of events but rather the dreamer's current, temporary position on a fixed soteriological path, combined with a snapshot of whatever specific bit of his karmic history triggered, by some unspecified mechanism, the dream. Neither that karmic history nor the dreamer's present position on the path would otherwise be knowable to him.

From Dreambooks to Narratives

The Yuelu Academy and Dunhuang manuscripts and the Buddhist *Pusa shuomeng jing* are important because they are our best early examples of what medieval dream-interpretation manuals looked like, and because they are, precisely, manuals, not theoretical or historical writings. The Yuelu Academy and Dunhuang documents are also important because they are manuscripts, preserving texts in their actual circulating states at a specific point in time, unmodified by intervening generations. But, as we have seen, what they can tell us about the actual practice of dream interpretation is sharply limited because they are only manuals and because their mode of interpretation is grid-like. Besides, in any culture there is something intrinsically odd about dream interpretations (oral or written) that reduce the dream to a single image, given that many dreams are mostly narrative, not just imagistic, in nature. Often we do not just see a single, static scene. We move through a sequence of actions or events in which we participate as more than passive observers, often with a strong emotional tone. This is another way of saying that dreambook-style interpretation is a very reductionist way of trying to bring order to dreams.

In many ways, extant Chinese narratives of dream interpretation convey much more information. They show us processes of divination as sequences of talk and action embedded in specific life situations and in social networks.[102] They portray people talking about dreams, creatively attaching meaning to them, and then responding. Surprisingly, they also often explain the actual logic of how dreams were deciphered, something the dreambooks never do. And they document a much wider range of hermeneutical methods than do the manuals. As Jean-Claude Schmitt writes of two very similar genres in medieval Europe, "The narratives consider dreams both in their totality and in a unique personal or social situation, while the keys [i.e., dreambooks] fragment the oneiric content into a myriad of discrete elements and isolated images, interpreting them according to an alternative logic, regardless of context."[103] The two sorts of texts have almost nothing to do with one another, to the point that Schmitt wonders if the European dreambooks, which were often associated with the prophet Daniel, were ever used at all.

The very existence of these many anecdotes tells us something important about the cultural place of dreams. The fact that such accounts were initially written down by someone, then preserved by other people in various textual formats, attests to the seriousness with which dreams were taken. And from the elaborate detail found in some of these stories we sense the delight people took in clever decipherings of dreams. The methods used by skilled interpreters had many of the qualities of games. Readers obviously relished instances in which the interpretive game was played consummately.

Let us now sample some of the many stories of dream divination that have come down to us from the early medieval period (and, in a few cases, from somewhat earlier). I proceed from simpler to more complex interpretive methods.

Once more, I am not interested in the context of any particular instance of dream interpretation. Even less am I interested in the question of the historicity of this or that report ("Did so-and-so really dream this?" "Was this really the dream's aftermath?"). Because I am reading across a body of narratives to map the range of ways in which dreams could be represented and credibly imagined as having been interpreted, and by whom, I treat the entire corpus of such narratives as a discourse shaped by and for social memory. What I am interested in is the set of ways it was possible to imagine interpreting dreams.

CHAPTER FOUR

Interpretations and Interpreters, Part II

I begin with a brief story in which a dream is not yet interpreted but merely reported and discussed. The passage affords us a glimpse of the sorts of social exchanges that generated the narratives we have about dreams and people's responses to them. The mother of a future well-regarded general of the Wu kingdom, Sun Jian 孫堅 (d. 191), while pregnant with him is said to have dreamed her intestines emerged and wrapped themselves around the Chang gate.[1] When she woke she was frightened. She spoke of her dream to a neighboring woman, who said, "How do you know it's not an auspicious omen?" In effect, the rest of Sun Jian's biography serves to confirm the neighbor's reassuring response.[2]

Anecdotes of Interpretation and Hermeneutical Modes

This is how almost every extant record of a dream began its life. Someone, upon waking, spoke of their dream to someone else—in this case not a family member but a neighbor—and a conversation ensued about what it might portend. Perhaps a record was made at the time. More likely this story was recalled (or perhaps invented) much later, after Sun Jian had risen from humble origins to become an effective battle commander.

Here now is one of the simplest interpretations imaginable of a non-direct dream. One of Wang Dao's 王導 (276–339)[3] grandsons, Wang Xun 珣,[4] dreamed a man gave him an enormous writing brush. On waking, Wang Xun told someone that the dream portended he would be asked to write something important. Soon afterwards the emperor died, and he was commissioned to help compose the encomium.[5] The interpretation works by simple metonymy: being given a brush indicates a writing commission; its large size correlates with the importance of the occasion. We see the dreamer telling of his dream to unnamed others and interpreting it himself.

Another instance of dream-telling comes from a story about Luo Han 羅含 (ca. 303–80). One day when young he dreamed a bird with strange markings flew into his mouth. Startled, he woke and told of it. Someone in his aunt's family, which was raising him, said, "A bird with markings indicates you will certainly produce refined writings." The boy applied himself even more diligently thereafter and did eventually become an official and author.[6] Here again we see the dreamer speaking of his dream to people close to him. In this case the interpretation is done by someone else. This reading of the meaning of the bird with markings was idiosyncratic, as far as I am aware.[7] I suspect that there must have been many such cases of individuals, families, or groups convinced, for whatever reason, that a certain dream correlate generally carried a particular meaning. We can assume that few such local, idiosyncratic interpretations made it into the archive. There must once have been many others. As we would expect to find, both of these semiotically simple interpretations are borne out by subsequent events, and this is pointedly noted.

In three more anecdotes we see dreamers confidently interpreting their own dreams in relatively simple ways. When the general Lü Guang 呂光 was advancing his troops to attack the capital of Kucha (384), an important oasis town on the northern silk route in the Tarim Basin, he is said to have dreamed one night of a golden elephant flying over the city wall. His interpretation: "This means the Buddha-god is leaving them. The barbarians must surely fall."[8] Again, the interpretation rests on simple metonymy, this time with an allusion to the famous story of Han emperor Ming's dream of a flying golden figure that turned out to be the Buddha.[9]

Zhou Pan 周磐 (49–121),[10] in his seventy-third year, held an assembly of his students. After a day of discussion he confided to his sons that he had dreamed of conversing with his former teacher in the southwest corner of his tomb.[11] He then sighed, said that his death was imminent, and requested a meager burial.[12] He died soon afterward without any sign of illness. For Zhou Pan, it seems, dreaming of either conversing with one's deceased teacher or doing so in the southwest corner of his tomb, or both, were signs of approaching death.[13] But the text does not elaborate. Even more laconic is the report that the famous general Guan Yu 關羽 (d. 219) dreamed that a boar bit his leg and, apparently on that basis, announced that he would die within the year.[14] No explanation is provided of how he reached this prediction, but events confirmed it.

Hermeneutics Explained

Unlike those we have seen so far, many anecdotes of dream interpretation do explain how a dream's meaning was derived. We may wonder why this is so. I believe the answer is that story-exchangers and readers relished these details, to the point of being as interested in the logic of interpretation as in the outcome of events. Each story we will now look at includes an account of how the interpreter decoded the dream.[15]

In the previous chapter I mentioned that in his *Fengsu tongyi*, Ying Shao (140–206) quotes from the *Annals of Master Yan* (*Yanzi chunqiu* 晏子春秋, pre-2nd century BCE)[16] the story of a dream interpretation. I return to that story now. Duke Jing of Qi suffered from an illness classified under the water sign. One night he dreamed of fighting with two suns and losing. When Master Yan next appeared at court, the duke told him of the dream and asked if it meant he would soon die. Yan asked to summon a diviner of dreams. When the diviner arrived, Yan explained why he had been summoned. The diviner wished to consult his manual, but Yan told him not to bother. The duke's illness, he said, was Yin, and the sun was Yang. One Yin cannot prevail over two Yangs: the illness would soon resolve. Tell this to the duke as your answer, Yan instructed. So the diviner went in for the audience, the duke narrated his dream, and the diviner replied as requested. Three days later the duke had recovered. He was about to reward the diviner when the latter revealed that the merit was not his: it was Master Yan who had told him what to say. The duke summoned Yan and was about to present him with the reward, but Yan said: "It is because the dream diviner relayed my response that you recovered, sir. If I had told it to you myself, you would not have believed me. So your recovery was due to the dream diviner's powers. The merit is not mine." The duke rewarded them both.[17]

Here, the interpretation is so simple that Yan can suggest dispensing with the diviner's manual: suns are Yang, illness is Yin. In the dream the Yin-afflicted dreamer lost a fight with the suns, so the interpretive output is that the illness will recede. More interesting is the psychological insight the story reflects. The dreamer, we might say, had more confidence in the optimistic prognosis when it was delivered by someone he saw as authoritative in such matters. There is even the suggestion that the duke's recovery owed more to his trust in the interpretation and the specialist than to whatever cosmic vibes the dream may have reflected—a divinatory placebo effect. That the wise Master Yan understood this is presented as more impressive than his ability to parse the dream.

In 279, a tomb in Ji commandery 汲郡 (present-day Jixian 汲縣, Henan) that had been sealed in 296 BCE was unearthed. The texts recovered from the tomb caused a stir among late Western Jin scholars,[18] likely stimulating interest in the collection of reports of "strange things" old and new.[19] Three of them concerned divination, but they were not manuals—they were collections of anecdotes. Two of these texts focused entirely on anecdotes of divination; the third mixed such tales with other narratives of uncanny events. Taken together, the contents of the three texts suggest that the use of divination by important clients had come to be seen either as a problem to be pondered or an exemplary tradition to be emulated—not, in any case, something taken for granted. The amassing of cases from authoritative sources would both clarify past uses of divination and justify its ongoing use at the time each compilation was made.

One of the works was *Gui zang* 歸藏, *Returning to Be Stored.*[20] Quotations from it had survived in several early medieval works, including Zhang Hua's 張華 (232–300) *Treatise on Curiosities* (*Bowu zhi* 博物志).[21] By the Song, scholars had doubted the authenticity of recompilations of such quotations.[22] But a bamboo-strip version unearthed in 1993 from a tomb at Wangjiatai 王家台 in Hubei Province overlaps considerably with the extant quotations. (The tomb occupant seems to have been a diviner himself, though there is no evidence as to how he used the text.) Most entries take the following form: In the past a protagonist, X, had another party, Y, prognosticate about a specific situation or course of action. Y pronounced it auspicious/inauspicious.[23] *Gui zang* differs from the *Classic of Changes* in one respect important for our purposes: the main content under each hexagram is usually a brief record of a specific historical or proto-historical instance of divination by named agents.[24] A second work recovered from the Ji tomb was called *Shi Chun* 師春, characterized thus in the *History of the Jin* biography of Shu Xi 束皙, an official involved in studying the documents: "One bundle. It inscribes the many instances of turtleshell and milfoil divination from the *Zuo Tradition*. 'Shi Chun' seems to be the name of the maker of the text."[25] *Shi Chun* testifies to the effort made by someone in late Warring States times to cull the cases of divination from the *Zuo Tradition* and amass them in a distinct compilation—testament to an effort to bring this set of arcane practices under some sort of textual order.

It is on a third text, however, that I wish to focus. *Suo yu* 瑣語 (*Trifling Anecdotes*)[26] is described in Shu Xi's biography as "eleven bundles [of bamboo strips]. A text of divinations, dreams, prodigies, and strange events from the many states" 十一篇, 諸國卜夢妖怪相書也.[27] Surviving quotations support this characterization. Two of them concern dream interpretation:

> Duke Ping of Jin dreamed he saw a red bear peering through his screen. He regarded it as evil and was taken ill. He sent someone to ask Zichan 子產 about it. Zichan said: "In antiquity Gong Gong's 共工 minister was called Fuyou 浮遊 (Floater). When he had been defeated by Zhuan Xu 顓頊, he threw himself into the Huai River and drowned.[28] His color was red, his speech fond of laughing, his movements fond of looking backward, his shape like a bear. He is frequently a curse to those under heaven. If he is seen in the hall, then the one who rules over the world will die. If he is seen before the hall, then the people of the country will be startled. If he is seen in the door, then ministers close to the ruler will be anxious. If he is seen in the courtyard, then there will be no harm. If he peered through my lord's screen, there will be illness but no harm. If you sacrifice to Zhuan Xu and Gong Gong, you will recover." The duke did as advised. His illness improved.[29]

> Duke Jing of Qi wanted to attack Song. Upon reaching Quling he dreamed he saw a great gentleman who was very tall, and there was a short man standing as a guest before him. The duke told Master Yan 晏子about this. Yan said, "What was your dream about?" The duke said, "A great gentleman who was very tall, big below and small above. He spoke very angrily and he liked to look upward." Yan said, "That must have

been Pan Geng 盤庚.[30] Pan Geng was over nine feet tall, big below and small above. His beard was white. When he spoke he liked to look upward and raise his voice." The duke said, "That is so. His guest was very short, big above and small below. He spoke very angrily and liked to look downward." Yan said, "That must have been Yi Yin 伊尹.[31] Yi Yin was very big but short, big above and small below. His beard was red. When he spoke he liked to look downward and lower his voice." The duke said, "That is so." Yan said, "This means they are angry about my lord's troops. It would be better to avoid [attacking]." So he did not attack Song after all.[32]

Both interpreters are familiar to us from other texts (and Yanzi has appeared above).[33] Both interpretations identify a strange dream figure with some quasi-divine personage of lore. First the figures are mapped onto an implied matrix of such personages based on particular aspects of their appearance or behavior in the dream. Then their behaviors are parsed, yielding in the first case a directive and prediction (sacrificing to two figures will result in recovery from illness), in the second a warning (not to attack). These commonalities across the two tales suggest an established mode of hermeneutics, although it may have been one known only to the maker of this text. In both cases the appearance and behavior of the dream figures are read as correlating to the dreamer's specific situation (an illness, a planned attack). The first story ends with a confirmatory detail: the diviner predicts recovery if the dreamer performs the sacrifice, and subsequent events confirm the prediction. The second ends with the dreamer taking the diviner's advice, with the implication that he was wise to do so.

One other detail warrants comment. In the first anecdote it is implied that the dream itself induced the illness for which the diviner prescribed a cure. In a great many dream narratives someone dreams something that, upon waking, they "regard as odious" or "detest" (*e zhi* 惡之),[34] or they dream of being attacked by an enemy, and the dream itself or their response to it results in illness or death. As noted above, such stories suggest that the protagonists' reactions to their dreams were seen as having effects of a sort we would be tempted to call psychosomatic.[35] Again Wang Fu's reflections are helpful: "If someone dreams of something auspicious, and he himself regards it as an occasion for great joy, and if these feelings spring from his heart and spirit, then the dream really will be auspicious. And if someone dreams of something inauspicious, and he himself regards it as an occasion for great fear and concern, and if these feelings spring from his heart and spirit, then the dream really will be inauspicious" 借如使夢吉事而己意大喜樂 [two-character lacuna], 發於心精, 則眞吉矣. 夢凶事而己意大恐懼憂悲, 發於心精, 即眞惡矣.[36] In a culture that had largely bought into the notion that dreams often portended future events and were triggered by external causes, to dismiss them as insignificant would have been difficult, and we can readily imagine dreamers' dread in the wake of baleful dreams. Dreaming itself—of anything—might be seen as a cause for perturbation, which is why some texts asserted that sages did not dream at all. Dreaming per se was both a cause and a symptom of worry.

Gui zang, *Shi Chun*, and *Suo yu* all resulted from the efforts of someone prior to 300 BCE to compile instances of successful divination from existing records and set them side by side. We have a manuscript of somewhat similar nature that was evidently made near the end of the time period treated here. Stein 2072, an untitled manuscript found at Dunhuang with both its beginning and ending missing, is a compilation in the *leishu* genre probably made in the late Tang or Five Dynasties period. Among its thirteen topical sections we find one titled "Dream divinations" 占夢.[37] The section comprises eleven anecdotes,[38] several of which are discussed elsewhere in these pages.

Wordplay

Judging from extant anecdotes, a great many dream interpretations centered on wordplay. Sometimes the play was on oral aspects of language, substituting homophones for the words for things seen in dreams. Sometimes it was on aspects of written language, "translating" dream scenes into graphs and then analyzing these into parts to form phrases. The Chinese case, then, goes beyond Patricia Cox Miller's observation that "in order to be subject to interpretation, a dream had to be told or written. In the most immediate sense, dreams were phenomena of language as well as of psychic imagination and divine intention."[39] In many instances in China it was further the case that certain linguistic aspects of dreams and of the words used to recount dreams were precisely the keys to decoding them.[40]

A relatively simple mode of such parsing was the transposition of homophonous words. Here is an example that also happens to include an apport, though that element is ignored by the diviner:

> In the Taiyuan period [376–97], Wang Rong 王戎 of Taiyuan[41] was named governor of Yulin. [On his way by boat to take up the post] he dropped anchor at Xinting and went to sleep there. He dreamed of a man who gave him seven mulberries, which he placed in his lapel. When he woke, he really had them in his possession.
>
> A diviner said: "The fruits are mulberry [*sang* 桑]. From this point on, including males and females, young and old, [your family] will have seven burials [*sang* 喪]."[42]

Another instance occurs in an anecdote concerning Liu Jingxuan 劉敬宣, eldest son of Liu Laozhi 劉牢之 (d. 402), who was an important figure in the tumultuous events surrounding Sun En's and Lu Xun's Daoist-inspired rebellion in the years 399–402.[43] The story has been preserved in all three of the major histories of the period.[44] After his father's demise, he was in dire straits when he dreamed[45] he made a bolus of dirt and swallowed it. Waking, he was delighted, saying, "The bolus [**hwan* 丸] is Huan 桓 [**hwan*, that is, Huan Xuan 桓玄]. Swallowing it means I will go back to my native soil." Within a couple of weeks Huan Xuan had been defeated and Liu Jingxuan was able to return to the capital. Here we have not only a play on homophonous words but also the transposition of an action in the dream to events in waking life: swallowing dirt correlates to returning to his native soil.

The following story was related in a now-lost *Annals of Jin* (*Jin yangqiu* 晉陽秋) by Sun Sheng (4th century) that was cited in a commentary to *Traditional Tales and Recent Accounts*. It was related as well in the *History of Jin* and in an early fifth-century collection of anomaly accounts, *A Garden of Marvels* (*Yi yuan* 異苑):

> Zhang Mao 張茂 once dreamed he received an elephant. He asked Wang Ya 王雅 about it. Wang said, "You're about to become governor of a large commandery, but it won't be a good thing. The elephant is a large animal (*da shou* 大獸), which takes the same final sound as 'governor' (*tai shou* 太守). This is how I know you'll be governor of a large commandery. But the elephant loses its life on account of its tusks."

Later Zhang did become governor of Wu commandery and was indeed killed by Shen Chong.[46]

The elephant of Zhang's dream figures twice in Wang's interpretation: for its size, indicating a large administrative unit, and for being killed for its tusks, indicating that Zhang himself will be killed. Surprisingly, it does not figure for the graph that names it, nor for the way that graph was pronounced, **zjang*. Instead, the way Wang derives Zhang's future governorship is that the elephant is a member of a class (beast, **syuw* 獸) the word for which rhymes with that of the word for the office (**syuw* 守, literally "protector" but part of the compound *taishou* 太守, "grand protector," governor).[47] The story ends, as most such stories do, by noting that subsequent events confirmed the prediction.

Here is an example of homophonous wordplay unusual in two ways: the divined dream itself includes the performance of a divination, and the protagonist returns to sleep to decode in a second dream the meaning of the first:

> During the [Song] Jingping period [423–24], Xun Maoyuan 荀茂遠 traveled [with relatives] to Nankang. That night he dreamed of a man with a horn on his head. The man cast divination stalks for Maoyuan, then said, "Upon reaching the capital, you will certainly obtain an office." When Maoyuan asked which office, the man said, "An office that originates from water." Then Maoyuan awoke.
>
> He could not make sense of what he had been told, so he went back to sleep and dreamed again. In this dream the army [with which he must have been traveling in this dream][48] arrived at the Yangzhou water gate, and he fell into the water and died. When the coffin had been prepared, he entered it to try it for himself, but it was uncomfortably small. He was then prepared for burial and interred beside the riverbank. He woke up with a start, depressed, and told his mother and elder brother about the dream.
>
> When they reached the water gate, Maoyuan indeed fell into the river and died. The funeral rites were exactly as he had dreamed.[49]

The story plays on both the homophony and the graphic similarity between **kwan* 官 (office) and **kwan* 棺 (coffin). In the first dream Xun hears *kwan* as "office," but what the diviner was really telling him—

accurately, as events showed—is that he would soon receive a coffin. Both dreams correctly foretell what will befall him, the first through wordplay, the second in a direct foreseeing. The second dream acts as a visual display of what the first one indirectly meant.

The play on **kwan* 官 and **kwan* 棺 was so common that it is the subject of bons mots attributed to Yin Hao 殷浩 (306–56, an important figure of his day who served as provincial governor and general)[50]:

> Someone asked why it is that, when someone is about to get an office, they dream of coffins, and when about to get wealth they dream of filth. Yin Hao replied: "Office (**kwan* 官) is basically stinking decay, so someone about to get it dreams of coffins (**kwan* 棺) and corpses. Wealth is basically shit and dirt, so someone about to get it dreams of filth and mess."[51]

Disparagement of the drudgery of office-holding was a popular pastime. This is an especially clever instance. But it is equally clever as a reason why dreaming of coffins (rather than of some other phenomenon named with a word pronounced *kwan*) indicates imminent promotion. We glimpse here the sort of dream-code rationale people must have often speculated about—and that is omitted from dreambooks.

A more complex sort of wordplay involved "translating" a dream scene into a word, which was then either rhymed with another word or analyzed into component parts, or both, to yield the interpretation. An example involving rhymes occurs in the biography of Yi Xiong 易雄, who although from a non-elite family had earned a fine reputation by his calm comportment when facing the Zhang Chang 張昌 rebels (303).[52] Later he organized the defense of the city where he was stationed[53] when Wang Dun 王敦 rebelled (322–24) and advanced on the capital. Captured and brought before Wang Dun at Wuchang, Yi Xiong calmly but firmly defended his actions as just, saying he looked forward after his execution to becoming a loyal ghost 忠鬼 and helping to avenge the Jin court. Momentarily shamed by this speech, Wang Dun released him. But when others congratulated Yi Xiong, he only laughed, saying, "Last night I dreamed I was driving a chariot with flesh hanging from its sides. Now, flesh must certainly have tendons [**kɨn* 筋]. 'Tendons' indicates 'axes' [**kɨn* 斤]. Axes on the sides of the chariot mean that I'm going to be killed." Not long afterward Wang Dun sent someone to murder him.[54]

Sometimes we find not homophony but a kind of metaphoric mapping.[55] Early in his eightieth year, Shen Qingzhi 沈慶之[56] dreamed that someone presented him with two bolts of silk, saying, "These bolts are a sufficient measure" 此絹足度. He told someone, "This old man won't survive the year. Two bolts equals eighty feet. 'Sufficient measure' means it can't be extended any further." He indeed died within the year.[57] Here, a quantity of measure mentioned in the dream is converted into different units and then transferred into terms of the dreamer's lifespan, and the meaning of an expression is also transferred onto lifespan.

Often a dream scene is converted into a graph, which proves key to the dream's interpretation. A relatively simple instance occurs in the biography of the Buddhist thaumaturge Fotudeng 佛圖澄 (d. 349).[58] The ethnic Jie 羯 ruler of the northern Later Zhao kingdom on whom he was attending, Shi Hu 石虎 (r. 333–49), once dreamed of seeing a flock of sheep carrying fish on their backs coming from the northeast. Upon waking, he asked Fotudeng about it, and the Master replied, "Inauspicious. The Xianbei 鮮卑 will take over the central plains." (This was, of course, later confirmed.) The sheep 羊 with fish 魚 on their backs form the graph *xian* 鮮 of Xianbei, and their southwestward movement presages the Xianbei/Murong expansion from their territorial base in Manchuria down into the central region.[59]

Similarly, the Western Jin literatus Wang Jun 王濬 (253–314) dreamed that he suspended three swords from the ceiling beam of his room and that soon there was a fourth hanging there as well. He awoke, startled, and considered it very baleful 意甚惡之. But his recorder, Li Yi, bowed and congratulated him: "The three swords form the character *zhou* 州 ["province"]. Wouldn't the addition 益 of a fourth sword mean that you are about to be appointed in Yi Province 益州?" Not long afterward the rebel Zhang Hong killed the regional inspector of Yi, and Wang Jun was appointed to replace him.[60]

Another case of dream images correlating to graphs occurs in a story about Cai Mao 蔡茂 (24 BCE–47 CE), an official under both the Western and Eastern Han[61] who dreamed of sitting in a large hall. From a rafter grew three ears of grain. He leapt up and grabbed the middle one but soon lost hold of it. He asked the recorder Guo He 郭賀 (d. 64), who worked under him, about it.[62] Guo stood up to congratulate him, saying: "The large hall is a form and correlate of palaces and bureaus 宮府之形象. That there were grains on the ceiling beams indicates the top salary level of an official. That you got the middle grain indicates you will obtain a position at court.[63] In characters 於字, 'grain' 禾 plus 'lost' 失 makes 'rank' 秩. So although you said you lost it, based on this you will receive a promotion. There is a vacancy at court, and you will fill it." Guo's prediction was borne out within the month.[64] Note that in both of these stories, Wang Jun and Cai Mao have their dreams interpreted by a subordinate on their staff.

In the biography of Deng You 鄧攸 (d. 326)[65] is told a story of his third-century ancestor, Deng Yin 殷. While serving as governor of Huainan 淮南 he once dreamed he was walking beside a river when he saw a girl. A tiger approached her from behind and severed her pouch[66] from her belt. A diviner thought that a girl 女 beside water 氵 formed the character *ru* 汝, and that, as for severing her pouch, a new tiger's head replacing an old one must indicate either Ruyin 汝陰 or Runan 汝南, two administrative jurisdictions. Afterward Deng Yin was indeed transferred to serve as governor of Ruyin.[67] So here we have two hermeneutic operations. Two components of the dream scene (the girl beside water) are joined and transposed into a graph, *ru* 汝. Then the tiger's displacement of the pouch in the dream is read as indicating a transfer of location from the dreamer's present post to either of two places whose names begin with *ru* 汝.

A related interpretive procedure involved converting a dream scene or image into a graph, then analyzing the graph into parts to reveal the dream's meaning. This is what has been called glyphomancy by some modern scholars, perhaps not felicitously.[68] For example, a man dreams of a pine tree growing on his belly and tells others: "The graph for 'pine' 松 is made up of 'ten' 十, 'eight' 八, and 'sire' 公. Eighteen years from now I will become a 'sire'"—that is, die.[69] Events confirmed this.[70] Guo Yu 郭瑀, a native of Dunhuang whose biography is included among the "recluses" of *History of the Jin*[71] and who was known as a teacher of the classics, dreamed of riding a green dragon into the sky. They came to a chamber and stopped. Waking, he sighed and said, "The dragon flies in the heavens, but in this case it stopped at a chamber. As a graph, 'chamber' 屋 is made up of 'corpse' 尸 with 'arrive' 至 underneath. A dragon flying to arrive at a corpse means I will die."[72]

In the following anecdote, each of the three graphs making up a person's name is analyzed to form a sentence:

> During the Jin there lived Zou Chen, a native of Nanyang. He began seeing in his dreams a man who called himself "Zhen Shuzhong" and said nothing else. This happened repeatedly. After some time had passed he realized what it meant, saying, "West of my house there is a mound of earth with broken tiles in it. There must be a dead person within. 'Zhen Shuzhong' 甄舒仲 means 'I am the person among the broken tiles west of your house'" 予舍西土瓦中人也. Upon examination this turned out to be true.
>
> So Zou reburied the man in generous fashion. Afterwards he dreamed that the man returned to thank him.[73]

The ghost initially seems incapable of normal speech, able to communicate only through this graph-based code, perhaps due to his unfortunate situation. Only after reburial is his tongue loosened. The story reads as if someone playing with these three graphs back-built a story with their analyzed form as the punchline. Zou Chen was, after all, a man of letters credited with (among other works) a study of the *Classic of Changes*.[74]

Cosmic Correlations and the Classic of Changes

Rather than wordplay, other methods used what might be called cosmic correlations. Consider the following episode in the biography of Xie An 謝安 (320–85).[75] He told associates of a dream he had during his assistantship under Huan Wen 桓溫 (312–73), who at the time held de facto power at the Eastern Jin court. He dreamed he was "riding in Wen's carriage. I traveled sixteen *li*, then saw a white chicken in the road and stopped. Riding in Huan Wen's carriage means that I have assumed his place. Sixteen *li* corresponds to sixteen years from that time down to today. The white chicken belongs to the direction *you* 酉. Now the shadow of Jupiter is in *you*.[76] I will die of illness and not recover!" Xie An did in fact die not long thereafter.[77] This interpretation involves transposing a measure of distance from the dream to a number of years in the dreamer's life. Then an animal seen in the dream is correlated to the position in the sky through which the counter-orbital correlate of Jupiter is passing.[78] Thus is derived the conclusion that the situation symbolized in the dream—riding a carriage sixteen units of distance, then stopping upon meeting a white chicken in the road—foreshadowed that Xie An had sixteen more years to live from that time.

Another such method was to "translate" a dream scene into a particular *Classic of Changes* hexagram, then use the classic's commentary on the hexagram as the basis for interpretation. Here is an example from *Records of the Three Kingdoms*:

> When Deng Ai 鄧艾 [d. 264] was preparing to attack Shu, he dreamed he was sitting atop a mountain near a flowing stream. He asked capital protector Yuan Shao about it.[79] Shao said, "According to the *Changes* hexagrams, being atop a mountain with water is *jian* 蹇.[80] The interpretation of the hexagram says: 'Favorable west and south. Unfavorable east and north.' Confucius said: 'It is auspicious [under these auspices] to travel west or south, for one will earn merit thereby. It is inauspicious to travel east or north, for the road will peter out.' If you proceed you will surely be subdued by Shu, and you will be in danger of not returning." Deng Ai was startled and displeased.[81]

He nevertheless accompanied Zhong Hui 鍾會 (d. 264) on his expedition against Shu in 263 and, "unjustly implicated in Zhong's attempted rebellion the following year, he was executed with all his sons. His wife and grandchildren were banished to Central Asia."[82]

In the *History of the Jin* biography of Fu Rong 苻融, youngest brother of Fu Jian 苻堅 (338–85) and commander of the Qin forces crushed in the battle of Fei River in 383 (in which Fu Rong died), comes one of the most remarkable anecdotes of dream interpretation to have survived from early medieval times.[83] A man named Dong Feng was headed homeward after three years of itinerant study when he stopped and stayed overnight at his wife's family's home. During the night she was murdered. The wife's older brother suspected Dong Feng and filed a complaint to have him arrested. Dong, unable to bear the interrogation, falsely confessed.

Fu Rong, in his capacity as commandant of convict labor, investigated the matter and doubted the confession, so he personally questioned Dong Feng.

> He asked Feng, "During your journey, did you note any anomalies or have any divinations performed" 頗有怪異及卜筮以不? Feng said, "On the night before I was departing, I dreamed I was riding a horse crossing a river southward. Then I turned around and headed north. Then from north to south again. The horse then stopped in the middle of the river, and although I goaded it, it wouldn't move. Looking down, I saw two suns beneath the water's surface. On its left side, the horse was white and wet 白而溼; on the right, it was black and dry 黑而燥. When I awoke I was afraid, assuming the dream was inauspicious. On the night before I began the return trip, I had the same dream again. I asked a diviner 筮者 about it, and he said: 'Beware of jail and trial. Keep away from the pillows. Avoid the baths.'
>
> "When I arrived, my wife prepared a bath for me. That night she gave me a pillow. I recalled what the diviner had said, but I didn't follow his advice. My wife then bathed herself, and we went to sleep on separate pillows."
>
> "I've got it!" Rong cried. "In the *Classic of Changes*, the *kan* 坎 trigram ☵ is water. Horses are the trigram *li* 離 ☲.[84] To dream of riding the horse south, then turning north, then south again, is going from *kan* to *li*. All three lines change to form *li*. *Li* is the middle daughter; *kan* is the middle son.[85] The two suns are a correlate of two men. The *kan* signifies the local law enforcement officer: the officer detained the husband while the wife died from blood loss. *Kan* is two Yins and one Yang; *li* is two Yangs and one Yin; they change places one after the other. *Li* below and *kan* above is Ferrying Complete 既濟 [hexagram 63 ䷾].[86] King Wen encountered this when imprisoned at Youli. With the proper rites he lived, but without them he'd have died.[87] As for the left side of the horse being wet: wetness indicates water. Water [氵] on the left and horse [馬] on the right forms the graph *feng* 馮. Two suns [日] form the graph *chang* 昌. It's Feng Chang 馮昌 who killed her!"
>
> Feng Chang was brought in on charges and confessed, saying: "Originally I was plotting with the wife to kill Dong Feng. We planned to use the pillow and the one who was freshly bathed as a sign.[88] Because of this I mistakenly struck the wife."

This is a complex decoding. First, Fu Rong "translates" the dream scene into trigrams. This translation is based on commonplace correlations between elements in the dream (horse, water) and specific trigrams. Then, from the dynamic relations between these trigrams, and next from their combination to form a particular hexagram, he draws further interpretive deductions. These are quite specific: the second line of the hexagram says, "The wife loses her headdress/hair," and the sixth says, "Wetting his head: danger."[89] Having come this far, Fu finally returns to the dream scene to "translate" its elements (water on the horse's flank, the horse, the two suns) into graphs, forming the surname and personal name of the murderer.

Named Professional Interpreters

In almost all known cases where someone seeking the meaning of a dream is said to have consulted a specialist diviner (usually termed simply 占者 or 占夢者) rather than a relative or friend, the diviner remains unnamed. Little is said about him or her other than to report the prognosis,[90] unless the writer wishes to make an argument about the diviner and the specific social situation being narrated, about divination in general, or about the dreamer. Such is the case, for example, in the biography of a prince of Liang named Chang 暢, who had had a series of nightmares. A retainer said he had the ability to deploy the Six Ding Spirits 六丁[91] and was skilled at divining dreams. So Chang had him divine several times. Because of this, his wet nurse and others said of themselves that they could see ghosts and spirits, so "together they divined *qi*, offering sacrifices and requesting good fortune" 共占氣, 祠祭求福. They deceived the prince by saying that the spirits had told them he would become emperor.[92] Such instances were probably not unusual. Specialists, particularly if claiming to wield an interpretive method that was esoteric, were in an excellent position to dupe people in powerful positions. That they might often do so had been a theme of historiography since at least Sima Qian.[93] Specialists in esoterica carefully managed their reputations and guarded access to the arts they claimed to possess,[94] and often moved from one area to the next, and this made it hard to invalidate their claims to divinatory accuracy, success in healing, or extraordinary longevity. Claims of having dreamed were a tool in the repertoire of ways in which practitioners of healing and other arts could persuade their communities of their powers.[95]

But in a few cases we have clusters of anecdotes about named dream interpreters. These allow us to glimpse the nature of the social interactions between dreamers and professional diviners, diviners' comportment in such situations, and the hermeneutical methods they used. After presenting the material on each diviner I will comment on these texts as a group.

Guan Lu

Guan Lu 管輅 (ca. 210–56) earned an unusually well-documented reputation as a skilled practitioner of several divination arts, including tortoise shell cracking (which may have continued to be an important method of divination through this period and beyond),[96] *Yijing*-based prognostications using milfoil stalks, astrology, physiognomy, and wind angles.[97] He was not primarily known for dream interpretations, but one striking anecdote survives showing him divining the dream of an important political figure, He Yan 何晏 (ca. 190–249).[98] The story begins when He Yan asks Guan Lu to use the hexagrams to see whether he will attain one of the Three Ducal Offices. He also mentions that he has repeatedly dreamed of several dozen blue flies gathering on the tip of his nose and not leaving even when he tried to shoo them away, and asks him to interpret this. Guan Lu responds:

> The nose is Mountain [Gen 艮, *Yijing* hexagram 52]. This is the "mountain in the midst of the heavens."[99] It's high but not steep, and thereby maintains its honored position.[100] Now blue flies, which are foul and odious, have gathered and alighted on it. The inevitable fate of one whose position is high is to be overthrown, and that of one who despises the powerful is to perish. Though changes and transformations produce each other, push either to its extreme, and harm will result. Though empty and full contain each other, if one overflows, the other will run dry. The sage, observing the nature of Yin and Yang, understands the principles underlying survival or perdition. He diminishes his gains, turning them into losses; he holds back his advances, turning them into

> retreats. For this reason, if Mountain is in the middle of earth, it's called Modesty [Qian 謙, hexagram 15], and if Thunder is above heaven, it's called Power of the Great [Dazhuang 大壯, hexagram 34]. Modesty means "taking from the excessive to make up the deficient." Power of the Great means "not treading on any path contrary to correct ritual."
>
> It is my humble wish that on the upper level you should search out the main idea of the six individual lines of each hexagram as given by King Wen, and on the lower level think over the interpretations of the judgments and counterparts as given by Confucius. Then the problem of whether or not you'll reach one of the Three Ducal Offices may be solved, and the blue flies driven away.

Deng Yang 鄧颺 (d. 249),[101] another important figure who was also in the company of the two men, dismissively replied, "This is the usual talk of an old scholar." Guan Lu retorted, "This 'old scholar' perceives that someone will not live. As for the 'usual talk,' he perceives that someone will not talk."[102] Both He Yan and Deng Yang were executed in 249.

As a dream interpretation, this is not especially interesting. Guan Lu opens by tying the dream imagery to a *Changes* hexagram, then uses the hexagram name to pull in a bit of physiognomy. But the bulk of his interpretation is made of up a moral cautionary speech, threaded with a few more hexagram allusions, to a man he sees[103] as endangered by his own actions. This admonitory use of divination moments must have been common, and can still be seen in many a Chinese temple today, where the invocator interpreting a medium's inchoate utterances for onlookers takes the opportunity to lecture them on morals, or where divination slips drawn at random yield mostly generic-seeming moral advice.

Zhou Xuan

Perhaps the most famous diviner of dreams from this period was Zhou Xuan 周宣 (d. ca. 238), a native of Le'an in what is now Shandong Province. His "biography" in *Records of the Three Kingdoms* is nothing but a string of episodes of his accurate dream interpretations.[104]

> Zhou Xuan, styled Konghe 孔和, was a native of Le'an and a subofficial functionary of the commandery. Governor Yang Pei 楊沛 [probably Zhou's supervisor in the commandery] dreamed that someone came to

him and said, "On the first day of the eighth month Duke Cao 曹公 [that is, Cao Cao (155–220)][105] will arrive. He will present you with a staff and fête you with medicinal wine." Pei had Zhou Xuan divine it. At the time the Yellow Turban rebellion had broken out. Xuan said: "A staff helps the weak to stand. Medicines cure illness. On the first day of the eighth month the rebels will be eliminated." When the day arrived the rebels were indeed defeated.

Later, Liu Zhen 劉楨 of Dongping dreamed of a snake with four legs living in a hollow in his gatehouse. He had Xuan divine it. Xuan said: "This is a dream concerning the realm, not your family. It means that women who are bandits will be killed." Soon two women bandits, one of the Zheng clan and one of the Qiang, were eliminated. [Zhou Xuan knew this] because snakes are usually an auspicious sign for women, but legs are something a snake is not supposed to have.

Emperor Wen [Cao Pi 曹丕 (187–226)] asked Xuan: "I dreamed that two tiles fell from the palace ceiling and transformed into a pair of ducks. What does it mean?" Xuan replied: "In the rear palace someone will die violently." But the ruler said, "I was only tricking you." Xuan responded: "Dreams are simply thoughts (*yi* 意).[106] If they can be described and put into words, they can be used to divine good or bad fortune." He had hardly finished speaking when the prefect of the yellow gate reported there had been a murder among the palace women.

Not long afterward Emperor Wen inquired again: "Last night I dreamed that a green vapor rose from the ground and filled the heavens." Xuan responded: "Somewhere under heaven a noblewoman will die unjustly." At the time the emperor had already dispatched a messenger to serve an imperial sentence on Lady Zhen 甄后. Upon hearing Xuan's words the emperor regretted his action and sent another messenger after the first one, but he did not arrive in time.

The emperor also asked: "I dreamed I was rubbing the image on a coin, trying to make it disappear, but the design only grew brighter. What does it mean?" Xuan grew distraught and made no answer, but the emperor asked again, so he replied: "This arises from a matter in your household. Although you wish for something, the imperial mother will not permit it. That is why the pattern only grows brighter despite your desire to rub it away." At that time the emperor wanted to discipline his younger brother Zhi 植 [107] and was pressuring his mother to allow it, but she would only permit a reduction in rank.[108]

The emperor made Xuan a palace attendant and appointed him to a post in the office of the grand astrologer.

Someone once asked Xuan: "Last night I dreamed I saw a straw dog. How would you divine it?" Xuan replied, "You are about to have something delicious to eat." Not long afterward the man was traveling and was invited to a sumptuous feast.

Later he approached Xuan again: "Last night I again dreamed I saw a straw dog. What about this?" Xuan said, "You will fall from a carriage and break a leg. Please take care!" Not long afterward it happened as Xuan had said.

Later he again asked Xuan, "Once again last night I dreamed I saw a straw dog. What about this?" Xuan replied, "Your house will be destroyed in a fire. Please take precautions!" Soon afterward a fire did indeed break out.

The man then told Xuan, "None of these three dreams really occurred. I was only testing you. How is it that your predictions were nevertheless accurate?" Xuan answered, "That was due to the spirits moving you to speak thus. It was therefore no different than if you had really dreamed those things" 此神靈動君使言，故與眞夢無異也. The man asked, "All three dreams were of straw dogs, yet you interpreted each differently. Why?" Xuan replied, "Straw dogs are objects used in sacrificing to spirits. That's how I knew after your first dream that you would attend a feast. After sacrificial offerings are concluded, straw dogs are run over by cart wheels. That's how I knew after your second dream that you would fall from a carriage and break your leg. After straw dogs are crushed by the cart, they are loaded up to be used as fuel for fire. That's how I knew after your last dream that your house would burn."

All of Zhou Xuan's relatings of dreams 敘夢[109] were of this sort. He hit the mark eight or nine times out of ten. People of the time likened his talents to those of Jianping in physiognomy.[110] The rest of his results were similarly efficacious, so I will not record them all here.

He died in the last years of Emperor Ming's reign.[111]

The crowning anecdote involving the dreams of straw dogs is, of course, both humorous and intended to illustrate Xuan's extreme skill. It might therefore seem pointless to attempt to extract the hermeneutic involved—but Xuan explains it! The succession of meanings derives from the sequences of uses to which straw dogs were put in the waking world. Somehow the things the spirits move the dreamer or talker to dream or talk about are correlated with the sequence of ways in which straw dogs are used in sacrificial ritual. This anecdote also reads as if (or could have been read as if) it were written to directly challenge the dreambook mode of interpretation, in which each dream sign has a single, fixed meaning.

Suo Dan

In the section of biographies devoted to practitioners of special arts 藝術 (not only divination but also various magical arts and paranormal feats) in chapter 95 of the *History of the Jin*, there is an entry devoted to one Suo Dan 索紞, native of Dunhuang, who specialized in dream interpretation. Judging from some of the figures mentioned, he flourished around 300.

> Suo Dan, styled Shuche 叔徹, was a native of Dunhuang. In his youth he traveled to the capital and received training at the imperial academy. He mastered a wide range of classics and other works and became a broadly knowledgeable scholar. He had particular ability in Yin/Yang astrology and numbers-based divinations. He was a minister of education and was appointed a palace attendant, but knowing that the central realm was about to collapse into disorder, he withdrew from the world and returned home. People of his home area flocked to have him divine their fortunes, to the point that his gate resembled a busy market. He said, "One should not involve oneself in too many affairs. The more one's affairs, the more one's troubles." So he fabricated false interpretations in order that, when his predictions failed to pan out, interest in him would cease. Dream interpretations 占夢 were the only sort of divination he did not stop providing. Such inquiries he did not refuse.
>
> The filial-and-incorrupt nominee Linghu Ce dreamed of standing on ice and conversing with others who were below the ice. Dan said: "To be above the ice is Yang, to be below it is Yin. So it's a matter of Yin and Yang. 'A knight who brings home his bride must do so before the ice melts':[112] it has to do with marriage. That you were above the ice but speaking with others below the ice means you were speaking on behalf of Yang with Yin—it's a matter of being a matchmaker. You will arrange a marriage for someone. The wedding will take place when the ice has melted." Ce replied, "I'm an old man. I don't serve as matchmaker." But he met the governor, Tian Bao, who engaged him to inquire on behalf of his son about the daughter of Ce's neighbor, Zhang Gongzheng. The wedding was held in the second month [of the lunar calendar].

The commandery recorder, Zhang Tuo, dreamed of riding a horse up a mountain. Upon returning, he rode around his home three times. All he saw were pine and cedar trees. He was unable to recognize where the gate was. Dan said: "The horse belongs to the [trigram] *li* 離, which is fire. Fire means disaster. A person ascending a mountain forms the graph *xiong* 凶 ["inauspicious"]. That you saw only pines and cypresses is the correlate [*xiang* 象] of a tomb gate. Not recognizing where the gate was indicates that there was no exit. Circling three times indicates three years. Three years from now you will certainly meet a great calamity." Tuo indeed was executed for plotting rebellion.

Suo Chong first dreamed that two coffins fell before him from the sky. Dan said: "Coffins indicate offices. You will be appointed by an important person in the capital. That there were two coffins indicates that you will subsequently be promoted further." Not long afterward, the minister of education Wang Rong 王戎[113] wrote a letter to the governor recommending Chong. At first the governor placed Chong in the labor section. Then he was selected as a Filial and Incorrupt. Later Chong dreamed that he saw a caitiff remove his upper garment and come to pay him a visit. Dan said: "If you remove the upper part of the graph 'caitiff' 虜, the lower part forms the graph 'male' 男. Barbarians are categorized as Yin. Your wife will bear a son." It turned out as he had said.

Song Jue dreamed there was someone in his inner quarters wearing crimson. Jue took a staff in each hand and beat the man severely with them. Dan said: "A person 人 in your inner quarters 内 forms the graph 'meat' 肉. The color of meat is crimson. The two staffs are the correlate 象 of chopsticks. That you beat the man severely indicates that you'll eat your fill of meat." Soon afterward this, too, was confirmed 驗.

Huang Ping asked Dan, "Last night I dreamed a horse was prancing inside my home. Several dozen people clapped their hands towards it. What does this portend?" Dan said: "The horse is fire. That it was prancing indicates a fire will break out. Those who were clapping towards it indicate firefighters." Ping hadn't even reached home when a fire broke out.

Suo Sui dreamed of seeing two horns in the east, each with writing on them concerning him. The larger horn was broken. The smaller one bore an inscription. [He donned them] in leather bags hanging from his belt, one in front and one behind. Dan said: "That the larger horn was broken indicates rotted coffin wood. That the smaller one bore an inscription means whatever the inscription said. As for the one in front, the front of the fringe is inauspicious [*xiong* 凶]. As for the one behind, behind indicates the back [*bei* 背]. You will have news of a death [*xiong bei* 凶背]."

At the time Sui's father was to the east of him. Three days afterward news of his father's death reached him.

The commandery personnel evaluator Zhang Miao was on his way to call at the provincial headquarters when one night he dreamed that a wolf ate one of his legs. Dan said: "To have the flesh [月 radical] eaten off one of your legs 脚 forms the graph *que* 卻 ["to go back"]." It then happened that caitiffs rebelled to the east, so Miao could not continue his journey.

Not one of his divinations failed to be confirmed by events 凡所占莫不驗.

The governor Yin Zhan 陰澹 asked him for his divination book 占書. Dan replied, "When I entered the imperial academy, I had a certain old man as my master. There was nothing he didn't know. He did not reveal his name and seemed to be a recluse. So I asked him about the art of divining dreams, and he went over it all with me. In actuality I don't possess a book about it." Yin Zhan appointed him libationer of the western pavilion but Dan declined the post. . . .[114] Yin Zhan presented him with a roll of silk as a gift and every month sent lamb meat and wine.

Dan died at home at the age of 75.[115]

Zhao Zhi

No discrete biography of Zhao Zhi 趙直 survives, but it is evident from several mentions in *Records of the Three Kingdoms* that he was active in Shu in the early third century and specialized in dream interpretation.

In the biography of Wei Yan (d. 234), a member of the staff of Zhuge Liang in the kingdom of Shu,[116] we find this anecdote:

> He dreamed that a horn grew from his head. He asked the diviner Zhao Zhi about it. Zhao Zhi lied to him, saying, "The *qilin* has a horn but doesn't use it. This is a correlate 象 indicating that if you don't fight, the rebels will defeat themselves." After he had withdrawn, Zhao Zhi said to others, "As a graph, 'horn' 角 has 'use' 用 beneath a sword 刀. To have a sword used on one's head is extremely inauspicious."[117]

After Zhuge Liang's death, Wei Yan and his family were indeed disgraced and executed at the behest of Zhuge's chief of staff, Yang Yi, who was Wei Yan's bitter enemy.

In Pei Songzhi's commentary to the biography of Yang Hong (d. 228), a provincial-level official in the state of Shu,[118] we find the following anecdote about one of his aides, He Zhi, styled Junsu:

> He Junsu once dreamed that a mulberry tree was growing in a well. He asked the dream diviner Zhao Zhi about it. Zhi said, "The mulberry isn't something that belongs in a well. It's about to be transplanted somewhere else. And the graph 'mulberry' 桑 is comprised of 'forty' plus 'eight' below. I'm afraid you will not live past that age." Zhi Junsu smiled and said, "If I can reach that age, I'll be satisfied."[119]

And in the biography of Jiang Wan (d. 246), an important official in the Shu kingdom,[120] there is this:

> After Jiang Wan had been dismissed,[121] he dreamed one night that a severed bull's head lay outside his gate, oozing blood. He considered it very baleful. He summoned and asked the dream diviner Zhao Zhi about it. Zhi said, "To see blood means that affairs will become clearer. The bull's horns plus its snout form the correlate of the graph *gong* 公 ["duke"]. Your rank will certainly reach the level of duke. This is a very auspicious sign 徵." Not long afterward he was appointed prefect of Shenfang.[122]

Yu Wen

In the *Treatise on Auspicious Omens* (*Xiangrui zhi* 祥瑞志) by Xiao Zixian 蕭子顯 (483–537), incorporated in his *History of the Southern Qi*, a series of dreams seen by the ruler is recorded.[123] Several of them are noted as having been interpreted by a certain Yu Wen 庾溫, on whom little else is known. The interpretations are reported only very laconically and need not detain us.[124] But the fact that the same individual is described as interpreting all the dreams clearly indicates he held a post with that function at the Southern Qi court. Yu Wen compiled these dream accounts along with other omens deemed politically significant into a *Ruiying tu* 瑞應圖 during the Yongming reign period (483–93), and this work served as the basis for Xiao Zixian's own more expansive treatise on dynastic omens incorporated into his history of the Southern Qi.[125]

Gleanings

What is recorded of these five individuals may not be entirely representative of the social situation, client interactions, and interpretive methods used by dream diviners generally in the early medieval period. (For one thing, there surely must have been many diviners of local repute who never gained enough prominence to be mentioned in the archive.) And these men were obviously deemed by their contemporaries to be especially skillful. Nevertheless, we might profitably consider these accounts as a group.

The clients were sometimes very highly placed officials—up to and including the emperor. In some cases the interpreters used their access to such officials to offer some moral suasion. When challenged, they sometimes stood their ground. Diviners working at court might help compile records of royal dreams to add to the mass of omens collected to legitimate the dynasty. Clients might also include members of the diviner's own clan, as seems to have been the case with Suo Dan. The diviners, for their part, were not social outsiders such as spirit-mediums (*wu* 巫) often were. But there was nonetheless some social distance between them and many of their clients.

Oneiromancers' relations with their clients could be quite delicate. They might shy away from leveling with clients in the case of inauspicious predictions. Clients were not above giving false reports of their dreams in order to test their diviners' skill. That the interpreters were nevertheless thought to have made accurate predictions (however this was theorized) testified to their abilities and arts, and so reports of such reputation-enhancing feats made it into the stories that circulated about them. Reputation management was a paramount concern for these specialists, whether it was for the purpose of attracting more clients or, as in the remarkable case of Suo Dan, limiting the crowds clamoring for access to him. Clients might press diviners for their methods, including the manuals on which they might be based, but diviners were apt to resist such demands. In all these ways the diviners' relations with their clients fit a cultural pattern in which men and women initiated into secret arts of divination, healing, or longevity would openly display the results of those arts, sometimes to large groups, while carefully guarding the methods by which they'd been obtained.[126] The exchange between the governor Yin Zhan and the diviner Suo Dan is a classic instance: the governor presses the adept for access to his manual. The adept claims to have no manual and pointedly does not offer to teach the governor orally, either. Unrelenting, the governor offers Suo a sinecure, which he declines. This does not deter the governor from sending the diviner monthly gifts.

Although these interpreters do not reveal the full basis for their accurate parsings of dreams, in the texts they do often explain at least some of the logic behind them. Guan Lu reads dream imagery by reference to *Changes* hexagrams. Zhou Xuan explains how he arrived at the meaning of a man's dream of a snake with legs. He also walks a client (and us) through a lengthy explanation of how he deciphered three successive dreams of straw dogs. Suo Dan reveals an array of hermeneutical principles: metonymy (evergreens are correlates of tomb gates), Yin/Yang binaries (above and below the ice), analogy (two sticks represent chopsticks), homophony, and the analysis of written characters. Their clients clearly wanted to know something of how they derived their predictions, and the diviners obliged. On the other hand, it was in diviners' interest to guard their actual methods for parsing dreams, and what they said about these methods in public might well have been designed to throw listeners off track.[127]

We learn little from these accounts of how these individuals acquired their skills. In Suo Dan's case, his knack is implied to have derived from his long study of Yin-Yang and numbers-based divination systems. A few tiny fragments of lore have come down to us concerning a "dream herb" (*meng cao* 夢草), said to resemble cattail (*pu* 蒲), whose leaves, when worn on one's person, allowed one to instantly discern whether a given dream was auspicious or baleful. Some texts add that Dongfang Shuo gave a bit of this plant to Han emperor Wu to help him dream of his beloved Lady Li. It therefore seems to have been both a material assist for dream interpretation and an incubatory device.[128] There were surely other such tricks of the trade, records of which have not, to my knowledge, survived.

One thing impossible to recover from these relatively terse accounts is the quality of the face-to-face interactions, "the nonverbal vocables, gestures, and movements"[129] of the diviner and the client. These subtle cues are known to be of great importance in divination and healing situations everywhere, but they are mostly unknowable at any great remove from the interaction. We can only imagine them hovering between the lines of the extant records.

It's clear from the material we've seen in this and the previous chapter that dream interpretation was ubiquitous and important. On the one hand, there was enough broad interest in knowing what dreams portended that, given sufficient skill or luck, one could make a living interpreting them for clients. On the other hand, dream interpretation was hardly the exclusive preserve of specialists: everyone seems to have engaged in it, regarding their own and others' dreams. Especially clever (and accurate) dream decodings, whether by specialists or laypersons, were prized enough to be enshrined in collective memory in formal histories, informal anecdotes, biographical writings, and records of striking conversations. Readers and story compilers took evident delight in the wordplay and hermeneutical maneuvers involved in adroit translations of obscure dream images.[130] It seems to me that dream culture was shot through with enjoyment of the supple play of hermeneutics and pleasure when the interpreter's prediction "hit the target," as some texts put it.[131]

Prospection and Retrospection

Let us now step back to ask not *how* the meanings of dreams were arrived at, but *what sorts of things* those meanings were. After a dream had been put through the interpretation process, what was its significance? What did its meaning come out looking like? What were nondirect dreams deeply about, once the surface symbolism had been penetrated?

First of all, what might be most striking to some readers is what they were *not* about. Due in part to the influence of Freud, some twentieth- and twenty-first century dreamers view their dreams as having primarily to do with themselves—with their latent fears, deep conflicts, desires, and unresolved past traumas. Or else dreams are simply a selection from among their recent diurnal activities. As Freud himself wrote, "It has been my experience that every dream without exception deals with oneself. Dreams are absolutely self-centered."[132] And one need not be a Freudian to see dreams this way. For Carl Jung, "Every interpretation of a dream is a psychological statement about certain of its contents," and the therapist arrives at this meaning for the dreamer "by a methodical questioning of the dreamer's own associations," a process Jung called "taking up the context": "This consists in making sure that every shade of meaning which each salient feature of the dream has for the dreamer is determined by the associations of the dreamer himself."[133] As the gestalt psychologist Frederick Perls said to a patient during a discussion of her dream, "This is your dream. Every part is a part of yourself."[134] Or, as the linguistic philosopher George Lakoff wrote when introducing his metaphor-based interpretations of the dreams of some friends of his, "The dream analyses to follow stress the importance of deep and extensive knowledge about the life of the dreamer. In each case, I have used a dream of someone I know very well, and it is only because I know the dreamer well that I feel confident of the interpretations."[135]

Efforts to understand dreams from an evolutionary perspective as instances of "costly signaling" literally view dreams as "signals" from the sleeping self to the waking self—the self talking to itself about itself in the strange language of dreams.[136] One of the major neuroscientific theories of the function of dreams nowadays sees dreams as the product of the brain's nocturnal consolidation of memories—the constant building and rebuilding of private knowledge structures.[137] Another sees dreams as primarily regulators of emotions.[138] Some researchers see dreams as "global, integrated models of the world" that are distinct from wakefulness precisely in being "exclusively internal simulations . . . created independently of the modulatory influence of information from the peripheral sensory organs," or in other words "offline simulations," for all their being "a complete behavioral space."[139] In short, many dominant contemporary views of dreams, particularly among academics—though certainly not the only view (as noted in chapter 1)—see them as being about the dreamer, as issuing from within the dreamer, and as authentically reflecting the dreamer's past experience or present concerns.

In China, the dreamer's emotions, worries, and current preoccupations were recognized as having the potential to shape dreams' contents. But I am aware of almost no recorded dream interpretations that consist chiefly of such things. When these aspects of the dreamer's life situation and psyche are mentioned, it is usually so that they can be *factored out* of the interpretation—because they were seen as irrelevant at best, distortive at worst. Thus we find Wang Fu writing: "When one thinks about something during the day and then dreams about it at night, one moment it may appear auspicious and the next moment it may seem inauspicious. The good or bad presage of such a dream is not to be relied upon. This is called a dream that recalls one's thoughts" 晝有所思, 夜夢其事, 乍吉乍凶, 善惡不信者, 謂之想.[140] Or again, "Only when [the dreamer's] energies have really been touched by something, really informed by spirits, will [accurate] divination be possible" 唯其時有精誠之所感薄, 神靈之所告者, 乃有占爾.[141] Personal factors were seen as red herrings, as signal interference. The stimulus of a usefully interpretable, prognosticatory dream (though not necessarily of a diagnostic dream) was expected to lie outside the dreamer, because it was supposed to reflect the otherwise murky shape of events and the hidden intentions of other actors. This is why recorded interpretations almost never reference the psychological state of the dreamer, nor the dreamer's past, nor are interpreters represented as inquiring about personal matters before offering their readings.[142] Instead, interpretations consisted almost entirely of predictions of future events, and were arrived at exclusively through analysis of selected aspects of the dream itself.

An analogy might help to clarify the point about what prospective dream interpretation was and wasn't. As a semiotic art, dream interpretation was set up analogously to crack divination (*bu* 卜). The dreamer was never thought of as the maker or fashioner of the dream, at least not if it held any divinatory significance, but was thought of as merely its vehicle. The dreamer was analogous to the tortoise carapace or ox scapula. The dream itself was analogous to the crack in the shell or bone. The interpreter of the dream was like the interpreter of the crack. But here the analogy trails off into fog. In the case of dreams, what is analogous to the heated rod that causes the crack, or to the person who applies the rod? If the simulacra comprised in dreams are the counterparts to future events, who or what established those semiotic correlations, and who or what caused the dreamer to dream those simulacra and not others? Almost all texts concerning dream interpretation are silent on these questions, but that didn't stop dreams from being read.[143] The legitimation of dream interpretations was based not on how they operated, not on their input or causal mechanisms, but on how well they worked—on their output.

The output, then, of the interpretation process was usually a prediction. Dreams were not taken to be expressions of latent fears or wishes of dreamers, but rather as indices of the direction of events. They were taken to be *prospective*, and their interpretation served the essential purpose of coping with the future.[144] (An important exception I noted in chapter 3 is the Buddhist *Pusa shuomeng jing*, which, like a few other texts glimpsed in chapter 2, is diagnostic, not predictive, in function.)[145] As we see in some of the entries in dreambook lists, the prediction could be as simple as "inauspicious," but most of the interpretations preserved in anecdotes are much more specific, and for good reason. The more specific the prediction, the more impressive the reading of the dream—and the more reaffirming of a cosmic pattern underlying the surface of events. The prediction and the eventual result are like the two halves of a tally. When the results match the prediction, the verb most often used is *yan* 驗, "confirmed," carrying an almost juridical force.

We could say, therefore, that dream interpretation was not really a psychological process at all, but a cosmo-semiotic one, working along the seams where the cosmos and the dreamer's life met. The dominant implied model of selfhood was not that of a container of subjectivity with a determinative past, but a dividual being open to cosmic influences,[146] ultimately bound into the pattern of events but possessing some limited scope for action. Dreams were simply one among many kinds of phenomena that afforded clues to the shape of things to come. It was that shape of things that the interpretations revealed and delivered. (Again, the contrast with Freud couldn't be starker: "And what of the value of dreams for our knowledge of the future? Of course that is out of the question. Instead, one should rather ask: for our knowledge of the past. For in every sense, dreams come from the past."[147]) Dream interpretation, like other contemporary forms of divination in China and like history writing, was a "rhetoric of order . . . imposed on a reality of violence and disorder."[148] It rested on hope in the readability of events based on clues such as dreams, available to those skilled in seeing through the surfaces of these nocturnal signs.

If dream prognostication was, then, a cosmo-semiotic rather than a psychological process, what was the nature of the cosmology implied and performed by it? It was, in short, a cosmology that saw cosmic order as utterly precarious. The constant reading of signs was made necessary not by confidence in an always already-in-place, immutable order of things, but by wariness of a world in which things were rarely what they appeared to be and were always in flux. Dream interpretation was "an art of suspicion."[149] As I began the previous chapter by noting, it was based on a locative worldview. In such a worldview, order cannot be assumed as a given: it must be constantly maintained and vigilantly guarded, for it is always a fleeting achievement bound, in the end, to fail. So, on the one hand, dream interpretation and other modes of divination were founded upon a "conceptualization of the cosmos as ultimately understandable and thus to some extent controllable—as opposed to the capricious interventions of unpredictable gods."[150] On the other hand, rather than seeing this conceptualization as an "optimistic" view of the cosmos,[151] as if cosmic order were taken as a fait accompli, I am inclined to agree with Michael Puett in seeing it as an *argument*.[152] Divination, including prognostication based on dream interpretation, is a mode of ritual, and ritual, operating in the subjunctive mode, the mode of "as if," represents the world as it should be, or as it is hoped to be, not as it is. It is fundamentally rhetorical in nature, in that it seeks to persuade participants and audiences of various things. And it is performative in nature, in that it does not take cosmic order for granted but seeks repeatedly to recreate, maintain, and sustain it under the constant threat of breakdown and the ongoing challenges of social opacity and divine inscrutability. The cosmos performed in most dream interpretation, as in most other modes of divination, was a locative cosmos. The need to perform an ordered world was grounded in the ever-latent potential for disorder.[153]

Divination was prospective. But records of instances of it were retrospective. Recognizing, or arguing for, order in the unfolding of events is a retrospective affair. Divinatory prospection and event-based retrospection are two sides of the same coin: "The historiographical imagination frequently engages with the past not for its own sake but for the way it presages some later point in the past."[154] Retrospection is how most of the dream accounts now embedded in the histories and chronicles, as well as most anecdotes of dream interpretation, came to enter the written record. Such writing was one way of ordering unruly, messy phenomena into a smooth narrative that functioned, in part, to project a sense of cosmic order. The predictability of the future based on readings of dreams and other signs suggested—narratively (and repeatedly) performed, we could say—an implicit order in the unfolding of events, a non-randomness in the cosmos.

Successful dream-based prediction was, then, not only a narrative device. And it was not only an argument for the efficacy of a particular method of interpretation or for the skill of a particular interpreter. More broadly, it was also an argument for a worldview. Retrospective narratives, what Schaberg calls proleptic anecdotes, demonstrated the efficacy of such prediction and contributed to the argument. As Schaberg observes of the makers of the *Zuo Tradition*, "All observable events are imbued with a quality of foreordination. The retrospective habit that ensures that only true predictions are recounted also imports into the past a sure but coy knowledge of the future. Observable details in general can take on an ominous quality, and the keys to interpretation are in the hands of the narrators. . . . Since the narrator builds anecdotes as predictions and puts the words of the predictions into the mouths of the ministers of that time, he disguises his own mastery of the past as their mastery of the present."[155] Every retrospective narrative of a successful prediction "serves the function of closure."[156]

This looping relationship between prospection and retrospection is easier to see with ethnographic examples. Anthropologist Michele Stephen, writing about which dreams her interlocutors chose to share with her and which they did not, astutely observes: "People described the examples that they were able to fashion into a personally meaningful account. They did not, or would only reluctantly, relate dreams they could not understand. Recent examples, where the link with waking events was yet to be realized, were thus not readily disclosed."[157] The following account is even more striking:

> In 1976 in Chowchilla, California a school-bus carrying 26 children (ages 5–14) home from summer school was hijacked at gun point. The children

> were transferred to vans with blackened windows. At the end of the day they were entombed in a truck-trailer that had been sunk in the ground and then covered with dirt. They escaped 16 hours later when two of the older boys dug them out. The children returned to their homes physically unharmed but continued to suffer emotionally from the effects of the event. . . . Omen formation emerged as one of the most common post-traumatic effects. . . . In the aftermath of the trauma, 19 of the 26 children (plus one who left the bus before the kidnapping) looked back and saw "omens" that would have warned them if only they had been alert. For a child whose coping mechanisms have been overwhelmed, *omen formation represents an attempt to retrospectively regain a sense of control by finding a "logic" in the events of the day* which correctly interpreted would have allowed the victim to choose a course of action that would have avoided the disaster. In some cases, something the child had done immediately prior to the kidnapping became a portent of the event to come. Otherwise minor behavior was endowed with ominous significance and the behavior became so indelibly associated with the trauma itself that it became . . . a "grafted appendage" of the event. . . . In some cases the ominous behavior suggests a sense of personal responsibility. . . . In other cases, the ominous event was seen simply as a warning sign and was derived from incidents that would have faded if the events of the day [had] unfolded in a normal manner. . . . The connection between the omen and the trauma appears to endow the omen with a continuing ability to signify. . . . [These formations] are conjoined items from different domains of experience. They are cognitive *constructs which turn events into signs and as a result establish a measure of distance and control*.[158]

For our purposes, we should note above all the essential function of the process: to attempt to "regain a sense of control" by construing the cosmos as ordered and sign-rich after all. Of course, this discussion of mine has tacitly assumed that foreknowledge is impossible, that it is only ever retrospective omen formation that happens. But this isn't known for a fact. "Premonitions are impossible, and they come true all the time."[159]

The Reception of Dreams

Do dreams mean things? From the emic perspectives reflected in the archive, we have seen that the answer was often (but certainly not always) yes. Those who saw dreams as meaningful typically imagined the meaning to inhere in the dream, awaiting extraction by a good interpreter. But from a (disenchanted?) perspective outside the cultural frame of late classical and medieval China, perhaps the question is badly formed. It would be better to say that dreams simply occurred, and to observe how people decided what, if anything, dreams meant, and what to do about it. As reception studies say of texts, films, and art objects, so too we may say of dreams that meaning does not inhere in them. Rather, interpreters attach meaning to them, create meaning based on them, and spin meaning out of them, sometimes in astonishingly creative ways. People are the (usually) involuntary makers of dreams, and then people—the dreamers themselves or, very often, other people—decide to fabricate meaning from what has been dreamed.[160]

One way to bring this point into sharper focus is to note cases in which we have record of disagreement about what a particular dream meant, or cases in which someone, for rhetorical reasons, feigned having had a dream in the first place. Such examples are few, but when we find them, they afford us precious and fleeting glimpses of some of the social processes that occurred off camera to produce the records we do have. We have already seen an instance in which a client deliberately gave a false dream report to test an interpreter's skills (the case of Zhou Xuan and his unnamed client who pretended to have dreamt three times of straw dogs), as well as an instance in which a harried diviner deliberately issued mistaken predictions[161] in order to reduce demand for his services (the case of Suo Dan) or because he feared a client's reaction (the case of Zhao Zhi). Here are summaries of two other cases.

> King Wen of Zhou saw a virtuous old man fishing and wished to hand over the government to him, but feared his clansmen wouldn't approve, so he feigned a dream in which his late father instructed him to do it. Accordingly, the measure was carried out to good effect, but then the old man ran away. Yan Yuan challenged Confucius on why King Wen had resorted to the ruse, and Confucius impatiently snapped that it was just an expediency.[162]

> When Confucius famously had his rough patch between Chen and Cai, he had no rice to eat. Yan Hui obtained some and was preparing it when Confucius noticed him reach for something in the pot and eat it. He pretended he hadn't seen it. After the food was cooked and Yan Hui presented it, Confucius rose and said, "Just now I dreamed of our late lord. Since this food is pure, I will offer some to him." Yan Hui replied, "That would not be acceptable. A while ago some ash fell into the pot. Because it's inauspicious to throw food out, I took it out of the pot and ate it." Confucius used the occasion to instruct his other disciples on the difficulty of truly knowing others.[163]

Not every reported dream occurred as reported; some reported dreams never occurred at all; and not all dream reports, and even fewer dream interpretations, were accepted at face value at the time they were first formed and circulated. "Just as people are expected to lie about their real intentions and motives, so too they are expected to lie about dreams."[164] That traces of these social facts made it into the archive at all only underlines the rhetorical weight carried in society by dreams and their interpretations.

The processes by which people interpreted dreams were ineluctably social, in several ways. The necessary first step was to convert the jumble of recalled impressions and story lines of the dream experience, something initially accessible only to the dreamer (except in the rare cases of different individuals having the same dream at the same time)[165] through the filter of waking memory, into words—already an interlocutory act even if the dreamer was initially recounting the dream only to himself. This is why we must always "distinguish the account of the dream from the dream experience":[166] the two are never the same. "It is not simply that our words do not do justice to what we dreamed," as Crapanzano writes, "it is that they change experiential register. They create a distance between the experience of the dream and its articulation. The dream loses its immediacy."[167] Or as Kevin Groark elegantly puts matters,

> At the moment of waking, a fascinating interpretive move occurs. For the first time, the person reflects on his or her dream experiences from the perspective of the waking self. The dreamer has gone from deeply immer-

> sive, embodied, disseminative first-person experiences in the dreamspace to a wakened state in which he or she "realizes" that these were the experiences of the soul, not of the self. . . . This perspectival tension between the first-person immediacy of the dream and its reframing as a quasi-third-person experience of the soul finds expression in dream narrative, in which it is indexed in several ways—all of which serve to shift the speaker from a central experiential position to one of distance and marginality.[168]

Then this verbal narrative was *shared* with someone else, and having been shared, it was released into the world and became potentially important for others. It became "party to the unfolding of reality,"[169] a reality constituted by social interactions. Most dreams, surely, were never remembered or spoken of, but any dream of which we have record was recounted to other people, presumably at first orally in most cases, then in writing. This initial telling of the dream is a complex moment in the process of interpretation, and I want to pause to consider it.

First, I suggest that both the dream and the telling are best thought of not as *expressions* of a self already fully and finally formed by other means, but rather as modes in which the self that is always in the process of formation is further discovered, constructed, or performed. Dream sharing is one aspect of the presentation of self in everyday life; it is a special mode of social interaction in its own right, subject to special restrictions or cautions. It is one among many modes of reputation management. "Dream accounts are performative"[170]—they are performances of selected dreams before selected audiences. Dreams might contain potentially explosive or dangerous information. "Were dreams . . . to be communicated freely, an endless web of fears and suspicions would be exposed."[171] Anyone claiming too much dream-derived knowledge is likely to arouse suspicion. For any given dreamer, his or her social roles will have often restricted the circle of interlocutors (we've seen, for example, a woman sharing her dream with a female friend, officials sharing their dreams with a single subordinate, a teacher sharing his dream with his children and students gathered for a valedictory occasion). It should not surprise us that not all dreams are shared, and of the ones that are, care will invariably have been taken in the choice of audience.[172] Writing of a type of healer who interprets both his own and clients' dreams as part of his toolbox of methods, Pamela Reynolds observes: "Dreams are used to bolster the aspirant healer's case; he garners them and presents them like signatures on petitions. In doing so he appropriates symbols. The symbols appear in his dreams. He selects which dreams to offer for interpretation. . . . He decides whether or not to act in accord with the interpretation."[173]

Of course, the way I have put things here assumes dreams themselves to be private—or if interactive, as seen in the next chapter, usually interactive with *extra-human* beings rather than with living members of the dreamer's own community. But it is not always so. In some cultures dreams themselves are understood as already interactive, a shared social space in addition to daily waking-life relations. Kevin Groark has written eloquently of how, among the Tzotzil Maya of Chiapas, Mexico, "the dreamspace . . . [is] an interpersonal realm in which the normally occluded motives and feelings of others (both human and extra-human) can be perceived and experienced through the medium of soul interactions"—many of these interactions decidedly hostile, often spilling back into the dreamer's waking life in the form of a range of symptoms, from general malaise to illness, anxiety, and even acute physical injury.[174] At this writing I have found relatively little evidence of such an understanding in China, although such oneiric interactions between living dreamers and *deceased* persons are easy to find, similarly resulting in many cases in the dreamer's illness or eventual death.[175] Throughout this book I sometimes refer to "psychosomatic" effects of dreams such as these, although in the wake of the sensitive, complex analyses offered by scholars such as Groark and Michele Stephen my doing so seems, at best, oversimplified and probably bears rethinking.

Second, the narration of the dream was already in its own right the performance of a certain interpretation of it. As we have seen Wang Fu remark, the terms in which the dream was initially recounted shaped whatever further interpretation was given. The other people to whom the dream was told were not simply passive receptacles of the words of the dream narrative: these interlocutors affected how, and whether, it was told. "They serve[d] as dream censors: embodiments of conscience and convention"[176]—intersubjective censors living not in the dreamer's head but in the human community. "Interlocutors—real, implied, or imagined—have a special hold over the dream. They take possession of it. They give it fixity."[177] "The people who are told dreams . . . tend to interfere with the dream-memory by suggesting neat constructions that are beguiling but fudge the dream's true outlines. The practically unavoidable dishonesty of dream-telling also . . . accounts for the bored suspicion often induced by other people's dreams: the aura has been dissipated because the tale has been tinkered with."[178] The interlocutors to whom dreams were initially recounted had a special role in co-authoring the narrative,[179] subtly shaping how it was told and what was made of it.

Third, someone—the dreamer, a relative, friend, colleague, subordinate official, a professional interpreter, or probably in many cases some combination of these—arrived at a statement of the "meaning" of the dream. This amounted, as we have seen, to a statement about something true regarding the present or future state of things, something hitherto unknown and otherwise unknowable but that had now been revealed through the interpreted dream. But even this was hardly the end of the social process. For one thing, there were surely always alternate interpretations, whether or not these were recorded and whether or not those records survive. What survives for us to read is the tip of an iceberg, most of which will remain forever submerged under the sea of time.[180] For another, whatever meaning ended up attributed to the dream was, in early medieval China as in most premodern societies, "a matter of negotiation. . . . Others had to be persuaded to accept the claim[s]"[181] made in this or that interpretation. The interpreter was not free to simply make things up at random or utter a string of nonsense. He was constrained by his audience's (and his own) expectation that there had to be a way of justifying the interpretation he had arrived at. It could not appear arbitrary or baseless. It needed to be non-obvious enough to elicit some surprise but not so outlandish as to seem to bear no relation to the tangle of events as well as to the details of the dream itself. Hence the exuberant attention in the written record to how particular interpretations were arrived at.

The recording of a dream, often along with the writing down of its interpretation, was another major step in the long, winding process of reception. It is likely that a dream deemed important was recorded in more than one version, some rougher but closer to the experience, others more polished but also more thoroughly subjected to genre conventions and audience expectations.[182] Dreams themselves were ephemeral, and their initial interpretations were probably initially conducted orally and face to face. But once committed to writing, whether in a fulsome narrative, a brief chronicle entry, a letter, an interpreter's log, or a family record, the dream and its paired interpretation were no longer the possession solely of the dreamer, the interpreter, or the writer. As a record, the dream along with its interpretation then escaped to become a thing in the world, eligible for its own biography, liable to be transmitted, received, used, and interpreted in unexpected ways, completely beyond the control of the initial recorder. "Writing possesses properties that call for vigilance. Left on its own, it may go off track."[183]

Finally, since most interpretations took a predictive stance, a key factor in how they were received by others was whether they were borne out by subsequent events. The initial interpretation was one half of a tally. Only once it had been matched to the other half—the way in which events actually unfolded, or the hitherto hidden information that subsequently come to light—was its status socially and epistemologically secured. Recognizing that the two tally halves fit was itself a social process. The hermeneutics of dreams, then, bore yet another inescapably social aspect, in that any given interpretation had to win over an audience of others, persuading them of both its veracity and the skill by which it had been derived. Dream interpretation was in many ways like an argument before the law: the detailed basis for assigning meanings and the playing out of predictions constituted essential evidence, but, finally, the judge and jury were the many other people before whom all of this was performed.

But still we have not reached the end of the social process of dream interpretation. For it kept rippling outward in social space and in generational time, as many hands were involved in the preservation, copying, editing, compiling, recompiling, anthologizing, and commenting on written records of such interpretive chains. Each instance in which an account of a dream interpretation was re-recorded or recompiled—whether in a biography of the dreamer or the interpreter, a compilation of anecdotes of uncanny happenings or of divination performances, a topically organized anthology, or a treatise—was an instance in which it had, in effect, won another sponsor. The sponsor selected it for inclusion in a larger work in order to make some point or other to readers. The reputation of that larger work—starting with its very survival or disappearance—depended on its reception by new generations of readers. And so the process rolled along, and still does, down to us, here, now. Of the making of dream records and dream interpretations there was, and is, no end.

CHAPTER FIVE

Visitations

Consider the following anecdote, attributed to a compilation made around 435.[1] A man named Dong Zhaozhi was crossing a river by boat when he noticed a twig floating on the current. An ant scurried back and forth on it, seemingly afraid. So Dong brought the ant on board. That night he dreamed a black-robed man thanked him, saying, "I am king among ants. Should you ever find yourself in trouble, please let me know." Years later Dong was falsely arrested. Remembering his dream, he gathered several ants into his palm and told them of his plight. He then dreamed again of the black-robed personage, who advised him to flee into the hills and await the official pardon that was coming by courier. Waking, he found that ants had chewed through his restraints, allowing him to escape. The pardon soon arrived.

I want to argue that this is not so much a story about dreams as a story about a relationship in which dreams figure importantly. The relationship is built on the exchange of help in dire circumstances. But it begins with an intersubjective encounter in which the human protagonist recognizes another self, a self that knows it is in trouble on the water. Significantly, some of the textual variants that have come down to us say that as it scurried to and fro on the twig the ant "feared for its life" 惶遽畏死; the ant thus becomes a narrative subject, a co-protagonist.[2] Other variants put this as an inference in the mind and speech of Dong: "Zhaozhi said [to himself], 'This means it is in fear for its life'" 昭之曰此畏死也; the ant is thus apprehended by the man, via what philosophers are wont to call a "theory of other minds," as a living subject like himself, whose behavior evinces an awareness of danger and the aim to stay alive.[3] It is a story, then, of the emergent relationship between two selves—a narrative of an ecology of selves.[4] Each of these protagonists has aims—most especially the aim to keep on living and thriving as long as possible. Each recognizes the other as an intentional being with aims similar to its own, and acts accordingly.

Each also recognizes the other as a member of a society with certain intelligible conventions. Although the man is initially unaware of the ant's status in its social world, he later, having learned of it, depends on it to make his own request for aid. And for his part the ant king is kept informed of events in human society by his far-flung network of formic subjects: this is how news of Dong's plight reaches him, and it's also how he knows that a pardon is on the way. This mutual recognition is what makes possible their exchange of life-saving assistance.

The two selves fall into a form, a pattern of gifting that, once entered into, links both parties even if it does not tightly bind them.[5] It is a form, the story invites us to think, that transcends species. It's not a conceptual or merely cultural structure imposed by the human party on the blank canvas of "nature" so much as an emergent feature of the process of interaction between the two selves, constraining both of them. We might even read the story as inviting us to consider whether, rather than a nature/culture binary in which cultures are plural but nature is singular, there is in fact only *one culture*—in which forms such as that of gift-giving link selves of diverse species—but *many natures*, in the sense of many *Umwelten*, many worlds-as-experienced depending on each species' distinctive sensorimotor capacities and how they shape its perception of and relation to their environment.[6] Some would read the story as a charming *projection* of a uniquely human, perhaps "Confucian" value (that of *bao* 報 or moral reciprocity) and of the uniquely human process of sign-making onto the sign-less, value-less, self-less, aim-less nonhuman world of nature. In such a reading, the story would have only human beings and human culture to be about. (Or, if one is a historian of Chinese literature, one might simply read the story as an instance of the "birth of fiction," in which case it has only the prehistory of a literary genre to be about.)

But I want to pursue a different reading. As Eduardo Kohn has argued, "The distinction . . . is not between an objective world, devoid of intrinsic significance, and humans who, as bearers of culture, are in a unique position to give meaning to it. . . . Rather, 'aboutness'—representation, intention, and purpose in their most basic forms—emerges wherever there is life; the biological world is constituted by the ways in which myriad beings—human and nonhuman—perceive and represent their surroundings. Significance . . . is not the exclusive province of humans."[7] And the narrative's two dream events are crucial to this reading.

Dreaming is a privileged mode of cross-kind communication, allowing the ant—normally presumably a user of indexical signs (to use Peirce's tripartite semiotic typology)[8]—to communicate in symbolic signs, that is, human language, as well.[9] That, we could say, is one affordance of dreaming.[10] Another is the opportunity for the ant to appear in human form and garb. Selves come clothed in bodies, and in dreams the clothing may be changed.[11] Dong presumably would not have understood ant signs, but the king of ants is able to cross the threshold and meet him more than halfway in dreams. This oneiric affordance usually moves in only one direction:[12] Dong does not appear in the ant's dream, addressing him in ant signs and wearing the physical form of an ant. Maybe that's simply because the record we have to read of the event is a record made by humans, and because we are humans, not ants.

The Visitation Paradigm

This story exemplifies what I call the *visitation paradigm* of the dreamscape. It has four working parts. The dream is an encounter with another being. The encounter is direct, not coded. The encounter is real; that is, it's not "just a dream," and something changes in the waking world as a result of it. And, most importantly for my argument in this chapter, the dream occurs in the context of, or creates the possibility for, a *relationship* between the one who dreams and the one who visits through the dream.

Strikingly unlike what we saw in the previous two chapters, here dreams do not *represent* anything about the world. They do not operate at the meta level. Dreams are rather "interlocutory *events*"[13] that take place *in* the world.[14] And, as we will see, they were experiences that changed the dreamer and left real traces in the waking world. They were dialogical in nature; they called for a response. Such dreams were "not . . . an escape from but . . . an engagement with the world."[15] They had evocative power, in that they spurred the dreamer to do things. They also had performative power: they themselves did things.

Rather than being private and isolative, then, these dreams again *connected* the dreamer to other selves, and even more intimately. Dreaming functioned as an interpersonal space—*and* the persons who might find each other there were not limited to living human persons. This is a view of dreaming that may surprise us (at least it has surprised me), but it turns out to be quite common, widely distributed in human history and geographic space. Kevin Groark captures it well:

> In many traditional societies, the dreamspace forms an alternate interpersonal sphere characterized by forms of social interaction and experience that are qualitatively different from waking life, yet intimately related to it. . . . Among the Tzotzil Maya, human sociality is explicitly understood to consist of both face-to-face relations (relations between physical selves) as well as relations between various self-extensions or soul-based "counterparts." *The dreamspace serves as an interpersonal realm in which the normally occluded motives and feelings of others (both human and extra-human) can be perceived and experienced through the medium of soul interactions*. . . . Dream experience allows for a translocation or shift in the focus of attention and intersubjective engagement from the relatively opaque phenomenal realm of physical bodies to the essential realm of souls. In doing so, it brings the extended intersubjective field of soul-based "counterpart relations" . . . into focus as part of the total field in which relationality is embedded.[16]

The Touch of the Real

Before proceeding, I pause to note an essential feature both of this dream-paradigm itself and of the way in which it was written about, or performed, in texts. The texts in question are typically anecdotal narratives; that's because dreams are seen as *events* that occurred at a particular point in time and involved a limited set of actors.[17] But furthermore and crucially, most of these anecdotes are framed in such a way that the reader is meant to assume the story isn't a parable, say, or a hypothetical case, but a report of *actual* past events. (Whether this or that reader believes the event actually occurred as reported is another matter entirely—a matter of her *reception* of it.)[18]

Now there are exceptions that prove this rule, and some of the most notable ones appear in *Zhuangzi* and another text that draws heavily on it, *Liezi*. For example, in the fourth chapter of *Zhuangzi* we find one of several passages advancing the theme of the usefulness of being useless. A carpenter and his apprentice pass by a shrine graced with a magnificent old oak tree. The apprentice asks why the carpenter didn't stop to admire the tree, and the carpenter irritably explains that it would be worthless as timber. That night the tree appears to the carpenter in a dream to mount a retort. It holds that perfecting the art of being useless has been very useful to it. The tree continues, "And besides, you and I are both things 物. What nonsense, that one of us should think it is the other which is the thing! And the worthless human who is about to die, what does he know of the worthless tree?" The carpenter wakes and tells of his dream. The apprentice wonders why the tree is standing at the shrine, providing shade and attracting admirers, if it's so intent on being of no use. The carpenter replies:

> Hush! Don't say it. It's simply using that as a pretext, thinks of itself as pestered by people who don't appreciate it. Aren't the ones which don't become sacred trees in danger of being clipped? Besides, it protects itself in a different way from the ordinary. If you try to judge it by conventional standards, you'll be way off![19]

It's hard to avoid the impression that this anecdote (like most others in *Zhuangzi* and *Liezi*) is meant to be taken as a parable or a thought experiment, not a report of an actual event. (One way we can see how the story is different is by comparing it with other anecdotes in the same text, many of which feature characters with unmistakably fictive or allegorical names, others of which feature familiar characters, such as Confucius, saying and doing things wildly incongruent with what the text presumes its readers are used to seeing those characters say and do. It's not a matter of divining authorial intention so much as doing intra- and intertextual reading. I *do not*, however, wish to be read as arguing that *Zhuangzi* espouses a worldview that rules out the possibility of trees being selves with aims.) The story is positioned at an oblique angle to the extra-textual flow of events in the world. It draws its energy not from the claim that the events it narrates actually happened but from the opposite—from its trust in the reader to see that the point being made isn't about an actual encounter between a carpenter and a tree but is instead an argument about transcending conventional views, and that the story is a fictive construct designed to make this point.[20] Yet, as a dream narrative, it shares all four elements of the visitation paradigm. For here, too, the dream constitutes an encounter between the dreamer and another being, and it is not in code. It changes its recipient. (Before the dream, the carpenter evaluates the tree as he would any other potential source of lumber; afterwards he has a new outlook, on the tree and on conventional standards generally. The dream-encounter thus leaves a real trace in the world.) And the dream occurs in the context of a relationship, however fleeting, between two beings.

Unlike this and similar parabolic dream narratives that use self-evidently fictive stories to argue stances on various topics, most texts we'll consider below insist that the events they narrate actually occurred—and this is crucial to their rhetorical construction. That is, they perform (and would usually have been read as) a different genre with a different stance toward the extra-textual world.[21] And some of them insist on this so strongly that they include details unmistakably meant to reinforce this "touch of the real."[22]

Take this one, for example:

> Liu Zhao served as governor of Hejian. While he held office there, his wife died. He buried her coffin in the garden of the headquarters building. When the Yellow Turban rebellion broke out [in 184], Zhao abandoned his office and fled.
>
> Later, a new governor arrived. He dreamed one night that a lady came to see him. Later she [came again and] left a pair of bracelets as a gift. The governor did not know what this sort of bracelet was called. The woman said, "These are Solomon's seal bracelets.[23] They are linked together with gold threads so that they bend and stretch on the wearer. They are truly rare. I must soon depart, so I bid you farewell with these. Tell no one of this!"
>
> Twenty days afterward, Liu Zhao's son, who had been sent to retrieve his mother's coffin for reburial, arrived. The current governor then realized the whole situation. When the son saw the bracelets he was overcome with grief.[24]

We are not told why Liu Zhao's deceased wife visits the new governor in his dreams, other than his sheer proximity to her resting place. In waking life, at least, such a visit would have been highly irregular; but this is the dream world, where anything is possible. What is clear is that her parting gift carries over into the waking world: to borrow the language of spiritualism, it's an apport.[25] That her son recognizes the rare bracelets adds two more layers of confirmation—that she really was the previous governor's wife, buried on the grounds, and that the gifts she left behind must surely, given their rarity, have come from inside her tomb. The implication is inescapable: dreaming of a dead person can sometimes be an encounter so tangibly *real* that physical objects can be transferred between worlds. The ontological mechanism enabling such apports remains unaddressed. But that it really occurred is asserted and then, lest we doubt, reconfirmed. The way in which the anecdote is constructed anticipates readers' doubt that the ghost-dream-to-waking-world object transfer really occurred, and in the face of such doubt it takes measures to assert the reality of the event. The dream did not represent the world but was itself an event in the world. Like all other dreams in the visitational paradigm, it was "party to the unfolding of reality."[26]

A few other examples will suffice. Here is another tale attributed to *A Record of Anomalies*:

> The magistrate of Jiaxing, Wu Shiji, suffered from malaria. Passing the temple at Wuchang by boat, he sent someone to beg pardon on his behalf[27] and to pray for the expulsion of the malaria-causing demon in him.[28] When he had traveled on to a point some twenty *li* past the temple, just as he was dozing off, he suddenly dreamed he saw a horseman riding up on the water behind him, seemingly with great urgency. When the rider saw Shiji, he dismounted and boarded the boat along with a subofficial functionary. They bound up a young boy and took him away. Shiji was soon cured of malaria.[29]

Here Wu Shiji's cure functions as the apport, the newly emergent phenomenon in the waking world that confirms (and is claimed to have been directly produced by) what happened in the dream. The process leading to the cure is set in motion by Wu's offering and request; that act opens the relationship with the god that moves him to respond as requested. The dream itself is in this instance not so much a communication as a real-time, temporary window onto the workings of the normally invisible spirit world that surrounds us: *this*, the dream shows, is how such cures work. That is, the dream briefly opens a portal through which the dreamer can see, as it swings into gear, the actual mechanism that will result in his cure—a mechanism usually imperceptible to him and to all who heard and read this anecdote (including me and, I presume, you). The metaphoric idiom in which that mechanism is couched is bureaucratic. Both the god's subordinates and the malaria-causing demon are clothed in human form, and the curative process takes the form of the arrest of an offender.[30] Again the affordance of the dream goes in only one direction: Wu does not necessarily see things as the demon or the god or, for that matter, the horse sees them. The anecdote argues the waking-world reality of what was seen in the dream. It also commends the efficacy of requests made to the Wuchang temple god.

Such arguments were a staple of the anecdote genre, used in stories shaped by various ideological and religious persuasions. An example from Wang Yan's 王琰 pro-Buddhist compilation, *Records of Signs from the Unseen Realm* (*Mingxiang ji* 冥祥記, ca. 490), reads thus:

> Zhao Xi of Huainan in the twentieth year of [Song] Yuanjia [443–44] was serving as assistant to the commander of the guard. He had a longstanding illness from which he feared he would not recover. With utmost mind he took refuge in the Buddha. That night he dreamed of a man of extraordinary appearance, like a god, who handed him from the rafter beam a small packet and a razor and said, "Take this medicine and use this razor,[31] and your illness will certainly be cured." Xi then woke up with a start, and he actually had possession of 果得 the medicine and the razor. He at once took the medicine, and his sickness was dispelled. He left the household and took the Dharma name Sengxiu. He lived past the age of eighty, and only then died.[32]

Two details serve to argue that the dream experience was veridical: Zhao's possession upon waking of the objects bestowed on him in the dream, and his recovery from chronic illness due (we are meant to infer) to the medicine received in the dream, with mention of his advanced longevity thrown in for good measure. And, as in the previous example, there's an implied recommendation to readers: there it was "be sure to pay respects to the temple god at Wuchang when passing by on the water," here it's "consider joining the sangha, especially when urged in a striking dream to do so."

Once we start noticing such features of dream anecdotes, they seem to be everywhere. Here are summaries of just a few from among several dozen other instances that have come down to us in the archive:

While stationed far from home a man dreams of having intercourse with his wife. When he returns home he finds her pregnant. The anecdote concludes: "It turned out to be as he [or they?] described" 後如其言矣, presumably meaning that husband and wife gave matching accounts of their oneiric encounter despite the distance between them.[33]

A divine personage appears in a dream and bestows on the sleeper a scepter (*ruyi* 如意) carved from black horn. The sleeper awakes to find the scepter resting by his head.[34]

A man while ill dreams that a person gives him a shirt, and upon waking the garment is at his side.[35]

Upon the conception of her future son, a woman dreams a monk addresses her as "mother" and gives her a flywhisk and an engraved book press. Awakening, she finds these objects beside her. When her son reaches the age of five she shows him the whisk and the press and he immediately recognizes them, but cannot recall from where. It later emerges that he had had them in his previous life as a renowned Dharma master.[36]

A man courts but is in the end rejected by a woman. Angered, he kills her. He dreams that she comes to return the gifts he'd given her during the courtship, and when he wakes they are all lying beside him.[37]

A monk illicitly casts a metal icon of the bodhisttva Sound Observer. When the casting is finished but the image is still in its mold, the monk is arrested (presumably for violating the proscription on private metal-founding). He concentrates on the bodhisttva, each day reciting one hundred times the *Lotus Sutra* chapter devoted to him. He dreams the icon comes to comfort him in his prison cell, and notices a small square hole in its chest. Not long afterwards he is pardoned. On returning to his monastery he discovers that the icon had broken out of its mold.[38]

A man dreams of being given a bolus of medicine, with instructions to swallow it with water. When he wakes, the medicine is in his hand. He takes it and recovers.[39]

A dead man appears in his widow's dream to thank her and their son for sponsoring the refurbishment of a Daoist temple as well as a ritual for his benefit, explaining that he has now been reborn in the heavens. He tells her that he's "leaving behind as a confirmation" 留以爲驗 a gilded melon knife. When she awakes she "does after all possess" 果得 the knife, and it's the very one that had been sealed in his coffin with him before his entombment.[40]

A man dreams he agrees to exchange heads with an exceedingly ugly interlocutor. When he wakes, he does indeed have the other man's head joined to his body, with the expected reactions of shock from colleagues and family.[41]

Waking up from a dream with someone else's head on one's shoulders is quite an apport!

Having noted these anecdotes' stance toward the real, I now want to ask: What were some of the contacts, communications, relationships, and exchanges that dreaming made possible? What variety of things did dreaming *afford*?

Dreaming's Affordances

One thing dreams afforded was a portal for *communication* across some distance, boundary, or ontological or taxonomic gap. Consider this story from the biography of Yan Han 顏含, which was widely anthologized as testament to the virtue of filiality.[42] During the funeral procession of Han's older brother, Ji, the banner wrapped itself around a tree and could not be loosened. The master of funeral ceremonies then fell to the ground and "declared Ji's words, saying 稱畿言曰: 'My allotted lifespan is not yet expired. It's just that I took too much medicine and damaged my five viscera. I am about to return to life,[43] so do not bury me.'" At this their father said an incantation in which he promised to take the coffin back home and not bury it yet. The banner then loosened itself from the tree. The coffin with Ji's body inside was returned home. That night Ji appeared to his wife in a dream, saying, "I'm about to revive. Hurry and open the coffin!" She spoke of it to the family. Then Ji's mother and others again dreamed of Ji imploring them to open the coffin, but the father still would not permit it. (Opening a coffin that had already been ritually sealed was a dangerous thing to do.) At this point Yan Han, still young at the time, declared, "Exceptional events have happened since ancient times. Now a numinous anomaly has occurred right here. Although opening the coffin is painful, isn't *not* opening it much worse?" So the parents gave permission. When they opened it they found confirmation that Ji was alive: he had scratched so persistently on the underside of the coffin lid that his fingernails were worn away. But his breathing was shallow, and he hovered near death. For several months he couldn't speak. When he required food or drink he would "communicate this through dreams" 託之以夢. The situation proved exhausting for everyone, so Han abandoned official life and stayed home to care for his brother for the next thirteen years.

Observe the modes of communication. Yan Ji, alive but unable to speak, first somehow signals an emergency through the stoppage of the funeral procession and the odd behavior of the funeral banner. (We are presumably meant to see him as the agent responsible for these anomalies. The mechanisms are not addressed, but this isn't the only extant instance of such.)[44] He delivers a verbal message through the master of the funeral ritual 喪者, seemingly by causing the man to fall to the ground, enter a trance, and "declare his words" in the first person, the way a god might speak through a medium. The paterfamilias responds by "pronouncing an incantation to him" 祝之. Not accidentally, these modes were typically used respectively for communications to and from gods and spirits in ritual settings. Shut inside his coffin, Ji of necessity avails himself of this other mode of communication from the available repertoire of such modes, and his father responds as people typically did in such communicative exchanges even though the interlocutor is atypical. Ji then resorts to a third method: he appears in dreams, addressing family members directly. (And this isn't the only anecdote of someone trapped inside a coffin sending simultaneous dreams to multiple relatives to communicate his plight.)[45] Freed from the coffin but failing to regain the power of speech, he continues to express himself through dreams.

That this regular communication through dreams is unelaborated upon suggests it was an unusual but not unknown trope. Rulers, for example, were enjoined or reputed to broadcast dreams as a way of summoning recluses to serve at court. The gap traversed was geographical distance, and the targeted recipients were not known in advance (since the intended dream recipients were recluses, no one knew exactly who or where they were). "To send dreams" (*tuo meng* 託夢) is the phrase most often used in such passages; sometimes it's "to grant dreams" (*chui meng* 垂夢).[46] I am not aware of a ritual practice for sending dreams to recipients, records of which have survived from elsewhere in the early medieval world,[47] but at least one passage implies that the thearch might accomplish this by giving sustained thought to his need for assistance.[48]

This prerogative was not restricted to rulers. We have several records of recently deceased persons "sending dreams" to their surviving kin to request help in the form of merit-making rituals and donations, or to pass along vital information about what really goes on in the afterlife domain.[49] Here the gap traversed was not simply one of geography, at least not in the usual sense. Nor was sending dreams a uniquely human achievement. Even animals might be credited with this capacity—not just of appearing and speaking in humans' dreams (this is common) but, much more unusually, of "sending" a dream to a human dreamer. Thus we find this laconic entry in *Inquest into the Spirit Realm* (*Soushen ji*): "*Pengyue* are a type of crab. Once upon a time one of them communicated a dream to a person 嘗通夢於人, and in it the crab referred to itself as 'chief chamberlain.' Today many people in Linhai call these crabs Chief Chamberlains."[50] Here we have two remarkable things in one twenty-three-character report: a crustacean joins the ranks of species able to transmit dreams to humans across a considerable taxonomic remove; and an instance is documented of a regional custom being newly introduced into waking life through a dream.

Beyond communication, this is another affordance of dreams: to launch new knowledge, texts, or traditions into society, or reintroduce old ones.[51] Ji Kang 嵇康 (fl. mid-3rd century)[52] famously went calmly to his execution, strumming a tune called the Guangling Melody 廣陵散 on his zither and voicing regret that he had stubbornly refused to teach it to anyone.[53] Less well known is the story of how he himself had acquired the melody in a dream—a story that comes down to us in the early fifth-century *Garden of Marvels* (*Yi yuan* 異苑) and is also attested in a quotation from that text in a Dunhuang manuscript (Stein 2072):

> Ji Kang, byname Shuye, a native of Qiao, when young was once sleeping during the daytime when he dreamed of a man over a pole tall who said he had been a court musician for the Yellow Thearch 黄帝. The man said his bones were lying in the woods three *li* east of a nearby inn. Someone had exposed them, he said, and he asked Kang to rebury them, promising to reward him richly for the assistance. Kang went to the place in question and indeed found white bones there. The tibia was three feet long. He collected the bones and reburied them.
>
> That night he dreamed again of the tall man. The man came to give him the Guangling melody. When Kang awoke, he played the song on his zither, and it sounded marvelous. He forgot none of it.[54]

Together, then, these two anecdotes—of how Ji Kang received the tune in a dream and died without transmitting it—neatly frame the melody within the esoteric dynamic: it originated in a dream, became famous through its attachment to a well-known figure, yet pointedly went with him into his tomb. Thus the tune was made famous at once for its beauty and for being unknowable. And yet knowledge of the Guangling Melody was always liable to be leaked back into the waking world through subsequent dreams and visions: in another anecdote we find Ji Kang, now a ghost himself, appearing and teaching the tune to an accomplished zither player.[55]

Through dreams, whole scriptures could be newly introduced into the world. One such case is the *Scripture of Sound Observer from the Era of Prince Gao* (*Gaowang Guanshiyin jing* 高王觀世音經), the text of which is attested in manuscripts found in Turfan and Dunhuang and is available in the apocrypha volume of the Taishō Buddhist canon.[56] Many versions of the story of this sutra's origin have come down to us. Some of them give the dreamer's name as Sun Jingde 孫敬德, others omit it, but all agree on this basic narrative: the man, a devotee of the bodhisattva Sound Observer (and who had earlier, some versions say, fashioned an icon of him), was accused and imprisoned. On the night before he was to be executed he performed a confession and vow. He then dreamed[57] that a monk appeared and orally taught him a sutra dedicated to the bodhisattva, urging him to recite it one thousand times. Waking, he recalled and began reciting the words. Moments before the executioner swung his blade the prisoner completed the thousandth recitation. Three times the blade broke into pieces. Because of this, the man was released. After arriving back home, he examined the icon and found three blade-shaped dents in its head. The sutra he was taught in the dream was copied out and circulated, the story concludes—and we are in a position to add that it was circulated widely enough to have come down to modern times. Some monastic cataloguers of sutras accepted this one as genuine, while others rejected it, but those who rejected it did so not because it was first transmitted in a dream per se but because it had been piped directly into China rather than passing through India first.[58] Claims of oneiric origin for Daoist scriptures, techniques, and other bits of esoteric knowledge were much more common.[59]

One could build a long list of dreaming's other affordances, but for brevity's sake I will mention only five.

Vital information can be conveyed. In a story type attested in both pro-Buddhist and pro-Daoist compilations of anecdotes, someone is in the process of constructing a religiously valorized object (an icon or temple) but lacks one essential pigment or building material. A figure visits in a dream to reveal where the missing items can be found.[60]

Relations with distant friends can be sustained, even when the friend is a nonhuman person. It was through two significant dreams that the official Wang Yan maintained contact with his cherished icon of the bodhisattva Sound Observer, which he'd been given as a child, during periods when they were separated by distance and by societal chaos.[61] Through one of the dreams, the icon, which he'd consigned to a monastery so that it would be in a secure, ritually pure place during renovation on his home, appeared to him displaced from its usual site. The icon, acting as a living self with aims, thus used an indexical sign to communicate its dire situation. Wang rushed to the monastery to retrieve it. Later that night several other icons were stolen from the monastery for their metal content. The implication is that the icon, and/or the powerful and beneficent being it embodied, had accurate foreknowledge of the robbers' plans and visited Wang Yan in his dream to warn him.

Vast distances can be traveled in an evening. The nun Huimu repeatedly visited Amitābha's Pure Land in her dreams, in one instance almost managing to climb up onto a lotus blossom and be reborn there. Implied is that it was only due to being awakened by visitors (these not from Porlock)[62] that her visits there were cut short.[63]

Intractable illnesses can be cured. In dreams, the underlying cause of a persistent illness, or its location in the body, might be revealed. Surgery might even be conducted in a dream! We saw an example in chapter 2, with the story of Zhu Fayi collected by Wang Yan in his *Records of Signs from the Unseen Realm.*[64]

People can share dreams. Given the understanding of dreams that underlies the visitation paradigm, it was quite possible for two or more people to have the same dream during the same night. Under a "modern" or Heraclitean view of dreams as private mental events, such cases seem impossible by definition, as well as inexplicable. But if dreams are imagined as real events in the world—simply the visitation of one being by another through the medium of the dream—then cases of "the same dream" (*tong meng* 同夢) become easily imaginable, if not ordinary. We have multiple records of cases where this was said to have happened.[65]

There is a stark contrast between the particularity and specificity of the initial dream experience (it happens to one person, in one circumstance) and, on the other hand, the subsequent wide diffusion and long preservation of the things revealed—and of the stories of how they were revealed. Although we no longer have the Guangling tune, we have the story of how we no longer have it, so that its very name continues to conjure a once marvelous thing no longer available in the world. We have an entire Buddhist sutra, still included in modern editions of the Chinese canon. Texts were launched, temple cults were begun, reputations of people and things were formed, and the stories of how these things happened continue to be read and discussed dozens of centuries later and around the world. Such is the power of some dreams and dream accounts.

Face to Face

Above all, dreaming afforded a portal for face-to-face encounters with Others across ontological, taxonomic, spatial, and linguistic gaps. It afforded *relationships*. Consider again the story of the ant king. It's not as if the ant was recognized at once by the human protagonist as a self with aims because that's how Chinese people viewed the *class* of beings known as ants. In many situations an ant might have gone unnoticed entirely. In others it might have been seen as an object, an instrument, or a nuisance. (In fact, some versions mention that other passengers on Dong's boat complain about his bringing a biting creature aboard and threaten to crush it. Out of pity he carefully shields the ant until the boat is safely docked.)[66] In this instance the ant's being seen as a self with aims emerges from the interaction of these two beings in their specific situation on the river. The ant scurries back and forth on the floating stick; the human being notices this unusual behavior, sizes up the situation, draws an inference about the ant's aims, and extends help. It's this pairing of human attention and action with the purposive behavior of the distressed ant that leads into a relationship that, facilitated by the communicative portal of dreaming, stretches over years.[67]

In this particular situation, the behavior of one self stood out to be noticed and responded to by another self. The relationship between Dong and the ant was irreducibly a series of interactions. In these interactions, face-to-face encounters were key. And it was in dreams that these encounters took their fullest form. I want to explore the implications of these features, which are hardly unique to the story of the ant king.

In his classic essay, "Ojibwa Ontology, Behavior, and World View," A. Irving Hallowell had this to say:

> Since stones are grammatically animate, I once asked an old man: Are *all* the stones we see about us here alive? He reflected a long while and then replied, "No! But *some* are." This qualified answer made a lasting impression on me. And it is thoroughly consistent with other data that indicate that the Ojibwa are not animists in the sense that they dogmatically attribute living souls to inanimate objects such as stones. The hypothesis which suggests itself . . . is that the allocation of stones to an animate grammatical category . . . does not involve a consciously formulated theory about the nature of stones. It leaves a door open that our orientation on dogmatic grounds keeps shut tight. Whereas we should never expect a stone to manifest animate properties of any kind under any circumstances, the Ojibwa recognize, *a priori*, potentialities for animation in certain classes of objects under certain circumstances. The Ojibwa

do not perceive stones, in general, as animate, any more than we do. The crucial test is experience. Is there any personal testimony available?[68]

Hallowell goes on to recount several anecdotes in which Anishinaabe people[69] saw stones move, or encountered stones with features suggesting eyes and a mouth, or saw stones opening their mouths as if to speak or disgorge objects. It is not, then, that the Anishinaabe "personify" nonhuman creatures or natural objects in general. This would imply two things that are not the case: that at some point Anishinaabe people first saw them as inanimate, material things, and only later began "personifying" them, and that how they see them is entirely a function of their membership in general classes. It is, instead, a matter of encounters in particular situations, and of subsequent socially circulated testimony—stories—about such experiences. Similarly, concerning the hunter-gatherer Nayaka people of South India, Nurit Bird-David writes:

> My argument is that Nayaka focus on events. Their attention is educated to dwell on events. They are attentive to the changes of things in the world in relation to changes in themselves. As they move and act in the forest, they pick up information about the relative variances in the flux of the interrelatedness between themselves and other things against relative invariances. When they pick up a relatively changing thing with their relatively changing selves—and, all the more, when it happens in a relatively unusual manner—they regard as devaru [that is, as a "superperson"][70] *this* particular thing within *this* particular situation. This . . . arises from the stories which Nayaka tell.[71]

With these points in mind, consider now a Chinese anecdote about a human being and a stone. Among the tales collected in *Arrayed Accounts of Marvels* (*Lieyi zhuan* 列異傳), attributed to Cao Pi 曹丕 (187–226), we find:

> A woman of the Dai clan in Yuning who had long been ill once went outdoors and, noticing a small stone, said to it, "If you have divinity and can cure my illness, I will worship you." That night she dreamed of a personage who said, "I am about to bestow blessings on you." Afterwards she gradually recovered. So she established a shrine for the deity, calling it the Shrine of the Stone Marquis.[72]

We are not told *why* the woman "notices" 見 the particular stone in question, only *that* she does. We sense a bit of weight hanging on "went outdoors" 出, perhaps implying that Ms. Dai had been shut in for a long time due to illness and that it was on this rare excursion that the stone caught her attention. In any case, here again it's not as if this lady is depicted as acting on a general cultural belief that stones are living beings who can cure ailments. Nor (I think) does the story wish to argue that just any object at all, if approached in this manner, would respond as this stone does. Rather, this particular stone catches her gaze and she responds by focusing her attention and intention on it, promising to serve it ritually if it possesses divine power and can cure her. This recognition and promise open the portal of a relationship, each party responding in turn to the other. She talks with the stone, and this

> "talking with" stands for attentiveness to variances and invariances in behavior and response of things in states of relatedness and for getting to know such things as they change through the vicissitudes over time of the engagement with them. To "talk with a [stone]" . . . is to perceive what *it* does as one acts towards it, being aware concurrently of changes in oneself and the [stone]. It is expecting response and responding, growing into mutual responsiveness and . . . possibly into mutual responsibility.[73]

In her dream the stone appears as a personage 人 declaring the intention to play its role in this emergent relationship. Again, dreaming is a key portal of communication, affording nonhuman selves the capacity to appear in human form and speak human language. The woman's recovery is taken as evidence that this intention was fulfilled, and she follows through by establishing the shrine. That the site acquired a name suggests that it came to be noticed and frequented by other people, gaining a local reputation. It is telling that the stone never confirms (or denies) its possession of divine power. We are left to wonder whether it was the interaction between the two parties that *performed* the stone's divinity into being. In other words, rather than see its divine power *either* already existing independently of the woman's response to it *or* as resulting from her sheer projection of power onto a "dumb object,"[74] we are invited to think of "divinity" here as *a type or aspect of the relationship* between the two parties, co-activated and sustained precisely by their interactions and in no other way.[75]

Another version of this anecdote that has come down to us is attributed to Gan Bao's *Inquest into the Spirit Realm*. I italicize details that differ importantly from the *Lieyi zhuan* version:

> A woman of the Dai clan in Yuzhang had long suffered from an incurable illness. She [once] noticed a small stone *with the form of a human being* 形像偶人. She told it: "*You have human form* 爾有人形. Are you divine? If you are able to cure my affliction, I will treat you very generously." That night she dreamed of a personage who said, "I am about to bestow blessings on you." Afterwards she gradually recovered from her illness. So she built a shrine at the foot of a mountain. *Members of the Dai clan served as the mediums there* 戴氏爲巫, so it came to be known as the Shrine to Marquis Dai.[76]

This version supplies a reason why the woman noticed this particular stone: it jumped out at her because of its unusual human-like form, a form that *she took as* hinting at its potential. (This *motif of the striking object* is a staple in Western thought experiments on how the phenomenon known as "religion" might first have emerged.)[77] The human form that the stone assumes in the woman's dream is simply an extension of how it appeared to her in waking experience. Members of the woman's family go on to serve as the mediums attached to the shrine—that is, as the literal mouthpieces through whom the god (or, more accurately, the being who was being treated by the Dai clan and other locals as what in English is termed a "god") spoke to human audiences. Whether through the portal of dreams or the bodies of mediums, this stone had words to speak in response (and only in response) to human devotional vows and action.

Taiping huanyu ji in turn attributes a slightly different version of this anecdote to *Soushen ji*. There, the chronically ill woman of the Dai clan had ventured out in search of medicines 覓藥 (presumably herbs in the wild) when she "noticed a stone *standing erect* and resembling human form 見一石立似人形. She *paid courtesies to it*" 禮之 and then spoke to it in terms similar to the above versions. So here the stone grabs the woman's attention both for its anomalous, human-like bodily form and for its erect stance. And she responds, as above, by engaging it as a fellow self, but here with the added mention of courtesies—a culturally patterned response, to which the stone responds in accordance with the pattern, both falling into a form.[78]

Finally, one other version of the tale is close to the *Lieyi zhuan* version—but adds a postscript. After the Shrine of the Stone Marquis is established, the text continues:

> Later, someone took the stone and threw it into a fire. Everyone said, "This is a divine stone 此神石. You ought not commit such an offense against it." The man said, "What 'divinity' is this stone 此石何神?" With that, he threw it into a well, [saying] "If it's really divine, then it should emerge from the well" 神當出井中. Next morning when everyone went to look, the stone had indeed emerged. The man who had seized it fell ill and died.[79]

The makers of this version were unwilling to simply leave the door open. By setting a test and having the stone-person pass it, they added narrative confirmation of the stone's divinity. This version also affords us an unmistakable glimpse of the *community of estimation* involved in bringing the shrine cult to life. The shrine has become a site where multiple individuals engage in relationships with the stone and each other—mutual responsiveness and possibly mutual responsibility.

If dreams enabled face-to-face interactions with stones, they also did so with a variety of other selves. One of these was the human dead. In a common story type, a living person is traveling or has just moved to a new home when he dreams of a once-living person whose remains lie nearby. The person explains that his or her tomb has been ruined, the bones lying exposed to the air or submerged in water, then requests help from the dreamer. An example:

> When Shang Zhongkan[80] was in Dantu, he dreamed of a man who said: "You, sir, are of a mind to succor creatures. If you could move me to a high, dry place, then your grace would extend even to a skeleton." The next day a coffin did indeed come floating down the river on the current. Zhongkan took it and reburied it atop a hill and made an offering of wine and food. That night in a dream he saw the same man return and bow to him in thanks.[81]

The being who appears in the dream is a *man*, not a skeleton, despite his humilific self-reference. Although his body has decayed, dreaming affords him his human form once again. What triggers the interaction, it seems at first, is simple physical proximity: the living man happens to be staying near the spot to which the dead man's coffin will soon be borne by the river current. The dead man's urgent concern is that his remains are not only wet but also floating loose in the world, unsecured in a tomb. For the living party in this relationship, such contact with the dead would normally be deemed greatly inauspicious, dangerous, ritually impure, and hence terrifying. But dreaming affords a sterile channel of contact that frames the interaction in a safe cultural form. Beyond physical proximity, it is the dead man's act of *recognizing* Shang as someone uniquely inclined to kindness, among all the other living persons presumably located near the point on the river where his coffin was about to alight, that enables the emergent relationship. This recognition parallels the Dai clanswoman's initial noticing of the stone—but here it's not the living human person but the extra-human person who does the noticing. From the local humanscape as seen through the eyes of the dead man, it's Shang who stands out for his kindness. The Dai clanswoman's need for help was her illness; the dead man's need for help is the compromised and exposed state of his remains. Upon awakening, Shang responds in one of the culturally patterned ways available to him in the repertoire. (He could have summoned a medium, say, to exorcise the ghost.) The dead man returns in a second dream to offer thanks, completing the pattern.

That this pattern recurs in a great many narratives suggests it was a key cultural scenario. A particularly lovely example (from among many others that could be adduced) has Wen Ying being approached in a dream while traveling. Again, it is proximity that initially triggers contact: the dead man's coffin lies underwater just a few paces away from where Wen has stopped for the night. The man appears in a dream to request removal to a high, dry place, and he unfolds his outer gown to show Wen that his clothes are soaked. Waking, Wen recounts the dream to the others in his party, but they dismiss it with the comment that dreams are false 虛. Wen goes back to sleep, and the man appears again to appeal for help, this time mentioning the exact location of his coffin. Upon waking, Wen's companions concede that it's worth checking to confirm 驗 what the dream revealed. They find the coffin where the dead man had said they would, rotted and half submerged. Wen comments, "You fellows called dreams false, but what has been passed down by the folk through generations cannot be without confirmation" 世俗所傳不可無驗. They relocate and rebury the coffin.[82]

The Perils of Contact

There are many anecdotes similar to the ones we just saw, but in which the proximity that triggers a dream-enabled relationship is a breaching of boundaries. The protagonist wittingly or unwittingly crosses a threshold, then—typically on the same night—is visited in a dream by the other party, who comes to deliver a warning or mete out retribution.

Here is a story collected in *A Garden of Marvels*:

> During the Jin, Wen Qiao was near the jetty at Niuzhu when he heard the sound of music coming from under the water. The water's depth there was unfathomable, and it had long been said that many strange creatures lived below. So he put a lamp inside a rhinoceros horn and shone light down into the water. Soon he caught sight of underwater creatures reflecting his light back. They were all of strange form and anomalous shape. Some rode horses or carriages; some wore red gowns and caps.
>
> That night, Qiao dreamed of a man who said, "We are rightly separated from you by the boundary between the paths of the unseen and the seen. Why, then, did you shine the light on us?" Qiao was filled with dread by the dream. He died not long afterward.[83]

The parameters are familiar: a human protagonist draws near, triggering the start of a relationship. Often in such stories the living human party approaches the site unawares, but here, having heard tell of the "many strange creatures" 多怪物 reputed to live underwater and having caught a bit of their music, the man deliberately peers down into the depths to see what he can see. In response, one of the "strange" extrahuman selves appears in a dream, assuming human form and addressing the dreamer in human speech. A series of interactions ensues—here, baleful ones, as the dreamer, after having been chastised for shining his light across "the boundary between the paths of the unseen and the seen" 幽明道隔, upon waking is filled with dread 意甚惡之 and dies soon afterwards. A connection is implied between the dream and his death, and we are left to wonder if this is another case of what we'd call the psychosomatic effects of a dream. The version of this story that ended up incorporated into Wen Qiao's biography in *History of the Jin* informs us that, having long had a bad tooth, he now had it extracted, and because of this was "hit by a wind" 中風, a pathogen often associated in medical texts with what we would term madness. He died within a week at age forty-two.[84]

Sometimes the breach is more blatant. Two examples follow, one involving the father of a noted lyric poet:

> The Temple of the Young Maiden at Qingxi is said to be that of the third younger sister of [the divine] Marquis Jiang 蔣侯.[85] Inside the temple is a thick grove of nut trees, in the tops of which birds often nest and raise their young.
>
> During the Taiyuan era of the Jin [376–97], Xie Qing of Chen commandery shot several of the birds from horseback with his crossbow. At once he felt a piercing sensation in his body. That night he dreamt of a girl shaking her sleeves and saying angrily, "I am the one who raised those birds. Why did you attack them?" Within a day Qing was dead.
>
> Qing's personal name was Huan. He was the father of Xie Lingyun.[86]

> Wu Kaozhi, a member of an encamped family[87] from Nankang, was cutting timber for building boats when he suddenly noticed a pregnant monkey in the tree of an earth-god shrine. He climbed up the tree in pursuit, scampering up nimbly as if flying. The tree was isolated, and there were other people on the ground below, so the monkey, realizing there was no escape, held on to a tree branch with her left hand while with her right hand she rubbed her abdomen. Kaozhi caught her, took her down to the ground, and killed her. When he cut open her abdomen there was a baby monkey inside that looked as if it had been about to be born.
>
> That night Kaozhi dreamed he saw a personage who called himself a god 稱神. The god reproached him for killing the monkey. Afterwards Kaozhi was ill for a week. At first he seemed deranged. Then he gradually transformed into a tiger, growing fur, whiskers, talons, and teeth; even his voice changed. He ended up running off into the mountains. No trace of him was ever found.[88]

The female monkey seems to have been signaling indexically that she was carrying a baby. In these and many similar anecdotes it's not just that the transgressor is punished for poaching temple resources. It's that those "resources" are themselves living beings—selves with aims—as are their overlords, who appear face to face and speak directly to the perpetrators thanks to the affordance of dreams.

The Other's Point of View

It was human beings, naturally, who told, wrote, compiled, and preserved these narratives. The stories are told from human points of view. But do they convey any sense of what the world looks like to the many kinds of extra-human selves who appeared to humans in dreams? If the Others are selves and subjects with aims, is there any way in which these stories afford us glimpses of what it's like to be them? Or do they at least afford glimpses of what humans imagined it must be like to be them?

Consider this example from *Further Records of an Inquest into the Spirit Realm* (*Soushen houji* 搜神後記), attributed to Tao Qian 陶潛 (365–427):

> Gu Zhan of Wu commandery was once out hunting when, coming to a hill, he heard a human voice exclaiming, "Drat! I'm down this year." So he and his companions searched for the source of the sound. On top of the hill they found an opening leading into an ancient tomb, and inside the tomb there crouched an old fox. Spread before him was a ledger-book to which he was pointing, as if counting up entries. The hunters loosed their dogs, and the dogs killed the fox.
>
> When the men retrieved the fox and examined it, they saw that there were no teeth left in its mouth, and the fur on its head had all turned white. The register turned out to be a list of the names of women lovers the fox had intended to defile. Red checkmarks indicated those who had already been defiled. Over a hundred women's names were in the ledger, and Zhan's own daughter's name was among them.[89]

The story affords us a glimpse of the spirit-fox's *Umwelt*, if not that of an ordinary fox. The spirit-fox is a self with aims. (This is why I have difficulty using the non-personal pronoun here.) His aims are unmistakably indicated by his speech, behavior, and the checklist he keeps in his den. He dwells on the edge of the living human community, in an old tomb. He has gained the capacity for human speech (the hunters hear "a human voice saying . . ." 人語聲云 . . .) and for written record keeping (they see him counting entries in "a ledger-book" 一卷簿書). The fox's advanced age, the story implies (in accordance with other bits of fox lore current at the time), is due in part to his success in repeated sexual conquests of humans. In this case no dream is necessary for this cross-species interaction to occur, because in waking life the spirit-fox has already transformed far enough toward human traits that he can speak, write, and, it's implied, morph at will into beguiling human form to seduce victims.

I don't suggest that a story such as this fully captures how a spirit-fox was supposed to see the world, or that it was intended to. It is not told from the spirit-fox's point of view. Yet I would argue that this and the many similar stories presume a view of such creatures as particular kinds of selves with particular aims. It was those aims that brought human beings into frequent contact with spirit-foxes—and not just contact, but relationships. The spirit-fox has an orientation in life, an *Umwelt* that is intelligible to us, if also at once sinister, vaguely menacing, and intriguing. Male fears around women's sexuality (and other men's, too) certainly colored the world in which such stories circulated, but that is not all these stories allow us to glimpse.[90]

This encounter with a spirit-fox, yielding a glimpse of the creature operating in its life-world, is possible because hunters approached its lair and overheard its speech in the wild. But dreaming afforded a much more thoroughgoing portal through which humans might experience the world from the embodied perspective of other kinds of selves. Probably the earliest extant and surely the most famous story of this type is that of the butterfly dream in *Zhuangzi*, discussed in the epilogue. But unlike the *Zhuangzi* tale, the following anecdote from *Miscellaneous Morsels from South of You* (*Youyang zazu* 酉陽雜俎), compiled by Duan Chengshi 段成式 (803–63), was strongly claimed by Duan to have actually occurred.

A man named Han Que had long savored pickled minced fish. He sent a servant to bring him some fish from a dam at a local lake. He then fell asleep and "dreamed he himself was a fish, forgetting himself in delight in the lake" 夢身爲魚, 在潭有相忘之樂.[91] Soon he experienced being netted by fishermen, flung into a pail, taken to market, and sold to the very servant whom he had sent to buy fish. The servant lifted him by the gills and strung him through the throat. When the servant arrived home with him, Han Que recognized his own wife, children, and servants. Someone put him on a chopping block and cut him in two. The pain was as if he were being skinned alive. Only when his head fell did he awaken. "His consciousness was muddled for a long time" 神凝良久.[92] When family members questioned him, he recounted the dream to them. He then summoned the servant and quizzed him on the details of his trip to buy the fish. "What [the servant] recounted was what he had dreamed" 具述所夢. Han Que responded by joining the sangha. To this entry Duan Chengshi adds a note that affords a glimpse of the interpersonal networks along which such anecdotes traveled before being set down in the written compilations where we now typically find them: "The home of my scribe, Chen Zhi, is in Yuezhou, close to the dam, and he himself witnessed this affair."[93]

This could be said to be an extreme case of the visitation paradigm: the dreamer, for the duration of the dream, is not visited by but *becomes* an extra-human self. (Note, however, that while a fish he still recognizes the servant from his human family. The transformation is not quite complete. There remains a human residue.) The experience leaves a deep trace in the waking world, spurring the dreamer to renounce his household life and take monastic vows. "Entertaining the viewpoints of other beings is dangerous business"[94] indeed.

Not One or Two but Many Worlds, with Passages

In *Xunzi* 荀子 (3rd century BCE)[95] we find a famous passage depicting a hierarchy of life, with human beings at the top:

> Water and fire have *qi* but are not alive 無生. Grasses and trees are alive but are without awareness 無知. Birds and beasts have awareness but are without a sense of rightness 無義. Human beings have *qi*, are alive, and

> have awareness, and moreover they have a sense of rightness. This is why they are valued over all else in the world.[96]

One wants to respond: *Valued by whom?* Slingerland, commenting summarily on this and similar passages, writes, "The picture that emerges from a consideration of pre-Qin Chinese texts is that consciousness and the ability to think and choose, centered in the *xin* [the mind or heart], is what makes a person a *person*, rather than an animal or inert object."[97] Observe, however, that by these lights, in stories in which animals and insects are shown possessing consciousness, memory, the ability to think and choose, and a sense of fairness or reciprocity, *animals and insects are persons, too*—just not human persons. The anecdotes may be read as both arguments for and reflections of a more expansive ecology of selves, and a more relational way of knowing within such an ecology, than the one envisioned in *Xunzi* and similar texts.

I would argue that if we adopted a broad view of the archive (in other words, if we expanded our engagement with it beyond the small circle of texts usually deemed "philosophical"), this more expansive ecology of selves, and the relational epistemology that was central to it, would be seen to be at least as prevalent and formative in China as the human-centered view reflected in the *Xunzi* passage and privileged in much discourse generated both within and about China. This is not the place to develop that big-picture argument. But I do wish to emphasize that this ecology and epistemology were not simply convenient narrative devices. They were not just literary forms imposed on an extra-textual world of life and thought to which they were alien. Rather, each of these many stories was produced out of lived experience. Each was circulated, retold, written, rewritten, compiled, and recompiled by countless individuals, each of whom had some *interest* in the account of events crystallized there. Each was a collaborative, collective product, telling us something about a way of viewing the world that was entertained as *possible*—as imaginable—by many persons. The claim is not, then, that any given anecdote accurately reports what happened, but that it preserves for us what some people thought had happened, thought it possible to have happened, and wished others to believe had happened. Each, in short, is an artefect of collective memory in the most literal sense; each is a product of narrative communities for whom the sorts of events depicted, and the worldviews in terms of which they made sense, were familiar.[98] It is because they were collectively produced and preserved that they testify to the sorts of things that were collectively thought possible. It's also for that reason that they were preserved in the archive: *they won sponsors.*

One way to see clearly what the visitation paradigm tells us about worldviews is to compare it to texts built around some other paradigms we have run across. In the exorcistic paradigm, for example, some Other appears to and interacts with the dreamer—in this respect, and in this respect only, resembling the visitation paradigm. But this Other remains an It, not a You, and, more to the point, it treats the dreamer as an It, as prey. The dream is an assault by a being that remains a stranger. It brings no useful information, and the Other certainly isn't visiting to offer help. The called-for response is for the dreamer to turn the tables by reasserting command and control, invoking higher-level beings to help drive off and contain the threat from without. In the prospective paradigm, the dreamer does not experience a face-to-face encounter with a recognizable other party, at least not one that's about what it appears on the surface to be about. Rather, the dreamer receives correlates that are understood as code. There is nothing personal about the dream. The dreamer is not a party to an emergent relationship so much as a tortoise carapace on which the cosmos is inscribing a signal. In the prospective paradigm, the dreamer sees elephant bones. In the visitation paradigm, the dreamer sees a living elephant—or an ant—and interacts with the elephant or the ant in ways constituting an unfolding relationship built around episodes of oneiric communication. In the prospective paradigm, the dream encrypts a statement at the meta level about something that may happen in the world; in the visitation paradigm, the dream is itself an event in the world, and the dreamer is visited by, or visits, another self, even if that self is initially a stranger of another kind.

This is why the language of visitation dreams is vivid language conveying the dream's emotional, and sometimes physical, impact on the dreamer. The dreamer undergoes a multisensory, sometimes revelatory, event. The narrative conveys not just a bit of content—what was shown in the dream, say—but also the dream's illocutionary force. And the dream is a medium for a relationship between two parties. It's not a divinatory indication but a party to the unfolding of reality. That the dreamer *sees and hears a speaker*, even if initially unknown, at once situates the recounted event not in the murky, abstract realm of correlates but in the comparatively straightforward realm of visitation.

In *Menschliches, Allzumenschliches* (1878), Friedrich Nietzsche penned a famous aphorism somewhat reminiscent of Tylor's thought experiment on the origins of "animism" (1871):

> Misunderstanding of the dream (*Mißverständnis des Traumes*). – The man of the ages of barbarous primordial culture (*der Mensch in den Zeitaltern roher uranfänglichen Kultur*) believed that in the dream he was getting to know a second real world (*eine zweite reale Welt*): here is the origin of all metaphysics (*der Ursprung aller Metaphysik*). Without the dream one would have had no occasion to divide the world into two (. . . *zu einer Scheidung der Welt gefunden*). The dissection into soul and body is also connected with the oldest idea of the dream, likewise the postulation of a life of the soul, thus the origin of all belief in spirits, and probably also of the belief in gods. "The dead live on, for they appear to the living in dreams": that was the conclusion one formerly drew, throughout many millennia.

Nietzsche, setting himself against his imagined primordial humanity, is sure that there is only one *Welt*. For many Chinese people, it was not that there were two worlds, the non-waking one a product of metaphysical deduction from dream experience—a faulty deduction, as for Nietzsche it turns out. Rather, there were many *Umwelten*, many worlds-as-experienced by extra-human persons who were, like us, selves with aims. But the many *Umwelten* were linked by portals allowing for the trans-formation of beings, for communication in speech, for giving gifts and teaching songs and requesting help and many other interactions. Perhaps the most important and ubiquitous of these portals was dreaming. In the common space of dreaming humans found themselves *connected in relationships* with a rich array of fellow sign-making, sign-interpreting selves. In this way dreaming was, among other things, a relational epistemology.

A FRAGMENTARY EPILOGUE

The Maps and the Butterfly

It is haunting to ponder the innumerable dreams that have been dreamed, but then forgotten, since the inception of the human species. In an important way, this book is about memory. Dreams that are forgotten can have no place in discourse. Only those that are remembered can be related, recorded, reported, discussed, interpreted, theorized about, and acted upon. What we have glimpsed is merely the tip of a gigantic iceberg that will always remain mostly submerged in the sea of time. It is an iceberg comprising not just humans' forgotten dreams but also the unspoken dreams of other species of living beings who join us in being dreamers.

We mustn't forget the non-dreamers—the people other than dreamers who figure in or outside the margins of the extant texts: those to whom dreams were told, and those who recorded and transmitted them. A cloud of witnesses, invisible brigades of anonymous text makers and shapers, they were at least as instrumental as the dreamers themselves in creating and preserving whatever has survived of the late classical and medieval Chinese archive of dreams.

One of the most famous passages in all of Chinese literature[1] is an enigmatic parable about a dream.

> Once Zhuang Zhou dreamt he was a butterfly, flitting and fluttering around, happy with himself and doing as he pleased, not knowing he was Zhou. Suddenly he woke and there he was, unmistakably Zhou. But he didn't know if he was Zhou who had dreamt he was a butterfly, or a butterfly dreaming he was Zhou. Between Zhou and the butterfly there is necessarily a distinction! This is what's known as the transformation of things.[2]

Naturally, this passage has been interpreted in many ways. I do not read it as "radical, philosophical skepticism," such that "Zhuangzi does not know whether he is a butterfly or a human being."[3] Instead I join many other interpreters in reading it as a story about "the transformation of things" 物化, with dreaming taking its place alongside other experiences that cause protagonists to question their previous certainties. In dreaming we (normally) don't know we are dreaming; it's only upon waking that we realize it. Just so, at any moment "we may 'wake up' to a higher insight which might invalidate whatever we think we know."[4] This is an instance of the transformation of things, acceptance of which is one of the central recommendations in *Zhuangzi*.[5] Another character, upon falling ill, demonstrates this acceptance when speaking to a friend who has come to console him:

> A child, obeying his father and mother, goes wherever he is told, east or west, north or south. And the Yin and Yang, how much more are they to a man than father or mother! Now that they have brought me to the verge of dying, if I should refuse to obey them, how perverse I would be! What fault is it of theirs? The Great Clod burdens me with form, labors me with life, eases me in old age, and rests me in death. So if I think well of my life, for the same reason I must think well of my death. When a skilled smith is casting metal, if the metal should leap up and say, "I insist on being made into a Moye!"[6] he would surely regard it as very inauspicious metal indeed. Now, having had the audacity to take on human form once, if I should say, "I don't want to be anything but a man! Nothing but a man!" the Fashioner of Transformations 造化者 would surely regard me as a most inauspicious sort of person. So now I think of heaven and earth as a great furnace, and the Fashioner of Transformations as a skilled smith. Where could he send me that would not be all right? I will go off to sleep peacefully, and then with a start I will wake up 成然寐，蘧然覺.[7]

Dreaming is a teacher, constantly reminding us that our perspective may shift as we ride along on the ceaseless process here playfully personified as the Fashioner of Transformations. In a dream, but only for the space of the dream, we may even cease to be ourselves and become a butterfly, embodier of metamorphosis. For *Zhuangzi* there is an order, a pattern, to the cosmos, but not one that we can ever definitively map. In fact, trying to map it is a sure way to lose sight of the whole. Better to "hide the world in the world" 藏天下於天下,[8] and accept the ceaseless changes of life with equanimity. The direction of transformation can never be predicted. Predicting it would require a locative worldview, but *Zhuangzi*'s is a thoroughly utopian view, urging that we *untie the bonds*. "The Fashioner of Things" 造物者, says Ziyu, another character who has fallen ill and is undergoing a series of unexpected transformations,

> "is making me all rolled up like this." Zisi said, "Do you detest it?"[9] Ziyu replied: "No! How could I detest it? . . . One obtains life at the proper time 得者時也; one loses it when it is fitting 失者順也. If you are content with the time and dwell in what is fitting 安時而處順, then anger and joy will not be able to enter you. This is what of old was called "untying the bonds" 縣解.[10]

Stepping back from the many details we have surveyed, we might ask: What essentially *were* the dreambooks, the methods and manuals of prognostication and diagnosis based on dreams, the anecdotes of dream visitation? Taken as one big heap, as if seen from a distance, what do they amount to? It is tempting to see them all as varied attempts to map the inherently mysterious phenomenon of dreaming, to enlist it in projects of order, to domesticate it. This is most easily visible in the dreambooks and diagnostic manuals, where the mapping took material form as tables or lists of signs laid out in uniform columns of words. Such texts are the high-water mark of the effort to domesticate dreams into grids of order.

In this locative rage for order I am reminded of a "document of the edict of the monthly ordinances for the four seasons in fifty articles" 詔書四時月令五十條, written in 5 CE with black ink in a carefully laid out grid of red lines on a white plaster wall in the postal station at Xuanyuan, an outpost near Dunhuang of the short-lived Xin dynasty. As Martin Kern notes, "it remains unclear . . . to whom exactly the edict might have spoken" its commands about what to do in each month of the year. Its function was "fundamentally rhetorical."[11] Placed at the border where imperial authority ended, it demarcated the ordered realm from neighboring cultures that lacked its agriculture, its cosmology and the mantic techniques based on it, its textual heritage, and its writing system.

But the peoples beyond the imperial realm were likely indifferent to these Ozymandian ordinances, just as dreams and dreaming cannot really be definitively mapped. Like that wall inscription at the Xuanyuan outpost, any grid posted at the border of waking life to try and order the outlying domain of dreams must ultimately fail. The butterfly escapes, fluttering above and across the map's earnest demarcations and out over the lone and level sands of formless desert. The transformations of things roll out as they will. This attempt to map the Chinese dreamscape cannot help but be similarly limited.

Notes

Preface

1. Robinson and Corbett, *Dreamer's Dictionary from A to Z*, is similar, and there are probably many other such books still on the market, in many languages. This is a cross-culturally-attested genre I discuss under the rubric *dreambook* in chapter 3.

Chapter 1

1. Gallagher and Greenblatt, "Introduction," 13.
2. Levine, *Forms*, 116.
3. See for example Barbara Tedlock, "Sharing and Interpreting Dreams in Amerindian Nations," 88, and Crapanzano, "Concluding Reflections," 175–76.
4. On the example of Augustine of Hippo, see Graf, "Dreams, Visions and Revelations," 227–28.
5. In a very cursory way, this is the approach taken, for example, in Han Shuai, *Meng yu mengzhan*, 15–34 (with medical texts added as an ism). A more detailed overview of dream culture, organized by historical period, may be found in Yang Jianmin, *Zhongguo gudai meng wenhua shi*.
6. As a case in point, note the tension that runs through Lin Fu-shih's "Religious Taoism and Dreams." On the one hand, Lin evidently feels pressed to identify *the single, "unique"* Daoist "attitude" or "belief" regarding dreaming, as if there should be only one. On the other hand, his favored candidate for this honor (which is to say, the belief that one should *not* dream at all, on which see Diény, "Le saint ne rêve pas") is belied by the variety of textual evidence he shows to be available even in a single large and supposedly representative compendium (*Yunji qiqian*, completed in 1019). He then feels compelled to reconcile the "unique belief" he has identified with the variety and complexity of the textual evidence he adduces. And so he dismisses the evidence as having resulted from Daoists' use of stories to "preach their beliefs" to outsiders, that is, lay people. So, dreaming is initially assumed to be a topic on which Daoists took a unitary stance, which was a matter of their "belief" about it; then the surprising variety of textual evidence on the subject is explained as resulting from the need for homiletics. I would argue that this approach is based on several mistaken assumptions and bedeviled by the implicit models (of "religions," of texts, and of people's relations to these) on which it's unconsciously based.
7. For more detailed discussions of these complex matters—discussions on which these few lines are based—see Campany, "On the Very Idea of Religions"; Campany, "Religious Repertoires and Contestation"; and Campany, "'Buddhism Enters China' in Early Medieval China."

8. I am loosely adapting the conception of cosmopolis from Pollock, *Language of the Gods in the World of Men* (esp. 10–19), and Sen, "Yijing and the Buddhist Cosmopolis of the Seventh Century." On the term Panhuaxia (analogous with "Panhellenic") see Beecroft, *Authorship and Cultural Identity in Early Greece and China*, 9.
9. Here and throughout, by "the archive" I simply mean the total body of texts that have come down to us from the period in question here, whether they have been transmitted or archeologically recovered.
10. Smith, *Drudgery Divine*, 117–18, emphasis added.
11. Dreamscape is an example of various "-scape" words that have proliferated in both academic and popular discourse in recent decades, perhaps thanks in part to Appadurai's "Disjuncture and Difference" and its delineation of five distinct "dimensions of global cultural flow." Appadurai explains, in terms relevant for our purposes: "I use terms with the common suffix scape to indicate first of all that these are not objectively given relations which look the same from every angle of vision, but rather that they are deeply perspectival constructs, inflected . . . by the historical, linguistic and political situatedness of different sorts of actors. . . . These landscapes . . . are the building blocks of what, extending Benedict Anderson, I would like to call 'imagined worlds. . . .' The suffix scape also allows us to point to the fluid, irregular shapes of these landscapes" (Appadurai, 296–97).
12. Niyazioglu, *Dreams and Lives in Ottoman Istanbul*.
13. Lam, *Spatiality of Emotion in Early Modern China*. Clearly for him, whatever "dreamscape" is, it names the earlier thing that got replaced by "theatricality," whatever that is. In one passage (25–26) he seems to mean by dreamscape the common ontological or epistemological ground on which mutual dreamers met during their dreams of each other, but this remains unclear, at least to me.
14. This is the sense of the term as used by Kempf and Hermann, "Dreamscapes: Transcending the Local in Initiation Rites," and by Evan Thompson, *Waking, Dreaming, Being*, 124. The word "selfscape" has been proposed for the central feature of one function of dreams, in which "some dreams reflect back to the dreamer how his or her current organization of self relates various parts of itself to its body, and to other people and the world" (Hollan, "Selfscape Dreams," 61). Compare Knudson, Adame, and Finocan, "Significant Dreams." This is a potentially useful notion but not one that I take up in this book.
15. Saussy, *Great Walls of Discourse*, 177.
16. In the sense first elaborated on in Austin, *How to Do Things with Words*.
17. Many more examples of the exorcistic, diagnostic, and spillover paradigms will be looked at in *Dreaming and Self-Cultivation* than are presented in these pages.
18. These five *paradigms* should not be confused with the *models* of what dreaming is presented in chapter 2. The models typically have only one feature each and concern only theories or metaphors for the nature of dreaming as a process or event.
19. "To dream is to imagine, not to have false perceptions. . . . When you imagine, you evoke something absent (something not directly stimulating you at that moment) and make it mentally present to your attention. . . . To form a mental image of a tiger is to imagine perceiving a tiger. The tiger appears from a certain angle or perspective, as it would if you were seeing it. To imagine that tigers can talk is to envision the world as being a certain way, namely, as containing talking tigers" (Evan Thompson, *Waking, Dreaming, Being*, 179–80). "So what exactly is a dream? A dream isn't a random false perception; it's a spontaneous mental simulation, a way of imagining ourselves a world" (Thompson, 184). "Perception . . . isn't online hallucination; it's sensorimotor engagement with the world. Dreaming isn't offline

hallucination; it's spontaneous imagination during sleep. We aren't dreaming machines but imaginative beings. We don't hallucinate at the world; we imaginatively perceive it" (Thompson, 188). Compare the somewhat similar proposals in Bulkeley, "Dreaming Is Imaginative Play in Sleep"; Bulkeley, *Big Dreams*, 136–40; Sosa, "Dreams and Philosophy"; Stephen, "Memory, Emotion, and the Imaginal Mind"; McGinn, *Mindsight*, 74–112; and Ichikawa, "Dreaming and Imagination." Convenient summaries of the competing theories of dreaming's function may be found in Windt, *Dreaming*; Bulkeley, "Dreaming Is Imaginative Play in Sleep," 1–2; Bulkeley, *Big Dreams*; Domhoff and Schneider, "Are Dreams Social Simulations?"; Barrett and McNamara, *New Science of Dreaming*; and Barrett, "An Evolutionary Theory of Dreams and Problem-Solving." I eschew providing an overview of recent science-based theories of what dreaming is or what it's for. Of the two concise, lay-targeted introductions to recent scientific inquiry into dreaming of which I'm aware, I have found Rock, *Mind at Night*, more useful than Robb, *Why We Dream*. See also Walker, *Why We Sleep*, 191–234.

20. Examples include but are certainly not limited to Ewing, "Dreams from a Saint"; Mittermaier, *Dreams That Matter*; Stephen, *A'aisa's Gifts*; Turner, *Experiencing Ritual*, 120–21, 219n11; Barbara Tedlock, "A New Anthropology of Dreaming"; and George, "Dreams, Reality, and the Desire and Intent of Dreamers." It is perhaps noteworthy that all six of these researchers are women.
21. A cogent discussion of this idea of the hermeneutic circle (and its implications) when it comes to studies of things Chinese may be found in Zhang Longxi, *Mighty Opposites*, 46–48.
22. Sahlins, *Apologies to Thucydides*, 4.
23. Sahlins, *Apologies to Thucydides*, 5, quoting Todorov, *Mikhail Bakhtin*, who was quoting Bakhtin.
24. Sahlins, *Apologies to Thucydides*, 5.
25. Older forms of dream divination continue to be practiced in some Chinese culture areas (see e.g., Laurence Thompson, "Dream Divination and Chinese Popular Religion"), while Western approaches have also been adopted (see Scharff, "Psychoanalysis in China").
26. Sahlins, *How "Natives" Think*, 151.
27. Lawrence Levine, *Unpredictable Past*, 280.
28. And between my initial writing of this sentence and its publication in the book you now hold, as if to plug this hole in my oneiric experience, I was indeed spoken to in words by a cat in a dream.
29. King and DeCicco, "Dream Relevance and the Continuity Hypothesis," 209.
30. Ullman, *Appreciating Dreams*, xxii. He dubs "our" dismissive attitude "dreamism."
31. Indeed, it has been rightly observed that contemporary North Americans and Europeans now have more studies available to them of the ideas about dreaming in many *other* societies and periods than in our own (see King and DeCicco, "Dream Relevance and the Continuity Hypothesis," 208). A groundbreaking but unfortunately unpublished study was Hall, "Beliefs about Dreams."
32. Morewedge and Norton, "When Dreaming Is Believing," 261.
33. Newman, "The Western Psychic as Diviner," 101.
34. Kunzendorf et al., "The Archaic Belief in Dream Visitations."
35. Mazandarani, Aguilar-Vafaie, and Domhoff, "Iranians' Beliefs about Dreams."
36. King and DeCicco, "Dream Relevance and the Continuity Hypothesis."
37. McNamara, Dietrich-Egensteiner, and Teed, "Mutual Dreaming."
38. See e.g., Schredl and Piel, "Interest in Dream Interpretation"; Schredl, "Frequency of Precognitive Dreams"; Schredl and Göritz, "Dream Recall Frequency"; Olsen,

Schredl, and Carlsson, "Sharing Dreams"; Vann and Alperstein, "Dream Sharing as Social Interaction"; Cohen and Zadra, "An Analysis of Laypeople's Beliefs." Still, we see great diversity. One study estimated that 8 percent of the German population have consulted self-help books about dream interpretation (Schredl, "Reading Books about Dream Interpretation"); another, based on the same survey sample, found that 54 percent of respondents see dreams as mere nonsense (Schredl, "Positive and Negative Attitudes towards Dreaming"). Some studies have broken attitudes toward dreaming into sets of distinct vectors (e.g., Beaulieu-Prévost, Simard, and Zadra, "Making Sense of Dream Experiences").

39. One scholar doing refreshingly non-survey-based, innovative work on intersections between dreaming and personal identity in the United States today is Jeanette Marie Mageo. See her *Dreaming Culture*; "Nightmares, Abjection, and American Not-Quite Identities"; "Subjectivity and Identity in Dreams"; and "Theorizing Dreaming and the Self."
40. For a good analysis, see Josephson-Storm, *Myth of Disenchantment*, 269–301.
41. A nice summation of the various elements of the Western-modern/Other-premodern dyadic complex as regards views of dreaming may be found in Schnepel, "In Sleep a King," 213–14.
42. Charles Taylor, "Western Secularity," 38–39, emphasis in original. Cf. Puett, "Social Order or Social Chaos," 109–13.
43. Bennett, *Enchantment of Modern Life*.
44. Latour, *We Have Never Been Modern*, 115.
45. Josephson-Storm, *Myth of Disenchantment*, 5.
46. Saussy, *Great Walls of Discourse*, 111. I adopt from him the term "own Other."
47. Saussy, *Great Walls of Discourse*, 185.
48. Since this isn't a book about my personal views of dreaming, I omit discussion of how my views have changed. Suffice it to say that I have become open to many more possible ways of seeing and responding to my own and others' dreams, practicing what John Keats called Negative Capability, "that is when man is capable of being in uncertainties, Mysteries, doubts, without any irritable reaching after fact and reason." Anthropologist Michele Stephen put it well: in contrast to the tendency "in both scientific and popular Western culture" to see mental phenomena such as dreams, visions, trances, and possession "as pathological, what . . . anthropological studies particularly underline is the very high value put upon such modes of thought in other cultures" (Stephen, *A'aisa's Gifts*, 107). "We should not be too ready to dismiss the possibility that dreams, divination, omens, and other fleeting intuitions may be subtle ways of bringing people in touch with valuable information and understandings not always available to public discursive formulation" (Stephen, 93). Cf. Bourguignon, "Dreams and Altered States of Consciousness."
49. Saussy, *Great Walls of Discourse*, 189. Compare: "The reader will encounter a great deal of 'we' and 'us' and see from the context that the implied speaker is someone coming to China from the outside. I do this for two reasons, and the reasons need to be explained. . . . One is to be honest: this book was written by a particular person at a particular time, and there is no point hiding that. The other is to adopt the role and play it to its point of inconsistency, to turn it inside out—for this, one has to start by getting inside it. If my provisional adoptions of the 'we/they' epistemological barrier succeed in making it unpersuasive, that will be a good thing. . . . There is not much help here for anyone who wants to know what makes the West different from China, or vice versa, but there is some encouragement for the person who is ready to start unlearning such distinctions" (Saussy, 12–13).

50. Pinney, "Things Happen," 257, quoting Latour, *We Have Never Been Modern*, 52. Compare the similar argument in Pinney, "Visual Culture," 82–83. I am reminded of Marshall Sahlins' critique of models in which "an understanding of the phenomenon is gained at the cost of everything that we know about it. We have to suspend our comprehension of what it is. But a theory ought to be judged as much by the ignorance it demands as by the knowledge it purports to afford" (*Use and Abuse of Biology*, 15–16).
51. Pinney, "Things Happen," 259.
52. Compare this comment by historian Carlo Ginzburg: "The historian reads into [images] *what he has already learned* by other means, or what he believes he knows, and wants to 'demonstrate'" (*Clues, Myths and the Historical Method*, 32, emphasis in original).
53. Pinney, "Things Happen," 261, emphasis added.
54. Pinney, 265.
55. Pinney here obliquely refers to the idea of *Volksgeist* as developed by Johann Gottfried Herder (1744–1803) and others. For provocative treatments see Lincoln, *Theorizing Myth*, 47–75; de Zengotita, "Speakers of Being"; and Bunzl, "Franz Boas and the Humboldtian Tradition."
56. Pinney, "Things Happen," 268–69.
57. I draw on Thomas Docherty's proposal for an art or literary criticism that respects the otherness of its objects. "I contend that it is necessary to adopt an ascetic stance or attitude towards a substantial *alterity* in the aesthetic which . . . is the founding condition of the very possibility of criticism itself. This is to make a claim not for the *autonomy* of art, but for its *heteronomy* vis-à-vis the Subject. . . . The dominant mode of criticism in our times is but a cover for a psychopolitical anxiety which has been addressed and countered by the production of a philosophy of *identity*: the main task of such criticism is to console the Subject . . . in the face of her or his anxiety that the world and its aesthetic practices may be evading our conscious control or apprehension. This book prefers to accept the threatening possibility that the world may not be 'there' *for* a Subject of consciousness, with the consequence that a new, pessimistic, and stoical attitude may be required in the critical engagement with an art whose condition is that it is of a fundamentally *different* order of being from that which is already known to and by consciousness" (Docherty, *Alterities*, vii). As related to waking life, that is, dreams can be regarded as *sputniks* in the sense discussed by Saussy, *Translation as Citation*, 9–10. This model of what dreams are vis-à-vis waking life also owes a debt to Nietzsche's statement on the "misunderstanding of dreams" ("Mißverständnis des Traumes") and others' reflections on it, including those of Müller, "Reguläre Anomalien im Schnittbereich zweier Welten," and Assmann, "Engendering Dreams," 288–91. I've found less useful the ruminations in Riches, "Dreaming as Social Process."
58. Lucretius, *On the Nature of Things*, 112–19, and Lucretius, *The Nature of Things*, 42–46. Vis-à-vis waking experience, dreams, that is, are "special" in the sense developed in Taves, *Religious Experience Reconsidered*, and borrowed in Campany, "'Religious' as a Category."
59. Groark, "Discourses of the Soul," 3, one of the subtlest and most sophisticated analyses I have seen for any culture of the special linguistic aspects of dream narration.
60. See for example Barbara Tedlock, "Sharing and Interpreting Dreams in Amerindian Nations," 92–94; Kracke, "Dream," 160; and Crapanzano, "Concluding Reflections," 184–85.
61. Mageo, "Theorizing Dreaming and the Self," 10.

62. Hollan, "Cultural and Intersubjective Context of Dream Remembrance and Reporting," 169.
63. Stewart, "Fields in Dreams," 878. I do not intend here to suggest that the contents of dreams are *completely* Other, just that they often sit at an oblique angle to the assumptions, rhythms, and patterns of waking life. A society's myths, for example, have often been found to turn up and be reflected upon in people's dreams (see Kracke, "Myths in Dreams, Thought in Images"). Dreams of course often engage elements of the dreamer's culture, albeit in non-predictable ways (see Burke, "L'histoire sociale des rêves," 339).
64. Kracke, "Afterword," 212.
65. "Dreams are dreamed and told in different worlds, whence dream-reports are infected with the hermeneutic difficulties analogous to those that anthropological accounts have with alien cultures" (Brann, *World of the Imagination*, 342).
66. Hacking, *Historical Ontology*, 236.
67. Yu, "Typical Dreams Experienced by Chinese People," and Yu, "We Dream Typical Dreams Every Single Night."
68. By these Linden means the long, narratively complex sort of dream typical of REM sleep shortly before waking, as opposed to (1) brief, sensorily rich but non-narrative dreams typical in the period just after sleep onset and (2) dreams typical of deeper, non-REM sleep, which may be heavily laden emotionally but are nonetheless non-narrative. See Linden, *Accidental Mind*, 209–11. Narrative dreams are the ones we're more likely to remember and discuss, "partly because they make for good stories, but also because of the structure of the sleep cycle: you are most likely to awaken, and therefore remember your dream, toward the end of the night's sleep when REM predominates" (Linden, 211).
69. Linden, *Accidental Mind*, 220.
70. See Stewart, *Dreaming and Historical Consciousness*.
71. Brann, *World of the Imagination*, 343.
72. "It is not the dream as dreamed that can be interpreted, but rather the text of the dream account" (Ricoeur, *Freud and Philosophy*, 5). Cf. Obeyesekere, *Work of Culture*, 55.
73. Tylor, *Religion in Primitive Culture*, 12–13.
74. Tylor, 13.
75. Stocking, *Delimiting Anthropology*, 116–46; Stocking, *Victorian Anthropology*, 191; and Bird-David, "'Animism' Revisited," 69–70.
76. Tylor, *Origins of Culture*, 155. On "survivals" as a hermeneutic trope employed by intellectuals to make sense of "popular" customs they claim not to understand, see Campany, "'Survival' as an Interpretive Strategy."
77. Stocking, *Delimiting Anthropology*, 140.
78. Tylor, *Religion in Primitive Culture*, 539.
79. Evans-Pritchard, *Theories of Primitive Religion*, 24, 43. "In the absence of any possible means of knowing how the idea of soul and spirit originated and how they might have developed, a logical construction of the scholar's mind is posited on primitive man, and put forward as the explanation of his beliefs. The theory has the quality of a just-so story like 'how the leopard got his spots'" (Evans-Pritchard, 25).
80. The phrases play key roles in the thought experiment at the heart of Rawls, *Theory of Justice*.
81. "Tylor's actual usage of the term 'culture' lacked a number of the features commonly associated with the modern anthropological concept: historicity, integration, behavioral determinism, relativity, and—most symptomatically—plurality. . . . Tylor's

culture was singular and hierarchical. . . . The modern anthropological usage was developed somewhat later, in the work of anthropologists with closer ties to the German tradition [of Franz Boas]" (Stocking, *Victorian Anthropology*, 302).

82. de Groot, *Religious System of China*.
83. Lohmann, "Introduction: Dream Travels and Anthropology," 2. Compare his assertion of "the general validity of Tylor's insight that dreaming and human belief in a supernatural realm are intimately connected" (Lohmann, "Supernatural Encounters," 207).
84. Yang Jianmin, *Zhongguo gudai meng wenhua shi*, 6–10, and Fu Zhenggu, *Zhongguo meng wenhua*, 193.
85. Sahlins, *How "Natives" Think*, 122, emphasis added. For a reflection on the debate between them, see Geertz, "Culture War."
86. Sahlins, 122, emphasis added.
87. Sahlins, 169. Compare: "Empirical?—yes, the pensée sauvage [Sahlins' ironic term for Hawaiians' way of thinking] is empirical. Does it involve universal human sensory capacities?—no doubt. But a sensory perception is not yet an empirical judgment, since the latter depends on criteria of objectivity which are never the only ones possible. One cannot simply posit another people's judgments of 'reality' *a priori, by means of common sense or common humanity*, without taking the trouble of an ethnographic investigation. Anthropology, too, will have to be empirical. There is no other way of knowing what other peoples are knowing" (Sahlins, 162–63, emphasis added).
88. Kracke, "Afterword," 215, emphasis added.
89. The quoted phrases are from Bird-David, "'Animism' Revisited," 78, discussing Guthrie, *Faces in the Clouds*.
90. Bird-David, "'Animism' Revisited," 68, 73.
91. Descola, *Beyond Nature and Culture*, 129.
92. Harvey, *Animism*, 9.
93. The following lines draw on Campany, "Two Religious Thinkers of the Early Eastern Jin," 179–81, and on Smith's retrospective essay "When the Chips are Down," in *Relating Religion*, 14–19.
94. Smith, *Map Is Not Territory*, 169–70. A particularly clear discussion of what a locative worldview meant in Han and early medieval China may be found in Redmond and Hon, *Teaching the "I Ching,"* 158–69.
95. Smith, *Map Is Not Territory*, 139.
96. Smith, 293.
97. For an excellent review of the history of the notion that religion is about bringing order to the human realm, and a contextualization of Smith's innovation in departing from it (including a critique of some of Smith's formulations), see Puett, "Social Order or Social Chaos."
98. Caroline Levine, *Forms*, 3.
99. Kohn, *How Forests Think*, 166.
100. Kohn, 161. Throughout this paragraph I both paraphrase and quote the discussion on pages 161–63.
101. Kohn, 162–63.
102. Bird-David, "'Animism' Revisited," 74; and see Gibson, "The Theory of Affordances."
103. Hoffmeyer, *Biosemiotics*, 171.
104. von Uexküll, *Foray into the Worlds of Animals and Humans*, 44–52. For a discussion of the concept's limits, see Kohn, "How Dogs Dream," 18n3.
105. Hoffmeyer, *Biosemiotics*, 26.

106. Kohn, *How Forests Think*, 73–74.
107. See Kracke, "Dreaming in Kagwahiv," and the critique in Price, "The Future of Dreams."
108. See Stephens, "Dreams of Aelius Aristides."
109. See Hughes, "Dreams of Alexander the Great."
110. See Hollan, "Personal Use of Dream Beliefs in the Toraja Highlands."
111. In fairness let me point out that in this book I do not address the more culturally nuanced uses of Freud in, e.g., Devereux, *Reality and Dream*; Devereux, *Ethnopsychoanalysis*; and Devereux, *Dreams in Greek Tragedy* (a fascinating work); or in Obeyesekere, *Medusa's Hair*, and Obeyesekere, *Work of Culture*—all of which are among the most sustained attempts to put Freud's theories and the discipline of anthropology into conversation with one another.
112. Stephens, "Dreams of Aelius Aristides," 77.
113. Stephens, 77. For a more sophisticated reading of Aristides, see Pearcy, "Theme, Dream, and Narrative."
114. See e.g., Harris, *Dreams and Experience in Classical Antiquity*, 91–122.
115. Here I agree with the similar choice made in Eggert, *Rede vom Traum*, despite other scholars' complaints about it (ter Haar review, 200), and I would defend the choice even more strongly for the earlier period with which my study deals. Still, it is not implausible to argue for a diachronic shift in attitudes toward dreaming based on limited and generically comparable sets of texts from two periods. An example of such an analysis done convincingly may be found in Jensen, "Dreaming Betwixt and Between." Dream accounts play a key role in arguing for the emergence, over little more than half a century, of a new notion of selfhood and of consciousness in Armstrong and Tennenhouse, "Interior Difference."
116. On this political aspect readers may fortunately consult Vance, "Divining Political Legitimacy in a Late Ming Dream Encyclopedia"; Wagner, "Imperial Dreams in China"; Fu Zhenggu, *Zhongguo meng wenhua*, 314–38; Soymié, "Les songes et leur interprétation"; Luo Xinhui, "Omens and Politics"; Fodde-Reguer, "Divining Bureaucracy"; and Shaughnessy, "Of Trees, a Son, and Kingship."
117. These are treated in *Dreaming and Self-Cultivation*.
118. See Richter, "Sleeping Time in Early Chinese Literature," and Richter, *Das Bild des Schlafes*.
119. See Montgomery, *Soul of an Octopus*, 37–39.

Chapter 2

1. For different surveys of this chapter's topic, ranging over much broader arrays of texts and longer timespans, see Fu Zhenggu, *Zhongguo meng wenhua*, 168–230, and Liu Wenying and Cao Tianyu, *Meng yu Zhongguo wenhua*, 233–314.
2. On the shifting positions on dreams found in the writings of Augustine of Hippo, see Graf, "Dreams, Visions and Revelations," 228. For an example of multiple models of dreams invoked by a speaker in a single conversation, see Stephen, *A'aisa's Gifts*, 162–63. Compare Crapanzano, *Hermes' Dilemma*, 244.
3. For elaboration of this point and discussion of its implications, see Campany, "On the Very Idea of Religions."
4. As S. R. F. Price explains, "Modern scientific theories of dreams, from the nineteenth-century pioneers to Freud and beyond, are primarily interested not in the consequences of dreams but in their genesis and causation," whereas for a Greek dream specialist such as Artemidorus, "interest lies in prediction, not introspection, and his account of the genesis of predictive dreams deliberately avoids deciding be-

tween inner and outer causes" ("The Future of Dreams," 18).

5. Tedlock, "Sharing and Interpreting Dreams in Amerindian Nations," 88, citing Rorty, *Contingency, Irony and Solidarity*, 14. Tedlock goes on to cite several other instances in which anthropologists have found multiple, inconsistent theories of dreaming even in the same small-scale community. The same point is made in Merrill, "Rarámuri Stereotype of Dreams."
6. "Serious translation problems are posed by indigenous terms indicating a segment of the self that becomes most aware in dreaming, alternately described as remaining inside or travelling outside the body of a dreamer" (Barbara Tedlock, "Dreaming and Dream Research," 26).
7. The model is by no means confined to ancient times: see for example Vance, "Exorcising Dreams and Nightmares in Late Ming China."
8. There were, and still are, many parallels in other cultures. For a few examples see Macrobius, *Commentary on the Dream of Scipio*, 92; Hadot, *Philosophy as a Way of Life*, 241; Graf, "Dreams, Visions and Revelations," 219–25; Spaeth, "'The Terror That Comes in the Night'"; and Hollan, "The Cultural and Intersubjective Context of Dream Remembrance and Reporting," 175–76.
9. On Shang-period graphs meaning "dream" or perhaps "nightmare," with examples of inscriptions, see Shima Kunio, *Inkyo bokuji sōrui*, 450, and Xu Zhongshu, *Jiaguwen zidian*, 836–37; for cursory overviews of Shang and subsequent graphic forms see also Luo Jianping, *Ye de yanjing*, 2–3, and Han Shuai, *Meng yu mengzhan*, 1–7. (On terms having to do with sleep see Richter, *Das Bild des Schlafes*, 17–37.) It seems significant that a graph meaning "illness" was written almost identically: both graphs include a human figure reclining on a bed; the one meaning "illness" has an additional couple of strokes. We might speculate that this implies that to dream was by default to experience a sort of malady or disturbance. Shirakawa Shizuka argues that the Shang graph actually depicts a spirit hovering over a sleeper on a bed (see Shirakawa, *Kōkotsu kimbungaku ronshū*, 449–76, and Harper, "Wang Yen-shou's Nightmare Poem," 255), but this theory does not seem to have gained wide acceptance among specialists in Shang-period writing, and I am not qualified to weigh its merit. In any event, such an etymology for words denoting "dream" is by no means unique to early China. For discussion of relevant Chinese etymologies see Liu Wenying, *Meng de mixin*, 157–59, and Liu Wenying and Cao Tianyu, *Meng yu Zhongguo wenhua*, 370ff. For an example from Mayan epigraphy see Groark, "Specters of Social Antagonism," 319.
10. On preclassical 隹 as a copula, see Pulleyblank, *Outline of Classical Chinese Grammar*, 22. On its explanatory, "due to" sense, often seen in inscriptions concerning dreams, see Takashima, "Negatives in the King Wu-ting Bone Inscriptions," 241–43, 394n34; Keightley, *Sources of Shang History*, 79–80; Keightley, *Ancestral Landscape*, 101–3; and Itō and Takashima, *Studies in Early Chinese Civilization*, 1:140–41, 1:310, 1:460–63. In classical and modern Chinese, as in many other languages (including English), the copula often has an explanatory function.
11. In some cases the ancestor mentioned in the charge would seem to have been too many generations removed from the dreamer to be recognized by appearance. Then again, in dreams anything is possible. Compare a passage in *Huainanzi* on the question, What if the dreamer has never seen his father? "The posthumous son does not yearn for his father, for there is no impression in his mind. He does not see his image as he dreams because he has never had his form in his eyes" 遺腹子不思其父, 無貌于心也; 不夢見像, 無形于目也 (*Huainanzi jishi*, 1200). Translation based on Brashier, *Ancestral Memory*, 204, and Major et al., *Huainanzi*, 682.

12. Itō and Takashima, *Studies in Early Chinese Civilization*, 2:143–44. For the apparent circumstances of this divination, as indicated on the reverse of the same plastron, see Itō and Takashima, 1:475. For another divination performed to see whether an exorcism should be done after a royal dream, see Itō and Takashima, 1:350. On inscriptions regarding spirits that cause (unpleasant) dreams, see Goldin, "Consciousness of the Dead," 75.
13. P2682 contains a medieval version of the demonological text *Baize jingguai tu* 白澤精怪圖, including illustrations of demons. The digital library of the Bibliothèque Nationale de France holds a digitized version; see https://gallica.bnf.fr/ark:/12148/btv1b83033424/f1.image.r=Pelliot%202682 [accessed March 3, 2020]. A thorough description of its contents is found in Kalinowski, ed., *Divination et société dans la Chine médiévale*, 455–58; see also Harper, "A Chinese Demonography of the Third Century B.C." One brief section deals with demon-induced dreams.
14. For the template's "so-and-so" (*mou* 某) the dreamer is to substitute his or her own name.
15. There is a pun here between the text's "broadcloth" (*fu* 幅) and "blessings" (*fu* 福) and "wealth" (*fu* 富). Quality textiles were, of course, themselves a form of wealth.
16. Translation is that of Harper, "Textual Form of Knowledge," 52; cf. Harper, "A Note on Nightmare Magic in Ancient and Medieval China," 72–73. Photographs, transcriptions, and annotations of the Shuihudi daybook passages may be consulted in *Shuihudi Qin mu zhujian*, plates 134–35 and pages 210, 247. See also the listings in Harper and Kalinowski, *Books of Fate and Popular Culture*, 449, 452. On this passage and others involving Qinqi and similar early dispellers of nightmares, see also Liu Zhao, *Chutu jianbo wenzi congkao*, 203–6, 213–16. On early exorcistic practices more generally see Harper, "Spellbinding"; Harper, "A Chinese Demonography of the Third Century B.C."; and Poo, "Ritual and Ritual Texts in Early China," 305–9.
17. Bo Qi 伯奇 is mentioned in the *Hou Han shu* treatise on ritual as the spirit who "eats dreams" (*Hou Han shu* 3128). His name was chanted as one of twelve demon names during the last-day-of-the-year Nuo exorcism. See Nishioka, "Akumu no zō," and Bodde, *Festivals in Classical China*, 81–117.
18. Harper, "Wang Yen-shou's Nightmare Poem," 242. I am indebted to this excellent translation and study. The Chinese text given here, as well as the line numbers, are provided by Harper; my translations occasionally differ in small ways.
19. Indeed, Harper has argued that the entire rhapsody (*fu* 賦) genre in Han times depends on "word magic" and the power of "language as enchantment" (Harper, "Wang Yen-shou's Nightmare Poem," 240), an argument that has tended to be ignored by historians of literature but deserves to be taken seriously. Rhetoric was sometimes seen in the ancient world as having magical power; see for example Barton, *Power and Knowledge*, 97.
20. On Dongfang Shuo, see Strickmann, "Saintly Fools and Taoist Masters"; Thomas Smith, "Ritual and the Shaping of Narrative"; Swartz, *Reading Philosophy, Writing Poetry*, 79–80; Campany, *To Live as Long as Heaven and Earth*, 341n191; and Campany, *Strange Writing*, 144–46, 318–21 (where the planet with which he was associated is misidentified).
21. Harper, "Wang Yen-shou's Nightmare Poem," 252n58.
22. Lines containing descriptive narrative are 4–9, 28, 35–37, and 43–49; three-syllable command lines are 10–27, 29–34, and 38–42. As Harper puts it, "the focus alternates between the dreamer's first person combat and general descriptions (employing a common narrative device in battle accounts)" (Harper, 253).

23. Compare: Coleridge's "*Kubla Khan* is a poem on the Romantic theme of lost inspiration that represents the loss occurring" (Perkins, "The Imaginative Vision of *Kubla Khan*," 44).
24. Harper, "Wang Yen-shou's Nightmare Poem," 276.
25. See Campany, *Dreaming and Self-Cultivation*.
26. Compare: "*The very act* [of dreaming] *involves risk to the dreamer*" (Stephen, *A'aisa's Gifts*, 124, emphasis in original).
27. *Han shu* 53.2428–29; BDQ, 349.
28. For examples see Campany, "Ghosts Matter," 27; Campany, *Strange Writing*, 377–84; and Campany, *A Garden of Marvels*, index s.v. "ghost."
29. *Shi* 石 as a term of measurement was originally a unit of weight but began in the Han to be sometimes used as a unit of capacity; see Wilkinson, *Chinese History*, 559–60.
30. *Jin shu* 88.2287–88. For a translation and discussion of the earlier part of Liu's story (breaking off before the dream episode), see Knapp, *Selfless Offspring*, 120–21.
31. This phrase, in precisely this wording, appears in the Sound Observer chapter of Dharmarakṣa's translation (285 CE) of the *Lotus Sutra* (*Zheng fahua jing*, 10:129c). For translations of Kumārajīva's version (early 5th century) of the same passage, see Hurvitz, *Scripture of the Lotus Blossom of the Fine Dharma*, 314–15, and Robert, *Le sûtra du Lotus*, 366–67.
32. My translation of this anecdote is based on FYZL 95.988b. The story is further discussed, and cognate versions listed, in Campany, *Signs from the Unseen Realm*, 132–33. I here omit the last line.
33. On these social and literary processes see Campany, "The Real Presence," and Campany, *Signs from the Unseen Realm*, 7–30.
34. In the classic study by Burlingame, "The Act of Truth (Saccakiriya)," an act of truth is "a formal declaration of fact, accompanied by command or resolution that the purpose of the agent shall be accomplished" (429). For other discussions and examples see Ch'en, "Filial Piety in Chinese Buddhism," 84–85; Mai, "Visualization Apocrypha," 76n35; Orsborn, "Chiasmus in the Early *Prajñāpāramitā*," 247; Ohnuma, "The Story of Rūpāvatī," 117–24; Campany, "Miracle Tales as Scripture Reception," 38; and especially Kimbrough, "Reading the Miraculous Powers of Japanese Poetry."
35. *Gaoseng zhuan* 353b17–20; translation modifying Link, "The Biography of Shih Tao-an," 34–35. The same anecdote was also picked up in *Ji shenzhou sanbao gantong lu* 52.426b8–c5 and FYZL 407a3–6. For more on Piṇḍola, see Campany, *Signs from the Unseen Realm*, 54–55, and Campany, "Abstinence Halls."
36. In the "Huailu" 懷盧 chapter of his *New Disquisitions* (*Xin yu* 新語). Chinese text and translation in Lu Jia, *Nouveaux discours*, 72; see also the translation and discussion in Goldin, "Xunzi and Early Han Philosophy," 148–52. On Lu Jia, see CL, 628–31, and BDQ, 415–16.
37. I discuss many such cases at length in *Dreaming and Self-Cultivation*.
38. On the date and early history of *Zuo zhuan* see ZT, xxxviii–lix. For the famous passage on multiple souls see ZT, 1426–27 (where the terms for the various types of souls are translated differently than here); Brashier, "Han Thanatology and the Division of 'Souls,'" 132, 148; Goldin, "The Consciousness of the Dead," 62–63; and Slingerland, *Mind and Body*, 74. On archeological evidence for the multiplicity of souls as early as the fifth century BCE, see Thote, "Shang and Zhou Funeral Practices." On the complexity, variability, and indeterminacy of late classical Chinese understandings of a person's postmortem components and their disposition in the tomb and the cosmos, see Brashier, "Han Thanatology"; Brashier, *Ancestral Memory*, 185–228; and Lo,

"From a Dual Soul to a Unitary Soul." Sterckx, "Searching for Spirit," points out that these terminologies spanned both ritual practice and texts of various genres and that we would do well to keep both sets of usages in mind.

39. In view of Klein, "Were There 'Inner Chapters' in the Warring States," this dating may be too early, in which case we would not, to my knowledge, have firmly datable textual evidence preceding the Western Han that dreaming is (caused by) spirit travel.
40. *Zhuangzi jijie*, 11; translation partially based on that of Graham, *Chuang-tzu*, 50.
41. Grand Purity 太清 in Daoist texts variously designates both the sage's state of pure responsiveness and a zone of the heavens (a zone from which scriptures and methods of practice emanated). See Campany, *To Live as Long as Heaven and Earth*, 33–36.
42. *Huainanzi jishi* 524–25, modifying the translation in Major et al., *Huainanzi*, 249. Although it doesn't involve dreaming, a roughly contemporary *Lüshi chunqiu* 呂氏春秋 passage talks about how the moving about of one's various souls causes perturbations in the self: If you live in Qin and the one you love lives in Qi, if that person dies, then the *qi* fixed in your mind will be ill at ease because your quintessence (that is, your *jing* 精) roams back and forth (Brashier, *Ancestral Memory*, 203).
43. I take it up in *Dreaming and Self-Cultivation*.
44. *Han shu* 100A.4214; translation modified from that in Knechtges, *Wen xuan*, 3:85. "True feelings" for 精誠 seems not to capture the underlying psychosomatic ontology; if we instead read 精成, then we would have the more neatly parallel line, "My essence took form and emerged during night sleep."
45. *Hongming ji* 52:55a: 予今據夢以驗形神不得共體. 當人寢時其形是無知之物. 而有見焉. 此神遊之所接也. Much has been written about these debates; see, for example, Balazs, "Der Philosoph Fan Dschen und sein Traktat gegen den Buddhismus"; Liebenthal, "The Immortality of the Soul in Chinese Thought"; Radich, "Ideas about 'Consciousness'"; Fu Zhenggu, *Zhongguo meng wenhua*, 77–85; de Rauw, "Beyond Buddhist Apology," 97–123; and Yoshikawa Tadao, *Liuchao jingshenshi yanjiu*, 396–400.
46. That is, they act as whistleblowers before the tribunals of the otherworld charged with overseeing the allotted lifespans of living persons, leading to the shortening of the practitioner's life. See Campany, "Living Off the Books," and Campany, "The *Sword Scripture*."
47. Bokenkamp, *Early Daoist Scriptures*, 322–26, translating *Huangtian Shangqing jinque dijun lingshu ciwen shangjing* 8b–11a. I have also consulted with profit Bokenkamp's "Image Work" and Zhan Shichuang, ed., *Meng yu dao*, 240–56, an overview of Daoist body gods as they relate to dreaming. A comparison with the theory of the dreaming self seen in book IX of Plato's *Republic* (also quoted in Cicero, *De divinatione*, 291) would pay dividends.
48. P3908, accessed March 3, 2020 at http://gallica.bnf.fr/ark:/12148/btv1b8300230n/f2.item.r=P%203908; Zheng Binglin, *Dunhuang xieben jiemeng shu*, 171, 179n5; and Liu Wenying and Cao Tianyu, *Meng yu Zhongguo wenhua*, 68–69.
49. Poirier's description of Australian aboriginal views of the self as it relates to dreaming applies here: it is a "notion of the person as separable . . . , as permeable to and consubstantial with non-human agents and essences, and composed of multiple relationships (that some might call 'identities'). . . . These relationships . . . are intrinsic to the bodily self. . . . In other words, they are constitutive of one's personhood. . . . The local notion of the person is . . . 'dividual.'" This "dividuality" of the person "makes for higher receptivity and communication in dreams" ("This Is Good Coun-

try," 114, 121). Of course, theories of the self as multiplex have also been developed in the modern West. See, for example, Taves, "Fragmentation of Consciousness," and Cataldo, "Multiple Selves, Multiple Gods."

50. Compare: "If the dream-self does not leave the body (i.e., if the person does not dream), then all the potential dangers of the other realm are avoided. In a healthy, normal state, the dream-self is not separated from the bodily self, even during sleep. Something must intervene to drive it out. In this sense, dreaming is an abnormal and vulnerable state" (Stephen, *A'aisa's Gifts*, 125).
51. For a review of literary passages touching on the relationship between sleep and death, see Richter, *Das Bild des Schlafes*, 196–209.
52. For example, Schmitt, "The Liminality and Centrality of Dreams in the Medieval West," 279–80; Stroumsa, "Dreams and Visions in Early Christian Discourse," 193; Gregor, "Far, Far Away My Shadow Wandered"; Firth, "The Meaning of Dreams in Tikopia"; Firth, "Tikopia Dreams"; Crapanzano, *Hermes' Dilemma*, 241, 244; Crapanzano, "Concluding Reflections," 180; Poirier, "This Is Good Country," 111; Groark, "Willful Souls," 105–7; Groark, "Toward a Cultural Phenomenology of Intersubjectivity," 285; Groark, "Social Opacity," 431–32; Stephen, *A'aisa's Gifts*, 116–18; Stephen, "Dreams of Change," 5–6; Hallowell, "Ojibwa Ontology, Behavior, and World View," 71–72; Tuzin, "The Breath of a Ghost," 563; Basso, "The Implications of a Progressive Theory of Dreaming," 88–89, 96–99; Herdt, "Selfhood and Discourse in Sambia Dream Sharing"; Lohmann, "Introduction: Dream Travels and Anthropology"; Barbara Tedlock, "Sharing and Interpreting Dreams in Amerindian Nations," 88–89; Lohmann, "Supernatural Encounters"; Kracke, "Afterword"; and in fact every essay in Lohmann, ed., *Dream Travelers*.
53. Dating based on the arguments presented in Graham, "The Date and Composition of *Lieh-tzu*." On *Liezi* regarding dreams see Fu Zhenggu, *Zhongguo meng wenhua*, 30–41.
54. *Liezi jishi* 102–3; translation partially based on that in Graham, *Book of Lieh-tzu*, 66–67.
55. A topic discussed at much greater length in *Dreaming and Self-Cultivation*.
56. On Han Zhong, see Campany, *To Live as Long as Heaven and Earth*, 243n410, and Campany, *Making Transcendents*, 132–34.
57. The same phrase, which I take as (part of) a title, appears in *Yunji qiqian* 82.10b1, where the context makes clear that this text consisted primarily of methods for expelling the three corpses from one's body. There, the same ensuing comments on "ambushing corpses" are quoted from the scripture. Note that in the TPYL 662.5a version of this passage, the word *se* 色 appears after *wu*, suggesting (if not simply a textual error) that the five sections (*pian*) each dealt in a different symbolic color.
58. On this deity and the system of lifespan adjudication alluded to here, see Campany, *To Live as Long as Heaven and Earth*, 47–60, and Campany, "Living Off the Books."
59. Campany, *To Live as Long as Heaven and Earth*, 245–46, based on texts in TPGJ 10/2, TPYL 662.5a, and other sources listed at Campany, 447–48. See also Campany, "Living Off the Books," 136–37, and *Baopuzi neipian jiaoshi* 125. For an early Christian example of a somewhat similar model of dreaming, see Stroumsa, "Dreams and Visions in Early Christian Discourse," 195.
60. In *Dreaming and Self-Cultivation* I take up this aspect of the Daoist discourse on corpse-caused dreams alongside Buddhist notions of the sort treated in Langenberg, *Birth in Buddhism*, 75–93, triangulating both with Julia Kristeva's notion of *abjection* as developed in her *Powers of Horror*.
61. I discuss these methods in *Dreaming and Self-Cultivation in China*.

62. For discussions of this text see Strickmann, "Dreamwork," 29–31; Brashier, "Han Thanatology," 142; and ECT, 196–215. For Chinese text and translation I have relied on Unschuld, *Huang Di Nei Jing Ling Shu*, 421–24, with modifications.
63. A modern commentator glosses this rather odd phrase as "all factors that excite the heart-mind and cause irritation, such as emotional excitation, hunger and satiation, as well as exhaustion" (Unschuld, *Huang Di Nei Jing Ling Shu*, 421n, slightly modified).
64. See Harper, "Dunhuang Iatromantic Manuscripts"; Harper, "Iatromancie"; and Harper, "Iatromancy, Diagnosis, and Prognosis in Early Chinese Medicine."
65. For a similar but more color-focused and five-phase-based scheme in a Buddhist framework, translated from Zhiyi's 智顗 (538–97) *Mohe zhiguan* 摩訶止觀, see Swanson, *Clear Serenity, Quiet Insight*, 1334. For a similar Indic Buddhist scheme, in the *Sutra of Golden Light* (*Jin guangming jing* 金光明經) as translated by Yijing 義淨 (635–713), see Salguero, "On Eliminating Disease," 37–38.
66. See *Zhubing yuanhou lun jiaozhu*, chapter 40; Furth, *A Flourishing Yin*, 90; and Chen Hsiu-fen, "Between Passion and Repression."
67. On Wang Chong's theories see Fu Zhenggu, *Zhongguo meng wenhua*, 41–56, and (cursorily) Zhan Shichuang, ed., *Meng yu dao*, 97–102. I borrow the translation of the title from Harper and Kalinowski, "Introduction," 9.
68. *Lunheng jiaoshi*, 22:931–33. For an excellent translation (with facing Chinese text) see Kalinowski, *Wang Chong, Balance des discours*, 271–74. Kalinowski does not translate the entirety of *Lun heng*, however.
69. Here Wang discusses two literary precedents of people who concentrated so much that they constantly saw a certain sort of thing, even when it wasn't there. One of these is Butcher Ding from the *Zhuangzi* inner chapters (*Zhuangzi jijie*, 28–30; Graham, *Chuang-tzu*, 63–64)—but Wang drastically or creatively misreads the story. In the *Zhuangzi* passage it's not that the butcher mentally projects ox bodies that aren't there but precisely the opposite: he concentrates so intently on the carcass before him that everything else falls away. His blade follows the natural patterns and seams 理 of the carcass.
70. *Lunheng jiaoshi*, 22:918–19.
71. *Lunheng jiaoshi*, 20:881–82. Consulting but departing from the translations in Ong, *Interpretation of Dreams*, 67–68; Forke, *Lun-hêng*, 1:191–201; and Zuffery, *Discussions critiques*, 155.
72. In his discourse on divination Wang allows that the simulacra (*xiang* 象) may be quite correct—that they may accurately "point at" 指 something—yet fail to be interpreted correctly due to the limitations of human skill. See the passage in *Lunheng jiaoshi* 24:1007, translated in Kalinowski, *Wang Chong, Balance des discours*, 193, and discussed in Raphals, *Divination and Prediction*, 187.
73. In the *Ji yao* discussion he grants that the category of "direct dreams" 直夢 is not an empty one but insists that no real encounter takes place in such dreams—it is only a matter of simulacra produced internally. He gives the example of someone dreaming of an acquaintance and then really encountering that person the next day. Presumably such dreams are "direct" in the sense that they are not coded, but *not* in the sense that they involve any real encounters with other beings. And on this point he departs from a large body of narratives that saw dreams precisely as *real* encounters, examples of which I treat in chapter 5.
74. See, for example, Kessels, "Ancient Systems of Dream-Classification"; Kilborne, "On Classifying Dreams"; Macrobius, *Commentary on the Dream of Scipio*, 87–92; Dodds, *Greeks and the Irrational*, 106–10; Neil, "Studying Dream Interpretation

from Early Christianity to the Rise of Islam"; Schmitt, "The Liminality and Centrality of Dreams in the Medieval West," 277–78; Cancik, "*Idolum* and *Imago*"; Cappozzo, *Dizionario dei sogni nel medioevo*; Walde, "Dream Interpretation in a Prosperous Age"; Price, "The Future of Dreams," 9–31; Harrisson, *Dreams and Dreaming in the Roman Empire*, 60–68, 189; Chandezon, Dasen, and Wilgaux, "Dream Interpretation, Physiognomy, Body Divination"; Hasan-Rokem, "Communication with the Dead in Jewish Dream Culture"; Kruger, *Dreaming in the Middle Ages*, 17–34; Harris, *Dreams and Experience in Classical Antiquity*, 229–78; Hollan, "Cultural and Intersubjective Context of Dream Remembrance and Reporting," 175–78; Reynolds, "Dreams and the Constitution of Self among the Zezuru," 22; Lamoreaux, *Early Muslim Tradition of Dream Interpretation*; Selove and Wanberg, "Authorizing the Authorless"; Szpakowska, "Dream Interpretation in the Ramesside Age"; Lorenz, *Brute Within*, 148–73 (for a satisfyingly exacting reading of Aristotle's various passages on *phantasia*); Guinan, "A Severed Head Laughed" (not on dreams specifically but excellent on the locative nature as well as the paradoxes inherent in lists, tables, and compendia of omens in ancient societies); O'Flaherty, *Dreams, Illusion and Other Realities*, 14–26; Harris-McCoy, *Artemidorus' "Oneirocritica,"* where we see this mid-second to early-third century author-practitioner not only assigning stable meanings to a vast number of dream contents but also, in many cases, giving rationales for the correlations. In later periods Chinese authors made increasingly ambitious attempts to taxonomize and catalogue dreams, dream theory, and dream lore. See Lackner, *Der chinesische Traumwald*, a sophisticated study of *Menglin xuanjie* 夢林玄解 (1636); Strassberg, *Wandering Spirits*, a study and translation of *Mengzhan yizhi* 夢占逸旨 (1562); Drettas, "Le rêve mis en ordre," an excellent study of both of these works along with *Mengzhan leikao* 夢占類考 (1585); Vance, "Textualizing Dreams in a Late Ming Dream Encyclopedia," a study of *Menglin xuanjie*; and Struve, *Dreaming Mind and the End of the Ming World* and "Dreaming and Self-Search during the Ming Collapse," both of which skillfully read dream records against their sociopolitical settings. Eggert, *Rede vom Traum*, similarly to Struve ranges across a broad range of texts in the late imperial period and focuses on literati. Wolfram Eberhard undertook a broadly sociological analysis of the dream content in very late Chinese literary works, mostly of the nineteenth and early twentieth centuries ("Chinesische Träume als soziologisches Quellenmaterial"). For an overview of various Chinese categorizations of dreams through the centuries, see Liu Mau-tsai, "Die Traumdeutung im alten China," 41–44.

75. See for example Hollan, "Cultural and Intersubjective Context of Dream Remembrance and Reporting," 175–76; Gregor, "Far, Far Away My Shadow Wandered," 713–16; Stewart and Strathern, "Dreaming and Ghosts among the Hagen and Duna," 54–55; and Reynolds, "Dreams and the Constitution of Self among the Zezuru," 22. Compare the nuanced sevenfold typology of visionary experiences based in Ndembu (and other local) understandings, and in the anthropologist's own, in Turner, *Experiencing Ritual*, 170–74.
76. The date of its composition has long been contested. Here it suffices to note that it was likely compiled before the Han dynasty, but perhaps only shortly before; recent theories favor the Qin (221–206 BCE) as the likely period. See ECT, 25–29, and Schaberg, "*Zhouli* as Constitutional Text," a provocative study of this work in its historical context.
77. Zheng Xuan 鄭玄 (127–200) glosses this category thus: "When one is not touched or moved by anything but, at rest, naturally dreams of something" 無所感動平安自夢. *Zhouli zhushu*, 380.
78. Literally "while awake." This is perhaps the least clear category; it's often rendered

as "daydreams," but this seems doubtful, at least if we take the understanding of Zheng Xuan into account. He glossed it thus: "While one is awake one [hears something] said, then dreams of it" 覺時道之而夢. Similarly, Zheng understood "yearning" dreams as reflecting recent waking experience: "When one dreams of what one has yearned for or thought on while awake" 覺時所思念之而夢. Of course, we should not assume that Zheng's take on what was meant by these categories reflects how they were intended by whoever set this passage down.

79. See Ong, *Interpretation of Dreams*, 132; SSHY, 104; Richard Smith, *Fortune-Tellers and Philosophers*, 247; Liu Guozhong, *Introduction to the Tsinghua Bamboo-Strip Manuscripts*, 184; Lackner, *Der chinesische Traumwald*, 36; Strassberg, *Wandering Spirits*, 12; Liu Mau-tsai, "Traumdeutung im alten China," 41–42; Brennan, "Dreams, Divination, and Statecraft," 75–77; Fukatsu, "Kodai chūgokujin no shisō to seikatsu," 952–53; Luo Jianping, *Ye de yanjing*, 5–10; Han Shuai, *Meng yu mengzhan*, 8–14; and Soymié, "Les songes et leur interprétation," 289–90.
80. See Nishioka, "Akumu no zō," and Harper, "Wang Yen-shou's Nightmare Poem," 268–69.
81. A few centuries later this same taxonomy would be parodied in the *Liezi* 列子 to make a very different rhetorical point, as discussed in *Dreaming and Self-Cultivation*.
82. On him see CL, 1166–70, and Pearson, *Wang Fu and the "Comments of a Recluse."*
83. Chinese text in *Qianfu lun jian jiaozheng*, 315–24. My renditions incorporate and are based on consideration of those in Richard Smith, *Fortune-Tellers and Philosophers*, 247; Raphals, *Divination and Prediction*, 187; Strickmann, "Dreamwork of Psycho-Sinologists," 27–28; and, primarily, Kinney, *Art of the Han Essay*, 119–21, whose excellent translations I adopt verbatim at several points. They do not incorporate those in Kamenarović, *Wang Fu: Propos d'un ermite*, 185–90, which are rather loose. For comments on this passage see Ong, *Interpretation of Dreams*, 132–40.
84. In its jumbled and incomplete state, the text first simply lists the ten categories, then runs quickly through them with brief elaborations, and finally takes up each one again, saying a bit more about it—except that in this final run-through, the first two categories (direct and indirect) have dropped out entirely, with most of the discussion of the third category also missing. Nor are the categories discussed in consistent sequence. So, for clarity, I synthesize what is said about each type.
85. See ZT, 1324–25.
86. Compare the lovely passage in Lucretius' exposition of Epicurean philosophy (ca. 55 BCE), book IV, lines 962ff., in which not only humans but also horses, dogs, and birds are said to be prone to dream of what occupied them during the day: "Whatever interest fascinates us, whatever thing we make / Our business, what occupies the mind when we're awake, / Whatever we're most focused on, it is that thing, it seems, / That we are likeliest to meet with also in our dreams" (Lucretius, *The Nature of Things*, 136–37). This is the so-called "continuity hypothesis" avant la lettre.
87. For the narrative see ZT, 417. For astute readings see Brennan, "Dreams, Divination, and Statecraft," 85–86, and Wai-yee Li, *Readability of the Past*, 267–68. See also Fukatsu, "Kodai chūgokujin no shisō to seikatsu," 944–45.
88. Here I am emending the text as suggested by several editors to restore the character 病 before 氣.
89. Foucault, *Order of Things*, xv. On its ubiquity, Zhang Longxi, *Mighty Opposites*, 19–54; Saussy, *Great Walls of Discourse*, 239n33; Slingerland, *Mind and Body*, 3, 25–26. Even Marshall Sahlins invokes this infamous passage, seemingly to suggest that it would be better to throw up our hands and admit the complete Otherness of another culture's categories than to assume a priori, "by means of common sense or com-

mon humanity," that other cultures' judgments and categories must be the same as our own (*How "Natives" Think*, 163).

90. Compare: "Philosophers of all epochs tried to explain the source and significance of dreaming. Aristotle, the Stoics, the Epicureans—all came up with totally different explanations: dreams had their origin in exterior reality, or were caused by divine influence, or by the dreamer's psyche, or the functions of his or her body. *Each of these explanations had an impact on the interpretability of dreams*" (Walde, "Dream Interpretation in a Prosperous Age," 122, emphasis added).
91. See Campany, *Strange Writing*, 252.
92. We find the Christian bishop Synesius in the early fifth century, for example, exhorting his followers: "Let all of us devote ourselves to the interpretation of dreams, men and women, young and old, rich and poor, private citizens and magistrates, inhabitants of the town and of the country, artisans and orators. No one is privileged, either by sex, age, fortune or profession. Sleep offers itself to all: it is an oracle always ready, and an infallible and silent counsellor" (Moreira, *Dreams, Visions, and Spiritual Authority in Merovingian Gaul*, 33). Moreira charts two sharply distinct traditions of access to the divine through dreams in Christian antiquity and the Middle Ages: one, exemplified in the Synesius passage, offered unrestricted access to all; the other, upheld for example by Augustine of Hippo, restricted access to those who merited favor. In China, several *Liezi* passages speak of dreaming as a social leveler. I deal with these in *Dreaming and Self-Cultivation*.
93. See Kinney, *Art of the Han Essay*, 123–24, and Kinney, "Predestination and Prognostication in the *Ch'ien-fu lun*," 31–33, 36. As Michael Loewe writes, "In his discussion of such subjects as fate and divination, [Wang Fu] is anxious to expose the weakness of evading responsibility or taking decisions owing to a belief that mantic methods form a substitute for moral scruple and judgment" (*Divination, Mythology and Monarchy in Han China*, 233).
94. This commentary has been translated in Bapat and Hirakawa, *Shan-Chien-P'i-P'o-Sha*; the passage on dreams, in chapter 12, is translated at 356–58. The same passage is mentioned in Strickmann, "Dreamwork," 38, and Strickmann, *Mantras et mandarins*, 294. Pinte, "On the Origin of Taishō 1462," concludes, based on an analysis only of the Chinese title (and references to it in other extant texts), that the standard equivalence drawn between this Chinese translation and the extant Pali *Samantapāsādikā* is false, and that another text was likely the source for the translation. He suggests Kashmir as the geographic origin (of both the text and the monk who brought it to China), based on the fact that Shanjian 善見 (which means not "good looking" but "to examine closely") was a name of the capital city of Kashmir. He does not deal with the work's contents.
95. This passage is quoted in FYZL 32 (53:533b–c) near the top of that work's section on dreams.
96. Bapat and Hirakawa (*Shan-Chien-P'i-P'o-Sha*, 357) render this category as "a dream that is prognostic," and Strickmann ("Dreamwork," 38) calls it "prophetic." I have not consulted the Pali text, but both of these seem to reverse the sense of the Chinese: these are dreams caused by thoughts whose seeds (to use a common Buddhist metaphor for karma) were planted by merit-making activity in *previous* lives.
97. We might understand *shi* 實 here not as real (as opposed to unreal) but as (karmically) efficacious. If this understanding is correct, then this usage of 實 differs from that in the next work discussed.
98. The language is reminiscent of how Herodotus wrote of dreams and omens as ways in which the gods "showed" or "indicated" coming events or recommendations. See Harrison, *Divinity and History*, 122–23.

99. Compare Tzohar, *Yogācāra Buddhist Theory of Metaphor*, 57. We find in this Buddhist discourse an unexpected parallel to Aristotle's theory of dreaming in *De insomniis*, that in sleep the soul, its waking consciousness (dominated by sensory perception) weakened, opens up to more subtle sensations (both internal and external to the dreamer) that are transmuted into dream images susceptible to divination. See Kany-Turpin and Pellegrin, "Cicero and the Aristotelian Theory of Divination by Dreams." A useful, well-annotated bilingual compilation of Aristotelian passages may be found in Gallop, *Aristotle on Sleep and Dreams*. In the case of the vinaya text, one dreams of committing actions, but they're too feeble to create karmic residue. In Aristotle's discussion, it's the slipping away of consciousness, likened to the greater of two fires, that creates greater "prescience due to the perceptual fineness of the dreaming state" (Kany-Turpin and Pellegrin, 225), likened to the light of a lesser fire not noticed while the subject is awake. Compare also Freud's "acquittal" of dreamed crimes: see Freud, *Interpretation of Dreams*, 411, and O'Flaherty, *Dreams, Illusion and Other Realities*, 47.
100. Even arhats were said to be capable of having erotic dreams and seminal emissions in their sleep, brought on by deities in female form; see Lamotte, *History of Indian Buddhism*, 274. In the context of a debate about the ontological status of the external world, against the position that dreams have no real efficacy in the extra-mental world Vasubandhu pointed to nocturnal emissions as a counterexample. See Tzohar, "Imagine Being a *Preta*," 341. For examples from early Christian monasticisms see Brakke, "Problematization of Nocturnal Emissions." Texts such as these represent Buddhist communities' wrestling with the extent to which dreamers "own" their dreams and are therefore responsible for what happens in them or, by contrast, are distanced from the dream-self and its oneiric deeds. On another culture's very different ways of wrestling with the same issue, see the excellent analyses in Groark, "Willful Souls," and Groark, "Discourses of the Soul."
101. *Mohe seng qilü* 摩訶僧祇律. See Yifa, *Origins of Buddhist Monastic Codes in China*, 6–7. On the confusing plethora of vinayas introduced in China around this time, see Bodiford, "Introduction," 1–9.
102. *Mohe seng qilü*, 22:263b.
103. For this dating I rely on *Encyclopedia of Buddhism*, 238, 377. On the categories of dreams in this text see pp. 238–39.
104. *Apidamo dapipa shalun*, 27:193c–194a. See *Encyclopedia of Buddhism*, 238–39, from which I have borrowed some wording. This text (192a–194c) has much else to say about dreams.
105. Although no narrative should be pushed too hard to extract a "theory," especially of something as nebulous as dreams, this work in particular must be treated with sensitivity when elucidating the ideas expressed in its dialogues. The sort of "pure conversation" (*qingtan* 清談) that *Shishuo xinyu* was apparently written to document was a spectacle of repartee, and this *form* of discourse was as important to contemporaries as the content of any given exchange. See especially Wai-yee Li, "*Shishuo xinyu* and the Emergence of Aesthetic Self-Consciousness," 241–49. In this example, in other words, the back-and-forth of the interlocutors—and the twists and turns of the narrative itself—count as much as what Yue Guang says regarding dreams.
106. The other version, in *Jin shu* 43.1244, lacks Yue Guang's brief but important elaboration of what he means by "causes." There it immediately follows another anecdote in which a guest at the home of Yue Guang left and never returned after being served wine, seeing a snake in the cup, and feeling apprehensive. Yue Guang realized the snake was actually the reflection from a pair of horns mounted on the wall. He subsequently invited the guest back and showed him the actual cause of the "snake."

Both anecdotes show Yue Guang alleviating others' anxieties by patiently explaining to them the causes of illusory phenomena. For brief remarks on this story see Ong, *Interpretation of Dreams*, 142.

107. I have largely followed the translation in SSHY, 104. This work's title may be understood variously and thus presents challenges for the translator. I have adopted the translation suggested by Dien ("On the Name *Shishuo xinyu*," 8) and Sanders ("New Note on *Shishuo xinyu*").

108. Note, however, that the protagonist of *Soushen ji* 10/5 dreams of entering an ant hole and touring the capacious-seeming buildings within. Presumably no one in waking life has ever entered an ant hole, either.

109. For example, Andrea Rock writes, "The surprise element in dreams stems from the fact that the [neural] networks during dreaming have no sensory input from the outside world to constrain the possible combination of neural patterns that can be activated" (*Mind at Night*, 123). Or, as Oliver Sacks elegantly put it, "Thus waking consciousness is dreaming—but dreaming constrained by external reality" (*An Anthropologist on Mars*, 57n7). Or again: "Dream states are unstable and poor in detail precisely because dream states, unlike normal, non-dream perceptual states, *are* produced by neural activity alone. Actual perceptual consciousness is anchored by the fact that we interact with, refer to, and have access to the environment. The stability of normal experience is explained by the involvement of the world in our experience" (Noë, *Action in Perception*, 214). See also Damasio, *Feeling of What Happens*, 250, 358n13; Hobson, *Dreaming as Delirium*, 65–66, 70–71; Brann, *World of the Imagination*, 337; Windt and Metzinger, "Philosophy of Dreaming and Self-Consciousness," 195–96; and Schwartz, "A Historical Loop of One Hundred Years." Something like the same question is taken up, in different matrices of assumptions, by Aristotle in *De insomniis* 461b21 (see Kany-Turpin and Pellegrin, "Cicero and the Aristotelian Theory of Divination by Dreams," 225) and in Egyptian-Greek texts from the second and third centuries (see Copenhaver, *Hermetica*, 27).

110. Liu Jun 劉峻 (462–521), the early commentator on *Shishuo xinyu*, drew on two categories of dreams in the *Zhou Rites* to suggest that by "thoughts" Yue Guang meant dreams caused by yearning (*si meng* 思夢), and by "causes" he meant "regular dreams" (*zheng meng* 正夢); see SSHY, 104n1. I can make little sense of this suggestion.

111. See SSHY, 629.

112. The *Zuo zhuan* story alluded to involves not one but two dreams: first, the duke of Jin dreams of a ghost threatening him with revenge on behalf of his (the ghost's) wronged ancestors. Later, after falling ill, the duke has another dream, this one personifying the illness as two boys conversing about strategy. See ZT, 787; Kalinowski, "Diviners and Astrologers under the Eastern Zhou," 360–62; Kalinowski, "La divination sous les Zhou orientaux," 122–24; and Miranda Brown, *Art of Medicine in Early China*, 32.

113. The Northern Dipper 北斗 was one of the places in the cosmos where people's lifespans were regulated and from whose dreaded offices were issued summonses to souls, triggering death. See Campany, "Return-from-Death Narratives," 111–13.

114. *Soushen ji* 10/10; XSSJ 158. On *Soushen ji* and its compiler, see CL, 263–66; Campany, *Strange Writing*, 55–62; and Campany, "Two Religious Thinkers of the Early Eastern Jin." For a complete translation, see DeWoskin and Crump, *In Search of the Supernatural*; translations from *Soushen ji* in this book are, however, my own.

115. *Soushen ji* 10/7. TPYL 946.4a cites it from "Yu Bao's [Yu 于 > Gan 干] *Soushen ji*" in identical form.

116. *Sanguo zhi* 64.1446. Many other examples of such reports could easily be adduced.
117. *Soushen ji* 10/9.
118. Robinson, *Heraclitus: Fragments*, 54–55, 138; translation slightly modified.
119. See Kirk and Raven, *Presocratic Philosophers*, 188, 207–9, 212–13.
120. As Shulman and Stroumsa note, "The modern assumption that dreaming is the most private and personal of modes is not shared by many of the cultures represented here" ("Introduction," 4).
121. Here concurring with one of the main thrusts of Slingerland, *Mind and Body*.
122. See Domhoff, *Emergence of Dreaming*, 71–72, 96–98; Domhoff, *Scientific Study of Dreams*; Erdelyi, "Continuity Hypothesis"; Bulkeley, "Meaningful Continuities between Dreaming and Waking"; Jenkins, "When Is a Continuity Hypothesis Not a Continuity Hypothesis?"; King and DeCicco, "Dream Relevance and the Continuity Hypothesis"; Sabourin et al., "Dream Content in Pregnancy and Postpartum"; Schredl, "Theorizing about the Continuity between Waking and Dreaming"; Black et al.,"Who Dreams of the Deceased?", 59–60; Bulkeley, *Lucrecia the Dreamer*, 120–31; Bulkeley, *Big Dreams*, 112–40; and Windt, *Dreaming*, 279–83. For a discussion focusing not on the contents of dreams but on spectrum-like continuities between the mental functioning involved in dreaming and in focused waking, see Hartmann, "Nature and Functions of Dreaming," 181–85. A related topic in oneirology is the theory of "the day residue" as the major source of dream material; see States, *Seeing in the Dark*, 169–87.
123. Hume, *Thirteen Principal Upanishads*, 134.
124. Here I have in mind Foucault, *Hermeneutics of the Subject*; Hadot, *Philosophy as a Way of Life*; and, on the Chinese case, Denecke, *Dynamics of Masters Literature*, 1–31, 326–46.
125. Linden, *Accidental Mind*, 216.

Chapter 3

1. *Han shu* 30.1773.
2. See for example Hollan, "Personal Use of Dream Beliefs in the Toraja Highlands," 170–73.
3. Johnston, "Delphi and the Dead," 297.
4. Johnston, 299–300.
5. Johnston, 300.
6. Dreams are not mentioned in the *Dao de jing* 道德經. There, the sage ruler is pictured as able to know things about the world without leaving his chamber, seemingly by a kind of meditative clairvoyance (as in chapter 47, for example—see Henricks, *Lao-tzu Te-Tao Ching*, 116–17). Divinatory prognostication is elliptically mentioned (as 前識) only to be rejected (chapter 38). I take up *Zhuangzi*'s and *Liezi*'s rhetorical uses of dreams in much greater detail in *Dreaming and Self-Cultivation*.
7. *Liezi jishi*, 129; translation by Graham, *Book of Lieh-tzu*, 82–83.
8. Despeux, "Physiognomie," gives a brief overview of mentions of the art in early texts, then focuses on the handful of relevant Dunhuang manuscripts. See also Zhu Pingyi, *Han dai de xiangren shu*; Li Ling, *Zhongguo fangshu xukao*; Xiao Ai, *Zhongguo gudai xiangshu yanjiu yu pipan*; Richard J. Smith, *Fortune-Tellers and Philosophers*, 187–201; Raphals, *Divination and Prediction*, 95–97, 256–57, 269–70, 350–51; Kinney, "Predestination and Prognostication in the *Ch'ien-fu lun*," 35–36; Csikszentmihalyi, *Material Virtue*, 127–41; Di Giacinto, *"Chenwei" Riddle*, 185–92; Galvany, "Signs, Clues and Traces"; and Goldin, "Xunzi and Early Han Philosophy," 135–66. It is startling to see physiognomy mentioned only once in passing in Hung and

Tsiang, eds., *Body and Face in Chinese Visual Culture*. The extensive Buddhist discourse on the thirty-two marks of the Buddha's body further enriched indigenous thinking about somatic divination. See McGovern, "On the Origins of the 32 Marks of a Great Man," and Zysk, *Indian System of Human Marks*. This sort of art was a fixture across the ancient and medieval world, exemplified for example in the pseudo-Aristotelian *Physiognomonica* (ca. 300 BCE?), and widely disseminated and commented on throughout the medieval centuries (see, e.g., Devriese, "Inventory of Medieval Commentaries on pseudo-Aristotle's *Physiognomonica*," and Devriese, "Physiognomy in Context"), as well as in the Islamic tradition (see Hoyland, "Physiognomy in Islam," and Swain, ed., *Seeing the Face, Seeing the Soul*). See also the excellent discussion in Barton, *Power and Knowledge*, 95–131.

9. *Zhuangzi jijie* 72–75; translation adapted from Graham, *Chuang-tzu*, 96–98, and Watson, *Complete Works of Chuang Tzu*, 94–97.
10. This is something I discuss in *Dreaming and Self-Cultivation*.
11. *Fangguang banruo jing*, 8:1a19; translation modified from Zürcher, *Buddhist Conquest of China*, 142. On Mokṣala and the translation see Zürcher, 62–65; on the famous monk Dao'an's expositions of it, Zürcher, 191. For further examples of dreams used as similes for impermanence, emptiness, and delusion, see Conze, *Short Prajñāpāramitā Texts*, 27, 115, 138, 197; Gotelind Müller, "Zum Begriff des Traumes und seiner Funktion," 362–63; Thompson, *Waking, Dreaming, Being*, 324 (and cf. 174); and Tzohar, *Yogācāra Buddhist Theory of Metaphor*, 209–19. A classic passage on the standard "ten analogies" 十喻 may be found in *Da zhidu lun*, 25:101c–105c. For brief discussions and examples of the standard formula see Swanson, *Clear Serenity, Quiet Insight*, 195–96, 338, 357, 523, 790.
12. *Weimojie suoshuo jing*, 14:539b15; translation modified from McRae, *Vimalakīrti Sutra*, 93. Compare the similar passage at 541b25, translated in McRae, 104. These standard similes were not always used to make the same epistemological or ontological point. Most texts use them as images of the unreality or the impermanence of phenomena; Yogācāra texts use them to demonstrate how the mind creates all apparent objects and endows them with the feeling of being external to us when in fact they are not—experiences thus can occur without the presence of objects outside or other than the mind itself. See Hattori, "Dream Simile in Vijñānavāda Treatises"; Jiang, *Contexts and Dialogue*, 53, 56, 78, 81, 174n24; Huntington, *Emptiness of Emptiness*, 163, 239n73; Williams, *Mahāyāna Buddhism*, 307n26; Thompson, *Waking, Dreaming, Being*, 168, 174, 358–60.
13. "The three realms are [merely] a lodging in the long night 三界爲長夜之宅, wherein mental consciousness is the protagonist of the great dream [of existence] 心識爲大夢之主. All impressions of existence which we now perceive are seen in that dream 今之所見群有皆於夢中所見. Upon awakening, delusory consciousness is extinguished, and the three realms are realized to be empty 獲曉即倒惑識滅三界都空." *Zhongguan lun shu* 42:29b3–7; translation modified from Zürcher, *Buddhist Conquest of China*, 142, 368n11, and Radich, "A 'Prehistory' to Chinese Debates," 108. Radich notes that the opening line of this passage seems to have been a slogan circulating in Yu's day.
14. On oracle bone divinations of Shang kings' dreams, see Keightley, *Ancestral Landscape*, 101–2, 111–12. An example of a royal dream that spurs a search for the man seen in the dream as having been sent by Di 帝 to assist him occurs in the *Shang Documents* 商書 section (specifically 說命上) of the *Shu jing* 書經 (*Documents Classic*), the date of which is very uncertain but is probably of Warring States or earlier provenance (see ECT, 377–78). Many examples occur in *Zuo zhuan*, formed by the

end of the fourth century BCE; see Wai-yee Li, "Dreams of Interpretation," and Wai-yee Li, *Readability of the Past*, 172–248. An example of Warring States dream divination occurs in the bamboo-strip manuscript held at Qinghua University that contains a chapter, "Cheng wu" 程寤 or "The Awakening at Cheng," of the lost *Yi Zhou shu* 逸周書, telling of how King Wen received the Zhou mandate of heaven by prognosticating his wife's dream. See Liu Guozhong, *Introduction to the Bamboo-Strip Manuscripts*, 179–92; Luo Xinhui, "Omens and Politics"; Fodde-Reguer, "Divining Bureaucracy," 21–22; and especially Shaughnessy, "Of Trees, a Son, and Kingship." Further examples could easily be added.

15. In the *Ji yao* discussion Wang Chong grants that the category of "direct dreams" 直夢 is not an empty one but insists—against the cultural grain—that no actual encounter takes place in such dreams; it is simply a case of simulacra produced internally. His example is dreaming of an acquaintance and then encountering that person the next day. Although his account is not completely clear, it seems such dreams are "direct" in that they are *not coded* and do not require interpretation, but not in that they involve real encounters with other beings. See *Lunheng jiaoshi* 918; Forke, *Lun-hêng*, 228; and Ong, *Interpretation of Dreams in Ancient China*, 69–70.
16. Other cultures have made a similar distinction between these two basic types of dreams. See Stephen, *A'aisa's Gifts*, 119–22; Barbara Tedlock, ed., "Sharing and Interpreting Dreams in Amerindian Nations," 90; Linden, *Accidental Mind*, 207; Renberg, *Where Dreams May Come*, 5–6n7, 28n78.
17. This question comes up in the study of any dream culture, and scholars have pointed to a range of answers. There have been societies with no dream-interpretation specialists, in which people interpret their own dreams (see for example Holy, "Berti Dream Interpretation," 87), but in many societies there have been specialists or manuals to consult.
18. See Barbara Tedlock, ed., "Sharing and Interpreting Dreams in Amerindian Nations," 88, and Mageo, "Theorizing Dreaming and the Self," 20.
19. For examples of notably ritualized interpretation in a group setting, see Owczarski, "Ritual of Dream Interpretation," and Pandya, "Forest Smells and Spider Webs."
20. On gossip among humans as functionally analogous to grooming among other primates see Smail, *On Deep History and the Brain*, 175–79.
21. On key scenarios see Ortner, "Patterns of History," 60–63, and Campany, *Signs from the Unseen Realm*, 47–48. I make use of this notion again below.
22. See van Zoeren, *Poetry and Personality;* Saussy, *Problem of a Chinese Aesthetic*, 13–150; Puett, "Sages, Gods, and History"; Puett, "Manifesting Sagely Knowledge"; and Beecroft, *Authorship and Cultural Identity*. Henderson, *Scripture, Canon, and Commentary*, 66, observes that in early China dream interpretation was not as closely connected to scriptural exegesis as it was in contemporaneous Western societies, yet goes on to say that "in China the reading of omens and oracles . . . apparently contributed as much to the development of the styles and strategies used by later textual commentators as did dream interpretation in some Western cultures." In a subsequent essay he elaborates: "The two enterprises [divination and textual exegesis] are interrelated in several ways, first . . . in that divination may be understood as a form of exegesis. Second, exegesis of a number of classical texts, and even some of those texts themselves, may be plausibly traced back to divinatory origins. Third, exegesis of canonical texts may perform some of the same functions as does divination, such as elucidating obscurities, giving foreknowledge, and adjudicating legal cases. Finally, classical exegetes often make assumptions about the character of their canons similar to those made by diviners regarding the character of their respective divina-

tory set, such as that it is comprehensive enough to cover all of reality" ("Divination and Confucian Exegesis," 79). In a similar vein, Fodde-Reguer compares what little is known of Qin-period dream semiotics with some roughly contemporary medical diagnostic procedures ("Divining Bureaucracy," 35–57). For a brief examination of parallels between the hermeneutics of dreams and of biblical texts in rabbinic culture, see Niehoff, "A Dream Which Is Not Interpreted Is Like a Letter Which Is Not Read." On techniques of dream interpretation shaping midrashic exegesis, see Greenstein, "Medieval Bible Commentaries," 216–17. On the relation between modes of dream interpretation and Christian exegeses of the Old Testament, see Wansbrough, *Quranic Studies*, 246.

23. Anthropologist Michael F. Brown has suggested something similar: "If dreaming is a kind of thinking, then it might profitably be studied in terms of its place in the total knowledge system of a culture. . . . If dreams are seen as symbolically charged, to what extent does dream symbolism resemble other forms of symbolic production found within the dreamer's society?" (Brown, "Ropes of Sand," 156).
24. There is no shortage of scholarship on omen interpretation. See, for example, Forte, *Political Propaganda and Ideology*; Lu Zongli, *Power of the Words*; Lippiello, *Auspicious Omens and Miracles*; Goodman, *Ts'ao P'i Transcendent*; Wechsler, *Offerings of Jade and Silk*; Kern, "Religious Anxiety and Political Interest in Western Han Omen Interpretation"; Hihara, "Saii to shin'i"; Strickmann, *Chinese Poetry and Prophecy*; Espesset, "Epiphanies of Sovereignty"; Cai, "Hermeneutics of Omens"; and Campany, "Two Religious Thinkers of the Early Eastern Jin."
25. For another example, in one of the stranger passages in the Shangqing Daoist *Declarations of the Perfected* (*Zhen'gao* 眞誥, 7.7a–b), one of the divine Mao brothers explains that he had earlier appeared in a dream to Xu Lian 許聯 (328–404) in the form of Lian's younger brother Xu Hui 翽 (341–ca. 370), "borrowing [Xu Hui's] *xiang* to convey the dream" 假 [翽之] 象以通夢. The reason he gives for having done so is discussed in *Dreaming and Self-Cultivation*.
26. See Schafer, *Pacing the Void*, 5, 55, 292n8; Peterson, "Making Connections," 80–81; Sharf, *Coming to Terms with Chinese Buddhism*, 147–49; Kory, "Cracking to Divine," 24–30; and Schilling, *Spruch und Zahl*, 372–424. A comparison with Aristotle's key term *phantasia* would be useful, since it is a term Aristotle invokes (1) when discussing appearances of things that aren't there (as in hallucinations and dreams), (2) when explaining how we retain memories of things no longer present, and (3) when linking action to desire. And there, too, according to the best modern accounts I'm aware of, the English word "image" has been too facilely laid over the indigenous term. See Nussbaum, *Aristotle's "De Motu Animalium,"* 221–69, and Lorenz, *Brute Within*, 133–37, 148–73. As seen below, this term was even connected to imagining distant elephants, just as was the Chinese *xiang*. Also useful would be a comparison with the Latin *imago* in such contexts; see Scioli and Walde, "Introduction."
27. Schafer, *Pacing the Void*, 55.
28. Peterson, "Making Connections," 80–81; Rutt, *Book of Changes*, 132, 408; Cheng, *Histoire de la pensée chinoise*, 276 (Cheng also uses *figuration*). Obert, "Imagination or Response?," understands *xiang* as "a figurative totality related to intuition, complete in itself and pregnant with meaning" (120–21). He renders *xiang* into German as *Erscheinungsgestalt* or *sinnhafte Erscheinungsgestalt* (*Welt als Bild*, 157–58, 212–15).
29. Lewis, *Writing and Authority*, 242, although elsewhere (e.g., 271) he reverts to translating *xiang* as "image."
30. Consulting the Chinese text in Henricks, *Lao-tzu Te-Tao Ching*, 214–15, 228–29, 102–3, 256–57 respectively, and slightly modifying his translations. In the chapter 41 passage,

however, Mawangdui manuscript B has 夭 where most other versions have 大, and 刑 where most versions have 形. I do not follow those manuscript readings (nor does Hendricks, although he doesn't discuss this). For a comparison of versions of this passage see Hachiya, *Rōshi*, 200.

31. See ECT, 115–17, and CL, 313–17.
32. Modifying the translation in Lewis, *Writing and Authority in Early China*, 271. Compare Sterckx, *Animal and the Daemon*, 214. On the *Han Feizi* chapters that comment on the *Dao de jing* see Queen, "*Han Feizi* and the Old Master." Curiously, Ibn Rushd, commenting (ca. 1170) on mental imaging and memory in Aristotle's *Parva naturalia*, also uses elephants as an example. People gifted at mental concentration and *phantasia*-formation can produce accurate mental images of things they haven't seen just from hearing others' descriptions. "In this manner," he writes, "it is possible for a person to form the image of an elephant without his ever having perceived one." Averroes, *Epitome of "Parva Naturalia,"* 28; Carruthers, *Book of Memory*, 75.
33. The *Fanlun* 氾論 chapter of *Huainanzi* notes that when creatures undergo transformations, the sage, due to his ability to mirror and flow with things, "makes images for them" 化則爲之象 (*Huainanzi jishi*, 961). For the context see Major et al., *Huainanzi*, 510. Likewise Guo Pu's preface argues that the sage "traces transformations to their origins to encompass change, assigns images to creatures to match their anomalousness" 原化以極變, 象物以應怪 (*Shanhai jing jiaozhu*, 479). I was alerted to both passages by Sterckx, *Animal and the Daemon*, 214.
34. The copy of a manuscript version of the *Changes* recovered from the tomb at Mawangdui (168 BCE) already includes the *Xi ci*. See ECT, 221; Shaughnessy, *I Ching*, 20–22, 187–211; and Shaughnessy, *Unearthing the Changes*, 4, 6.
35. Wang Bi's theories have been extensively studied. Of particular relevance here is the discussion in Gu Ming Dong, *Chinese Theories of Reading and Writing*, 113–50.
36. *Zhouyi zhushu* 7.9b–10a; translation modifying Rutt, *Book of Changes*, 413; cf. Lynn, *Classic of Changes*, 56–57. Kong Yingda 孔穎達 (574–648) glosses the "mysteries" 賾 as "things hidden deeply and hard to perceive" 賾謂幽深難見.
37. *Zhouyi zhushu* 7.18a–b; translation based on Rutt, *Book of Changes*, 419, and Lynn, *Classic of Changes*, 67.
38. Kong Yingda, commenting on "The Master said, 'The sages established *xiang* to convey all meanings,'" writes: "Although speech does not fully convey meaning, establishing *xiang* enables it to be fully conveyed" 雖言不盡意, 立象可以盡之也 (*Zhouyi zhushu* 7.18b). Cf. Klein, "Constancy and the *Changes*," 215–16, and Richard J. Smith, *Fathoming the Cosmos*, 40.
39. Crapanzano, *Hermes' Dilemma*, 145–46. For a fascinating discussion of the ontology and epistemology involved in dream interpretation in the medieval Islamic tradition, see Sviri, "Dreaming Analyzed and Recorded."
40. There, too, it is a matter of words (*yan* 言) versus meaning or ideas (*yi* 意). See *Zhuangzi jijie*, 244; Graham, *Chuang-tzu*, 190.
41. Egan, "Nature and Higher Ideals," 288–89. See also Hon, "Hexagrams and Politics," 81; Chua, "Tracing the Dao"; and Gu Ming Dong, *Chinese Theories of Reading and Writing*, 113–50.
42. I have in mind here the comments in Kohn, *How Forests Think*, 172–73.
43. Jonathan Z. Smith, *Imagining Religion*, 44.
44. Jonathan Z. Smith, 47.
45. See Hasan-Rokem, "Communication with the Dead in Jewish Culture," 222, for a list of standard dream symbols and their meanings in rabbinic literature; Price, "The Future of Dreams," 17, on the tripartite typology developed by Herophilus, a

third-century BCE physician; Harrisson, *Dreams and Dreaming in the Roman Empire*, 189; Mageo, "Theorizing Dreaming and the Self," 18 (on "dream thesauruses"); Lamoreaux, *Early Muslim Tradition of Dream Interpretation*; and Oppenheim, "Interpretation of Dreams in the Ancient Near East." Artemidorus' *Oneirocritica* (mid-2nd to early-3rd century CE) was nothing less than an explicit, encyclopedic attempt to bring a comprehensive taxonomic order once and for all into the unruly realm of dreams and their interpretation. See Harris-McCoy, *Artemidorus' Oneirocritica*, 3, 19–25; Walde, "Dream Interpretation in a Prosperous Age," who notes that this is "the only extant [substantial] work of ancient dream interpretation" (124) and that it was one of the first books to be printed in Europe, after the Bible; Kessels, "Ancient Systems of Dream-Classification"; Näf, "Artemidor"; and Näf, *Traum und Traumdeutung im Altertum*. Macrobius (fl. late 4th–early 5th century CE), who in his commentary on Cicero's famous account of the dream of Scipio in book 6 of the *Republic* introduced a five-part classification, in some ways similar to that of Artemidorus but in other ways quite different, was another authority on dreams whose work would resonate through the European Middle Ages. See Macrobius, *Commentary on the Dream of Scipio*, 87–92; Cancik, "*Idolum* and *Imago*"; and Schmitt, "The Liminality and Centrality of Dreams in the Medieval West," 278–79. Useful treatments of Cicero's writings on divination in the context of his time include Beard, "Cicero and Divination"; Kany-Turpin and Pellegrin, "Cicero and the Aristotelian Theory of Divination by Dreams"; Schultz, "Argument and Anecdote in Cicero's *De divinatione*"; and Schultz, *Commentary on Cicero "De Divinatione I"*. Strickmann insightfully comments: "Les inventaires et les listes permettaient de *contrôler le chaos* de la vie onirique" (*Mantras et mandarins*, 305, emphasis added).

46. See for example Hollan, "Cultural and Intersubjective Context of Dream Remembrance and Reporting," 175–76; Hollan, "Personal Use of Dream Beliefs in the Toraja Highlands," 171; Gregor, "Far, Far Away My Shadow Wandered," 713–16; Stewart and Strathern, "Dreaming and Ghosts among the Hagen and Duna," 54–55; Reynolds, "Dreams and the Constitution of Self among the Zezuru," 22; Mannheim, "A Semiotic of Andean Dreams"; Crapanzano, *Hermes' Dilemma*, 243; Basso, "The Implications of a Progressive Theory of Dreaming," 103–4; and George-Joseph and Smith, "Dream World in Dominica." Often the typologies and classifications are only implicit, unavailable for total recall on any given occasion but nevertheless implied by repeated patterns of interpretation. Stephen, for example, on the same page can write about the Mekeo people that, on the one hand, "There exists no elaborate typology of dreams that people can reel off for the ethnographer," and on the other hand, "Many . . . dream symbols are widely known to everyone and it is easy initially to gain the impression that dream interpretation is in essence a matter of knowing an extensive repertoire of symbolic equivalents" (*A'aisa's Gifts*, 119).

47. See ECT, 483–86; CL, 1868–73; and Milburn, *Spring and Autumn Annals of Master Yan*, 3–67.

48. See *Fengsu tongyi*, 331–32, following the editor's suggested textual emendations. The term used for the manual is simply "book(s)" (*shu* 書). For a translation see Nylan, "Ying Shao's 'Feng Su T'ung Yi,'" 522–24. See also Strassberg, *Wandering Spirits*, 4. I return to this anecdote below. See Wang Zijin, *Changsha jiandu yanjiu*, 366, for discussion of several *Shi ji* passages mentioning dream interpretation manuals and specialists.

49. These are *Huangdi changliu zhanmeng* 黃帝長柳占夢 in eleven rolls and *Gande changliu zhanmeng* 甘德長柳占夢 in twenty rolls (*Han shu* 30.1772). Because these works are lost, we cannot be sure that they took the form of lists of dream signs and

their meanings, but they are grouped in the catalog alongside other works on divination that appear from their titles to have been manuals. Ban Gu based this treatise, which incorporates lists of titles held in the imperial library, on an earlier work by Liu Xin (46 BCE–23 CE). See ECT, 130. On the treatise's importance in the classification of divinatory and mantic arts, see Kalinowski, ed., "Introduction générale," 11–13; Kalinowski, "Divination and Astrology," 342–44; and Raphals, "Divination in the *Han shu* Bibliographic Treatise." On its larger ideological, political, and religious context, see Kalinowski, ed., "Technical Traditions in Ancient China," 225–28, and Fukatsu, "Kodai chūgokujin no shisō to seikatsu," 957. And on the gap between this heavily ideological list of works and the textual realities of the era see in particular Harper, "Warring States Natural Philosophy," 822–23, and Kern, "Early Chinese Divination and Its Rhetoric," 262–63. As Kern observes, "The [imperial] library was as much—and probably more—engaged in censoring as it was in curating" (263).

50. See *Sui shu* 29.1037–38. All these titles sound quite generic, although works attributed to such notable figures as Jing Fang 京房, Cui Yuan 崔元, and Zhou Xuan 周宣 are listed there as already lost by the Sui. It is possible that other works on divination listed in this catalog also dealt with dreams, though this is not explicitly indicated in any of the other titles. On the date of completion of the "treatises" (*zhi* 志) sections of the *Sui shu,* including the bibliographic catalog, see Twitchett, *Writing of Official History under the T'ang*, 22, and Wilkinson, *Chinese History*, 751. Drège and Drettas ("Oniromancie," 370) conclude from the dwindling number of such titles in subsequent catalogs that the genre may have declined in popularity during the Tang, but I do not share their confidence in this inference.

51. See Twitchett, *Writing of Official History under the T'ang*, 22n67, and Wilkinson, *Chinese History*, 730. I return to this passage below when discussing the diviner Suo Dan.

52. *Jin shu* 95.2494–95. In this case the diviner responds that he owns no such book but learned the art of dream interpretation orally from a teacher. What is telling is that the governor assumes he must have used a manual.

53. Liu Wenying, *Zhongguo gudai de mengshu*, gives a rather brief overview of premodern Chinese dreambooks and anthologizes passages from them; an even briefer sampling is given in Han Shuai, *Meng yu mengzhan*, 55–60.

54. *Qianfu lun jian jiaozheng*, 318–19; translations following Kinney, *Art of the Han Essay*, 122. If Wang Fu derived these equivalences from written lists, he may have synthesized the signs into these groups to compress the discussion. Similarly, in his *Ji yao* chapter Wang Chong rattles off in passing a few seemingly standard equivalences; see *Lunheng jiaoshi*, 916, and Drège and Drettas, "Oniromancie," 391.

55. See Zhu Hanmin and Chen Songchang, *Yuelu shuyuan cang Qin jian*, 1–2, and Fodde-Reguer, "Divining Bureaucracy," 42–43.

56. I consulted the reordering of strips carried out by Anna-Alexandra Fodde-Reguer, who was assisted by Miranda Brown. The text was consistently written on only one side of the strips, making the sequence of passages harder to reconstruct. Even if the ordering of slips remains uncertain, however, the text's general nature is quite clear, and the importance of the sequencing is lessened by the fact that in most cases one or two discrete listings of dream contents with their interpretations are given on each slip, with no overrun to a second slip.

57. This is the opening portion of the text on the slip numbered 1514. See the photograph, transcription, and annotations at Zhu Hanmin and Chen Songchang, *Yuelu shuyuan cang Qin jian*, 153, and the transcription and translation at Fodde-Reguer, "Divining Bureaucracy," 123, 125. Throughout this discussion, my translations have

benefited, but sometimes differ slightly, from those given in Fodde-Reguer, "Divining Bureaucracy," 125–27.

58. Perhaps the slip that immediately preceded slip 1514 in the text's original arrangement, as maintained by both Zhu Hanmin and Chen Songchang, *Yuelu shuyuan cang Qin jian*, 152–53, and Fodde-Reguer, "Divining Bureaucracy," 123, 125.
59. This line appears on slip 0102. See Zhu Hanmin and Chen Songchang, *Yuelu shuyuan cang Qin jian*, 152, and Fodde-Reguer, "Divining Bureaucracy," 123, 125. For an example of a Shang oracle bone inscription that notes the timing of a royal dream (though it does not venture an interpretation of its significance based on the timing), see Itō and Takashima, *Studies in Early Chinese Civilization*, 1:462.
60. Here following Fodde-Reguer, "Divining Bureaucracy," 123, in reading *guan* 官 rather than the *gong* 宮 transcribed by Zhu Hanmin and Chen Songchang, *Yuelu shuyuan cang Qin jian*, 153. The character appears in the topmost position of strip 1526, which is partly split away.
61. These lines of text run across slips 1514 and 1526. See Zhu Hanmin and Chen Songchang, *Yuelu shuyuan cang Qin jian*, 153, and Fodde-Reguer, "Divining Bureaucracy," 123, 125.
62. This is slip 0015. See Zhu Hanmin and Chen Songchang, *Yuelu shuyuan cang Qin jian*, 164, and Fodde-Reguer, "Divining Bureaucracy," 124, 127.
63. This is slip 0029, the top half of which is missing. I follow the transcription and glosses given in Zhu Hanmin and Chen Songchang, *Yuelu shuyuan cang Qin jian*, 158. Other strips on which different interpretations of the same dream content are given based on the dreamer's gender include 0049, 1513, and 1495.
64. On the daybook genre in this period, see Harper and Kalinowski, eds., *Books of Fate and Popular Culture*; Harkness, "Cosmology and the Quotidian"; Kern, "Early Chinese Divination and Its Rhetoric," 265–73.
65. The passage appears in the second (or 乙) daybook. Reproductions of these slips can be seen in *Shuihudi Qin mu zhujian*, plates 134–35 (slips 189–93), with transcriptions and annotations on p. 247. Compare Harper, "Textual Form of Knowledge," 53, and Harper and Kalinowski, *Books of Fate and Popular Culture*, 452. Contrary to what Raphals says about this passage ("the emphasis is shifted from magical techniques for stopping nightmares to predicting them by means of the sexagenary cycle" [*Divination and Prediction*, 187]), the cosmic correlates are provided not to predict dreams but to interpret ones that have already occurred, and this hemerological key does not replace the method for dispelling nightmares but supplements it. The interpretive key and the ritual prescription perform utterly different functions. Compare the techniques for interpreting dreams based on their posited nexus of connection to the stars discussed in Idel, "Astral Dreams in Judaism."
66. There does not yet appear to be scholarly consensus on which manuscripts constitute witnesses to which texts, so the following list of titles and the specific manuscripts in which they are attested should be considered provisional. [1] 新集周公解夢書 (*New Collection of the Duke of Zhou's Book for Interpreting Dreams*). (a) P3908: for transcription see Zheng Binglin, *Dunhuang xieben jiemeng shu jiaolu yanjiu*, 171–202; for detailed description and analysis see Drège and Drettas, "Oniromancie," 396–97. For translation see Drège, "Clefs des songes de Touen-houang," 213–34. (b) S5900: for transcription see Zheng Binglin, *Dunhuang xieben jiemeng shu jiaolu yanjiu*, 167–70. For description and analysis see Drège and Drettas, "Oniromancie," 401. (c) P3571 verso. For description and analysis see Drège and Drettas, "Oniromancie," 395. [2] 周公解夢書 (*The Duke of Zhou's Book for Interpreting Dreams*). (a) P3105 recto: For description and analysis see Drège and Drettas, "Oniromancie," 393–94. (b) P3281 verso:

For description and analysis see Drège and Drettas, "Oniromancie," 394–95. Transcription: Zheng Binglin, *Dunhuang xieben jiemeng shu jiaolu yanjiu*, 219–32. (c) P3685 verso: For description and analysis see Drège and Drettas, "Oniromancie," 395–96. Transcription: Zheng Binglin, *Dunhuang xieben jiemeng shu jiaolu yanjiu*, 219–32. (d) S2222 recto: For description and analysis see Drège and Drettas, "Oniromancie," 399–400. Transcription: Zheng Binglin, *Dunhuang xieben jiemeng shu jiaolu yanjiu*, 203–18. (e) Two fragments held by the India Office, British Library (C118): For description and analysis see Drège and Drettas, "Oniromancie," 401. [3] 先賢周公解夢書 (*Book for Interpreting Dreams from Former Worthies and the Duke of Zhou*).(a) P3105 recto: For description and analysis see Drège and Drettas, "Oniromancie," 394. (b) What Zheng Binglin calls Fragment 58. Transcription: Zheng Binglin, *Dunhuang xieben jiemeng shu jiaolu yanjiu*, 238–43. [4] Untitled. (a) S620 recto. For description and analysis see Drège and Drettas, "Oniromancie," 398–99. Transcription: Zheng Binglin, *Dunhuang xieben jiemeng shu jiaolu yanjiu*, 262–89. (b) P3990 verso. For description and analysis see Drège and Drettas, "Oniromancie," 398. Transcription: Zheng Binglin, *Dunhuang xieben jiemeng shu jiaolu yanjiu*, 290–93. [5] 解夢書(*Book for Interpreting Dreams*). (a) S2222 verso. For description and analysis see Drège and Drettas, "Oniromancie," 400–401. (b) P2829 recto. For description and analysis see Drège and Drettas, "Oniromancie," 393. [6] Untitled hemerological interpretive key (differing in its details from that given in P3908) with a preface containing theoretical remarks on dreams, attested uniquely in P3571 verso. For transcription see Zheng Binglin, *Dunhuang xieben jiemeng shu jiaolu yanjiu*, 294–99, and for description and analysis see Drège and Drettas, "Oniromancie," 384–86, 395. [7] S2072, an untitled collection of anecdotes, which I take up below. Zheng Binglin, *Dunhuang xieben jiemeng shu jiaolu yanjiu*, 303–10. For an earlier-published overview of some of this material, see Drège, "Notes d'onirologie chinoise," 272–76. For a useful study of Dunhuang composite manuscripts (multiple texts copied onto single rolls), see Galambos, "Composite Manuscripts in Medieval China."

67. Some have speculated that the rolls were more likely to have been used by professional diviners while the codices were for private use (Drège and Drettas, "Oniromancie," 371).

68. This text is attested in P3908. For the digital version made available by the Bibliothèque Nationale de France, see https://gallica.bnf.fr/ark:/12148/btv1b8300230n.r=P%203908?rk=128756;0 [accessed March 3, 2020]. For a transcription see Zheng Binglin, *Dunhuang xieben jiemeng shu jiaolu yanjiu*, 171–202; for detailed description and analysis, see Drège and Drettas, "Oniromancie," 396–97. For a translation, see Drège, "Clefs des songes de Touen-houang," 213–34. This work is partially attested as well in S5900 (for transcription see Zheng Binglin, *Dunhuang xieben jiemeng shu jiaolu yanjiu*, 167–70, and for description and analysis see Drège and Drettas, "Oniromancie," 401). For brief comments on the material and visual aspects of this and similar texts, see Drettas, "Deux types de manuscrits mantiques." Drège and Drettas ("Oniromancie," 395) note similarities between the formatting of the hemerological correlations given in P3571 verso and those found in P3908 ("pour une rubrique similaire . . ."), but Zheng Binglin (*Dunhuang xieben jiemeng shu jiaolu yanjiu*, 295–96) points out correctly that its interpretations of signs and those found in P3908 vary widely in their contents. The titles of several other manuals of various sorts recovered at Dunhuang include the phrase "new collection of" (*xin ji* 新集), apparently to emphasize to readers in that outpost area that the particular version of the work offered in the manuscript was up-to-date—that is, that it reflected the best textual knowledge currently available in the distant central plains (see Zheng Binglin, *Dunhuang xieben jiemeng shu jiaolu yanjiu*, 178).

69. The terms for which include *zhang* 章, *bu* 部, and *pian* 篇.
70. On the history of the *leishu* genre, see Liu Quanbo, *Wei Jin nanbeichao leishu bianzuan yanjiu*; Cheng Lesong, *Zhonggu daojiao leishu yu daojiao sixiang*; Wilkinson, *Chinese History*, 955–62; and Elman, "Collecting and Classifying."
71. Drège and Drettas, "Oniromancie," 379–80.
72. See Drège and Drettas, 390–92.
73. The method developed by Frederick Perls holds that since every last detail of each dream—every character, even every object—is a fragmented projection of the dreamer's consciousness, it holds meaning that may be recovered during the process of analysis. This "re-owning" of the fragments is, for Perls, the goal of dream interpretation. I return briefly to this method in the conclusion to chapter 4. See Perls, *Gestalt Therapy Verbatim*, 67, and Coolidge, *Dream Interpretation as a Psychotherapeutic Technique*, 78–87. My thanks to Linda F. Campany for these references.
74. On "hemerological" and its history as a category, see Harper and Kalinowski, "Introduction," 1–9.
75. The two manuscripts in question are P3908 and P3571 verso, the latter of which is only a fragment. See the tables in Drège and Drettas, "Oniromancie," 384–86. For transcriptions of these hemerological lists see Zheng Binglin, *Dunhuang xieben jiemeng shu jiaolu yanjiu*, 176–77 (P3908) and 294 (P3571 verso). P3908 is further complicated by the inclusion of not one but multiple hemerological schemes.
76. See ZT, 1716–17, and the discussion in Brennan, "Dreams, Divination, and Statecraft," 86–87. Both the *Zuo zhuan* narrative itself and the early medieval commentary on it by Du Yu 杜預 (222–84) go into considerable detail about the significance of the dream's timing, using the stem-and-branch as well as the five-phases systems to unpack what it portends. Neither explication says a word about the naked singing boy.
77. To cite a single example, see Harper, "Physicians and Diviners," 99, discussing manuscripts from the Shuihudi tomb sealed in 217 BCE.
78. This is the view taken by Drège and Drettas, "Oniromancie," 380–81.
79. See for example Harper, "A Chinese Demonography of the Third Century B.C.," and Harper, "Spellbinding."
80. In *Analects* 7.5, a passage discussed in *Dreaming and Self-Cultivation*. On representations of the Duke of Zhou, see Nylan, "Many Dukes of Zhou in Early Sources." Drège, "Clefs des songes de Touen-houang," 213n28, raises the possibility that the figure referred to in these titles was in fact not the early Zhou paragon but rather the noted Jin-era dream interpreter Zhou Xuan 周宣 (on whom I will say more in the next chapter, in the section Named Professional Interpreters). This possibility is not taken up in the more recent Drège and Drettas, "Oniromancie," but, absent new evidence, I think it cannot be ruled out, especially since the ancient Duke of Zhou, while mentioned as a subject of Confucius' dreams, was not himself (to my knowledge) credited with acumen in dream interpretation, whereas Zhou Xuan was famous for it and was credited with authoring at least one known (now lost) single-roll dreambook himself (see the listing at *Sui shu* 29:1037).
81. See Campany, "Secrecy and Display in the Quest for Transcendence," and Campany, *Making Transcendents*, 88–129.
82. A point also made in Fodde-Reguer, "Divining Bureaucracy," 21–22.
83. *Qianfu lun jian jiaozheng*, 320–21, following the editor's suggested emendations and his explications of the wording. Translation is that of Kinney, *Art of the Han Essay*, 122.
84. *Qianfu lun jian jiaozheng*, 322. Translation slightly modified from Kinney, *Art of the Han Essay*, 123.

85. In Wang Fu's case, of course, there is nothing comparable to Freud's notion of the "censor."
86. *Qianfu lun jian jiaozheng*, 322. Translation modified from Kinney, *Art of the Han Essay*, 123. Compare the observation in *On Prophecy in Sleep*, attributed to Aristotle, that those especially skilled in interpreting dreams (for *anybody* can interpret *vivid* dreams) are those who are good at detecting likenesses. "By likenesses I mean that the mental pictures are like reflections in water. . . . If there is much movement, the reflection is not like the original, nor the images like the real object. Thus he would indeed be a clever interpreter of reflections who could quickly discriminate, and envisage these scattered and distorted fragments of the images as representing a man, say, or a horse or any other object." Similarly in dreams: movement destroys the clarity of the images in them. (Here are *phantasmata* again, the components in dreams that somehow signify meanings outside the dreams, in many ways reminiscent of 象.) We could wish for a clearer explication of precisely what constitutes the "movement" (*kinesis*) in dreams that disturbs the clarity of their images, paralleling the effect of water's movement on the reflections in it. Aristotle, *On the Soul, Parva Naturalia, On Breath*, 385.
87. The dreamer's feelings and temperament are important in order that they may be factored out of the interpretive equation, rather than factored in. Wang Fu views them as red herrings. I return to this point in the conclusion to chapter 4.
88. Drège and Drettas, "Oniromancie," 380.
89. Johnston, "Delphi and the Dead," 300.
90. Similar remarks about one of the functions of dream interpretation in a very different sort of society may be found in Hollan, "Personal Use of Dream Beliefs in the Toraja Highlands," 173.
91. As mentioned by Strickmann, *Mantras et mandarins*, 306–7. Compare: "When a culture contributes syntax [to dreams], a dream paradigm is inscribed within the dream itself. Thus it is often said that people in Jungian analysis have archetypal dreams, while those in psychoanalysis have dreams replete with the kind of symbolism central to Freud's view of the dream. Haitians . . . think they dream of that world the Haitian system of dream interpretation suggests they will find" (Mageo, "Theorizing Dreaming and the Self," 17–18). And: "Systems of dream interpretation may have a rather distinctive character. . . . Inasmuch as it momentarily represents a very relevant part of the sleeper's cultural surround, the interpretational system appears to have an inordinately large part in constructing the dream's manifest content. The individual is struck by the poignant accuracy of the diviner's interpretation, not realizing that the dream content was itself a partial artifact of his (the dreamer's) prior knowledge of the interpretational system" (Tuzin, "The Breath of a Ghost," 560–61). For that matter, social-scientific quantitative studies of dream content across cultures have found that the majority of reported dreams fall into a small number of typical themes—although such studies have tended so far to be based on small sample sizes (e.g., Yu, "We Dream Typical Themes Every Single Night," and Yu, "Typical Dreams Experienced by Chinese People").
92. Several extant Daoist texts correlate certain dream images with fixed meanings, but I have not yet found any that match this Buddhist text in the extensiveness of such a listing. They are treated in *Dreaming and Self-Cultivation*.
93. See Forte, "South Indian Monk Bodhiruci"; Weinstein, *Buddhism under the T'ang*, 44.
94. On this collection see Pagel, *Bodhisattvapiṭaka*; Pedersen, "Notes on the *Ratnakūṭa* Collection"; and Chang, *Treasury of Mahāyāna Sūtras*. Several parts of this large compilation are attested in Dunhuang manuscripts, including a beautiful, complete copy on a paper scroll (still attached to its wooden roller, S351) of its *juan* 117, com-

prising the first half of *Baofa pusa hui* 寶髻菩薩會/*Ratnacūḍaparipṛcchā*, corresponding to T 310.47a, 11:657a–665a; see Pagel, *Bodhisattvapiṭaka*, 435. However, so far as I have been able to determine, this dream text is unattested among them except in P3017, a list of errata and corrections to the entire collection, titled *Jinzi dabao [ji]jing neilüe chu jiaocuo ji shangsun zishu* 金字大寶「積」經內略出交錯及傷損字數. On the first sheet of this manuscript a few minor emendations are listed under *juan* 15 and 16, corresponding to brief passages in the *Shuomeng jing*. Beside the heading as given in *juan* 15, interestingly, the attribution of the translation to Dharmarakṣa is repeated. See https://gallica.bnf.fr/ark:/12148/btv1b83007111/f1.item.r=大寶積經.zoom [accessed March 3, 2020].

95. See the listing in *Kaiyuan shijiao lu* 55:493b18, in the section given over to works translated in the Wu and Jin eras (see 477b13). There the sutra is titled *Pusa shuomeng jing* 菩薩說夢經 in two rolls. Zhisheng's comment reads: "The 'Fashang record' 法上錄 [this refers to Fei Zhangfang's catalog of 598] says it was produced by Dharmarakṣa. A detailed [examination] of the text suggests not. But we go by the earlier catalog to list it." The Palace edition of the canon likewise says that the attribution to Dharmarakṣa stems from Fei Zhangfang's catalog. A version of this sutra exists in Tibetan; see Harrison, "Mediums and Messages," 136–37. At this writing it is unclear to me whether the Tibetan text discussed by Esler ("Note d'oniromancie tibétaine") is the same one treated by Harrison.
96. According to Harrison ("Mediums and Messages," 137–38), the Tibetan version lists 106 signs. Esler mentions that the text he discusses has 108 signs. It is, of course, unsurprising in a Buddhist context to find a list totaling 108 items. Judging from Harrison's brief characterization of the Tibetan text, there are certainly overlaps but also significant differences between the Tibetan and Chinese versions.
97. Some dream signs given in the initial list lack corresponding interpretations in the subsequent, main section. Conversely, some interpretations in the main section are of dream content not found in the opening list of signs. The order of signs is sometimes jumbled, the wording in the list of signs does not always match that in the main section, and the text is unusually poorly punctuated, even by the standards of the Taishō edition. In *Dreaming and Self-Cultivation* I undertake a more detailed analysis of this text and translate selected entries.
98. For example, sign 95, dreaming of explaining the Dharma for many persons (89b9).
99. 89a3–12.
100. On these "obstructions" see Dayal, *Bodhisattva Doctrine in Buddhist Sanskrit Literature*, 103, 121–22; Gethin, *Buddhist Path to Awakening*, 173–82.
101. See Strickmann, "*Consecration Sūtra*"; Strickmann, *Mantras et mandarins*, 330–31; and Guggenmos, "A List of Magic and Mantic Practices." The second scroll of *Zhancha shan'e yebao jing* has been translated, not entirely satisfactorily, in Rulu, *Teachings of the Buddha*, 108–18.
102. Compare: "Divination operates on a[n] item by item basis and is utilized by an individual or a group to address a specific situation. Divinatory practice functions in a culture according to a structure and set of beliefs that is shared and public and at the same time it needs to convey meaning that resonates with singular significance. As a result, divinatory meaning is mutable. Not only can a reading signify differently to individuals within the same belief system, meanings can easily reverse" (Guinan, "A Severed Head Laughed," 20). I would add only that, even in small-scale cultures, and certainly in one as large and diverse as that of early medieval China, there was not even a single "structure and set of beliefs that is shared and public." There were, rather, many.

103. Schmitt, "The Liminality and Centrality of Dreams in the Medieval West," 276. Drège and Drettas touch on the greater complexity of narratives as compared with dreambooks ("Oniromancie," 383).

Chapter 4

1. Which gate the story is referring to is not entirely clear, but it may well be the Chang gate 閶門 in the wall surrounding the city of Suzhou, which had stood since ancient times. See HYD 12:124. On Sun Jian, see BDL, 769.
2. *Sanguo zhi* 46.1093. In his 429 commentary to Chen Shou's *Sanguo zhi*, Pei Songzhi 裴松之 cites the story from a *History of Wu* (*Wu shu* 吳書), presumably the text by that title attributed to Zhou Chu 周處 (236–97), on whom see CL, 2274–76.
3. Wang Dao was a key figure in the founding of the Eastern Jin government south of the Yangzi in 317. His official biography appears in *Jin shu* 65, and it is from that collection of anecdotes that this example is taken. For a biographical sketch, see SSHY, 626.
4. For a biographical sketch of Wang Xun (350–401), known for being close to the Jin emperor Xiaowu (Sima Yao, r. 373–96) and to Buddhist monks, see SSHY, 619. See also Zürcher, *Buddhist Conquest of China*, 211–13, 395nn151, 153.
5. *Jin shu* 65.1756.
6. *Jin shu* 92.2403. Luo Han served in administrative positions under Yu Liang and Huan Wen. Most of his writings are lost, but a treatise on rebirth, *Gengsheng lun* 更生論 (ca. 370), is preserved in the Buddhist compendium *Hongming ji* (52:27b–c) by Sengyou 僧祐 (435–518). See SSHY, 587, and Zürcher, *Buddhist Conquest of China*, 16, 135–36.
7. Zheng Binglin, *Dunhuang xieben jiemeng shu jiaolu yanjiu*, 311–57, provides a useful index of the dream correlates mentioned in the Dunhuang dreambooks, which of course constitute only a small (and perhaps regionally distinctive) sampling of what must have been a much larger corpus of standard correlations. In any case, this one does not appear among them.
8. *Jin shu* 122.3055. For the military background, see Graff, *Medieval Chinese Warfare*, 69. Lü's conquest of Kucha resulted in the famed translator Kumārajīva being taken to Chang'an, with large consequences for the history of Buddhism in China. See Zürcher, *Buddhist Conquest of China*, 226; and Tsukamoto, *History of Early Chinese Buddhism*, 253, 745, 869.
9. See Campany, *Signs from the Unseen Realm*, 68–71.
10. For a biographical sketch, see BDL, 1146.
11. The commentator Li Xian 李賢 (in his commentary presented to the throne in 677; see Wilkinson, *Chinese History*, 714) glosses 陰堂 as "dark room" and says that 奥 indicates the southeast corner. I follow HYD 11:1028a in understanding 陰堂 as referring to the teacher's tomb and Wang Li, *Gu Hanyu zidian*, 184, in understanding 奥 as referring to the southwest corner of a room.
12. Such requests were frequent during this period. See Knapp, "Heaven and Death according to Huangfu Mi"; Zhang Jiefu, *Zhongguo sangzang shi*, 119–55; Poo Muchou, *Muzang yu shengsi*, 254–68; and Bokenkamp, *Ancestors and Anxiety*, 53–56.
13. *Hou Han shu* 39.1311; cf. TPYL 551.4a. Li Xian comments that this is a "correlate of death" 死之象. For a useful study of the biography of the *Hou Han shu*'s author, Fan Ye 范曄 (398–446), see Eicher, "Fan Ye's Biography in the *Song shu*."
14. *Sanguo zhi* 36.942, quoting *Records of Shu* 蜀記.
15. A brief treatment of this section's subject matter may be found in Ong, "Image and Meaning."

16. See ECT, 483–86; CL, 1868–73; and Milburn, *Spring and Autumn Annals of Master Yan*, 3–67. On Yan Ying 晏嬰 of the state of Qi (d. ca. 500) and the early compilation of stories about him, see Milburn, *Spring and Autumn Annals of Master Yan*, 68–453. On Yan Ying in *Zuo zhuan*, see Schaberg, *A Patterned Past*, 102, 129, 150, 230–32, 277, 279–80; Wai-yee Li, *Readability of the Past*, 22–25, 352–55; and Pines, "From Teachers to Subjects."
17. See *Fengsu tongyi*, 331–32, following the editor's suggested textual emendations, which are considerable—the *Fengsu tongyi* text as it stands is rather garbled. For a translation of the passage see Nylan, "Ying Shao's 'Feng Su T'ung Yi,'" 522–24. For a translation from the transmitted *Yanzi chunqiu* text itself, see Milburn, *Spring and Autumn Annals of Master Yan*, 196–98. For another record of a dream interpretation by Master Yan for Duke Jin of Qi, this one preserved in the third-century *Bowu zhi*, see Greatrex, *Bowu zhi*, 128.
18. For a detailed account of the excavation and the editing of the texts found in it, see Shaughnessy, *Rewriting Early Chinese Texts*, 131–84. The texts included several not directly relevant here, including the famous *Traditions of Mu, Son of Heaven* (*Mu tianzi zhuan* 穆天子傳).
19. As noted in Campany, "Two Religious Thinkers of the Early Eastern Jin," 202; Shaughnessy, *Rewriting Early Chinese Texts*, 167; and Campany, *A Garden of Marvels*, xxix–xxx.
20. See Shaughnessy, *Unearthing the Changes*, 141–88, which includes a thorough discussion of the 1993 excavation and the text and its history as well as translations of all the fragments; Shaughnessy, *Rewriting Early Chinese Texts*, 148–49, 156–60; and Shaughnessy, "Wangjiatai *Gui cang*," which centers on the relation between *Gui zang* and *Zhou yi* 周易.
21. On *Bowu zhi* see Greatrex, *Bowu zhi*, and Campany, *Strange Writing*, 49–52, 127–28, 280–94.
22. See Shaughnessy, *Unearthing the Changes*, 147, and Shaughnessy, "Wangjiatai *Gui cang*," 95–97.
23. See the summary characterization of the text's entries in Shaughnessy, *Unearthing the Changes*, 152. On the other formats evidenced in the bamboo strips, see Shaughnessy, *Unearthing the Changes*, 158–61.
24. See Shaughnessy, "Wangjiatai *Gui cang*," 99, 104, and Shaughnessy, *Unearthing the Changes*, 152–53.
25. *Jin shu* 51:1433. Compare the slightly more detailed characterization written by Du Yu 杜預 in 282 CE, translated in Shaughnessy, *Rewriting Early Chinese Texts*, 145, and again at 163; here it is made clear that the sequence of instances and the sense or wording of each instance were identical across the *Zuo zhuan* and *Shi Chun*.
26. See Unger, "Die Fragmente des So-Yü," and Shaughnessy, *Rewriting Early Chinese Texts*, 166–71. Both of these discussions offer translations of some of the fragments. (Shaughnessy translates one that Unger missed.) See also Campany, *Strange Writing*, 33–34.
27. *Jin shu* 51:1433; translation from Shaughnessy, *Rewriting Early Chinese Texts*, 167.
28. On myths surrounding Gong Gong, Zhuan Xu, and the cosmic flood, see Lewis, *Flood Myths of Early China*; Wang Qing, *Zhongguo shenhua yanjiu*, 146–50; and Luan Baoqun, *Zhongguo shenguai dacidian*, 149. At this writing I have failed to locate other mentions of Fuyou.
29. TPYL 908.2b–3a; Unger, "Die Fragmente des So-Yü," 374–75. Translation modified from that of Shaughnessy, *Rewriting Early Chinese Texts*, 169 (where the Chinese

text is also provided). A version of the same anecdote, with some significant differences of detail, appears in *Zuo zhuan*: see ZT, 1423, and discussions in Wai-yee Li, *Readability of the Past*, 237, and Brown, *Art of Medicine in Early China*, 34.

30. Pan Geng was an ancient Shang king; a chapter of the *Book of Documents* (*Shang shu* 尚書) records an oration he was purported to have given to the people of his realm. See Allan, *Buried Ideas*, 301; Keightley, *These Bones Shall Rise Again*, 164, 182; and Lewis, *Construction of Space in Early China*, 144–45.
31. On Yi Yin, see Sterckx, *Food, Sacrifice, and Sagehood in Early China*, 65–74; Sterckx, "Le pouvoir des sens," 76–79; Luan Baoqun, *Zhongguo shenguai dacidian*, 631; Lewis, *Construction of Space in Early China*, 272; Campany, *Strange Writing*, 38–39, 115, 316. A version of this story was incorporated into Zhuang Hua's *Bowu zhi*; see *Bowu zhi jiaozheng*, 84 (item 250), and Greatrex, *Bowu zhi*, 128.
32. TPYL 377.4b, 378.3b; Unger, "Die Fragmente des So-Yü," 374–75.
33. Zichan, minister of the state of Zheng, in *Zuo zhuan* is frequently depicted as a skilled practitioner of reasoned persuasion. See Lewis, *Construction of Space in Early China*, 29–32, 53, 145–47; Schaberg, *A Patterned Past*, 82–84, 143–44, 147; Wang, *Cosmology and Political Culture in Early China*, 83, 102, 104, 124; Wai-yee Li, *Readability of the Past*, 358–69; and Hunter, *Confucius Beyond the "Analects,"* 52, 105, 116.
34. On some uses of *e* in early medieval texts see Liu Zhao, *Chutu jianbo wenzi congkao*, 220–21.
35. Of course, the nature of the relationship between *psyche* and *soma* that underlies our word might or might not correspond closely to what we would find if we sifted through large numbers of Chinese texts. On the other hand, the notion that those texts lack *any* distinction or contrast between mind and body—the "myth of holism"—has been quite zestily, and I think successfully, refuted in Slingerland, *Mind and Body*, esp. 22–61.
36. *Qian fu lun jian jiaozheng*, 318. Cf. the translation in Kinney, *Art of the Han Essay*, 121.
37. For discussions of the dreams-related portion of the text see Zheng Binglin and Yang Ping, *Dunhuang ben mengshu*, 265–70; Drège and Drettas, "Oniromancie," 383; and especially Zheng Binglin, *Dunhuang xieben jiemeng shu jiaolu yanjiu*, 303–10. An excellent digitization is available online under the auspices of the International Dunhuang Project; see http://idp.bl.uk/idp.a4d [accessed March 3, 2020].
38. The story of Ji Kang's oneiric receipt of the Guangling tune (discussed in chapter 5), and another story involving Guo Pu's 郭璞 oneiric bestowal of a multicolored writing brush on Jiang Wentong (the fifth anecdote in the series), in fact involve no dream *interpretation*. Instead these two stories tell of direct visitations in which knowledge or an object is transferred through the dream into the waking world. Their underlying notion of dreams is structured, that is, not by the prospective but by the visitation paradigm. The other nine stories do all involve interpretation.
39. Miller, *Dreams in Late Antiquity*, 39.
40. There were parallels elsewhere in the ancient world: see, for example, Hughes, "Dreams of Alexander the Great," 175, and Harris-McCoy, *Artemidorus' Oneirocritica*, 5, 39, 321. Wordplay was key to Freud's view of how dreams mean; see *Interpretation of Dreams*, index s.v. "jokes," "puns," "words," for many examples. A scholar who has investigated the linguistics of dream puns writes, "It is as though the mind while dreaming is deliberately searching for opportunities to pun, so that it can present abstract ideas through imagery" (Rock, *Mind at Night*, 131).
41. Not to be confused with the better-known Wang Rong 王戎 (234–305) who was one of the Seven Sages of the Bamboo Grove (on whom see SSHY, 621, and *Jin shu*

43.1231–35), nor with Wang Rong 融 (468–94), who was a noted fifth-century author (on whom see CL, 1208–13).

42. *Yi yuan* 7/23; TPGJ 276/13. Translated in Campany, *A Garden of Marvels*, 96.
43. For a biographical synopsis on Liu Laozhi, see SSHY, 584. On the rebellion and Liu Laozhi's role in quelling it, see Graff, *Medieval Chinese Warfare*, 86–87; Miyakawa, "Local Cults around Mount Lu at the Time of Sun En's Rebellion," 83; Miyakawa, "Son On, Ro Jun no ran ni tsuite"; Miyakawa, "Son On, Ro Jun no ran hokō"; Zürcher, *Buddhist Conquest of China*, 154–56; and Lewis, *China between Empires*, 67–69.
44. *Jin shu* 84.2192; *Song shu* 47.1411; *Nan shi* 17.474.
45. The *Song shu* version says he "repeatedly dreamed" 尋夢.
46. Translation modified from SSHY, 271. See also *Jin shu* 78.2065 and *Yi yuan* 7/15 (translated in Campany, *A Garden of Marvels*, 94–95). Drège, "Clefs des songes de Touen-houang," 245, discusses the tale.
47. The characters 大 and 太 were often used interchangeably, though they did not rhyme in this period.
48. The text here mentions *buwu* 部伍, meaning military units (see HYD, 10.651), so apparently in the dream he was marching or being transported by boat with a detachment of soldiers.
49. *Yi yuan* 7/31; TPYL 396.3a.
50. See SSHY, 635.
51. SSHY 123–24; my translation partially borrows from Mather's. Part of Yin Hao's reply is constructed on a rhyme. "Wealth is basically shit and dirt" alludes to a passage in *Guo yu* 國語. This play on *kwan* 官 "office" and *kwan* 棺 "coffin" recurs below. The same anecdote appears in *Jin shu* 77.2043, translated in Drège and Drettas, "Oniromancie," 283.
52. On the rebellion see *Jin shu* 100.2612–14 and Zürcher, *Buddhist Conquest of China*, 347n4.
53. Perhaps Chongling 舂陵, today's Zaoyang City in Hubei Province, where he served as prefect.
54. *Jin shu* 89.2314–15.
55. For a sophisticated rhetorical analysis of some modes of dream hermeneutics, see Hasar, "Metaphor and Metonymy in Ancient Dream Interpretation."
56. He had a distinguished military career but was later forced to commit suicide. See the biographies in *Song shu* 77.1996 ff. and *Nan shi* 37.353 ff.
57. *Song shu* 77.2004. This anecdote was also anthologized in Liu Jingshu's *zhiguai* compilation, *A Garden of Marvels* (*Yi yuan*), where it appears as one of two anecdotes recounted in item 7/32.
58. On him see Zürcher, *Buddhist Conquest of China*, 181–85, and Wright, *Studies in Chinese Buddhism*, 34–72 (this episode appears on p. 61).
59. On the historical situation see Graff, *Medieval Chinese Warfare*, 56–69, and Vovin, Vajda, and de la Vaissière, "Who Were the Kjet (羯)?"
60. *Jin shu* 42.1208. This anecdote was also included in the compilation of eleven dream-related anecdotes in the untitled *leishu* recovered at Dunhuang, Stein 2072; see Zheng Binglin, *Dunhuang xieben jiemeng shu jiaolu yanjiu*, 303. On Wang Jun, see CL, 1199–200.
61. See BDL, 27–28.
62. See BDL, 282. His biography appears in *Hou Han shu* 26:908–9, just after Cai Mao's.
63. Literally, "among [those officials who gather at] the central platform" 中台 at court.
64. *Hou Han shu* 26.908; versions appear in *Soushen ji* 10/3 and in the untitled *leishu*

recovered at Dunhuang, S2072, discussed above (see Zheng Binglin, *Dunhuang xieben jiemeng shu jiaolu yanjiu*, 304). The latter cites *Hou Han shu* as its source.

65. See SSHY, 608–9, for a biographical synopsis.
66. These leather pouches worn from the belt, called *pannang* 鞶囊, often took the shape of, or were decorated with, embroidered tiger heads. See HYD 12.212. The corresponding passage cited in TPYL 398.2b and BTSC 76.3b–4a from a different *Jin shu* (the one authored by Wang Yin 王隱), and the citation of the passage in TPYL 691.7a, say that the unspecified "beast" 獸 in the received version was a tiger. I translate accordingly.
67. *Jin shu* 90.2338. Quoted in TPYL 261.3a and 691.7a. A slightly different version is quoted from a different work of the same title by Wang Yin 王隱 in TPYL 398.2b and BTSC 76.
68. For studies see de Groot, "On Chinese Divination by Dissecting Written Characters"; Vance, "Deciphering Dreams"; Strassberg, "Glyphomantic Dream Anecdotes"; and Bauer, "Chinese Glyphomancy (*ch'ai-tzu*)." For a critique of the term "glyphomancy" as applied to these interpretation techniques (mostly based on the author's dissatisfaction with calling Chinese characters "glyphs"), which are often denominated in Chinese as *cezi* 測字 or *xiangzi* 相字, see Drettas, "Le rêve mis en ordre," 314n164.
69. The dead were often addressed in such honorific terms.
70. Commentary to *Sanguo zhi* 48.1167, the biography of Sun Hao 孫皓 (d. 284), last ruler of the Wu kingdom, citing a passage from *History of Wu* (*Wu shu* 吳書), probably that of Zhou Chu. The dreamer is not Sun Hao but the Wu minister Meng Ren.
71. He is mentioned in passing in Berkowitz, *Patterns of Disengagement*, 207.
72. *Jin shu* 94.2455. Summarized in Drettas, "Le rêve mis en ordre," 333n177.
73. *Yi yuan* 6/4, translated in Campany, *A Garden of Marvels*, 89, modified here. Versions are cited from *Jin shu* in TPYL 883.3b and TPGJ 276/14, and indeed the story is also found in the extant *Jin shu* 92.2380. It is translated and discussed in Strassberg, "Glyphomantic Dream Anecdotes," 183 (my translation was arrived at independently). For a biographical note on Zou Chen (d. 299?) see CL, 2360–61.
74. See CL, 2360–61.
75. Xie An was a dominant literary, political, cultural, and military figure during the Eastern Jin period. See CL, 1568–71; Zürcher, *Buddhist Conquest of China*, 112–13, 117–18, 134, 141, 189; Graff, *Medieval Chinese Warfare*, 84–86; and Chennault, "Lofty Gates or Solitary Impoverishment," 269–70.
76. "Shadow of Jupiter" translates *taisui* 太歲, sometimes rendered as "year star" and equated with the planet Jupiter but here surely used in its more technical sense of the planet's counter-orbital correlate, moving across the sky in the opposite direction. *You* 酉 is the position or direction in the sky (one of twelve) through which *taisui* is moving at the time Xie An is speaking, See Wilkinson, *Chinese History*, 515–16, and Hou, "Chinese Belief in Baleful Stars," 205–9.
77. *Jin shu* 79.2076. A version also appears in *Youming lu*, item 100 (LX 268).
78. For a more complex dream decoding involving the mapping of dream correlates onto astrological stations, see the biography of Liu Yao 劉曜 in *Jin shu* 103.2699, quoted in TPYL 328.4a. The same story is quoted from *Qian Zhao lu* 前趙錄 in TPYL 400.5a–b.
79. This is not the better-known general Yuan Shao 袁紹 (d. 202) who played an important role in the military conflicts attending the waning years of the Eastern Han, on whom see BDL, 1009–11.

80. This is hexagram 39 ䷦; its name means "stumbling" or "adversity." Its lower constituent trigram is *gen* ☶, mountain, and the upper is *kan* ☵, water. See Lynn, *Classic of Changes*, 375–80, and Rutt, *Book of Changes*, 262.
81. *Sanguo zhi* 28.781. For biographical sketches of Deng Ai, a noted surveyor and general for the Wei kingdom, see BDL, 109, and SSHY, 608.
82. SSHY, 608.
83. See *Jin shu* 114.2934; partially quoted from *Jin shu* in TPYL 639.4a–b and from a *Daiji* 載記 (presumably short for *Fu Jian daiji*) in TPYL 728.3a–b. TPYL 639 omits part of Fu Rong's explication of the dream. A version also appears in the section on dream divinations in Dunhuang manuscript S2072, an untitled *leishu* discussed above; it cites *Leilin* 類林 (a Tang work) as its source (see the International Dunhuang Project's website at http://idp.bl.uk/database/stitched.a4d?recnum=2071 [accessed March 3, 2020] and Zheng Binglin, *Dunhuang xieben jiemeng shu jiaolu yanjiu*, 303). This appended biography is unfortunately not included in Rogers, *Chronicle of Fu Chien*. The anecdote translated here is followed by another one further demonstrating Fu Rong's skill in divinatory crime detection, but the second one doesn't involve dreams.
84. These are indeed the standard correlations.
85. That is, the *li* trigram has a broken line, correlating to Yin and the female, in the middle; the *kan* trigram has a solid line, correlating to Yang and the male, in the middle.
86. This hexagram's name may also be understood more simply as "already completed," as in Shaughnessy, *I Ching*, 81.
87. King Wen of Zhou was said to have produced a rearrangement of the *Yi* hexagrams while imprisoned at Youli by King Zhou of Shang. He was released thanks to the payment of ransom by Sanyi Sheng. "With the proper rites he lived, but without them he'd have died" 有禮而生, 無禮而死 may be an allusion to a line in the *Li yun* 禮運 chapter of *Li ji* 禮記, "He who loses [the rites] dies, while he who holds to them lives" 失之者死, 得之者生. At this writing I am otherwise unable to trace the specific allusion apparently being made in this line.
88. The word order varies here across the textual versions, leading me to suspect that whatever the precise sign involving bathing and pillows was to be, from the text as it stands it was no clearer to medieval redactors than it is to me.
89. The Mawangdui manuscript has "hair" in the second line, while the received version of the text has "headdress" (see Shaughnessy, *I Ching*, 81, 298; compare Lynn, *Classic of Changes*, 538–44, and Rutt, *Book of Changes*, 286). I am grateful to Ed Shaughnessy for discussing this passage with me and sparing me from errors.
90. As noted by Drège and Drettas, "Oniromancie," 246. Some passages in which a dreamer is said to have consulted an unnamed diviner and a prediction is given (but without any explanation of the logic of the interpretation) include *Hou Han shu* 10A.418, 12.504, 59.1920, 65.2144, 74A.2393; *Sanguo zhi* 9.288, 18.547, 63.1425; *Jin shu* 95.2489; *Song shu* 19.559; *Nan Qi shu* 26.479; *Soushen ji* 10/8; and *Yi yuan* 7/30. Named individuals interpreting others' dreams include, for example, *Shuyi ji* 78 (LX 189–90) and *Yi yuan* 7/20, where Fu Jian is the dreamer and the interpreter is his wife.
91. On these spirits and the divinatory and self-cultivational techniques associated with them, see Kalinowski, "La littérature divinatoire dans le *Daozang*," 91–95; Pregadio, *Encyclopedia of Taoism*, 695–97; and Campany, *To Live as Long as Heaven and Earth*, 72–75.
92. *Hou Han shu* 50.1676.
93. See Campany, *Making Transcendents*, 125, 178, 201, 210, 221.

94. This is a topic approached from multiple angles in Campany, *Making Transcendents.*
95. Compare: "Dreams are used to bolster the aspirant healer's case; he garners them and presents them like signatures on petitions" (Reynolds, "Dreams and the Constitution of Self among the Zezuru," 26).
96. This is the central argument of Kory, "Cracking to Divine."
97. See Richard J. Smith, *Fathoming the Cosmos and Ordering the World*, 98–100; DeWoskin, *Doctors, Diviners, and Magicians*, 91–134; and SSHY, 576.
98. On whom see SSHY, 557–58.
99. Pei Songzhi here cites books on physiognomy to the effect that the nose in physiognomy is the correlate (*xiang* 象) of mountains.
100. Mather (SSHY, 299) suggests this alludes to a passage in the third chapter of the "Book of Filial Piety."
101. On whom see SSHY, 608.
102. Translation based on that in SSHY, 299–300. Cf. the translation in DeWoskin, *Doctors, Diviners, and Magicians*, 111–14.
103. In a related passage cited from another text, *Guan Lu biezhuan* 管輅別傳, in the commentary to *Sanguo zhi* we read in detail of how Guan diagnosed both men's impending death by observing their *qi* as manifest in their bodily comportment. For a translation see DeWoskin, *Doctors, Diviners, and Magicians*, 113–14.
104. *Sanguo zhi* 29:810–11; translation modified from DeWoskin, *Doctors, Diviners, and Magicians*, 138–40. The straw dog anecdote is also translated in Drège and Drettas, "Oniromancie," 247, and the coin-rubbing anecdote in SSHY, 506–7.
105. One of the Yellow Turban armies—or a rebel force that was at least loosely affiliated with the Yellow Turban groups—surrendered to Cao Cao in Yan Province in the northeast in 192. See de Crespigny, *Imperial Warlord*, 62–67.
106. Bearing in mind the discussion above of the relationship between simulacra 象 and their meanings 意, we could perhaps also read here 意 as "meanings."
107. For a biographical sketch of Cao Zhi's (192–232) life, see CL, 90–106.
108. This particular anecdote also appears at *Sanguo zhi* 5.157.
109. Harper ("Wang Yen-shou's Nightmare Poem," 243n9) treats *xu meng* 敘夢 as a technical term for the oneiromancer's skill in "relating" the meanings of dreams he is commissioned to interpret. Note that it serves as a subheading of the *Taiping yulan* section on dreams (scroll 397).
110. This is Zhu Jianping 朱建平 (d. ca. 224), a noted physiognomist in the kingdom of Wei. See his biography in *Sanguo zhi* 29:808–10, translated in DeWoskin, *Doctors, Diviners, and Magicians*, 134–37.
111. Cao Rui 曹叡 ruled as Wei emperor Ming from 226 to early 239.
112. Suo Dan is here quoting a pair of lines from a song in the *Classic of Odes* (*Shi jing* 詩經), Mao number 34. The stanza reads: "On one note the wild-geese cry / A cloudless dawn begins to break / A knight that brings home his bride / Must do so before the ice melts." Translation from Waley, *Book of Songs*, 30.
113. Wang Rong (234–305) was the youngest member of the group known as the Seven Sages of the Bamboo Grove. Later in life he entered political service, rising all the way to the presidency of the imperial secretariat and (in 303) receiving an appointment as minister of education. See SSHY, 621, and *Jin shu* 43.1231–35.
114. I omit his polite speech declining the appointment.
115. *Jin shu* 95.2494–95. In Ming- and Qing-period works Suo Dan was credited—certainly falsely—with a work called *Yusuo huiyi* 玉瑣煇遺. See Drettas, "Le rêve mis en ordre," 116–19.
116. See BDL, 857 (where his surname is misprinted).

117. *Sanguo zhi* 40.1003.
118. See BDL, 951.
119. *Sanguo zhi* 41.1014, citing a now-lost work.
120. On whom see BDL, 378.
121. He was dismissed for offending Liu Bei, the ruler of the Shu kingdom, with his drunkenness and sloppy administration. The background is given earlier in the biography (*Sanguo zhi* 44.1057) and summarized in BDL, 378.
122. *Sanguo zhi* 44.1057. This anecdote shows up in the untitled Dunhuang *leishu* compilation (S2072) discussed above. See Zheng Binglin, *Dunhuang xieben jiemeng shu jiaolu yanjiu*, 304.
123. On Xiao Zixian see CL, 1560–63, and Tian, *Beacon Fire and Shooting Star*, 152–61. On this treatise see Lippiello, *Auspicious Omens and Miracles*, 125.
124. *Nan Qi shu* 18.353–54.
125. See *Nan Qi shu* 18.349, where Xiao writes that he incorporated Yu Wen's earlier, Yongming-period work into his own.
126. See Campany, "Secrecy and Display in the Quest for Transcendence," and Campany, *Making Transcendents.*
127. See Barton, *Power and Knowledge*, 86, on the gap between explanations given and methods actually used in the case of Artemidorus.
128. One such passage shows up in *Record of [Han Emperor Wu's] Penetration into the Mysteries [of Outlying Realms]* (*Dongming ji* 洞冥記 item 3.2); see Wang Guoliang, *Han Wu Dongming ji yanjiu*, 85–86, and Thomas E. Smith, "Ritual and the Shaping of Narrative," 632–33 (on *Dongming ji* as a whole see also the annotated translation in Thomas E. Smith, "Ritual and the Shaping of Narrative," 588–652, and brief discussions in Campany, *Strange Writing*, 95–96, 144–46). Another is to be found in Wang Jia's *Uncollected Records* (*Shiyi ji* 拾遺記), *juan* 6 (on this text see Campany, *Strange Writing*, 64–67, 306–18), anthologized in TPYL 397.6b. See also TPGJ 408/40, citing *Youyang zazu* 酉陽雜俎, and a passage in *Yunxian zaji* 雲仙雜記, *juan* 10 (a Tang work). A few other mentions of this plant survive in later sources. There are societies in which specialists in healing sleep on an item of clothing or other object belonging to the patient; during sleep, they are shown the source of the illness (see, e.g., Tonkinson, "Ambrymese Dreams," 89–90).
129. Newman, "Western Psychic as Diviner," 98.
130. Michael Nylan has demonstrated Yang Xiong's (53 BCE–18 CE) sense of pleasure in studying and writing about texts handed down from the ancients (Nylan, *Yang Xiong and the Pleasures of Reading*). Wai-yee Li has similarly written of the pleasure of riddles, of parsing out the message concealed in indirect discourse ("Riddles, Concealment, and Rhetoric").
131. Archery was a common metaphor in classicist discourse (in both the *Zhong yong* 中庸 and in Yang Xiong's writings, among others) for the ongoing processes of mastery characteristic of moral self-cultivation and textual learning, as mentioned in Nylan, *Yang Xiong and the Pleasures of Reading*, 78. Perhaps that is why both the *Zhuangzi* and the *Liezi* contain the story of an archer who, while possessing extreme skill at shooting and handling his bow and arrows under controlled conditions, panics when approaching the edge of a mountain cliff. See Watson, *Complete Works of Chuang Tzu*, 230–31, and Graham, *Book of Lieh-tzu*, 38–39. This archer, unlike a proper Daoist sage, is unable to "hide himself in heaven" 聖人藏於天, as another *Liezi* passage puts it (*Liezi jishi*, 51; Graham, *Book of Lieh-tzu*, 38).
132. Freud, *Interpretation of Dreams*, 246.
133. Jung, *Dreams*, 69–71.

134. Perls, *Gestalt Therapy Verbatim*, 163.
135. Lakoff, "How Metaphor Structures Dreams," 89. For a critique of Lakoff's approach to dream interpretation, see Bulkeley, *Big Dreams*, 131–36.
136. See McNamara, Harris, and Kookoolis, "Costly Signaling Theory of Dream Recall and Dream Sharing." They also, however, understand the sharing of dreams with others as performing a similar function: "When a dreamer shares a dream with another, the dreamer may use his or her dreams to convey unfakeable and, therefore, more trustworthy, emotional *signals about the Self* when dealing with others. . . . The dreamer can then signal that he or she is sharing something that was not invented by the dreamer. Like emotions, dreams are considered to be involuntary products of the mind. They are thus less fakeable than other forms of discourse. When you combine emotions and dreams into the sharing of an emotional or bizarre dream, the audience who hears the dream knows that regardless of content, the dream will convey important emotional and social *information about the mind of the dreamer*" (118, emphasis added). At least in the Chinese archive this view of dream reporting would have to be set against strong examples of *faking* dreams, however. There, even a figure such as Confucius was not above falsely reporting a dream to achieve some rhetorical or instructional end.
137. See, for example, Rock, *Mind at Night*, 77–100; States, *Dreaming and Storytelling*; States, *Seeing in the Dark*.
138. Rock, *Mind at Night*, 101–20.
139. Windt and Metzinger, "Philosophy of Dreaming and Self-Consciousness," 202.
140. *Qianfu lun jian jiaozheng*, 317.
141. *Qianfu lun jian jiaozheng*, 320, modifying the translation in Kinney, *Art of the Han Essay*, 122. Cf. Brashier, *Ancestral Memory in Early China*, 206.
142. Drège and Drettas, "Oniromancie," 390–91, make this point specifically about the interpretations attributed in *Jin shu* 95 to Suo Dan. But it seems to have been the norm. The same point has been made concerning Artemidorus' extensive record concerning dream interpretation: "Artemidorus did not interpret dreams in order to gain psychological insight into the dreamer" (Price, "The Future of Dreams," 17–18).
143. Recall that the diviner Zhou Xuan explained to the client who falsely said he had dreamed of straw dogs, yet who received three successive accurate divinations based on what he'd told Zhou Xuan, that "that was due to the spirits moving you to speak thus 此神靈動君使言. It was therefore no different than if you had really dreamed those things." So here, at least, is the ghost of a vague theory of why people dream dreams that turn out, upon being correctly divined, to harbor clues to the future.
144. For a provocative discussion of the human condition as fundamentally rooted in prospection, see Seligman, Railton, Baumeister, and Sripada, *Homo Prospectus*. Anthropologist Ellen Basso writes, "While the regressive theory of dreaming adopted by psychoanalysis emphasizes adaptation to past experiences, a progressive view of dreaming . . . suggests the salience of anxiety about the future for determining dream imagery" ("Implications of a Progressive Theory of Dreaming," 87).
145. And thus it is an example of the same basic semiotic paradigm of knowledge—"an attitude oriented towards the analysis of specific cases which could be reconstructed only through traces, symptoms, and clues," or in other words "the deciphering of signs of various kinds" (Ginzburg, *Clues, Myths, and the Historical Method*, 95)—but applied toward a diagnostic, not a prognostic, function. I deal with other diagnostic texts in *Dreaming and Self-Cultivation*.
146. Which is not to say that this implied self *lacked boundaries* (Slingerland, *Mind and Body*, has well cautioned us against this orientalizing notion; compare Descola, *Be-*

yond Nature and Culture, 121) but only that its bounds were to some extent porous, as one would expect in most models of selfhood. For a compelling study of the influence of cell biology on modern models of selves and nations, see Otis, *Membranes*.

147. Freud, *Interpretation of Dreams*, 412.
148. Wai-yee Li, *Readability of the Past*, 4. Compare ibid., 173: "The assumption that clues to a human situation can be interpreted and thereby facilitate efficacious action underlies many narratives in *Zuo zhuan*." See also Vogelsang, "The Shape of History," 579–80.
149. Galvany, "Signs, Clues and Traces," 165. Galvany in this passage is speaking of arts of physiognomy, but, as we have seen, the reading of dreams was built on the same principles as the reading of faces and bodies: seeing through the surfaces of things, their *xiang* 象, to extract the thought or meaning—the *yi* 意—within. For a beautiful study of how Tzotzil Maya of Chiapas, Mexico, negotiate social opacity in the context of "a marked preoccupation with questions of surface and depth, inner and outer, and public and private" (428), see Groark, "Social Opacity."
150. Kern, "Early Chinese Divination and Its Rhetoric," 266.
151. As do, for example, Keightley, *These Bones Shall Rise Again*, 111–15; Keightley, "The 'Science' of the Ancestors," 174–77; Kern, "Early Chinese Divination and Its Rhetoric," 266 (quoting Keightley approvingly); and Roth, "The Classical Daoist Concept of *Li* 理 (Pattern)."
152. See for example these works by Puett: "Ritual Disjunctions," esp. 221; "Ritualization as Domestication," esp. 366–67; *To Become a God*, esp. 14–15; "Genealogies of Gods, Ghosts and Humans," esp. 161–62, 165, 176–77, 180; "Innovation as Ritualization," 27–36; and "Haunted World of Humanity." See also Seligman, Weller, Puett, and Simon, *Ritual and its Consequences*, 17–42.
153. See Seligman, Weller, Puett, and Simon, *Ritual and Its Consequences*, 30–31.
154. Schaberg, *A Patterned Past*, 195.
155. Schaberg, *A Patterned Past*, 194.
156. Wai-yee Li, *Readability of the Past*, 269.
157. Stephen, *A'aisa's Gifts*, 113.
158. Guinan, "A Severed Head Laughed," 24–26, emphasis added. A famous example of retrospective omen formation is Abraham Lincoln's dream, mere hours before his death, of traveling on a ship, and its reception by people as news of his death and the retelling of his dream spread across the country. See White, *Midnight in America*, 151–72.
159. Knight, "The Premonitions Bureau," 44, a riveting account of a psychiatrist's attempts to document instances of accurate premonitions.
160. A catch: one way people fabricate meaning from dreams is by telling themselves that the meanings made by people are in fact intrinsic to dreams.
161. But apparently he did not offer fake interpretations of dreams, only when conducting other modes of divination.
162. *Zhuangzi jijie* 181–82; Watson, *Complete Works of Chuang Tzu*, 228–30.
163. Knoblock and Riegel, *Annals of Lü Buwei*, 418. A briefer example would be the charge that the Zhou touted a dream of King Wu annihilating Yin "to seduce the masses" (Knoblock and Riegel, *Annals of Lü Buwei*, 266–68), implying either that the dream hadn't really happened or that if it had, its announcement was made for merely rhetorical reasons. My thanks to Mick Hunter for these references.
164. Stephen, *A'aisa's Gifts*, 139. For examples of disputes over the veracity of dream claims by individuals in particular circumstances, see Groark, "Toward a Cultural Phenomenology of Intersubjectivity," 287.

165. Instances of such *tong meng* 同夢 are discussed briefly in chapter 5. To my knowledge, such cases are almost always built on the visitation, not the prospective, paradigm, for reasons that will become clearer in chapter 5.
166. Crapanzano, "Concluding Reflections," 182.
167. Crapanzano, 182. See also Crapanzano, "Betwixt and Between of Dreams." Compare: "When we interpret the dreams of others, the process of interpretation has always already begun before we get there. . . . We begin our interpretation when the dreamer has already formulated a narrative, one which may have been reformulated through successive retellings. But . . . before the narrative comes the rethinking of the dream by the awakening dreamer, and before the dream is even over comes the dreamer's interpretation of its ongoing events" (Dennis Tedlock, "Mythic Dreams and Double Voicing," 104).
168. Groark, "Discourses of the Soul," 708.
169. Poirier, "This Is Good Country," 117.
170. Mageo, "Theorizing Dreaming and the Self," 20.
171. Stephen, *A'aisa's Gifts*, 139.
172. Drawing here on Goffman, *Presentation of Self in Everyday Life*; Vann and Alperstein, "Dream Sharing as Social Interaction"; Herdt, "Selfhood and Discourse in Sambia Dream Sharing"; Barbara Tedlock, ed., "Zuni and Quiché Dream Sharing and Interpreting"; and Goodale, "Tiwi Island Dreams."
173. Reynolds, "Dreams and the Constitution of Self among the Zezuru," 26.
174. Groark, "Toward a Cultural Phenomenology of Intersubjectivity," 285–87; Groark, "Social Opacity," 431; and especially Groark, "Specters of Social Antagonism." Stephen, *A'aisa's Gifts*, similarly writes of a society in which waking, face-to-face interactions are overwhelmingly smooth, calm, and harmonious, but in which more complex hostilities, resentments, and even attacks often occur among members of the community in dreams, with similarly serious emotional and somatic effects carrying back into waking life.
175. Instances where two persons interact in the same dream are occasionally found in the Chinese archive and are briefly discussed in chapter 5. To my knowledge, however, such cases are rare.
176. Crapanzano, "Concluding Reflections," 193.
177. Crapanzano, 193.
178. Brann, *World of the Imagination*, 343.
179. I have in mind here the detailed demonstration in Ochs and Capps, *Living Narrative*, of how interlocutors in conversations effectively join in shaping narratives as they emerge. See the discussion in Campany, *Making Transcendents*, 10–11.
180. For an ethnographic example of how a single dream was dealt with differently in a dreambook, as well as by three semi-professional dream interpreters in Taiwan in 1969, see Drège, "Notes d'onirologie chinoise," 276–77.
181. Keen, "Dreams, Agency, and Traditional Authority in Northeast Arnhem Land," 129.
182. Compare the analysis by Pearcy ("Theme, Dream, and Narrative") of the complex relationship between the finished, meant-for-circulation version(s) of Aristides' *Sacred Tales* and the personal records Aristides kept of his dreams, to which he refers at many points but which are rhetorically distinct in multiple ways from the publicized document. For studies of Aristides see also Harris and Holmes, eds., *Aelius Aristides*, and Petsalis-Diomidis, *Truly Beyond Wonders*. A reading of narrative documents from the ancient world that is likewise sensitive to the rhetoricity of genres and the distinctiveness of informal notes as opposed to (un)finished, circulated versions of records may be found in Larsen, *Gospels before the Book*. For excellent ethnographic observations of a collectively maintained, communal record of dreams

and waking visions, see Mittermaier, "The Book of Visions," and Mittermaier, *Dreams that Matter*, 118–39.

183. Svenbro, *Phrasikleia*, 211.

Chapter 5

1. The work in question is *Qi Xie's Records* (*Qi Xie ji* 齊諧記), attributed to Dongyang Wuyi 東陽无疑 (fl. ca. 435). This story is translated in Campany, *A Garden of Marvels*, 24–25. Textual witnesses include CXJ 20.493; YWLJ 97.1689; TPYL 479.7b and 643.9b–10a; and TPGJ 473/8. On *Qi Xie ji* see Campany, *A Garden of Marvels*, 24; Campany, *Strange Writing*, 80–81; Li Jianguo, *Tang qian zhiguai xiaoshuo shi*, 388; and Wang Guoliang, *Wei Jin nanbeichao zhiguai xiaoshuo yanjiu*, 323. The same narrative appears in the standard twenty-chapter recension of *Soushen ji* (as item 20/8), but Li Jianguo rejects this attribution since all the above-listed versions give *Qi Xie ji* as their source and none gives *Soushen ji* (see XSSJ 764).
2. Specifically, the versions in CXJ 20 (惶遽垂死), TPYL 643 (惶遽畏死), and TPGJ 473 (遑遽畏死). I should point out that here and below, when mentioning variant versions of the same anecdotes, I do so on the assumption that each version that has come down to us was an artefact of social memory; each therefore has value in assessing what people claimed to have happened, or what they thought might possibly happen. It's not a question, then, of trying to ascertain which version was "original" or "correct." For more on this point see Campany, *Signs from the Unseen Realm*, 17–30, and works cited there.
3. Specifically, the versions in YWLJ 97 and TPYL 479, both of which have 昭之曰此畏死也. Incidentally, our waking "theory of mind" has been shown to carry over robustly into our dreams as well; see Kahn and Hobson, "Theory of Mind in Dreaming."
4. In the sense developed in Kohn, "How Dogs Dream," and Kohn, *How Forests Think*.
5. Following Descola (*Beyond Nature and Culture*, 307–35), I see the relationship here as one involving gifting, not exchange. "Unlike exchange, the gift is above all a one-way gesture that consists in abandoning something to someone without expecting any compensation other than that, possibly, of gratitude on the part of the receiver. . . . Reciprocal benefaction is never guaranteed where a gift is concerned" (Descola, 313). But I would add that in China the expectation of a commensurate return has often been stronger than Descola suggests. On the one hand, Dong's initial gesture was not made with the expectation of a return; but on the other hand, the ant king's response to it was, in the Chinese context, hardly unexpected, either (except in the obvious way that he was an ant with extraordinary power to be of assistance).
6. On this concept see the classic discussion in von Uexküll, *Foray into the World of Animals and Humans*, and the use made of it, for example, in Kohn, *How Forests Think*, 84, and Kohn, "How Dogs Dream," 4–5, 7, 9; see also Gallagher, *How the Body Shapes the Mind*, and Noë, *Action in Perception*. Deacon explains it memorably: "Because an organism is the locus of the work that is responsible for generating the constraints that constitute information about its world, what this information can be about is highly limited, specific, and self-centered. Like the treasure hunter with his metal detector, an organism can only obtain information about its environment that its internally generated dynamic processes are sensitive to—von Uexküll's *Umwelt*, the constellation of self-centered species-relevant features of the world" (Deacon, *Incomplete Nature*, 410). See also the excellent discussions in Hoffmeyer, *Biosemiotics*, 171–211; Wheeler, *Whole Creature*, 120–22; and Horowitz, *Inside of a Dog*, 20–32. Central to my approach here is Descola, *Beyond Nature and Culture*.

7. Kohn, "How Dogs Dream," 5. Compare Hoffmeyer: "Processes of sign and meaning cannot, as is often assumed, become criteria for distinguishing between the domains of nature and culture. Rather, cultural sign processes must be regarded as special instances of a more general and extensive biosemiosis that continuously unfolds and acts in the biosphere" (Hoffmeyer, *Biosemiotics*, 4).
8. A sign, for Peirce, is "something which stands to somebody for something in some respect or capacity" (Kohn, *How Forests Think*, 29; Hoffmeyer, *Biosemiotics*, 20; cf. Sherman, *Neither Ghost nor Machine*, 60: "Information is always *significant for* a self *about* its circumstances"). Understood thus, "not all signs have languagelike properties, and . . . not all the beings who use them are human" (Kohn, *How Forests Think*, 29). Peirce distinguished three general classes of signs. *Icons* are usually likenesses of their objects (e.g., photographs). *Indexes*, rather than being likenesses of the objects they represent, point to them (e.g., weathervanes as indices of wind direction). *Symbols* refer to their objects indirectly as a function of their systematic and conventional relationship to other symbols (e.g., words in a human language). "Unlike iconic and indexical modes of reference, which form the bases for all representation in the living world, symbolic reference is, on this planet at least, a form of representation that is unique to humans" (Kohn, *How Forests Think*, 31–32). Or, as Robert Yelle summarized the types, "Icon, index, and symbol denote sign-relations based upon, respectively, qualitative resemblance, existential connection (connection in fact), and arbitrary determination" ("Peircean Icon and the Study of Religion," 241). See also Peirce, *Essential Peirce*, 13–17; Liszka, *General Introduction to the Semeiotic of Charles Sanders Peirce*, 18–52.
9. Compare: "Dreaming is understood to be a privileged mode of communication through which, via souls, contact among beings inhabiting different ontological realms [that is, different *Umwelten*] becomes possible" (Kohn, "How Dogs Dream," 12).
10. On the notion of *affordances* as intended here and below, see chapter 1 and Gibson, "The Theory of Affordances"; Levine, *Forms*, 6–11; and Bird-David, "'Animism' Revisited."
11. On the variability of the forms under which beings appear to people in dreams, see for example Schweitzer, "Phenomenological Study of Dream Interpretation."
12. Compare Kohn, *How Forests Think*, 167.
13. Mittermaier, *Dreams That Matter*, 171, emphasis added.
14. In part I'm using here the language of Eduardo Kohn, who observes that for the Runa people of Ecuador's Upper Amazon "dreams are not representations of the world. Rather, they are events that take place in it. As such, they are not exactly commentaries about the future or the past but, more accurately, form part of a single experience that spans temporal domains and states of consciousness" (Kohn, "How Dogs Dream," 12). It is not (*pace* Bourguignon, "Dreams That Speak") that these dreams come "preinterpreted"—a way of putting it that is still too close to the interpretive, prospective paradigm—but rather that these dreams don't need interpretation in the first place, whether within the dream experience or subsequently.
15. Mittermaier, *Dreams That Matter*, 142. In this paragraph I draw repeatedly on her discussion on pages 140–72. Other useful treatments of this general type of dream include Faure, *Visions of Power*, 128–29 (where he distinguishes "two models" of dreaming, the performative and the hermeneutic; the latter is what was treated in the previous two chapters, and the former is what's treated in this one); Crapanzano, *Hermes' Dilemma*, 244 ("visitational dreams"); Harris, *Dreams and Experience in Classical Antiquity*; Moreira, *Dreams, Visions, and Spiritual Authority in*

Merovingian Gaul; Ewing, "Dreams from a Saint"; Gerona, *Night Journeys*; Cicero, *De divinatione*, 285–87 (two lovely anecdotes).

16. Groark, "Toward a Cultural Phenomenology of Intersubjectivity," 285, emphasis added.
17. On the nature of anecdotes in China, see the essays collected in van Els and Queen, *Between History and Philosophy*, and in Chen and Schaberg, *Idle Talk*.
18. These sorts of anecdotes are often treated by modern scholars as "fiction" not because scholars can demonstrate that that's how they were read at the time they were told and compiled—they can't—but because they "believe that, since the tales themselves cannot be true (given their content), they must be fiction" (Allen, *Shifting Stories*, 33). But, of course, what is believed possible, likely, or conceivable changes over time, a point lost on many historians of what is too neatly segregated off as Chinese "literature."
19. *Zhuangzi jijie* 41–42. I have adapted the translations of Watson (*Complete Works of Chuang Tzu*, 63–65) and Graham (*Chuang-tzu*, 72–73).
20. Compare the remarks in Goldin, "Non-Deductive Argumentation in Early Chinese Philosophy," esp. 49–51.
21. For elaboration of this point, see Campany, *A Garden of Marvels*, xix–xxvi and xxxiv–xxxvii; Campany, *Making Transcendents*, 8–22; and Campany, *Signs from the Unseen Realm*, 14–30. Each anecdote is, to borrow a term from folklore studies, a *memorate*: "a second-, third-, or fourth-hand narrative of events portrayed as having happened to someone in particular, and . . . a narrative that engages issues of sufficient importance to sustain the interest of narrative communities across multiple links in the chain of transmission" (Campany, *Signs from the Unseen Realm*, 17n63).
22. I borrow the phrase, and the argument about why it matters, from Greenblatt, "Touch of the Real."
23. Presumably so named because the gold threads of the bracelets resembled the rhizomes of Solomon's seal, an herb that figured in medical recipes as well as herbal methods of longevity. See Campany, *To Live as Long as Heaven and Earth*, 25–26, 223n323.
24. *A Record of Anomalies* (*Luyi zhuan* 錄異傳) by an unknown compiler (see Campany, *Strange Writing*, 94). The text is preserved in TPGJ 316/7; translation modified from Campany, *A Garden of Marvels*, 21.
25. A term from nineteenth- and early twentieth-century spiritualist discourse, an apport ("what is brought over") is a physical object purported to have been carried over from one dimension to another. See Dodds, *Greeks and the Irrational*, 106. Physical apports have in common with lucid dreams this quality of "bringing over" things from the (ostensibly private) dreaming to the (public) waking state. Addressing experiments in the late 1970s and early 1980s by Keithe Hearne and Stephen LeBerge, in which lucid dreamers carried out preplanned eye-movement signals to indicate when they had entered a lucid dreaming state, Evan Thompson writes: "These ingenious experiments were momentous. They showed that the subjects were genuinely asleep when they signaled their lucid dreams; they enabled subjects to report on their dreams while the dreams were happening, instead of just retrospectively; *they effected a kind of transworld communication from the private dream world to the public waking world*; and they opened up a new way to investigate consciousness whose prospects we've barely begun to tap" (Thompson, *Waking, Dreaming, Being*, 154–55, emphasis added).
26. Poirier, "This is Good Country," 117.

27. This request for pardon 辭謝 is probably for not appearing personally (due to his condition) to present his offerings and request, perhaps also for whatever sin he thought had resulted in his affliction.
28. Diseases were often attributed to the work of demons and gods (this one is termed simply 鬼); this tale is not unusual in that respect.
29. LX 416; TPGJ 318/13; TPYL 743.2b–3a.
30. The arrest implies that the malaria-causing demon was acting illicitly. But in many cases disease-causing agents were seen as operating licitly on the orders of gods. For an example, see Campany, "Taoist Bioethics in the Final Age," 82.
31. The razor is for shaving the head prior to monastic ordination. It functions as a synecdochic suggestion to leave the household, a suggestion on which the protagonist acts.
32. Translation based on source texts in FYZL 22.453b; LX 439; Wang Guoliang, *Mingxiang ji yanjiu*, 101; and Wakatsuki, Hasegawa, and Inagaki, *Hōon jurin no sōgōteki kenkyū*, 154–55. See also Campany, *Signs from the Unseen Realm*, 225.
33. Attributed to *Records of the Hidden and Visible Worlds* (*Youming lu* 幽冥錄) credited to Liu Yiqing 劉義慶 (d. 444) in TPGJ 276/27; also attested in *Yi yuan* 異苑 7/21. The protagonist is one Xu Jing 徐精. On Liu Yiqing, see Zhang Zhenjun, "Observations."
34. *Yi yuan* 7/26; TPYL 703.4a and 398.6b–7a. The protagonist is Guo Dengzhi 郭澄之, who has a brief biography in *Jin shu* 92.2406 (this anecdote does not appear there).
35. *Soushen ji* 10/6; translated in DeWoskin and Crump, *In Search of the Supernatural*, 120.
36. *Lidai sanbao ji* 49:97a–b; *Gaoseng zhuan* 50:370c–371a. Discussed in "Campany, "Buddhist Revelation and Taoist Translation," 5.
37. *Soushen ji* 11/6; translated in DeWoskin and Crump, *In Search of the Supernatural*, 126.
38. Wang Yan's *Mingxiang ji*; translated in Campany, *Signs from the Unseen Realm*, 166.
39. *Youming lu* 243 (LX 309), TPGJ 276/39; translated in Zhang Zhenjun, *Hidden and Visible Realms*, 60.
40. *Numinous Confirmations in Support of Daoism* (*Daojiao lingyan ji* 道教靈驗記) 121.19a–20a, by Du Guangting 杜光庭 (early 10th century). The dead man is Qin Wan 秦萬. On this compilation see Verellen, "Evidential Miracles in Support of Taoism," and Miyazawa, "'Dōkyō reigen ki' ni tsuite.'"
41. *Youming lu* 141 (279–80); translated in Zhang Zhenjun, *Hidden and Visible Realms*, 30. For other examples from the pre-Tang *zhiguai* corpus see Campany, *Strange Writing*, 354.
42. *Jin shu* 88.2285; the story also appears in Gan Bao's *Soushen ji* 15/10; cf. TPGJ 383/4, XSSJ 359–61. Yan Han, renowned in part for the filiality exemplified in this anecdote, was ninth-generation ancestor to Yan Zhitui 顏之推 (531–after 591), who was noted for his essays in the genre of advice to be handed down to his descendants, *Family Instructions of Mr. Yan* (*Yan shi jiaxun* 顏氏家訓). See Dien, *Pei Ch'i shu 45*; Dien, "Yen Chih-t'ui (531–591+)"; Dien, "Custom and Society"; and Teng, *Family Instructions for the Yen Clan*.
43. Operating in the background here are ideas common at the time about why we die when we do and what happens next. See Campany, "Return-from-Death Narratives," and Campany, "Living Off the Books."
44. See, for example, the story of Fan Shi in *Hou Han shu* 81.2677: from within the coffin he halts his own funeral procession (by stopping the coffin's motion) until a distant friend can arrive.

45. Another instance—this one interpreted as a politically relevant omen—is recorded in *Jin shu* 29.907 and *Song shu* 34.1005.
46. Unlike *tuo meng*, which works in only one direction (from the sender of the dream), *chui meng* could also humilifically name the phenomenon from the dreamer's point of view, with the sense that a sage or deity deigned to grant a dream visitation. See for example Liu Xie's 劉勰 (d. after 519) preface to his famous *Wenxin diaolong* 文心雕龍, where he speaks of having been granted a dream of traveling with Confucius (the passage is translated and discussed in Richter, "Empty Dreams and Other Omissions"), and a passage in *Daojiao lingyan ji* (2.9a–10a), in which a princess who'd earlier vowed to sponsor the refurbishing of an abbey is reminded of her vow in a dream she describes as having been "granted" her by the divine Azure Lad.
47. Ritual practices for the sending of long-distance messages via dreams (*oneiropompoi*) in the late antique Mediterranean world included offerings to the moon goddess, the use of demons as message carriers, miniature animals fashioned from wax, a "dream-sending sympathy doll," and a practice involving killing a falcon or a cat, whose spirit then served as dream messenger; lamps factored in many of these methods. See Eitrem, "Dreams and Divination in Magical Ritual," 179–82; Johnston, *Ancient Greek Divination*, 161–66; and Johnston, "Sending Dreams, Restraining Dreams."
48. *Jin shu* 82.2145, "thinking on [his need for] assistance he sends forth dreams" 思佐發夢. Other passages include *Jin shu* 52.1452, 56.1543; *Sanguo zhi* 11.356, 19.570, 21.616, 38.968, 65.1546; and *Nan Qi shu* 54.930.
49. For a Daoist example, see the story of Qin Wan anthologized from Du Guangting's *Daojiao lingyan ji* in *Yunji qiqian* 121.19a–20a, and for a Buddhist one, see the story collected in FYZL 94.980b and TPGJ 134/6. In both cases the deceased person sending the dream is guilty of having cheated in commercial exchanges by falsifying measurements. Other instances include TPGJ 375/19 (from the Tang compilation *Zhitian lu* 芝田錄), TPGJ 439/16 (from FYZL); YWLJ 18.332 (夜託夢以交靈, from Cai Yong's 蔡邕 [d. 192] "Rhapsody on Curbing Excess" ["Jianyi fu" 檢逸賦], on which see CL, 64: here we have the not unexpected notion that the sending of a dream results in an intercourse of spirits between the sender and the receiver); and *Shishuo xinyu* 2/97, where, in a commentarial passage not translated by Mather, we find cited a commentary to the Buddhist polemical compilation *Bianzheng lun* (52:539c) that recounts the story of how Kong Qiong 孔瓊, although not a Buddhist, accompanied others to a temple on Buddha's birthday to release living beings and perform the penitence ritual. After his death he "sends a dream" to his son to inform him that because of these acts he has been released from suffering in the purgatories. The passage cites Kong's *biezhuan* 別傳 as its source.
50. *Soushen ji* 13/13; XSSJ 449–50.
51. Powerful examples of dreams launching new socio-religious movements in the waking world are treated in Burridge, *Mambu*, and Burridge, *New Heaven, New Earth*. Burridge shows that "issues of status, politics, and power are inevitably implicated in the passage of dreams outwards from a reported individual experience and in their diffusion and potentially transformative impact on a given group or society" (Tonkinson, "Ambrymese Dreams," 88). Dream reports can make or break leaders' reputations as well (Robbins, "Dreaming and the Defeat of Charisma"; Schnepel, "In Sleep a King"). Compare the role played by dreams in certain societies of "potentiating" knowledge gained while awake; see, e.g., Devereux, *Ethnopsychoanalysis*, 249–64.
52. The dates of his birth and death continue to be debated. See CL, 1407–19.

53. Probably the most famous telling of this story is the one preserved in *Traditional Tales and Recent Accounts*; see SSHY, 190–91, and compare *Jin shu* 49.1374. Some accounts have him strumming a different tune. See CL, 1409–10, and Holzman, *La vie et la pensée de Hi K'ang*, 49–51. Although it's sometimes asserted that a zither tune by this name predated Ji Kang, I find no evidence for this. HYD 1266B defines the tune in terms of its origin with Ji Kang, citing his *Jin shu* biography. The other sources cited there suggest it was most famous for having been kept secret and *not* transmitted by Ji Kang, thus bruited in the world for its beauty yet forever cut off from being known (this is the esoteric dynamic!)—except occasionally through dreams, as we'll see below. Ji Kang left a rhapsody on the zither; in it he mentions the Guangling Melody, giving it pride of place in a list of songs. See Knechtges, *Wen xuan* 3:297.
54. *Yi yuan* 7/14; translation modified from Campany, *A Garden of Marvels*, 94. For an annotated transcription of the tale as it appears in the Dunhuang manuscript S2072, which cites *Yi yuan* as its source, see Zheng Binglin, *Dunhuang xieben jiemeng shu*, 308. For the digital version of this manuscript made available by the International Dunhuang Project, see http://idp.bl.uk/database/oo_scroll_h.a4d?uid=2093002176;recnum=2071;index=3 [accessed March 3, 2020]. In a different story Ji is given the song by a ghost who is drawn to approach by the sound of Ji's skillful zither playing. The ancient but unidentified ghost, appearing not in a dream but in a waking visitation, after listening appreciatively takes up Ji's instrument and plays several unfamiliar tunes, including the Guangling. These he teaches to Ji on the condition he never transmit them. See Ji Kang's biography in *Jin shu* 49.1374, as well as *Linggui zhi* 靈鬼志 8 (LX 198–99), attested in TPGJ 317 and TPYL 579. The tale is translated in CCT, 123–24.
55. *Youming lu* 222 (LX 302–3, based on TPGJ 324/4); translated in Zhang Zhenjun, *Hidden and Visible Realms*, 165–66.
56. T 85:1425b–1426a. The Dunhuang manuscript version is embedded in Pelliot 3920. In all extant versions, the scripture is quite short and contains a list of names of Buddhas and bodhisattvas, the promise that reciting the scripture will save the reciter from various perils, and verses praising Sound Observer. See Makita, *Rikuchō kōitsu Kanzeon ōkenki no kenkyū*, 159–78; Makita, *Gikyō kenkyū*, 272–89 (which includes a transcription of the Turfan manuscript version); and Campany, "Buddhist Revelation and Taoist Translation," 10–13.
57. Most versions say outright that he dreamed the transmission, others that it came in a sudden experience that was "like a dream" 如夢 or "indistinct, like a dream" 依稀如夢. The former include FYZL 17 (53:411b–c), *Xu gaoseng zhuan* 29 (50:692c–693a), *Shijia fangzhi* 3 (51:972b), *Kaiyuan Shijiao lu* 10 (55:581b), *Bianzheng lun* 7 (52:537b–c), *Wei shu* 84.1860, *Bei shi* 30.1099, and TPGJ 111/14 (where the tale is attributed, probably wrongly, to *Mingxiang ji*). The latter include FYZL 14 (53:389c), *Ji shenzhou sanbao gantong lu* 2 (52:427a–b), and *Da Tang neidian lu* 10 (55:339a–b). To my knowledge, *Beishan lu* 7 (52:619c) is the only version of the tale that frames the encounter with the monk neither as a dream nor as "like a dream"; there, the mysterious monk simply appears, transmits the sutra, then vanishes.
58. See Campany, "Buddhist Revelation and Taoist Translation," 12–13.
59. To mention just one example, Du Guangting included in his compilation of pro-Daoist miracle tales an instance in which a pious young girl, who habitually burned incense and lit votive lamps before the household icon of Xuanyuan 玄元, dreamed that Lord Lao 老君, accompanied by a retinue, came and "orally bestowed" on her a *Divine Scripture of the Nine Celestial Kings* (*Jiu tianwang shen jing* 九天王神經).

See *Daojiao lingyan ji* 10.3a–6b and (for what is merely a brief extract) *Yunji qiqian* 119:15a–b.

60. For Buddhist examples see Campany, *Signs from the Unseen Realm*, 162–63, 240–41. For a Daoist one see *Yunji qiqian* 117.14a–b.
61. See Campany, *Signs from the Unseen Realm*, 63–67.
62. Coleridge's famous preface to his poem "Kubla Khan," which he maintained to have come to him in a dream-like reverie (he writes of himself in the third person): "On awakening he appeared to himself to have a distinct recollection of the whole, and taking his pen, ink, and paper, instantly and eagerly wrote down the lines that are here preserved. At this moment he was unfortunately called out by a person on business from Porlock, and detained by him above an hour, and on his return to his room, found, to his no small surprise and mortification, that though he still retained some vague and dim recollection of the general purport of the vision, yet, with the exception of some eight or ten scattered lines and images, all the rest had passed away like the images on the surface of a stream into which a stone had been cast, but, alas! without the after restoration of the latter!"
63. See Campany, *Signs from the Unseen Realm*, 212–14.
64. Based on FYZL 95.988b. The story is further discussed, and cognate versions listed, in Campany, *Signs from the Unseen Realm*, 132–33.
65. A few examples: *Jin shu* 29.907, 88.2285; *Song shu* 34.1005 (a nice instance), 79.2037; *Nan Qi shu* 3.43, 45.791 (everyone in a city has the same dream); *Soushen ji* 10/11; the story (from an indeterminate early medieval compilation) translated in Campany, *A Garden of Marvels*, 129–30. Slightly different is the phenomenon one researcher terms "telepathic *rêve à deux*," "when two or more individuals who are unknown to each other effect a psychological relationship in their seemingly separate dreams which seems to transcend the conventionally conceived barriers of time, space and ordinary sense perception" (Eisenbud, "Dreams of Two Patients," 262).
66. These lines appear in the version preserved as item 20/8 in the received *Soushen ji*; in YWLJ 97.1689 they are attributed to *Qi Xie ji*.
67. Compare Bird-David, "'Animism' Revisited," 75.
68. Hallowell, "Ojibwa Ontology, Behavior, and World View," 54–55. For an astute unpacking and appreciation of Hallowell's essay and its aims, see Strong, "A. Irving Hallowell and the Ontological Turn."
69. Switching to the autonym now used by these indigenous people of what's now Canada and the northern United States.
70. *Not*, however, *supernatural* person. See Bird-David, "'Animism' Revisited," 71, and Astor-Aguilera, "Maya-Mesoamerican Polyontologies," 143, as over against Lohmann, "The Supernatural Is Everywhere."
71. Bird-David, "'Animism' Revisited," 74.
72. *Lieyi zhuan* 39 (LX 144; TPYL 51.6a–b).
73. Bird-David, "'Animism' Revisited," 77, substituting "stone" where she writes "trees."
74. Sahlins, *How "Natives" Think*, 153.
75. There were stories circulating in this period, a few of which have survived, that can be read as suggesting precisely this. See Campany, "'Religious' as a Category," 363–66.
76. *Soushen ji* 4/20; XSSJ 109–10; TPGJ 294/15.
77. See Campany, "'Religious' as a Category," 346–49.
78. *Taiping huanyu ji* 106.8b.
79. BTSC 160.17a–b, attributing the text to *Liexian zhuan* 列仙傳, obviously an error for *Lieyi zhuan* 列異傳 (as noted by Li Jianguo, XSSJ 109).

80. The name might well be an error for Yin Zhongkan, a noted intellectual figure. See Zürcher, *Buddhist Conquest of China*, 213.
81. *Yi yuan* 7/28. The text continues with another version of the story, not relevant here. See Campany, *A Garden of Marvels*, 97–98.
82. *Soushen ji* 16/8, translated in DeWoskin and Crump, *In Search of the Supernatural*, 187; TPGJ 317/4; FYZL 32 (53:536a–b). For further discussion of this scenario, with examples, see Campany, *Strange Writing*, 377–84, and Campany, "Ghosts Matter," 26–28.
83. *Yi yuan* 7/19. Compare a story in which a fisherman ties up one night to an old sunken boat, said to be one of Cao Cao's fleet, whose top protrudes from the water when the river runs low. He hears the sounds of string and wind instruments and detects an unusual fragrance. The moment he falls asleep he dreams of someone racing toward him, shouting, "Do not approach the royal entertainers!" 勿近官妓. YWLJ 44.794 (citing *Xu soushen ji*); TPGJ 322/7 (citing *Guang gujin wuxing ji* 廣古今五行記); TPYL 399.9a (included in LX 204, citing *Linggui zhi* 靈魂志—this version adds that the fisherman woke with a start and hurriedly moved his boat); *Soushen houji* 6/3; XSSJ 569; and Campany, *Strange Writing*, 370.
84. *Jin shu* 67.1795, which is cited three times in TPYL (71.4b–5a, 885.2a–b, and 890.2a). One of these texts probably was based on the other—the *Jin shu* passage may well have been based on the *Yi yuan* tale (historians sometimes used *zhiguai* narratives as sources, and vice versa). TPGJ 294/2 alludes to the story, citing a text simply titled *Zhiguai* 志怪, as does TPGJ 422/3, citing a text simply titled 傳奇. The story seems to have functioned as a stock example of the hazards of idly testing the boundary between the visible and normally invisible worlds. On Wen Qiao see SSHY, 599–600, and CL, 1309–12. On *feng* 風 as a pathogen, see Chen Hsiu-fen, "Wind Malady as Madness in Medieval China."
85. Marquis Jiang was an important regional god in the southeast, mentioned in passages across many texts. See Lin Fu-shih, "The Cult of Jiang Ziwen in Medieval China," and Miyakawa Hisayuki, "Local Cults around Mount Lu."
86. *Yi yuan* 5/10, also anthologized in TPGJ 295.6 and TPYL 350.2a. Xie Lingyun 謝靈運 (385–443), a lyric poet, was descended from a noted northern émigré family of the southern aristocracy. See Owen, ed., *Cambridge History of Chinese Literature*, 1:234–38, and CL, 1599–1623.
87. *Yingmin* 營民 or *yinghu* 營户 refers not to people on a camping holiday but to dispossessed families or individuals, often refugees, who were detained to work on the lands of their captors. It was a status only slightly above that of slave. See HYD 7.266a, 267a.
88. From the compilation *Shuyi ji* by Zu Chongzhi (429–500). LX 192; TPYL 910.4a. Compare the different version in TPGJ 131/17.
89. XSSJ, 535–36. Cited from *Xu soushen ji* in TPYL 909.7b.
90. On the enormous body of fox lore, see Chan, *Discourse on Foxes and Ghosts*; Huntington, *Alien Kind*; Huntington, "Foxes and Sex in Late Imperial Chinese Narrative"; Kang, *Cult of the Fox*; Kang, "The Fox [*hu* 狐] and the Barbarian [*hu* 胡]"; Heine, "Putting the 'Fox' Back in the 'Wild Fox Kōan'"; and Li Shouju, *Huxian xinyang yu huli gushi*.
91. An echo of the *Zhuangzi* butterfly dream is detectable here, as "Zhuangzi" describes himself during the dream as "happy with himself and doing as he pleased, not knowing he was Zhou" 自喻適志與, 不知周也.
92. Another intertextual echo of the butterfly dream parable. There, "Zhuangzi" after waking becomes momentarily confused about whether he had been Zhuangzi

dreaming he was a butterfly or whether he was now a butterfly dreaming he was Zhuangzi. But the *Zhuangzi* passage, like this story, doesn't leave things there.

93. The story, minus Duan's closing note about its source, is anthologized in TPGJ 282/8. My summary draws on the translation in Reed, *A Tang Miscellany*, 136. The story is internally dated to 837.
94. Kohn, "How Dogs Dream," 7.
95. The text was assembled by Liu Xiang (77 BCE–6 BCE) from earlier bits; how much earlier is hard to say. See Hutton, *Xunzi*, xviii–xix, and ECT, 178.
96. *Xunzi jijie* 164. Adapting the translations in Hutton, *Xunzi*, 76, and Slingerland, *Mind and Body*, 112.
97. Slingerland, *Mind and Body*, 111.
98. For elaboration of these points, with citations of supporting scholarship, see Campany, *Making Transcendents*, 8–22, and Campany, *Signs from the Unseen Realm*, 23–30.

Epilogue

1. It is often cited by scholars who cite little else from the Chinese archive. See, for example, O'Flaherty, *Dreams, Illusion and Other Realities*, 250, and Thompson, *Waking, Dreaming, Being*, 198–202. O'Flaherty doesn't venture much of an interpretation, and, to my mind, Thompson's interpretation fails to grasp the story's point.
2. *Zhuangzi jijie* 26–27; translation based on Graham, *Chuang-tzu*, 61, and Watson, *Complete Works of Chuang Tzu*, 49.
3. Schwitzgebel, "Zhuangzi's Attitude Toward Language," 86.
4. Harbsmeier, *Language and Logic*, 257. Interpretations of the passage that I have found persuasive include Wai-yee Li, "Dreams of Interpretation," 30–31; Kupperman, "Spontaneity and Education of the Emotions in the *Zhuangzi*," 189; Hansen, "Guru or Skeptic," 148; Chong, *Zhuangzi's Critique of the Confucians*, 46–50; and especially Lusthaus, "Aporetics Ethics in the *Zhuangzi*," 165–72. My reading is also informed by Puett, "Nothing Can Overcome Heaven," although he does not discuss this passage specifically.
5. See Raphals, "Debates about Fate in Early China," 33.
6. A famed sword, or swordmaker, of legend, associated with the king of Wu. On sword lore of the ancient kingdoms of Wu and Yue, see Milburn, *Glory of Yue*, 273–93; Milburn, "The Weapons of Kings," and Brindley, *Ancient China and the Yue*, 181–85.
7. *Zhuangzi jijie* 64; translation largely following Watson, *Complete Works of Chuang Tzu*, 85.
8. *Zhuangzi jijie* 59; translation from Watson, *Complete Works of Chuang Tzu*, 81.
9. Here is 惡之 again: "do you detest it/find it odious/find it disgusting/are you nauseated by it" or perhaps even, in a demonological and ritual context (but not in *Zhuangzi*), "do you regard it as polluting?"
10. *Zhuangzi jijie* 63; translation modified from Puett, "Nothing Can Overcome Heaven," 253, and Watson, *Complete Works of Chuang Tzu*, 84. The same object-verb phrase occurs at the end of chapter 3, where it names a process playfully imagined as being divinely helped along: "When the master arrived, it was his time; when he left, the master did so compliantly. Dwelling in timeliness and located in compliance, he could not be penetrated by sadness or joy. The ancients called this 'being unleashed by the gods'" 適來，夫子時也，適去，夫子順也．安時而處順，哀樂不能入也，古者謂是帝之縣解 (*Zhuangzi jijie* 31; translation modified from Saussy, *Translation as Citation*, 91). Another Zhuangzian figure for the same idea is the "fasting of the mind" (*xinzhai* 心齋)

mentioned in chapter 4. Note Erica Fox Brindley's provocative discussion of this idea as involving, first, the metaphorical construction of the self as a receptacle and, second, the emptying out from it of one's own priorities and notions, allowing for "the collection of *external* agency *within* the receptacle of the body. . . . He who fasts [the mind] allows for the emptying of *qi* . . . [from] the body. Being stripped of its operational fuel, the body no longer has anything by which to guide itself. It then becomes possible for . . . the Dao, playfully . . . suggested in this passage as an 'agent, envoy, or assignment' (*shi* 使), to collect there and replace it as the motivational agent" (Brindley, *Individualism in Early China*, 56, emphasis added; note her comments on the sense of 使 in this passage on page 166n6).

11. Kern, "Early Chinese Divination and Its Rhetoric," 270–71; Sanft, "Edict of Monthly Ordinances."

Bibliography

Works Cited by Abbreviation

BDL de Crespigny, Rafe, ed. *A Biographical Dictionary of Later Han to the Three Kingdoms (23–220 AD)*. Leiden: E. J. Brill, 2007.

BDQ Loewe, Michael, ed. *A Biographical Dictionary of the Qin, Former Han and Xin Periods (221 BC–AD 24)*. Leiden: E. J. Brill, 2000.

BTSC *Beitang shuchao* 北堂書鈔. Compiled by Yu Shinan 虞世南. Facsimile reprint in 2 vols. of 1888 edition. Taipei: Wenhai chubanshe, 1962. Cited by scroll and folio page number.

CCT Kao, Karl S. Y., ed. *Classical Chinese Tales of the Supernatural and the Fantastic: Selections from the Third to the Tenth Century*. Bloomington: Indiana University Press, 1985.

CL Knechtges, David R., and Taiping Chang, eds. *Ancient and Early Medieval Chinese Literature: A Reference Guide*. 4 vols. Leiden: E. J. Brill, 2010–14.

CXJ *Chuxue ji* 初學記. Compiled by Xu Jian 徐堅 et al. 3 vols., continuously paginated. Beijing: Zhonghua shuju, 1962. Cited by juan and page number.

DZ *Zhengtong daozang* 正統道藏. Shanghai: Shangwu, 1923–26; reprinted Taipei: Xinwenfeng, 1977. Texts in this canon are cited first by the number assigned them in Schipper and Verellen, *The Taoist Canon*, then by scroll and folio page number.

ECT Loewe, Michael, ed. *Early Chinese Texts: A Bibliographical Guide*. Berkeley: Society for the Study of Early China, 1993.

FYZL *Fayuan zhulin* 法苑珠林 by Daoshi 道世. T 2122.

HDW *Hanji dianzi wenxian ciliao ku* 漢籍電子文獻資料庫 (Scripta Sinica database). Academia Sinica 中央研究院, Taipei, Taiwan. http://sinology.teldap.tw/index.php/a/material

HWCS *Han Wei congshu* 漢魏叢書. Compiled by Cheng Rong 程榮. Printed in 1592. Place of publication and printing house unknown; copy held at the Joseph Regenstein Library (East Asia Collection), University of Chicago.

HYD *Hanyu dacidian* 漢語大辭典. Edited by Luo Zhufeng 罗竹风. Shanghai: Shanghai cishu chubanshe, 1986.

LX Lu Xun 魯迅. *Gu xiaoshuo gouchen* 古小說鉤沈. Beijing: Renmin wenxue chubanshe, 1954.

P Prefix to the numbers assigned to manuscripts in the Pelliot collection, Bibliothèque nationale de France. These were accessed electronically through the digital library of the Bibliothèque nationale and its partners: gallica.bnf.fr.

S Prefix to the numbers assigned to manuscripts in the Stein collection, British Museum. These were accessed electronically through the website of the International Dunhuang Project: idp.bl.uk.

SSHY Mather, Richard B. *Shih-shuo Hsin-yü: A New Account of Tales of the World*.

2nd edition. Ann Arbor: Center for Chinese Studies, University of Michigan, 2002.

T *Taishō shinshū daizōkyō* 大正新脩大藏經. Edited by Takakusu Junjirō 高楠順次郎, Watanabe Kaigyōku 渡辺海旭, and Ono Gemmyō 小野玄妙. 100 vols. Tokyo: Taishō Issaikyō Kankōkai, 1924–1935; reprinted Taipei: Xinwen feng, 1983. In citing texts from this canon I give the romanized title, volume number, and page numbers assigned to them in it.

TPGJ *Taiping guangji* 太平廣記. Compiled by Li Fang 李昉 et al. 4 vols. Shanghai: Shanghai guji chubanshe, 1990. Cited by scroll and serial position of the cited item in the scroll (e.g., "387.1" indicates the first passage anthologized in scroll 387).

TPYL *Taiping yulan* 太平御覽. Compiled by Li Fang 李昉 et al. Facsimile reprint of Shangwu yinshuguan 1935 printing from a Song copy. 4 vols. Beijing: Zhonghua shuju, 1992. Cited by scroll and folio page number.

XSSJ Li Jianguo 李劍國. *Xinji Soushen ji, xinji Soushen houji* 新輯搜神記, 新輯搜神後記. 2 vols., continuously paginated. Beijing: Zhonghua shuju, 2007.

YWLJ *Yiwen leiju* 藝文類聚. Compiled by Ouyang Xun 歐陽詢 et al. Modern edition by Wang Shaoying 王紹楹. 2 vols., continuously paginated. Beijing: Zhonghua shuju, 1965. Cited by scroll and page number.

ZT Durrant, Stephen, Wai-yee Li, and David Schaberg. *Zuo Tradition: Zuozhuan*. 3 vols., continuously paginated. Seattle: University of Washington Press, 2016.

Works Cited by Title

The dynastic histories consulted are all in the widely available editions published by Zhonghua shuju in Beijing. I do not separately list their places or dates of publication.

Apidamo dapipo shalun 阿毘達摩大毘婆沙論. T 1545.

Baopuzi neipian jiaoshi 抱朴子內篇校釋. Edited by Wang Ming 王明. 2nd edition. Beijing: Zhonghua shuju, 1985.

Bei shi 北史 by Li Yanshou 李延壽.

Beishan lu 北山錄. T 2113.

Bencao gangmu 本草綱目. Hanji dianzi wenxian ciliao ku 漢籍電子文獻資料庫 (Scripta Sinica) electronic edition.

Bianzheng lun 辯正論. T 2110.

Bowu zhi 博物志 by Zhang Hua 張華. *Bowu zhi jiaozheng* 博物志校正. Edited by Fan Ning 范寧. Beijing: Zhonghua shuju, 1980.

Da baoji jing 大寶積經. T 310.

Da Tang neidian lu 大唐內典錄 by Daoxuan 道宣. T 2149.

Da zhidu lun 大智度論. T 1509.

Daojiao lingyan ji 道教靈驗記 by Du Guangting 杜光庭. DZ 590 + *Yunji qiqian* scrolls 117–21.

Dongming ji 洞冥記. See Wang Guoliang, *Han Wu Dongming ji yanjiu*.

Encyclopedia of Buddhism. Edited by Robert E. Buswell, Jr. New York: Macmillan, 2004.

Fangguang banruo jing 放光般若經. T 221.

Fengsu tongyi 風俗通義 by Ying Shao 應劭. *Fengsu tongyi jiaozhu* 風俗通義校注. Edited by Wang Liqi 王利器. 2 vols., continuously paginated. Beijing: Zhonghua shuju, 1981.

Gaoseng zhuan 高僧傳 by Huijiao 慧皎. T 2059.
Gaowang Guanshiyin jing 高王觀世音經. T 2898.
Han shu 漢書 by Ban Gu 班固, Ban Biao 班彪, et al.
Hanyu dacidian 漢語大辭典. Edited by Luo Zhufeng 罗竹风. Shanghai: Shanghai cishu chubanshe, 1986.
Hongming ji 弘明集 by Sengyou 僧祐. T 2102.
Hou Han shu 後漢書 by Fan Ye 范曄.
Huainanzi jishi 淮南子集釋. Edited by He Ning 何寧. 3 vols., continuously paginated. Beijing: Zhonghua shuju, 1998.
Huangdi neijing lingshu 黄帝内經靈樞. See Unschuld, *Huang Di Nei Jing Ling Shu*.
Huangtian Shangqing jinque dijun lingshu ciwen shangjing 皇天上清金闕帝君靈書紫文上經. DZ 639.
Ji shenzhou sanbao gantong lu 集神州三寶感通錄 by Daoxuan 道宣. T 2106.
Jin shu 晉書 by Fang Xuanling 房玄齡 et al.
Jing Chu suishi ji 荊楚歲時記 by Zong Lin 宗懍. In *Suishi xisu ziliao huibian* 歲時習俗資料彙編. Taipei: Yiwen yinshuguan, 1970. Accessed via Hanji dianzi wenxian ciliao ku 漢籍電子文獻資料庫 (Scripta Sinica) electronic edition.
Kaiyuan shijiao lu 開元釋教錄 by Zhisheng 智昇. T 2154.
Liang shu 梁書 by Yao Silian 姚思廉.
Lidai sanbao ji 歷代三寶紀 by Fei Zhangfang 費長房. T 2034.
Lieyi zhuan 列異傳 by Cao Pi 曹丕. LX.
Liezi jishi 列子集釋. Edited by Yang Bojun 楊伯峻. Beijing: Zhonghua shuju, 1979.
Linggui zhi 靈鬼志 by a Mr. Xun 荀氏. LX.
Lunheng jiaoshi 論衡校釋. Edited by Huang Hui 黄暉. Beijing: Zhonghua shuju, 1990.
Lunyu jijie yishu 論語集解義疏. Compiled by Huang Kan 皇侃. 2 vols. Taipei: Guangwen shuju, 1969.
Luyi zhuan 錄異傳. LX.
Mingxiang ji 冥祥記 by Wang Yan 王琰. See Campany, *Signs from the Unseen Realm*.
Mohe seng qilü 摩訶僧祇律. T 1425.
Nan Qi shu 南齊書 by Xiao Zixian 蕭子顯.
Nan shi 南史 by Li Yanshou 李延壽 and Li Dashi 李大師.
Pusa shuomeng jing 菩薩説夢經. T 310, 11:80c–91b.
Qi min yao shu 齊民要術 by Jia Sixie 賈思勰. Congshu jicheng 叢書集成 edition. Shanghai [?]: Shangwu yinshuguan, 1939.
Qi Xie ji 齊諧記 by Dongyang Wuyi 東陽无疑. LX.
Qianfu lun jian jiaozheng 潛夫論箋校正. Edited by Peng Duo 彭鐸, annotated by Wang Jipei 汪繼培. Beijing: Zhonghua shuju, 1985.
Sanguo zhi 三國志 by Chen Shou 陳壽.
Shanhai jing jiaozhu 山海經校注. Edited by Yuan Ke 袁珂. Shanghai: Shanghai guji chubanshe, 1980.
Shanjianlü piposha 善見律毘婆沙. T 1462.
Shenxian zhuan 神仙傳 by Ge Hong 葛洪. See Campany, *To Live as Long as Heaven and Earth*.
Shijia fangzhi 釋迦方志 by Daoxuan 道宣. T 2088.
Shishuo xinyu by Liu Yiqing 劉義慶. *Shishuo xinyu jianshu* 世説新語箋疏. Edited by Yu Jiaxi 余嘉錫. 2nd ed. Shanghai: Shanghai guji. Accessed through HDW.
Shiyi ji 拾遺記 by Wang Jia 王嘉. Zengding Han Wei congshu 增訂漢魏叢 edition.
Shuihudi Qin mu zhujian 睡虎地秦墓竹簡. Edited by Yu Haoliang 于豪亮 et al. Beijing: Wenwu chubanshe, 1990.

Shuijing zhu 水經注 by Li Daoyuan 酈道元. Edited by Yang Shoujing 楊守敬 and Xiong Huizhen 熊會貞. 3 vols., continuously paginated. Nanjing: Jiangsu guji chubanshe, 1989.
Shuyi ji 述異記 by Zu Chongzhi 祖沖之. LX.
Song shu 宋書 by Shen Yue 沈約.
Soushen houji 搜神後記 by Tao Qian 陶潛. Congshu jicheng 叢書集成 edition. Shanghai: Commercial Press, 1935–37. *See also* XSSJ.
Soushen ji 搜神記 by Gan Bao 干寶. *Xinjiao Soushen ji* 新校搜神記. Edited by Yang Jialuo 楊家駱. Taipei: Shijie shuju, 1982. See also XSSJ.
Sui shu 隋書 by Wei Zheng 魏徵.
Taiping huanyu ji 太平寰宇記 by Yue Shi 樂史. Ming-period 烏絲欄鈔本 woodblock print edition. Accessed through HDW.
Wei shu 魏書 by Wei Shou 魏收.
Weimojie suoshuo jing 維摩詰所說經. T 475.
Xu gaoseng zhuan 續高僧傳 by Daoxuan 道宣. T 2060.
Xu Soushen ji. See *Soushen houji*.
Xunzi jijie 荀子集解. Compiled by Wang Xianqian 王先謙. 2 vols., continuously paginated. Beijing: Zhonghua shuju, 1987.
Yanzi chunqiu 晏子春秋. See Milburn, *Spring and Autumn Annals of Master Yan*.
Yi yuan 異苑 by Liu Jingshu 劉敬叔. In *Xuejin taoyuan* 學津討原, compiled by Zhang Pengyi 張鵬一. Facsimile reprint in *Baibu congshu jicheng* 百部叢書集成, edited by Yan Yiping 嚴一萍. Taipei: Yiwen yinshuguan, 1966.
Youming lu 幽冥錄 by Liu Yiqing 劉義慶. LX.
Yunji qiqian 雲笈七籤. DZ 1032.
Zhancha shaneyebao jing 占察善惡業報經. T 839.
Zhen'gao 真誥. DZ 1016.
Zheng fahua jing 正法華經. T 263.
Zhongguan lun shu 中觀論疏. T 1824.
Zhouli zhushu 周禮注疏. Shanghai: Shanghai guji chubanshe, 1990.
Zhouyi zhushu 周易注疏. Shanghai: Shanghai guji chubanshe, 1990.
Zhuangzi jijie. 莊子集解. Edited by Wang Xianqian 王先謙 and Liu Wu 劉武. Beijing: Zhonghua shuju, 1987.
Zhubing yuanhou lun jiaozhu 諸病源候論校注. Accessed through HDW.

Works Cited by Author

Africa, Thomas W. "Psychohistory, Ancient History, and Freud: The Descent into Avernus." *Arethusa* 12 (1979): 5–34.
Allan, Sarah. *Buried Ideas: Legends of Abdication and Ideal Government in Early Chinese Bamboo-Slip Manuscripts*. Albany: State University of New York Press, 2015.
Allen, Sarah M. *Shifting Stories: History, Gossip, and Lore in Narratives from Tang Dynasty China*. Cambridge, MA: Harvard University Asia Center, 2014.
Appadurai, Arjun. "Disjuncture and Difference in the Global Cultural Economy." *Theory, Culture & Society* 7 (1990): 295–310.
Aristotle. *The Complete Works of Aristotle: The Revised Oxford Translation*. Edited by Jonathan Barnes. 2 vols. Princeton: Princeton University Press, 1984.

———. *On the Soul, Parva Naturalia, On Breath*. With an English translation by W. S. Hett. Loeb Classical Library 288. 2nd edition. Cambridge, MA: Harvard University Press, 1957.

Armstrong, Nancy, and Leonard Tennenhouse. "The Interior Difference: A Brief Genealogy of Dreams, 1650–1717." *Eighteenth-Century Studies* 23 (1990): 458–78.

Artemidorus. *See* Harris-McCoy, Daniel E.

Assmann, Aleida. "Engendering Dreams: The Dreams of Adam and Eve in Milton's *Paradise Lost*." In *Dream Cultures: Explorations in the Comparative History of Dreaming*, edited by David Shulman and Guy G. Stroumsa, 288–302. New York: Oxford University Press, 1999.

Astor-Aguilera, Miguel. "Maya-Mesoamerican Polyontologies: Breath and Indigenous American Vital Essences." In *Rethinking Relations and Animism: Personhood and Materiality*, edited by Miguel Astor-Aguilera and Graham Harvey, 133–55. London and New York: Routledge, 2018.

Astor-Aguilera, Miguel, and Graham Harvey, eds. *Rethinking Relations and Animism: Personhood and Materiality*. London and New York: Routledge, 2018.

Austin, J. L. *How to Do Things with Words*. Cambridge, MA: Harvard University Press, 1962.

Averroes. *Epitome of "Parva Naturalia."* Translated and edited by Harry Blumberg. Cambridge, MA: Medieval Academy of America, 1961.

Balazs, Stephan. "Der Philosoph Fan Dschen und sein Traktat gegen den Buddhismus." *Sinica* 7 (1932): 220–34.

Bapat, P. V., and Akira Hirakawa. *Shan-Chien-P'i-P'o-Sha: A Chinese Version by Saṅghabhadra of Samantapāsādikā*. Poona: Bhandarkar Oriental Research Institute, 1970.

Barrett, Deirdre. "An Evolutionary Theory of Dreams and Problem-Solving." In *The New Science of Dreaming*, Volume 3: *Cultural and Theoretical Perspectives*, edited by Deirdre Barrett and Patrick McNamara, 133–53. Westport, CT: Praeger, 2007.

Barrett, Deirdre, and Patrick McNamara, eds. *The New Science of Dreaming*, Volume 3: *Cultural and Theoretical Perspectives*. Westport, CT: Praeger, 2007.

Barton, Tamsyn S. *Power and Knowledge: Astrology, Physiognomics, and Medicine under the Roman Empire*. Ann Arbor: University of Michigan Press, 1994.

Basso, Ellen B. "The Implications of a Progressive Theory of Dreaming." In *Dreaming: Anthropological and Psychological Interpretations*, edited by Barbara Tedlock, 86–104. 2nd edition. Santa Fe: School of American Research Press, 1992.

Bateson, Gregory. *Steps to an Ecology of Mind*. 2nd edition. Chicago: University of Chicago Press, 2000.

Bauer, Wolfgang. "Chinese Glyphomancy (*ch'ai-tzu*) and Its Uses in Present-Day Taiwan." In *Legend, Lore, and Religion in China*, edited by Sarah Allan and Alvin P. Cohen, 71–96. San Francisco: Chinese Materials Center, 1979.

Beard, Mary. "Cicero and Divination: The Formation of a Latin Discourse." *Journal of Roman Studies* 76 (1986): 33–46.

Beaulieu-Prévost, Dominic, Catherine Charneau Simard, and Antonio Zadra. "Making Sense of Dream Experiences: A Multidimensional Approach to Beliefs about Dreams." *Dreaming* 19.3 (2009): 119–34.

Beecroft, Alexander. *Authorship and Cultural Identity in Early Greece and China: Patterns of Literary Circulation*. Cambridge: Cambridge University Press, 2010.

Bennett, Jane. *The Enchantment of Modern Life: Attachments, Crossings, and Ethics*. Princeton: Princeton University Press, 2001.

Berkowitz, Alan J. *Patterns of Disengagement: The Practice and Portrayal of Reclusion in Early Medieval China*. Stanford: Stanford University Press, 2000.

Bird-David, Nurit. "'Animism' Revisited: Personhood, Environment, and Relational Epistemology." *Current Anthropology* 40, special issue 1 (February 1999): S67–S91.

Black, Joshua, et al. "Who Dreams of the Deceased? The Roles of Dream Recall, Grief Intensity, Attachment, and Openness to Experience." *Dreaming* 29.1 (2019): 57–78.

Bodde, Derk. *Festivals in Classical China: New Year and Other Annual Observances during the Han Dynasty, 206 B.C.–A.D. 220*. Princeton: Princeton University Press, 1975.

Bodiford, William M. "Introduction." In *Going Forth: Visions of Buddhist Vinaya*, edited by William M. Bodiford, 1–16. Honolulu: University of Hawai'i Press, 2005.

Bokenkamp, Stephen R. *Ancestors and Anxiety: Daoism and the Birth of Rebirth in China*. Berkeley: University of California Press, 2007.

———. *Early Daoist Scriptures*. Berkeley: University of California Press, 1997.

———. "Image Work: Dream Interpretation in a Late Fourth Century Daoist Text." Paper presented at the workshop Visions of the Night: Dreams, Dreamers, and Religion in Medieval Societies, University of Southern California, April 2009.

Bourguignon, Erika. "Dreams and Altered States of Consciousness in Anthropological Research." In *Psychological Anthropology*, edited by F. L. K. Hsu, 403–34. Cambridge, MA: Schenkmann, 1972.

———. "Dreams That Speak: Experience and Interpretation." In *Dreaming and the Self: New Perspectives on Subjectivity, Identity, and Emotion*, edited by Jeannette Marie Mageo, 133–53. Albany: State University of New York Press, 2003.

Brakke, David. "The Problematization of Nocturnal Emissions in Early Christian Syria, Egypt, and Gaul." *Journal of Early Christian Studies* 3.4 (1995): 419–60.

Brann, Eva T. H. *The World of the Imagination: Sum and Substance*. Lanham, MD: Rowman & Littlefield, 1991.

Brashier, K. E. *Ancestral Memory in Early China*. Cambridge, MA: Harvard University Press, 2011.

———. "Han Thanatology and the Division of 'Souls.'" *Early China* 21 (1996): 125–58.

Bremmer, Jan. *The Early Greek Concept of the Soul*. Princeton: Princeton University Press, 1983.

Brennan, John. "Dreams, Divination, and Statecraft: The Politics of Dreams in Early Chinese History and Literature." In *The Dream and the Text: Essays on Literature and Language*, edited by Carol Schreier Rupprecht, 73–102. Albany: State University of New York Press, 1993.

Brindley, Erica Fox. *Ancient China and the Yue: Perceptions and Identities on the Southern Frontier, c. 400 BCE–50 CE*. Cambridge: Cambridge University Press, 2015.

———. *Individualism in Early China: Human Agency and the Self in Thought and Politics*. Honolulu: University of Hawai'i Press, 2010.

Brown, Michael F. "Ropes of Sand: Order and Imagery in Aguaruna Dreams." In *Dreaming: Anthropological and Psychological Interpretations*, edited by Barbara Tedlock, 154–70. 2nd edition. Santa Fe: School of American Research Press, 1992.

Brown, Miranda. *The Art of Medicine in Early China: The Ancient and Medieval Origins of a Modern Archive*. Cambridge: Cambridge University Press, 2015.

Bulkeley, Kelly. *Big Dreams: The Science of Dreaming and the Origins of Religion*. New York: Oxford University Press, 2016.

———. "Dreaming Is Imaginative Play in Sleep: A Theory of the Function of Dreams." *Dreaming* 29.1 (2019): 1–21.

———. *Lucrecia the Dreamer: Prophecy, Cognitive Science, and the Spanish Inquisition*. Stanford: Stanford University Press, 2018.
———. "The Meaningful Continuities between Dreaming and Waking: Results of a Blind Analysis of a Woman's 30-Year Dream Journal." *Dreaming* 28.4 (2018): 337–50.
Bunzl, Matti. "Franz Boas and the Humboldtian Tradition: From *Volksgeist* and *Nationalcharakter* to an Anthropological Concept of Culture." In *"Volksgeist" as Method and Ethic: Essays on Boasian Ethnography and the German Anthropological Tradition*, edited by George W. Stocking, Jr., 17–78. History of Anthropology 8. Madison: University of Wisconsin Press, 1996.
Burke, Peter. "L'histoire sociale des rêves." *Annales: Histoire, sciences sociales* 28 (1973): 329–42.
Burlingame, E. W. "The Act of Truth (Saccakiriya): A Hindu Spell and Its Employment as Psychic Motif in Hindu Fiction." *Journal of the Royal Asiatic Society of Great Britain and Ireland* 49 (1917): 429–67.
Burridge, Kenelm. *Mambu: A Study of Melanesian Cargo Movements and Their Ideological Background*. New York: Harper & Row, 1960.
———. *New Heaven, New Earth: A Study of Millennarian Activities*. Oxford: Basil Blackwell, 1969.

Cai Liang. "The Hermeneutics of Omens: The Bankruptcy of Moral Cosmology in Western Han China (206 BCE–8 CE)." *Journal of the Royal Asiatic Society* 3 (2015): 1–21.
Campany, Robert Ford. "Abstinence Halls (*Zhaitang* 齋堂) in Lay Households in Early Medieval China." *Studies in Chinese Religions* 1.2 (2015): 1–21.
———. "'Buddhism Enters China' in Early Medieval China." In *Old Society, New Belief: Religious Transformation of China and Rome, ca. 1st–6th Centuries*, edited by Poo Mu-chou, Harold Drake, and Lisa Raphals, 13–34. New York: Oxford University Press, 2017.
———. "Buddhist Revelation and Taoist Translation in Early Medieval China." *Taoist Resources* 4.1 (1993): 1–29.
———. "Dreaming and Self-Cultivation." Unpublished manuscript, last updated April 4, 2020.
———. *A Garden of Marvels: Tales of Wonder from Early Medieval China*. Honolulu: University of Hawai'i Press, 2015.
———. "Ghosts Matter: The Culture of Ghosts in Six Dynasties *Zhiguai*." *Chinese Literature: Essays, Articles, Reviews* 13 (1991): 15–34.
———. "Living Off the Books: Fifty Ways to Dodge *Ming* 命 in Early Medieval China." In *The Magnitude of "Ming": Command, Allotment, and Fate in Chinese Culture*, edited by Christopher Lupke, 129–50. Honolulu: University of Hawai'i Press, 2005.
———. "Long-Distance Specialists in Early Medieval China." In *Literature, Religion, and East-West Comparison: Essays in Honor of Anthony C. Yu*, edited by Eric Ziolkowski, 109–24. Newark, DE: University of Delaware Press, 2005.
———. *Making Transcendents: Ascetics and Social Memory in Early Medieval China*. Honolulu: University of Hawai'i Press, 2009.
———. "Miracle Tales as Scripture Reception: A Case Study involving the *Lotus Sutra* in China, 370–750 CE." *Early Medieval China* 24 (2018): 24–52.
———. "On the Very Idea of Religions (in the Modern West and in Early Medieval China)." *History of Religions* 42 (2003): 287–319.
———. "The Real Presence." *History of Religions* 32.3 (1993): 233–72.

———. "'Religious' as a Category: A Comparative Case Study." *Numen* 65 (2018): 333–76.
———. "Religious Repertoires and Contestation: A Case Study Based on Buddhist Miracle Tales." *History of Religions* 52.2 (2012): 99–141.
———. "Return-from-Death Narratives in Early Medieval China." *Journal of Chinese Religions* 18 (1990): 91–125.
———. "Secrecy and Display in the Quest for Transcendence in China, ca. 220 B.C.E.–350 C.E." *History of Religions* 45 (2006): 291–336.
———. *Signs from the Unseen Realm: Buddhist Miracle Tales from Early Medieval China*. Honolulu: University of Hawai'i Press, 2012.
———. *Strange Writing: Anomaly Accounts in Early Medieval China*. Albany: State University of New York Press, 1996.
———. "'Survival' as an Interpretive Strategy: A Sino-Western Comparative Case Study." *Method and Theory in the Study of Religion* 2.1 (1990): 1–26.
———. "The *Sword Scripture*: Recovering and Interpreting a Lost 4th-Century Daoist Method for Cheating Death." *Daoism: Religion, History and Society* 道教研究學報 6 (2014): 33–84.
———. "Taoist Bioethics in the Final Age: Therapy and Salvation in the *Book of Divine Incantations for Penetrating the Abyss*." In *Religious Methods and Resources in Bioethics*, edited by Paul Camenisch, 67–91. Dordrecht: Kluwer Academic Publishers, 1994.
———. *To Live as Long as Heaven and Earth: A Translation and Study of Ge Hong's Traditions of Divine Transcendents*. Berkeley: University of California Press, 2002.
———. "Two Religious Thinkers of the Early Eastern Jin: Gan Bao 干寶 and Ge Hong 葛洪 in Multiple Contexts." *Asia Major* 3rd ser. 18 (2005): 175–224.
Cancik, Hubert. "*Idolum* and *Imago:* Roman Dreams and Dream Theories." In *Dream Cultures: Explorations in the Comparative History of Dreaming,* edited by David Shulman and Guy G. Stroumsa, 169–88. New York: Oxford University Press, 1999.
Cappozzo, Valerio. *Dizionario dei sogni nel medioevo: Il Somniale Danielis in manoscritti letterari*. Firenze: Leo S. Olschki Editore, 2018.
Carruthers, Mary. *The Book of Memory: A Study of Memory in Medieval Culture*. 2nd edition. Cambridge: Cambridge University Press, 2008.
Castaneda, Carlos. *The Art of Dreaming*. New York: HarperCollins, 1993.
Cataldo, Lisa M. "Multiple Selves, Multiple Gods? Functional Polytheism and the Postmodern Religious Patient." *Pastoral Psychology* 57 (2008): 45–58.
Chan, Leo Tak-hung. *The Discourse on Foxes and Ghosts: Ji Yun and Eighteenth-Century Literati Storytelling*. Honolulu: University of Hawai'i Press, 1998.
Chandezon, Christophe, Véronique Dasen, and Jérôme Wilgaux. "Dream Interpretation, Physiognomy, Body Divination." In *A Companion to Greek and Roman Sexualities*, edited by Thomas K. Hubbard, 297–313. Oxford: Blackwell, 2014.
Chang, Garma C. C., ed. *A Treasury of Mahāyāna Sūtras: Selections from the Mahāratnakūta Sūtra*. University Park: Pennsylvania State University Press, 1983.
Chen Hsiu-fen. "Between Passion and Repression: Medical Views of Demon Dreams, Demonic Fetuses, and Female Sexual Madness in Late Imperial China." *Late Imperial China* 32 (2011): 51–82.
———. "Wind Malady as Madness in Medieval China: Some Threads from the Dunhuang Medical Manuscript." In *Medieval Chinese Medicine: The Dunhuang Medical Manuscripts*, edited by Vivienne Lo and Christopher Cullen, 345–62. London and New York: RoutledgeCurzon, 2005.
Chen, Jack W., and David Schaberg, eds. *Idle Talk: Gossip and Anecdote in Traditional China*. Berkeley: University of California Press, 2014.

Ch'en, Kenneth. "Filial Piety in Chinese Buddhism." *Harvard Journal of Asiatic Studies* 28 (1968): 81–97.
Cheng, Anne. *Histoire de la pensée chinoise*. Paris: Éditions du Seuil, 1997.
Cheng Lesong 程樂松. *Zhonggu daojiao leishu yu daojiao sixiang* 中古道教類書與道教思想. Beijing: Zhongjiao wenhua chubanshe, 2017.
Chennault, Cynthia L. "Lofty Gates or Solitary Impoverishment? Xie Family Members of the Southern Dynasties." *T'oung Pao* 85 (1999): 249–327.
Chong, Kim-chong. *Zhuangzi's Critique of the Confucians: Blinded by the Human*. Albany: State University of New York Press, 2016.
Chua, Jude Soo-Meng. "Tracing the Dao: Wang Bi's Theory of Names." In *Philosophy and Religion in Early Medieval China*, edited by Alan K. L. Chan and Yuet-Keung Lo, 53–70. Albany: State University of New York Press, 2010.
Cicero. *De divinatione*. Translated by William Armistead Falconer. Cambridge, MA: Harvard University Press, 1923.
Cohen, Ariela, and Antonio Zadra. "An Analysis of Laypeople's Beliefs Regarding the Origins of Their Worst Nightmare." *International Journal of Dream Research* 8.2 (2015): 120–28.
Conze, Edward. *The Short Prajñāpāramitā Texts*. London: Luzac, 1973.
Coolidge, Frederick L. *Dream Interpretation as a Psychotherapeutic Technique*. Boca Raton, FL: CRC Press, 2006.
Copenhaver, Brian P. *Hermetica*. Cambridge: Cambridge University Press, 1992.
Crapanzano, Vincent. "The Betwixt and Between of Dreams." In *Hundert Jahre "Die Traumdeutung": Kulturwissenschaftliche Perspektiven in der Traumforschung*, edited by Burkhard Schnepel, 232–59. Köln: Rüdiger Köppe Verlag, 2001.
———. "Concluding Reflections." In *Dreaming and the Self: New Perspectives on Subjectivity, Identity, and Emotion*, edited by Jeannette Marie Mageo, 175–97. Albany: State University of New York Press, 2003.
———. *Hermes' Dilemma and Hamlet's Desire: On the Epistemology of Interpretation*. Cambridge, MA: Harvard University Press, 1992.
Csikszentmihalyi, Mark. *Material Virtue: Ethics and the Body in Early China*. Leiden: E. J. Brill, 2004.

Damasio, Antonio R. *The Feeling of What Happens: Body and Emotion in the Making of Consciousness*. New York: Harcourt Brace, 1999.
Dayal, Har. *The Bodhisattva Doctrine in Buddhist Sanskrit Literature*. London: Routledge & Kegan Paul, 1932; reprinted Delhi: Motilal Banarsidass, 1978.
Deacon, Terrence W. *Incomplete Nature: How Mind Emerged from Matter*. New York: Norton, 2013.
de Crespigny, Rafe. *A Biographical Dictionary of Later Han to the Three Kingdoms (23–220 AD)*. Leiden: E. J. Brill, 2007.
———. *Imperial Warlord: A Biography of Cao Cao 155–220 AD*. Leiden: E. J. Brill, 2010.
de Groot, J. J. M. "On Chinese Divination by Dissecting Written Characters." *T'oung Pao* 1 (1890): 239–47.
———. *The Religious System of China*. 6 vols. Leiden: E. J. Brill, 1892–1910.
Denecke, Wiebke. *The Dynamics of Masters Literature: Early Chinese Thought from Confucius to Han Feizi*. Cambridge, MA: Harvard University Asia Center, 2010.
Descola, Philippe. *Beyond Nature and Culture*. Translated by Janet Lloyd. Chicago: University of Chicago Press, 2013.
Despeux, Catherine. "Physiognomie." In *Divination et société dans la Chine médiévale*, edited by Marc Kalinowski, 513–55. Paris: Bibliothèque nationale de France, 2003.

Devereux, Georges. *Dreams in Greek Tragedy: An Ethno-Psycho-Analytical Study*. Berkeley: University of California Press, 1976.

———. *Ethnopsychoanalysis: Psychoanalysis and Anthropology as Complementary Frames of Reference*. Berkeley: University of California Press, 1978.

———. *Reality and Dream: Psychotherapy of a Plains Indian*. New York: New York University Press, 1969.

———, ed. *Psychoanalysis and the Occult*. New York: International Universities Press, 1953.

Devriese, Lisa. "An Inventory of Medieval Commentaries on pseudo-Aristotle's *Physiognomonica*." *Bulletin de philosophie médiévale* 59 (2017): 215–46.

———. "Physiognomy in Context: Marginal Annotations in the Manuscripts of the *Physiognomonica*." *Recherches de théologie et philosophie médiévales* 84.1 (2017): 107–41.

DeWoskin, Kenneth J. *Doctors, Diviners, and Magicians of Ancient China: Biographies of "Fangshih."* New York: Columbia University Press, 1983.

DeWoskin, Kenneth J., and J. I. Crump, Jr., trans. *In Search of the Supernatural: The Written Record*. Stanford: Stanford University Press, 1996.

De Zengotita, Thomas. "Speakers of Being: Romantic Refusion and Cultural Anthropology." In *Romantic Motives: Essays on Anthropological Sensibility*, edited by George W. Stocking, Jr., 74–123. History of Anthropology 6. Madison: University of Wisconsin Press, 1989.

Dien, Albert E. "Custom and Society: *The Family Instructions of Mr. Yan*." In *Early Medieval China: A Sourcebook*, edited by Wendy Swartz, Robert Ford Campany, Yang Lu, and Jessey J. C. Choo, 494–510. New York: Columbia University Press, 2014.

———. "On the Name *Shishuo xinyu*." *Early Medieval China* 20 (2014): 7–8.

———. *Pei Ch'i shu 45: Biography of Yen Chih-t'ui*. Bern: Herbert Lang, 1976.

———. "Yen Chih-t'ui (531–591+): A Buddho-Confucian." In *Confucian Personalities*, edited by Arthur F. Wright and Dennis Twitchett, 44–64. Stanford: Stanford University Press, 1962.

Diény, Jean-Pierre. "Le saint ne rêve pas: de Zhuangzi à Michel Jouvet." *Études chinoises* 20 (2001): 127–99.

Di Giacinto, Licia. *The "Chenwei" Riddle: Time, Stars, and Heroes in the Apocrypha*. Gossenberg: Ostasien Verlag, 2013.

Docherty, Thomas. *Alterities: Criticism, History, Representation*. Oxford: Clarendon, 1996.

Dodds, E. R. *The Greeks and the Irrational*. Berkeley: University of California Press, 1951.

Domhoff, G. William. *The Emergence of Dreaming: Mind-wandering, Embodied Simulation, and the Default Network*. New York: Oxford University Press, 2018.

———. *The Scientific Study of Dreams: Neural Networks, Cognitive Development, and Content Analysis*. Washington, DC: American Psychological Association, 2003.

Domhoff, G. William, and Adam Schneider. "Are Dreams Social Simulations? Or Are They Enactments of Conceptions and Personal Concerns? An Empirical and Theoretical Comparison of Two Dream Theories." *Dreaming* 28.1 (2018): 1–23.

Drège, Jean-Pierre. "Clefs des songes de Touen-houang." In *Nouvelles contributions aux études de Touen-houang*, edited by Michel Soymié, 205–49. Genève: Droz, 1981.

———. "Notes d'onirologie chinoise." *Bulletin de l'École française d'Extrême-Orient* 70 (1981): 271–89.

Drège, Jean-Pierre, and Dimitri Drettas. "Oniromancie." In *Divination et société dans la Chine médiévale*, edited by Marc Kalinowski, 369–404. Paris: Bibliothèque nationale de France, 2003.

Drettas, Dimitri. "Deux types de manuscrits mantiques: Prognostication par tirage au sort et clefs des songes." In *La fabrique du lisible: la mise en texte des manuscrits de la Chine ancienne et médiévale*, edited by Jean-Pierre Drège and Costantino Moretti, 123–28. Paris: Institut des Hautes Études Chinoises, Collège de France, 2014.

———. "Le rêve mis en ordre: Les traités onirologiques des Ming à l'épreuve des traditions divinatoire, médicale et religieuse du rêve en Chine." PhD diss., École Pratique des Hautes Études, 2007.

Durrant, Stephen, Wai-yee Li, and David Schaberg. *Zuo Tradition: Zuozhuan*. 3 vols., continuously paginated. Seattle: University of Washington Press, 2016.

Eberhard, Wolfram. "Chinesische Träume als soziologisches Quellenmaterial." *Sociologus* new series 17.1 (1967): 71–91.

Egan, Ronald. "Nature and Higher Ideals in Texts on Calligraphy, Music, and Painting." In *Chinese Aesthetics: The Ordering of Literature, the Arts, and the Universe in the Six Dynasties*, edited by Zong-qi Cai, 277–309. Honolulu: University of Hawai'i Press, 2004.

Eggert, Marion. *Rede vom Traum: Traumauffassungen der Literatenschicht im späten kaiserlichen China*. Münchener Ostasiatische Studien 64. Stuttgart: Steiner, 1993.

Eicher, Sebastian. "Fan Ye's Biography in the *Song shu*: Form, Content, and Impact." *Early Medieval China* 22 (2016): 45–64.

Eisenbud, Jule. "The Dreams of Two Patients in Analysis as a Telepathic *Rêve-à-Deux*." In *Psychoanalysis and the Occult*, edited by Georges Devereux, 262–76. New York: International Universities Press, 1953.

Eitrem, Samson. "Dreams and Divination in Magical Ritual." In *Magica Hiera: Ancient Greek Magic and Religion*, edited by Christopher A. Faraone and Dirk Obbink, 175–87. New York: Oxford University Press, 1991.

Eliade, Mircea. *Myth and Reality*. Translated by Willard R. Trask. New York: Harper & Row, 1963.

Elman, Benjamin. "Collecting and Classifying: Ming Dynasty Compendia and Encyclopedias (*leishu*)." *Extrême-Orient, Extrême-Occident* hors-série (2007): 131–57.

Erdelyi, Matthew Hugh. "The Continuity Hypothesis." *Dreaming* 27.4 (2017): 334–44.

Esler, Dylan. "Note d'oniromancie tibétaine: Réflexions sur la chapitre 4 du *Bsam-gtan mig-sgron* de Gnubs-chen sangs-rgyas ye-shes." *Acta Orientalia Belgica* 25 (2012): 317–28.

Espesset, Grégoire. "Epiphanies of Sovereignty and the Rite of Jade Disc Immersion in Weft Narratives." *Early China* 37 (2014): 393–443.

Evans-Pritchard, E. E. *Theories of Primitive Religion*. Oxford: Clarendon Press, 1965.

Ewing, Katherine Pratt. "Dreams from a Saint: Anthropological Atheism and the Temptation to Believe." *American Anthropologist* n.s. 96 (1994): 571–83.

Faure, Bernard. *Visions of Power: Imagining Medieval Japanese Buddhism*. Translated by Phyllis Brooks. Princeton: Princeton University Press, 1996.

Firth, Raymond. "The Meaning of Dreams in Tikopia." In *Essays Presented to C. G. Seligman*, edited by E. E. Evans-Pritchard, R. Firth, B. Malinowski, and I. Schapera, 63–74. London: Kegan Paul, 1934.

———. "Tikopia Dreams: Personal Images of Social Reality." *Journal of the Polynesian Society* 110 (2001): 7–29.

Fodde-Reguer, Anna-Alexandra. "Divining Bureaucracy: Divination Manuals as Technology and the Standardization of Efficacy in Early China." PhD diss., University of Michigan, 2014.

Forke, Alfred. *Lun-hêng*. 2 vols. Reprint of 1907–11 edition. New York: Paragon Book Gallery, 1962.
Forte, Antonino. *Political Propaganda and Ideology in China at the End of the Seventh Century*. Napoli: Istituto Universitario Orientale, 1976.
———. "The South Indian Monk Bodhiruci (d. 727): Biographical Evidence." In *A Life Journey to the East: Sinological Studies in Memory of Giuliano Bertuccioli (1923–2001)*, edited by Antonino Forte and Federico Masini, 77–116. Kyoto: Scuola Italiana di Studi sull' Asia Orientale, 2002.
Foucault, Michel. *The Hermeneutics of the Subject: Lectures at the Collège de France, 1981–1982*. Edited by Frédéric Gros. Translated by Graham Burchell. New York: Picador, 2001.
———. *The Order of Things: An Archaeology of the Human Sciences*. New York: Vintage, 1970.
Freud, Sigmund. *The Interpretation of Dreams*. Translated by Joyce Crick, with an introduction by Ritchie Robertson. Oxford: Oxford University Press, 1999.
Fu Zhenggu 傅正谷. *Zhongguo meng wenhua* 中國夢文化. Beijing: Zhongguo shehui kexue chubanshe, 1993.
Fukatsu Tanefusa 深津胤房. "Kodai chūgokujin no shisō to seikatsu: yume ni tsuite" 古代中國人の思想と生活：夢について. In *Uno Testuto sensei hakuju shukuga kinen Tōyōgaku ronsō* 宇野哲人先生白壽祝賀記念東洋學論叢, 939–61. Tokyo: Uno Testuto sensei hakuju shukuga kinen kai, 1974.
Furth, Charlotte. *A Flourishing Yin: Gender in China's Medical History, 960–1665*. Berkeley: University of California Press, 1999.

Galambos, Imre. "Composite Manuscripts in Medieval China: The Case of Scroll P.3720 from Dunhuang." In *One-Volume Libraries: Composite and Multiple-Text Manuscripts*, edited by Michael Friedrich and Cosmia Schwarke, 355–78. Berlin: De Gruyter, 2016.
Gallagher, Catherine, and Stephen Greenblatt. "Introduction." In *Practicing New Historicism*, edited by Catherine Gallagher and Stephen Greenblatt, 1–19. Chicago: University of Chicago Press, 2000.
Gallagher, Shaun. *How the Body Shapes the Mind*. Oxford: Oxford University Press, 2005.
Gallop, David. *Aristotle on Sleep and Dreams: A Text and Translation with Introduction, Notes and Glossary*. Warminster: Aris & Phillips, 1996.
Galvany, Albert. "Signs, Clues and Traces: Anticipation in Ancient Chinese Political and Military Texts." *Early China* 38 (2015): 151–94.
Geertz, Clifford. "Culture War." *New York Review of Books*, November 30, 1995, 4–6.
George, Marianne. "Dreams, Reality, and the Desire and Intent of Dreamers as Experienced by a Fieldworker." *Anthropology of Consciousness* 6 (1995): 17–33.
George-Joseph, Gizelle, and Edward W. L. Smith. "The Dream World in Dominica." *Dreaming* 18.3 (2008): 167–74.
Gerona, Carla. *Night Journeys: The Power of Dreams in Transatlantic Quaker Culture*. Charlottesville: University of Virginia Press, 2004.
Gethin, Rupert M. L. *The Buddhist Path to Awakening*. Oxford: Oneworld, 2001.
Gibson, James J. "The Theory of Affordances." In *Perceiving, Acting, and Knowing*, edited by R. E. Shaw and J. Bransford, 67–82. Hillsdale, NJ: Lawrence Erlbaum Associates, 1977.
Ginzburg, Carlo. *Clues, Myths, and the Historical Method*. Translated by John and Anne C. Tedeschi. Baltimore: Johns Hopkins University Press, 2013.

Goffman, Erving. *The Presentation of Self in Everyday Life*. New York: Doubleday, 1959.
Goldin, Paul Rakita. "The Consciousness of the Dead as a Philosophical Problem in Ancient China." In *The Good Life and Conceptions of Life in Early China and Græco-Roman Antiquity*, edited by R. A. H. King, 59–92. Berlin: De Gruyter, 2015.
———. "Non-Deductive Argumentation in Early Chinese Philosophy." In *Between History and Philosophy: Anecdotes in Early China*, edited by Paul van Els and Sarah A. Queen, 41–62. Albany: State University of New York Press, 2017.
———. "Xunzi and Early Han Philosophy." *Harvard Journal of Asiatic Studies* 67.1 (2007): 136–66.
Goodale, Jane C. "Tiwi Island Dreams." In *Dream Travelers: Sleep Experiences and Culture in the Western Pacific*, edited by Roger Ivar Lohmann, 149–67. New York: Palgrave Macmillan, 2003.
Goodman, Howard L. *Ts'ao P'i Transcendent: The Political Culture of Dynasty-Founding in China at the End of the Han*. Seattle: Scripta Serica, 1998.
Graf, Fritz. "Dreams, Visions and Revelations: Dreams in the Thought of the Latin Fathers." In *Sub Imagine Somni: Nighttime Phenomena in Greco-Roman Culture*, edited by Emma Scioli and Christine Walde, 211–29. Pisa: Edizioni ETS, 2010.
Graff, David. *Medieval Chinese Warfare, 300–900*. London: Routledge, 2001.
Graham, A. C. *The Book of Lieh-tzu: A Classic of the Tao*. 2nd edition. New York: Columbia University Press, 1990.
———. *Chuang-tzu: The Inner Chapters*. London: George Allen & Unwin, 1981.
———. "The Date and Composition of *Lieh-tzu*." In *Studies in Chinese Philosophy and Philosophical Literature*, 216–82. Albany: State University of New York Press, 1990.
Greatrex, Roger. *The Bowu zhi: An Annotated Translation*. Stockholm: Skrifter utgivna av Föreningen för Orientaliska Studier, 1987.
Greenblatt, Stephen. "The Touch of the Real." In *The Fate of "Culture": Geertz and Beyond*, edited by Sherry B. Ortner, 14–29. Berkeley: University of California Press, 1999.
Greenstein, E. L. "Medieval Bible Commentaries." In *Back to the Sources*, edited by B. Holtz, 212–59. New York: Summit, 1984.
Gregor, Thomas. "'Far, Far Away My Shadow Wandered': The Dream Symbolism and Dream Theories of the Mehinaku Indians of Brazil." *American Ethnologist* 8 (1981): 709–20.
Groark, Kevin. "Discourses of the Soul: The Negotiation of Personal Agency in Tzotzil Maya Dream Narrative." *American Ethnologist* 36 (2009): 705–21.
———. "Social Opacity and the Dynamics of Empathic In-Sight among the Tzotzil Maya of Chiapas, Mexico." *Ethos* 36 (2008): 427–48.
———. "Specters of Social Antagonism: The Cultural Psychodynamics of Dream Aggression among the Tzotzil Maya of San Juan Chamula (Chiapas, Mexico)." *Ethos* 45 (2017): 314–41.
———. "Toward a Cultural Phenomenology of Intersubjectivity: The Extended Relational Field of the Tzotzil Maya of Highland Chiapas, Mexico." *Language and Communication* 33 (2013): 278–91.
———. "Willful Souls: Dreaming and the Dialectics of Self-Experience among the Tzotzil Maya of Highland Chiapas, Mexico." In *Toward an Anthropology of the Will*, edited by Keith M. Murphy and C. Jason Throop, 101–22. Stanford: Stanford University Press, 2010.
Gu Ming Dong. *Chinese Theories of Reading and Writing: A Route to Hermeneutics and Open Poetics*. Albany: State University of New York Press, 2005.

Guggenmos, Esther-Maria. "A List of Magic and Mantic Practices in the Buddhist Canon." In *Coping with the Future: Theories and Practices of Divination in East Asia*, edited by Michael Lackner, 151–95. Leiden: E. J. Brill, 2018.

Guinan, Ann Kessler. "A Severed Head Laughed: Stories of Divinatory Interpretation." In *Magic and Divination in the Ancient World*, edited by Leda Ciraolo and Jonathan Seidel, 7–30. Leiden: E. J. Brill, 2002.

Guthrie, Stewart. *Faces in the Clouds: A New Theory of Religion*. New York: Oxford University Press, 1995.

Hachiya Kunio 蜂屋邦夫. *Rōshi* 老子. Tokyo: Iwanami shoten, 2008.

Hacking, Ian. *Historical Ontology*. Cambridge, MA: Harvard University Press, 2002.

Hadot, Pierre. *Philosophy as a Way of Life*. Edited with an introduction by Arnold I. Davidson. Translated by Michael Chase. Oxford: Blackwell, 1995.

Hall, David H. "Beliefs about Dreams and Their Relationship to Gender and Personality." PhD diss., Wright Institute Graduate School of Psychology, 1996.

Hallowell, A. Irving. "Ojibwa Ontology, Behavior, and World View." In *Primitive Views of the World*, edited by Stanley Diamond, 49–82. New York: Columbia University Press, 1964. [Originally published 1960.]

Han Shuai 韓帥. *Meng yu mengzhan* 夢與夢占. Tianjin: Tianjin renmin chubanshe, 2011.

Hansen, Chad. "Guru or Skeptic? Relativistic Skepticism in the *Zhuangzi*." In *Hiding the World in the World: Uneven Discourses on the "Zhuangzi,"* edited by Scott Cook, 128–62. Albany: State University of New York Press, 2003.

Harbsmeier, Christoph. *Language and Logic*. Volume 7, part 1 of *Science and Civilisation in China*. Edited by Kenneth Robinson. Cambridge: Cambridge University Press, 1998.

Harkness, Ethan Richard. "Cosmology and the Quotidian: Day Books in Early China." PhD diss., University of Chicago, 2011.

Harper, Donald. "A Chinese Demonography of the Third Century B.C." *Harvard Journal of Asiatic Studies* 45 (1985): 459–98.

———. "Dunhuang Iatromantic Manuscripts: P. 2856 R° and P. 2675 V°." In *Medieval Chinese Medicine: The Dunhuang Medical Manuscripts*, edited by Vivienne Lo and Christopher Cullen, 134–64. London: Routledge, 2005.

———. "Iatromancie." In *Divination et société dans la Chine médiévale*, edited by Marc Kalinowski, 471–512. Paris: Bibliothèque nationale de France, 2003.

———. "Iatromancy, Diagnosis, and Prognosis in Early Chinese Medicine." In *Innovation in Chinese Medicine*, edited by Elisabeth Hsu, 99–120. Cambridge: Cambridge University Press, 2001.

———. "A Note on Nightmare Magic in Ancient and Medieval China." *T'ang Studies* 6 (1988): 69–76.

———. "Physicians and Diviners: The Relation of Divination to the Medicine of the *Huangdi neijing* (Inner Canon of the Yellow Thearch)." In *Extrême-Orient, Extrême-Occident: Cahiers de recherches comparatives* vol. 21: *Divination et rationalité en Chine ancienne,* edited by Karine Chemla, Donald Harper, and Marc Kalinowski, 91–110. Paris: Presses Universitaires de Vincennes, 1999.

———. "Spellbinding." In *Religions of China in Practice*, edited by Donald S. Lopez, Jr., 241–50. Princeton: Princeton University Press, 1996.

———. "The Textual Form of Knowledge: Occult Miscellanies in Ancient and Medieval Chinese Manuscripts, Fourth Century B.C. to Tenth Century A.D." In *Looking at It from Asia: The Processes That Shaped the Sources of History of Science*, edited by Florence Bretelle-Establet, 37–80. Paris: Springer, 2010.

———. "Wang Yen-shou's Nightmare Poem." *Harvard Journal of Asiatic Studies* 47 (1987): 239–83.

———. "Warring States Natural Philosophy and Occult Thought." In *The Cambridge History of Ancient China*. Vol. 1, *From the Origins of Civilization to 221 B.C.*, edited by Michael Loewe and Edward L. Shaughnessy, 813–84. Cambridge: Cambridge University Press, 1999.

Harper, Donald, and Marc Kalinowski. "Introduction." In *Books of Fate and Popular Culture in Early China: The Daybook Manuscripts of the Warring States, Qin, and Han*, 1–10. Leiden: E. J. Brill, 2017.

Harper, Donald, and Marc Kalinowski, eds. *Books of Fate and Popular Culture in Early China: The Daybook Manuscripts of the Warring States, Qin, and Han*. Leiden: E. J. Brill, 2017.

Harris, William V. *Dreams and Experience in Classical Antiquity*. Cambridge, MA: Harvard University Press, 2009.

Harris, William V., and Brooke Holmes, eds. *Aelius Aristides between Greece, Rome, and the Gods*. Leiden: E. J. Brill, 2008.

Harris-McCoy, Daniel E. *Artemidorus' Oneirocritica: Text, Translation, and Commentary*. Oxford: Oxford University Press, 2012.

Harrison, Paul M. "Mediums and Messages: Reflections on the Production of Mahāyāna Sūtras." *Eastern Buddhist* 35 (2003): 116–51.

Harrison, Thomas. *Divinity and History: The Religion of Herodotus*. Oxford: Clarendon, 2000.

Harrisson, Juliette. *Dreams and Dreaming in the Roman Empire: Cultural Memory and Imagination*. London: Bloomsbury, 2013.

Hartmann, Ernest. "The Nature and Functions of Dreaming." In *The New Science of Dreaming*, Volume 3: *Cultural and Theoretical Perspectives*, edited by Deirdre Barrett and Patrick McNamara, 171–92. Westport, CT: Praeger, 2007.

Harvey, Graham. *Animism: Respecting the Living World*. 2nd edition. New York: Columbia University Press, 2017.

Hasan-Rokem, Galit. "Communication with the Dead in Jewish Dream Culture." In *Dream Cultures: Explorations in the Comparative History of Dreaming*, edited by David Shulman and Guy G. Stroumsa, 213–32. New York: Oxford University Press, 1999.

Hasar, Rahman Veisi. "Metaphor and Metonymy in Ancient Dream Interpretation: The Case of Islamic-Iranian Culture." *Journal of Ethnology and Folkloristics* 11.2 (2017): 69–83.

Hattori, Masaaki. "The Dream Simile in Vijñānavāda Treatises." In *Indological and Buddhist Studies: Volume in Honour of Professor J.W. de Jong on his Sixtieth Birthday*, edited by L. A. Hercus et al., 235–41. Sidney: Australian National University, 1982.

Heine, Steven. "Putting the 'Fox' Back in the 'Wild Fox Kōan': The Intersection of Philosophical and Popular Religious Elements in the Ch'an/Zen Kōan Tradition." *Harvard Journal of Asiatic Studies* 56.2 (1996): 257–317.

Henderson, John B. "Divination and Confucian Exegesis." In *Extrême-Orient, Extrême-Occident: Cahiers de recherches comparatives* vol. 21: *Divination et rationalité en Chine ancienne*, edited by Karine Chemla, Donald Harper, and Marc Kalinowski, 79–89. Paris: Presses Universitaires de Vincennes, 1999.

———. *Scripture, Canon, and Commentary: A Comparison of Confucian and Western Exegesis*. Princeton: Princeton University Press, 1991.

Henricks, Robert G. *Lao-tzu Te-Tao Ching: A New Translation Based on the Recently Discovered Ma-wang-tui Texts*. New York: Ballantine, 1989.

Herdt, Gilbert. "Selfhood and Discourse in Sambia Dream Sharing." In *Dreaming: Anthropological and Psychological Interpretations*, edited by Barbara Tedlock, 55–85. 2nd edition. Santa Fe: School of American Research Press, 1992.
Hihara Toshikuni 日原利國. "Saii to shin'i 災異と讖緯." *Tōhōgaku* 43 (1972): 31–43.
Hobson, J. Allan. *Dreaming as Delirium: How the Brain Goes Out of Its Mind*. 1994; reprinted Cambridge, MA: MIT Press, 1999.
Hoffmeyer, Jesper. *Biosemiotics: An Examination into the Signs of Life and the Life of Signs*. Translated by Jesper Hoffmeyer and Donald Favareau. Edited by Donald Favareau. Scranton, PA: University of Scranton Press, 2008.
Hollan, Douglas. "The Cultural and Intersubjective Context of Dream Remembrance and Reporting: Dreams, Aging, and the Anthropological Encounter in Toraja, Indonesia." In *Dream Travelers: Sleep Experiences and Culture in the Western Pacific*, edited by Roger Ivar Lohmann, 169–87. New York: Palgrave Macmillan, 2003.
———. "The Personal Use of Dream Beliefs in the Toraja Highlands." *Ethos* 17 (1989): 166–86.
———. "Selfscape Dreams." In *Dreaming and the Self: New Perspectives on Subjectivity, Identity, and Emotion*, edited by Jeannette Marie Mageo, 61–74. Albany: State University of New York Press, 2003.
Holy, Ladislav. "Berti Dream Interpretation." In *Dreaming, Religion and Society in Africa*, edited by M. C. Jędrej and Rosalind Shaw, 86–99. Leiden: E. J. Brill, 1992.
Holzman, Donald. *La vie et la pensée de Hi K'ang (223–262 ap. J.-C.)*. Leiden: E. J. Brill, 1957.
Hon, Tze-Ki. "Hexagrams and Politics: Wang Bi's Political Philosophy in the *Zhouyi zhu*." In *Philosophy and Religion in Early Medieval China*, edited by Alan K. L. Chan and Yuet-Keung Lo, 71–95. Albany: State University of New York Press, 2010.
Horowitz, Alexandra. *Inside of a Dog: What Dogs See, Smell, and Know*. New York: Scribner, 2009.
Hou, Ching-lang. "The Chinese Belief in Baleful Stars." In *Facets of Taoism: Essays in Chinese Religion*, edited by Holmes Welch and Anna Seidel, 193–228. New Haven: Yale University Press, 1979.
Hoyland, Robert. "Physiognomy in Islam." *Jerusalem Studies in Arabic and Islam* 30 (2005): 361–402.
Hucker, Charles O. *A Dictionary of Official Titles in Imperial China*. Stanford: Stanford University Press, 1985.
Hughes, J. Donald. "The Dreams of Alexander the Great." *Journal of Psychohistory* 12 (1984): 168–92.
Hume, Robert Ernest. *The Thirteen Principal Upanishads*. 2nd edition. London: Oxford University Press, 1931.
Hung, Wu, and Katherine R. Tsiang, eds. *Body and Face in Chinese Visual Culture*. Cambridge, MA: Harvard University Press, 2005.
Hunter, Michael. *Confucius beyond the "Analects."* Leiden: E. J. Brill, 2017.
Huntington, C. W., Jr. *The Emptiness of Emptiness: An Introduction to Early Indian Mādhyamika*. With Geshé Namgyal Wangchen. Honolulu: University of Hawai'i Press, 1989.
Huntington, Rania. *Alien Kind: Foxes and Late Imperial Chinese Narrative*. Cambridge, MA: Harvard University Asia Center, 2003.
———. "Foxes and Sex in Late Imperial Chinese Narrative." *Nan nü* 2.1 (2000): 78–128.
Hurvitz, Leon. *Scripture of the Lotus Blossom of the Fine Dharma (The Lotus Sutra)*. Revised edition. New York: Columbia University Press, 2009.
Hutton, Eric. *Xunzi: The Complete Text*. Princeton: Princeton University Press, 2014.

Ichikawa, Jonathan. “Dreaming and Imagination.” *Mind and Language* 24 (2009): 103–21.
Idel, Moshe. “Astral Dreams in Judaism: Twelfth to Fourteenth Centuries.” In *Dream Cultures: Explorations in the Comparative History of Dreaming*, edited by David Shulman and Guy G. Stroumsa, 235–51. New York: Oxford University Press, 1999.
Itō Michiharu 伊藤道治 and Takashima Ken-ichi 高嶋謙一. *Studies in Early Chinese Civilization: Religion, Society, Language and Palaeography*. Edited by Gary F. Arbuckle. 2 vols., separately paginated. Osaka: Intercultural Research Institute, Kansai Gaidai University, 1996.

Jenkins, David. “When is a Continuity Hypothesis Not a Continuity Hypothesis?” *Dreaming* 28.4 (2018): 351–55.
Jensen, Christopher Jon. “Dreaming Betwixt and Between: Oneiric Narratives in Huijiao and Daoxuan’s *Biographies of Eminent Monks*.” PhD diss., McMaster University, 2018.
Jiang, Tao. *Contexts and Dialogue: Yogācāra Buddhism and Modern Psychology on the Subliminal Mind*. Honolulu: University of Hawai’i Press, 2006.
Johnston, Sarah Iles. *Ancient Greek Divination*. Chichester: Wiley-Blackwell, 2008.
———. “Delphi and the Dead.” In *Mantikê: Studies in Ancient Divination*, edited by Sarah Iles Johnston and Peter T. Struck, 283–307. Leiden: E. J. Brill, 2005.
———. “Sending Dreams, Restraining Dreams: *Oneiropompeia* in Theory and Practice.” In *Sub Imagine Somni: Nighttime Phenomena in Greco-Roman Culture*, edited by Emma Scioli and Christine Walde, 63–80. Pisa: Edizioni ETS, 2010.
Josephson-Storm, Jason Ā. *The Myth of Disenchantment: Magic, Modernity, and the Birth of the Human Sciences*. Chicago: University of Chicago Press, 2017.
Jung, Carl G. *Dreams*. Translated by R. F. C. Hull. Princeton: Princeton University Press, 2010.

Kahn, David, and Allan Hobson. “Theory of Mind in Dreaming: Awareness of Feelings and Thoughts of Others in Dreams.” *Dreaming* 15.1 (2005): 48–57.
Kalinowski, Marc. “Divination and Astrology: Received Texts and Excavated Manuscripts.” In *China’s Early Empires: A Re-appraisal*, edited by Michael Nylan and Michael Loewe, 339–66. Cambridge: Cambridge University Press, 2010.
———, ed. *Divination et société dans la Chine médiévale*. Paris: Bibliothèque nationale de France, 2003.
———. “La divination sous les Zhou orientaux (770–256 avant notre ère).” In *Religion et société en Chine ancienne et médiévale*, edited by John Lagerwey, 101–64. Paris: Cerf, 2009.
———. “Diviners and Astrologers under the Eastern Zhou: Transmitted Texts and Recent Archaeological Discoveries.” In *Early Chinese Religion, Part One: Shang through Han (1250 BC–220 AD)*, edited by John Lagerwey and Marc Kalinowski, 341–96. Leiden: E. J. Brill, 2009.
———. “Introduction générale.” In *Divination et société dans la Chine médiévale*, edited by Marc Kalinowski, 7–33. Paris: Bibliothèque nationale de France, 2003.
———. “La littérature divinatoire dans le *Daozang*.” *Cahiers d’Extrême-Asie* 5 (1989–90): 85–114.
———. “Technical Traditions in Ancient China and *Shushu* Culture in Chinese Religion.” In *Religion and Chinese Society*, vol. 1: *Ancient and Medieval China*, edited by John Lagerwey, 223–48. Hong Kong: Chinese University Press, 2004.
———. *Wang Chong, Balance des discours: Destin, providence et divination*. Paris: Les Belles Lettres, 2011.

Kamenarović, Ivan P. *Wang Fu: Propos d'un ermite (Qianfu lun)*. Paris: Les Éditions du Cerf, 1992.

Kang, Xiaofei. *The Cult of the Fox: Power, Gender, and Popular Religion in Late Imperial and Modern China*. New York: Columbia University Press, 2005.

———. "The Fox [*hu* 狐] and the Barbarian [*hu* 胡]: Unraveling Representations of the Other in Late Tang Tales." *Journal of Chinese Religions* 27 (1999): 35–68.

Kany-Turpin, José, and Pierre Pellegrin. "Cicero and the Aristotelian Theory of Divination by Dreams." In *Cicero's Knowledge of the Peripatos*, edited by William W. Fortenbaugh and Peter Steinmetz, 220–45. Rutgers University Studies in Classical Humanities IV. New Brunswick, NJ: Transaction Publishers, 1989.

Kao, Karl S. Y., ed. *Classical Chinese Tales of the Supernatural and the Fantastic: Selections from the Third to the Tenth Century*. Bloomington: Indiana University Press, 1985.

Keen, Ian. "Dreams, Agency, and Traditional Authority in Northeast Arnhem Land." In *Dream Travelers: Sleep Experiences and Culture in the Western Pacific*, edited by Roger Ivar Lohmann, 127–47. New York: Palgrave Macmillan, 2003.

Keightley, David N. *The Ancestral Landscape: Time, Space, and Community in Late Shang China (ca. 1200–1045 B.C.)*. Berkeley: Institute of East Asian Studies, University of California, 2000.

———. "The 'Science' of the Ancestors: Divination, Curing, and Bronze-Casting in Late Shang China." *Asia Major* 3rd series 14.2 (2001): 143–87.

———. *Sources of Shang History: The Oracle-Bone Inscriptions of Bronze Age China*. Berkeley: University of California Press, 1978.

———. *These Bones Shall Rise Again: Selected Writings on Early China*. Edited by Henry Rosemont Jr. Albany: State University of New York Press, 2014.

Kempf, Wolfgang, and Elfriede Hermann. "Dreamscapes: Transcending the Local in Initiation Rites among the Ngaing of Papua New Guinea." In *Dream Travelers: Sleep Experiences and Culture in the Western Pacific*, edited by Roger Ivar Lohmann, 61–85. New York: Palgrave Macmillan, 2003.

Kern, Martin. "Early Chinese Divination and Its Rhetoric." In *Coping with the Future: Theories and Practices of Divination in East Asia*, edited by Michael Lackner, 255–88. Leiden: E. J. Brill, 2018.

———. "Religious Anxiety and Political Interest in Western Han Omen Interpretation." *Chūgoku shigaku* 中國史學 10 (2000): 1–31.

Kessels, A. H. M. "Ancient Systems of Dream-Classification." *Mnemosyne* 4th ser. 22 (1969): 389–424.

Kilborne, Benjamin. "On Classifying Dreams." In *Dreaming: Anthropological and Psychological Interpretations*, edited by Barbara Tedlock, 171–93. 2nd edition. Santa Fe: School of American Research Press, 1992.

Kimbrough, R. Keller. "Reading the Miraculous Powers of Japanese Poetry: Spells, Truth Acts, and a Medieval Buddhist Poetics of the Supernatural." *Japanese Journal of Religious Studies* 32.1 (2005): 1–33.

King, David B., and Teresa L. DeCicco. "Dream Relevance and the Continuity Hypothesis: Believe It or Not?" *Dreaming* 19.4 (2009): 207–17.

Kinney, Anne Behnke. *The Art of the Han Essay: Wang Fu's Ch'ien-fu lun*. Tempe: Center for Asian Studies, Arizona State University,1990.

———. "Predestination and Prognostication in the *Ch'ien-fu lun*." *Journal of Chinese Religions* 19 (1991): 27–45.

Kirk, G. S., and J. E. Raven. *The Presocratic Philosophers*. Cambridge: Cambridge University Press, 1957.

Klein, Esther S. "Constancy and the *Changes:* A Comparative Reading of *Heng xian*." *Dao* 12 (2013): 207–24.

———. "Were There 'Inner Chapters' in the Warring States? A New Examination of Evidence about the *Zhuangzi*." *T'oung Pao* 96 (2011): 299–369.

Knapp, Keith. "Heaven and Death according to Huangfu Mi, a Third-Century Confucian." *Early Medieval China* 6 (2000): 1–31.

———. *Selfless Offspring: Filial Children and Social Order in Medieval China*. Honolulu: University of Hawai'i Press, 2005.

Knechtges, David R. *Wen xuan, or Selections of Refined Literature. Vol. 2, Rhapsodies on Sacrifices, Hunting, Travel, Sightseeing, Palaces and Halls, Rivers and Seas.* Princeton: Princeton University Press, 1987.

———. *Wen xuan, or Selections of Refined Literature. Vol. 3, Rhapsodies on Natural Phenomena, Birds and Animals, Aspirations and Feelings, Sorrowful Laments, Literature, Music, and Passions*. Princeton: Princeton University Press, 1996.

Knight, Sam. "The Premonitions Bureau." *The New Yorker*, 4 March 2019: 38–47.

Knoblock, John, and Jeffrey Riegel. *The Annals of Lü Buwei: A Complete Translation and Study*. Stanford: Stanford University Press, 2000.

Knudson, Roger M., Alexandra L. Adame, and Gillian M. Finocan. "Significant Dreams: Repositioning the Self Narrative." *Dreaming* 16.3 (2006): 215–22.

Kohn, Eduardo. "How Dogs Dream: Amazonian Natures and the Politics of Transspecies Engagement." *American Ethnologist* 34.1 (2007): 3–24.

———. *How Forests Think: Toward an Anthropology beyond the Human*. Berkeley: University of California Press, 2013.

Kory, Stephan N. "Cracking to Divine: Pyro-Plastromancy as an Archetypal and Common Mantic and Religious Practice in Han and Medieval China." PhD diss., Indiana University, 2012.

Kracke, Waud. "Afterword: Beyond the Mythologies, a Shape of Dreaming." In *Dream Travelers: Sleep Experiences and Culture in the Western Pacific*, edited by Roger Ivar Lohmann, 211–35. New York: Palgrave Macmillan, 2003.

———. "Dream: Ghost of a Tiger, a System of Human Words." In *Dreaming and the Self: New Perspectives on Subjectivity, Identity, and Emotion*, edited by Jeannette Marie Mageo, 155–64. Albany: State University of New York Press, 2003.

———. "Dreaming in Kagwahiv: Dream Beliefs and Their Psychic Uses in an Amazonian Indian Culture." In *The Psychoanalytic Study of Society*, edited by Werner Muensterberger and L. Bryce Boyer, 119–71. New Haven: Yale University Press, 1979.

———. "Myths in Dreams, Thought in Images: An Amazonian Contribution to the Psychoanalytic Theory of Primary Process." In *Dreaming: Anthropological and Psychological Interpretations*, edited by Barbara Tedlock, 31–54. 2nd edition. Santa Fe: School of American Research Press, 1992.

Kristeva, Julia. *Powers of Horror: An Essay on Abjection*. Translated by Leon S. Roudiez. New York: Columbia University Press, 1982.

Kroll, Paul W. *A Student's Dictionary of Classical and Medieval Chinese*. Leiden: E. J. Brill, 2015.

Kruger, Steven F. *Dreaming in the Middle Ages*. Cambridge: Cambridge University Press, 1992.

Kunzendorf, Robert G., et al. "The Archaic Belief in Dream Visitations as It Relates to 'Seeing Ghosts,' 'Meeting the Lord,' as well as 'Encountering Extraterrestrials.'" *Imagination, Cognition and Personality* 27.1 (2007–08): 71–85.

Kupperman, Joel. "Spontaneity and Education of the Emotions in the *Zhuangzi*." In *Essays on Skepticism, Relativism, and Ethics in the "Zhuangzi,"* edited by Paul

Kjellberg and Philip J. Ivanhoe, 183–95. Albany: State University of New York Press, 1996.

Lackner, Michael. *Der chinesische Traumwald: Traditionelle Theorien des Traumes und seiner Deutung im Spiegel der ming-zeitlichen Anthologie Meng-lin hsüan-chieh*. Frankfurt: Peter Lang, 1985.

———, ed. *Coping with the Future: Theories and Practices of Divination in East Asia*. Leiden: E. J. Brill, 2017.

Lakoff, George. "How Metaphor Structures Dreams: The Theory of Conceptual Metaphor Applied to Dream Analysis." *Dreaming* 3 (1993): 77–98.

Lam, Ling Hon. *The Spatiality of Emotion in Early Modern China: From Dreamscapes to Theatricality*. New York: Columbia University Press, 2018.

Lamoreaux, John C. *The Early Muslim Tradition of Dream Interpretation*. Albany: State University of New York Press, 2002.

Lamotte, Étienne. *History of Indian Buddhism from the Origins to the Śaka Era*. Translated by Sara Webb-Boin. Louvain: Peeters, 1988.

Langenberg, Amy Paris. *Birth in Buddhism: The Suffering Fetus and Female Freedom*. New York: Routledge, 2017.

Larsen, Matthew D. C. *Gospels before the Book*. New York: Oxford University Press, 2018.

Latour, Bruno. *We Have Never Been Modern*. Translated by Catherine Porter. Cambridge, MA: Harvard University Press, 1993.

Levine, Caroline. *Forms: Whole, Rhythm, Hierarchy, Network*. Princeton: Princeton University Press, 2015.

Levine, Lawrence W. *The Unpredictable Past: Explorations in American Cultural History*. New York: Oxford University Press, 1993.

Lewis, Mark Edward. *China between Empires: The Northern and Southern Dynasties*. Cambridge, MA: Harvard University Press, 2009.

———. *The Construction of Space in Early China*. Albany: State University of New York Press, 2006.

———. *The Flood Myths of Early China*. Albany: State University of New York Press, 2006.

———. *Writing and Authority in Early China*. Albany: State University of New York Press, 1999.

Li Jianguo 李劍國. *Tang qian zhiguai xiaoshuo shi* 唐前志怪小說史. Tianjin: Nankai Daxue chubanshe, 1984.

Li Ling 李零. *Zhongguo fangshu xukao* 中國方術續考. Beijing: Dongfang, 2000.

Li Shouju 李壽菊. *Huxian xinyang yu huli jing gushi* 狐仙信仰與狐狸精故事. Taipei: Taiwan xuesheng shuju, 95.

Li Wai-yee. "Dreams of Interpretation in Early Chinese Historical and Philosophical Writings." In *Dream Cultures: Explorations in the Comparative History of Dreaming*, edited by David Shulman and Guy G. Stroumsa, 17–42. New York: Oxford University Press, 1999.

———. *The Readability of the Past in Early Chinese Historiography*. Cambridge, MA: Harvard University Press, 2007.

———. "Riddles, Concealment, and Rhetoric in Early China." In *Facing the Monarch: Modes of Advice in the Early Chinese Court*, edited by Garret P. S. Olberding, 100–132. Cambridge, MA: Harvard University Asia Center, 2013.

———. "*Shishuo xinyu* and the Emergence of Aesthetic Self-Consciousness in the Chinese Tradition." In *Chinese Aesthetics: The Ordering of Literature, the Arts, and the

Universe in the Six Dynasties, edited by Zong-qi Cai, 237–76. Honolulu: University of Hawai'i Press, 2004.

Liebenthal, Walter. "The Immortality of the Soul in Chinese Thought." *Monumenta Nipponica* 8 (1952): 327–96.

Lin Fu-shih 林富士. "The Cult of Jiang Ziwen in Medieval China." *Cahiers d'Extrême-Asie* 10 (1998): 357–75.

———. "Religious Taoism and Dreams: An Analysis of the Dream-data Collected in the *Yün-chi ch'i-ch'ien*." *Cahiers d'Extrême-Asie* 8 (1995): 95–112.

Lincoln, Bruce. *Theorizing Myth: Narrative, Ideology, and Scholarship*. Chicago: University of Chicago Press, 1999.

Linden, David J. *The Accidental Mind*. Cambridge, MA: Harvard University Press, 2007.

Link, Arthur. "The Biography of Shih Tao-an." *T'oung Pao* 46 (1958): 1–48.

Lippiello, Tiziana. *Auspicious Omens and Miracles in Ancient China: Han, Three Kingdoms and Six Dynasties*. Sankt Augustin: Institut Monumenta Serica, 2001.

Liszka, James Jakób. *A General Introduction to the Semeiotic of Charles Sanders Peirce*. Bloomington: Indiana University Press, 1996.

Liu Guozhong 劉國忠. *Introduction to the Tsinghua Bamboo-Strip Manuscripts*. Translated by Christopher J. Foster and William N. French. Leiden: E. J. Brill, 2016.

Liu Mau-tsai. "Die Traumdeutung im alten China." *Asiatische Studien* 16 (1963): 35–65.

Liu Quanbo 刘全波. *Wei Jin nanbeichao leishu bianzuan yanjiu* 魏晋南北朝类书编纂研究. Beijing: Minzu chubanshe, 2018.

Liu Wenying 劉文英. *Meng de mixin yu meng de tansuo* 夢的迷信與夢的探索. Beijing: Zhongguo shehui kexue chubanshe, 1989.

———. *Zhongguo gudai de mengshu* 中國古代的夢書. Beijing: Zhonghua shuju, 1990.

Liu Wenying 劉文英 and Cao Tianyu 曹田玉. *Meng yu Zhongguo wenhua* 夢與中國文化. Beijing: Renmin chubanshe, 2003.

Liu Zhao 劉釗. *Chutu jianbo wenzi congkao* 出土簡帛文字叢考. Taipei: Taiwan guji, 2004.

Lo, Yuet Keung. "From a Dual Soul to a Unitary Soul: The Babel of Soul Terminologies in Early China." *Monumenta Serica* 56 (2008): 23–53.

Loewe, Michael. *A Biographical Dictionary of the Qin, Former Han and Xin Periods (221 BC–AD 24)*. Leiden: E. J. Brill, 2000.

———. *Divination, Mythology and Monarchy in Han China*. Cambridge: Cambridge University Press, 1994.

Lohmann, Roger Ivar. "Introduction: Dream Travels and Anthropology." In *Dream Travelers: Sleep Experiences and Culture in the Western Pacific*, edited by Roger Ivar Lohmann, 1–18. New York: Palgrave Macmillan, 2003.

———. "Supernatural Encounters of the Asabano in Two Traditions and Three States of Consciousness." In *Dream Travelers: Sleep Experiences and Culture in the Western Pacific*, edited by Roger Ivar Lohmann, 189–210. New York: Palgrave Macmillan, 2003.

———. "The Supernatural Is Everywhere: Defining Qualities of Religion in Melanesia and Beyond." *Anthropological Forum* 13 (2003): 175–85.

———, ed. *Dream Travelers: Sleep Experiences and Culture in the Western Pacific*. New York: Palgrave Macmillan, 2003.

Lorenz, Hendrik. *The Brute Within: Appetitive Desire in Plato and Aristotle*. Oxford: Clarendon, 2006.

Lu Jia 陸賈. *Nouveaux discours*. Edited and translated by Béatrice l'Haridon and Stéphane Feuillas. Paris: Les belles lettres, 2012.

Lu Xun 魯迅. *Gu xiaoshuo gouchen* 古小說鉤沈. Beijing: Renmin wenxue chubanshe, 1954.

Lu Zongli. *Power of the Words: Chen Prophecy in Chinese Politics, AD 265–618*. Bern: Peter Lang, 2003.

Luan Baoqun 栾保群. *Zhongguo shenguai dacidian* 中国神怪大辞典. Beijing: Renmin chubanshe, 2009.

Lucretius. *On the Nature of Things*. Translated by W. H. D. Rouse, revised by Martin F. Smith. Cambridge, MA: Harvard University Press, 1992.

———. *The Nature of Things*. Translated with notes by A. E. Stallings. London: Penguin, 2007.

Luo Jianping 羅建平. *Ye de yanjing: Zhongguo meng wenhua xiangzheng* 夜的眼睛：中國夢文化象征. Chengdu: Sichuan renmin chubanshe, 2005.

Luo Xinhui 羅新慧. "Omens and Politics: The Zhou Concept of the Mandate of Heaven as Seen in the *Chengwu* 程寤 Manuscript." In *Ideology of Power and Power of Ideology in Early China*, edited by Yuri Pines, Paul R. Goldin, and Martin Kern, 49–68. Leiden: E. J. Brill, 2015.

Lusthaus, Dan. "Aporetics Ethics in the *Zhuangzi*." In *Hiding the World in the World: Uneven Discourses on the "Zhuangzi,"* 163–206. Edited by Scott Cook. Albany: State University of New York Press, 2003.

Lynn, Richard John. *The Classic of Changes: A New Translation of the I Ching as Interpreted by Wang Bi*. New York: Columbia University Press, 1994.

Macrobius. *Commentary on the Dream of Scipio*. Translated and edited by William Harris Stahl. New York: Columbia University Press, 1990.

Mageo, Jeannette Marie. *Dreaming Culture: Meanings, Models, and Power in U.S. American Dreams*. New York: Palgrave Macmillan, 2011.

———. "Nightmares, Abjection, and American Not-Quite Identities." *Dreaming* 27.4 (2017): 290–310.

———. "Subjectivity and Identity in Dreams." In *Dreaming and the Self: New Perspectives on Subjectivity, Identity, and Emotion*, edited by Jeannette Marie Mageo, 23–40. Albany: State University of New York Press, 2003.

———. "Theorizing Dreaming and the Self." In *Dreaming and the Self: New Perspectives on Subjectivity, Identity, and Emotion*, edited by Jeannette Marie Mageo, 3–22. Albany: State University of New York Press, 2003.

Mai, Cuong T. "Visualization Apocrypha and the Making of Buddhist Deity Cults in Early Medieval China: With Special Reference to the Cults of Amitābha, Maitreya, and Samantabhadra." PhD diss., Indiana University, 2009.

Major, John S., Sarah A. Queen, Andrew Seth Meyer, and Harold D. Roth. *The Huainanzi: A Guide to the Theory and Practice of Government in Early Han China*. New York: Columbia University Press, 2010.

Makita Tairyō 牧田諦亮. *Gikyō kenkyū* 疑經研究. Kyoto: Kyoto University, Jinbun kagaku kenkyūsho, 1976.

———. *Rikuchō kōitsu Kanzeon ōkenki no kenkyū* 六朝古逸觀世音應驗記の研究. Kyoto: Hyōrakuji shoten, 1970.

Mannheim, Bruce. "A Semiotic of Andean Dreams." In *Dreaming: Anthropological and Psychological Interpretations*, edited by Barbara Tedlock, 132–53. 2nd edition. Santa Fe: School of American Research Press, 1992.

Mather, Richard B. *Shih-shuo Hsin-yü, A New Account of Tales of the World*. 2nd edition. Ann Arbor: Center for Chinese Studies, University of Michigan, 2002.

Mazandarani, Amir Ali, Maria E. Aguilar-Vafaie, and G. William Domhoff. "Iranians' Beliefs about Dreams: Developing and Validating the 'My Beliefs About Dreams' Questionnaire." *Dreaming* 28.3 (2018): 225–34.

McGinn, Colin. *Mindsight: Image, Dream, Meaning*. Cambridge, MA: Harvard University Press, 2004.

McGovern, Nathan. "On the Origins of the 32 Marks of a Great Man." *Journal of the International Association of Buddhist Studies* 39 (2016): 207–47.

McNamara, Patrick, Erica Harris, and Anna Kookoolis. "Costly Signaling Theory of Dream Recall and Dream Sharing." In *The New Science of Dreaming*, Volume 3: *Cultural and Theoretical Perspectives*, 117–32. Westport, CT: Praeger, 2007.

McNamara, Patrick, Luke Dietrich-Egensteiner, and Brian Teed. "Mutual Dreaming." *Dreaming* 27.2 (2017): 87–101.

McRae, John R., tr. *The Vimalakīrti Sutra*. BDK English Tripiṭika 26-I. Berkeley: Numata Center for Buddhist Translation and Research, 2004.

Merrill, William. "The Rarámuri Stereotype of Dreams." In *Dreaming: Anthropological and Psychological Interpretations*, edited by Barbara Tedlock, 194–219. 2nd edition. Santa Fe: School of American Research Press, 1992.

Milburn, Olivia. *The Glory of Yue: An Annotated Translation of the "Yuejue shu."* Leiden: E. J. Brill, 2010.

———. *The Spring and Autumn Annals of Master Yan*. Leiden: E. J. Brill, 2016.

———. "The Weapons of Kings: A New Perspective on Southern Sword Legends in Early China." *Journal of the American Oriental Society* 128.3 (2008): 423–37.

Miller, Patricia Cox. *Dreams in Late Antiquity: Studies in the Imagination of a Culture*. Princeton: Princeton University Press, 1994.

Mittermaier, Amira. "The Book of Visions: Dreams, Poetry, and Prophecy in Contemporary Egypt." *International Journal of Middle East Studies* 39 (2007): 229–47.

———. *Dreams That Matter: Egyptian Landscapes of the Imagination*. Berkeley: University of California Press, 2011.

Miyakawa Hisayuki 宮川尚志. "Local Cults around Mount Lu at the Time of Sun En's Rebellion." In *Facets of Taoism: Essays in Chinese Religion*, edited by Holmes Welch and Anna Seidel, 83–122. New Haven: Yale University Press, 1979.

———. "Son On, Ro Jun no ran hokō" 孫恩盧循の亂補考. In *Suzuki hakushi koki kinen Tōyōgaku ronsō* 鈴木博士古稀記念東洋學論集, 533–48. Tokyo, 1972.

———. "Son On, Ro Jun no ran ni tsuite" 孫恩盧循の亂について. *Tōyōshi kenkyū* 東洋史研究 30.2 (1971): 1–30.

Miyazawa Masayori 宮沢正順. "'Dōkyō reigen ki' ni tsuite" 道教靈驗記について. *Sankō bunka kenkyūjo nempō* 三康文化研究所年報 18 (1986): 1–38.

Montgomery, Sy. *The Soul of an Octopus: A Surprising Exploration into the Wonder of Consciousness*. New York: Atria, 2015.

Moreira, Isabel. *Dreams, Visions, and Spiritual Authority in Merovingian Gaul*. Ithaca: Cornell University Press, 2000.

Morewedge, Carey K., and Michael I. Norton. "When Dreaming Is Believing: The (Motivated) Interpretation of Dreams." *Journal of Personality and Social Psychology* 96 (2009): 249–64.

Müller, Gotelind. "Zum Begriff des Traumes und seiner Funktion im chinesischen buddhistichen Kanon." *Zeitschrift der Deutschen Morgenländischen Gesellschaft* 142 (1992): 343–77.

Müller, Klaus E. "Reguläre Anomalien im Schnittbereich zweier Welten." *Zeitschrift für Parapsychologie und Grenzgebiete der Psychologie* 34 (1992): 33–50.

Näf, Beat. "Artemidor—ein Schlüssel zum Verständnis antiker Traumberichte?" In *Sub Imagine Somni: Nighttime Phenomena in Greco-Roman Culture*, edited by Emma Scioli and Christine Walde, 185–209. Pisa: Edizioni ETS, 2010.

———. *Traum und Traumdeutung im Altertum*. Darmstadt: Wissenschaftliche Buchgesellschaft, 2004.

Neil, Bronwen. "Studying Dream Interpretation from Early Christianity to the Rise of Islam." *Journal of Religious History* 40.1 (2016): 44–64.

Newman, Deena I. J. "The Western Psychic as Diviner: Experience and the Politics of Perception." *Ethnos* 64 (1999): 82–106.

Niehoff, Maren. "A Dream Which Is Not Interpreted Is Like a Letter Which Is Not Read." *Journal of Jewish Studies* 43 (1992): 58–84.

Nishioka Hiromu 西岡弘. "Akumu no zō" 惡夢の贈. In *Ikeda Suetoshi hakushi koki kinen Tōyōgaku ronshū* 池田末利博士古稀記念東洋學論集, 313–28. Hiroshima: Ikeda Suetoshi hakushi koki kinen gikyōkai, 1980.

Niyazioğlu, Asli. *Dreams and Lives in Ottoman Istanbul: A Seventeenth-Century Biographer's Perspective*. London: Routledge, 2017.

Noë, Alva. *Action in Perception*. Cambridge, MA: MIT Press, 2004.

Nussbaum, Martha Craven. *Aristotle's "De Motu Animalium."* Princeton: Princeton University Press, 1978.

Nylan, Michael. "The Many Dukes of Zhou in Early Sources." In *Statecraft and Classical Learning: The Rituals of Zhou in East Asian History*, edited by Benjamin A. Elman and Martin Kern, 94–128. Leiden: E. J. Brill, 2010.

———. *Yang Xiong and the Pleasures of Reading and Classical Learning in China*. American Oriental Series 94. New Haven, CT: American Oriental Society, 2011.

———. "Ying Shao's 'Feng Su T'ung Yi': An Exploration of Problems in Han Dynasty Political, Philosophical and Social Unity." PhD diss., Princeton University, 1982.

Obert, Mathias. "Imagination or Response? Some Remarks on the Understanding of Images and Pictures in Pre-Modern China." In *Dynamics and Performativity of Imagination: The Image between the Visible and the Invisible*, edited by Bernd Huppauf and Christoph Wulf, 116–34. New York: Routledge, 2009.

———. *Welt als Bild: Die theoretische Grundlegung der chinesischen Berg-Wasser-Malerei zwischen dem 5. und dem 12. Jahrhundert*. München: Verlag Karl Alber Freiburg, 2007.

Obeyesekere, Gananath. *Medusa's Hair: An Essay on Personal Symbols and Religious Experience*. Chicago: University of Chicago Press, 1981.

———. *The Work of Culture: Symbolic Transformation in Psychoanalysis and Anthropology*. Chicago: University of Chicago Press, 1990.

Ochs, Elinor, and Lisa Capps. *Living Narrative: Creating Lives in Everyday Storytelling*. Cambridge, MA: Harvard University Press, 2001.

O'Flaherty, Wendy Doniger. *Dreams, Illusion and Other Realities*. Chicago: University of Chicago Press, 1984.

Ohnuma, Reiko. "The Story of Rūpāvatī: A Female Past Birth of the Buddha." *Journal of the International Association of Buddhist Studies* 23.1 (2000): 103–46.

Olivelle, Patrick. *Saṃnyāsa Upaniṣads: Hindu Scriptures on Asceticism and Renunciation*. New York: Oxford University Press, 1992.

Olsen, Michael Rohde, Michael Schredl, and Ingegerd Carlsson. "Sharing Dreams: Frequency, Motivations, and Relationship Intimacy." *Dreaming* 23.4 (2013): 245–55.

Ong, Roberto Keh. "Image and Meaning: The Hermeneutics of Traditional Chinese Dream Interpretation." In *Psycho-Sinology: The Universe of Dreams in Chinese Culture*, edited by Carolyn T. Brown, 47–54. Washington, D.C.: Woodrow Wilson International Center for Scholars, 1988.

———. *The Interpretation of Dreams in Ancient China*. Bochum: Studienverlag Brockmeyer, 1985.

Oppenheim, A. Leo. "The Interpretation of Dreams in the Ancient Near East, with a Translation of an Assyrian Dream-Book." *Transactions of the American Philosophical Society* 46 (1956): 179–373.

Orsborn, Matthew Bryan. "Chiasmus in the Early *Prajñāpāramitā*: Literary Parallelism Connecting Criticism and Hermeneutics in an Early *Mahāyāna Sūtra*." PhD diss., University of Hong Kong, 2012.

Ortner, Sherry B. "Patterns of History: Cultural Schemas in the Foundings of Sherpa Religious Institutions." In *Culture Through Time: Anthropological Approaches*, edited by Emiko Ohnuki-Tierney, 57–93. Stanford: Stanford University Press, 1990.

Otis, Laura. *Membranes: Metaphors of Invasion in Nineteenth-Century Literature, Science, and Politics*. Baltimore: Johns Hopkins University Press, 1999.

Owczarski, Wojciech. "The Ritual of Dream Interpretation in the Auschwitz Concentration Camp." *Dreaming* 27.4 (2017): 278–89.

Owen, Stephen, ed. *The Cambridge History of Chinese Literature, Volume 1: To 1375*. Cambridge: Cambridge University Press, 2010.

Pagel, Ulrich. *The Bodhisattvapiṭaka: Its Doctrines, Practices and Their Position in Mahāyāna Literature*. Tring: Institute of Buddhist Studies, 1995.

Pandya, Vishvajit. "Forest Smells and Spider Webs: Ritualized Dream Interpretation among Andaman Islanders." *Dreaming* 14 (2004): 136–50.

Pearcy, Lee T. "Theme, Dream, and Narrative: Reading the *Sacred Tales* of Aelius Aristides." *Transactions of the American Philological Association* 118 (1988): 377–91.

Pearson, Margaret J. *Wang Fu and the "Comments of a Recluse."* Tempe: Center for Asian Studies, Arizona State University, 1989.

Pedersen, K. Priscilla. "Notes on the *Ratnakūṭa* Collection." *Journal of the International Association of Buddhist Studies* 3 (1980): 60–66.

Peirce, Charles. *The Essential Peirce: Selected Philosophical Writings. Volume 2 (1893–1913)*. Bloomington: Indiana University Press, 1998.

Perkins, David. "The Imaginative Vision of *Kubla Khan*: On Coleridge's Introductory Note." In *Samuel Taylor Coleridge*, edited by Harold Bloom, 39–50. 2nd edition. New York: Bloom's Literary Criticism, 2010.

Perls, Frederick. *Gestalt Therapy Verbatim*. Compiled and edited by John O. Stevens. Moab, UT: Real People Press, 1969.

Peterson, Willard J. "Making Connections: 'Commentary on the Attached Verbalizations' of the *Book of Change*." *Harvard Journal of Asiatic Studies* 42 (1982): 67–116.

Petsalis-Diomidis, Alexia. *Truly Beyond Wonders: Aelius Aristides and the Cult of Asklepios*. Oxford: Oxford University Press, 2010.

Pines, Yuri. "From Teachers to Subjects: Ministers Speaking to the Rulers, from Yan Ying 晏嬰 to Li Si 李斯." In *Facing the Monarch: Modes of Advice in the Early Chinese Court*, edited by Garret P. S. Olberding, 69–99. Cambridge, MA: Harvard University Asia Center, 2013.

Pinney, Christopher. "Things Happen: Or, From Which Moment Does That Object Come?" In *Materiality*, edited by Daniel Miller, 256–72. Durham: Duke University Press, 2005.

———. "Visual Culture." In *The Material Culture Reader*, edited by Victor Buchli, 81–104. Oxford: Berg, 2002.

Pinte, Gudrun. "On the Origin of Taishō 1462, the Alleged Translation of the Pāli *Samantapāsādikā*." *Zeitschrift der Deutschen morgenländischen Gesellschaft* 160 (2010): 435–49.

Poirier, Sylvie. "'This Is Good Country. We Are Good Dreamers': Dreams and Dreaming in the Australian Western Desert." In *Dream Travelers: Sleep Experiences and Culture in the Western Pacific*, edited by Roger Ivar Lohmann, 107–25. New York: Palgrave Macmillan, 2003.

Pollock, Sheldon. *The Language of the Gods in the World of Men: Sanskrit, Culture, and Power in Premodern India*. Berkeley: University of California Press, 2006.

Poo Mu-chou 浦慕州. *Muzang yu shengsi—Zhongguo gudai zongjiao zhi xingsi* 墓葬與生死—中國古代宗教之省思. Taibei: Lianjing, 1993.

———. "Ritual and Ritual Texts in Early China." In *Early Chinese Religion, Part One: Shang through Han (1250 BC–220 AD)*, edited by John Lagerwey and Marc Kalinowski, 281–313. Leiden: E. J. Brill, 2009.

Pregadio, Fabrizio, ed. *The Encyclopedia of Taoism*. 2 vols., continuously paginated. London: Routledge, 2008.

Price, S. R. F. "The Future of Dreams: From Freud to Artemidorous." *Past & Present* 113 (1986): 3–37.

Puett, Michael J. "Genealogies of Gods, Ghosts and Humans: The Capriciousness of the Divine in Early Greece and Early China." In *Ancient Greece and China Compared*, edited by G. E. R. Lloyd and Jingyi Jenny Zhao, 160–85. Cambridge: Cambridge University Press, 2018.

———. "The Haunted World of Humanity: Ritual Theory from Early China." In *Rethinking the Human*, edited by J. Michelle Molina and Donald K. Swearer, 95–110. Cambridge, MA: Center for the Study of World Religions, Harvard University, 2010.

———. "Innovation as Ritualization: The Fractured Cosmology of Early China." *Cardozo Law Review* 28 (2006): 23–36.

———. "Manifesting Sagely Knowledge: Commentarial Strategies in Chinese Late Antiquity." In *The Rhetoric of Hiddenness in Traditional Chinese Culture*, edited by Paula M. Varsano, 303–31. Albany: State University of New York Press, 2016.

———. "'Nothing Can Overcome Heaven': The Notion of Spirit in the *Zhuangzi*." In *Hiding the World in the World: Uneven Discourses on the "Zhuangzi,"* edited by Scott Cook, 248–62. Albany: State University of New York Press, 2003.

———. "Ritual Disjunctions: Ghosts, Philosophy, and Anthropology." In *The Ground Between: Anthropologists Engage Philosophy*, edited by Veena Das, Michael Jackson, Arthur Kleinman, and Bhrigupati Singh, 218–33. Durham: Duke University Press, 2014.

———. "Ritualization as Domestication: Ritual Theory from Classical China." In *Grammars and Morphologies of Ritual Practices in Asia*, section 2: *Ritual Discourse, Ritual Performance in China and Japan*, edited by Lucia Dolce, Gil Raz, and Katja Triplett, 365–76. Wiesbaden: Harrassowitz Verlag, 2010.

———. "Sages, Gods, and History: Commentarial Strategies in Chinese Late Antiquity." *Antiquorum Philosophia* 3 (2009): 71–88.

———. "Social Order or Social Chaos." In *The Cambridge Companion to Religious Studies*, edited by Robert A. Orsi, 102–29. Cambridge: Cambridge University Press, 2012.

———. *To Become a God: Cosmology, Sacrifice, and Self-Divinization in Early China*. Cambridge, MA: Harvard University Press, 2002.

Pulleyblank, Edwin G. *Outline of Classical Chinese Grammar*. Vancouver: University of British Columbia Press, 1995.

Queen, Sarah A. "*Han Feizi* and the Old Master: A Comparative Analysis and Translation of *Han Feizi* Chapter 20, 'Jie Lao,' and Chapter 21, 'Yu Lao.'" In *Dao Companion to the Philosophy of Han Feizi*, edited by Paul R. Goldin, 197–256. Dordrecht: Springer, 2013.

Radich, Michael. "Ideas about 'Consciousness' in Fifth and Sixth Century Chinese Buddhist Debates on the Survival of Death by the Spirit, and the Chinese Background to *Amalavijñāna*." In *A Distant Mirror: Articulating Indic Ideas in Sixth and Seventh Century Chinese Buddhism*, edited by Chen-kuo Lin and Michael Radich, 471–512. Hamburg: Hamburg University Press, 2014.

———. "A 'Prehistory' to Chinese Debates on the Survival of Death by the Spirit, with a Focus on the Term *shishen* 識神/*shenshi* 神識." *Journal of Chinese Religions* 44 (2016): 105–26.

Raphals, Lisa. "Debates about Fate in Early China." *Études chinoises: Revue de l'Association française d'études chinoises* 33.2 (2014): 13–42.

———. *Divination and Prediction in Early China and Ancient Greece*. Cambridge: Cambridge University Press, 2013.

———. "Divination in the *Han shu* Bibliographic Treatise." *Early China* 32 (2008–9): 45–102.

de Rauw, Tom. "Beyond Buddhist Apology: The Political Use of Buddhism by Emperor Wu of the Liang Dynasty (r. 502–549)." PhD dissertation, Ghent University, 2008.

Rawls, John. *A Theory of Justice*. Cambridge, MA: Harvard University Press, 1971.

Redmond, Geoffrey, and Tze-ki Hon. *Teaching the "I Ching" (Book of Changes)*. Oxford: Oxford University Press, 2014.

Reed, Carrie E. "Motivation and Meaning of a 'Hodge-Podge': Duan Chengshi's *Youyang zazu*." *Journal of the American Oriental Society* 123.1 (2003): 121–45.

———. *A Tang Miscellany: An Introduction to "Youyang zazu."* New York: Peter Lang, 2003.

Renberg, Gil H. *Where Dreams May Come: Incubation Sanctuaries in the Greco-Roman World*. 2 vols., continuously paginated. Leiden: E. J. Brill, 2017.

Reynolds, Pamela. "Dreams and the Constitution of Self among the Zezuru." In *Dreaming, Religion and Society in Africa*, edited by M.C. Jędrej and Rosalind Shaw, 21–35. Leiden: E. J. Brill, 1992.

Riches, David. "Dreaming as Social Process, and Its Implications for Consciousness." In *Questions of Consciousness*, edited by A. Cohen and N. Rapport, 101–16. London: Routledge, 1995.

Richter, Antje. *Das Bild des Schlafes in der altchinesischen Literatur*. Hamburger Sinologische Schriften 4. Gossenberg: Ostasien Verlag, 2015.

———. "Empty Dreams and Other Omissions: Liu Xie's *Wenxin diaolong* Preface." *Asia Major* 3rd series 25.1 (2012): 83–110.

———. "Sleeping Time in Early Chinese Literature." In *Night-time and Sleep in Asia and the West: Exploring the Dark Side of Life*. Edited by Brigitte Steger and Lodewijk Brunt, 24–44. London: Routledge, 2004.

Ricoeur, Paul. *Freud and Philosophy: An Essay on Interpretation*. Translated by Denis Savage. New Haven: Yale University Press, 1970.

Robb, Alice. *Why We Dream: The Transformative Power of Our Nightly Journey*. Boston: Houghton Mifflin Harcourt, 2018.

Robbins, Joel. "Dreaming and the Defeat of Charisma: Disconnecting Dreams from Leadership among the Urapmin of Papua New Guinea." In *Dream Travelers: Sleep*

Experiences and Culture in the Western Pacific, edited by Roger Ivar Lohmann, 19–41. New York: Palgrave Macmillan, 2003.
Robert, Jean-Noël. *Le sûtra du Lotus*. Paris: Fayard, 1997.
Robinson, Lady Stearn, and Tom Corbett. *The Dreamer's Dictionary from A to Z: 3,000 Magical Mirrors to Reveal the Meaning of Your Dreams*. New York: Warner Books, 1974.
Robinson, T. M. *Heraclitus: Fragments: A Text and Translation with a Commentary*. Toronto: University of Toronto Press, 1987.
Rock, Andrea. *The Mind at Night: The New Science of How and Why We Dream*. New York: Basic Books, 2004.
Rogers, Michael C. *The Chronicle of Fu Chien: A Case of Exemplar History*. Berkeley: University of California Press, 1968.
Rorty, Richard. *Contingency, Irony and Solidarity*. Cambridge: Cambridge University Press, 1989.
Roth, Harold D. "The Classical Daoist Concept of *Li* 理 (Pattern) and Early Chinese Cosmology." *Early China* 35–36 (2012–13): 157–84.
Rulu. *Teachings of the Buddha: Selected Mahāyāna Sutras*. Np: AuthorHouse, 2012.
Rutt, Richard. *The Book of Changes (Zhouyi)*. New York: RoutledgeCurzon, 1996.

Sabourin, Catherine, et al. "Dream Content in Pregnancy and Postpartum: Refined Exploration of Continuity between Waking and Dreaming." *Dreaming* 28.2 (2018): 122–39.
Sacks, Oliver W. *An Anthropologist on Mars: Seven Paradoxical Tales*. New York: Knopf, 1995.
Sahlins, Marshall. *Apologies to Thucydides: Understanding History as Culture and Vice Versa*. Chicago: University of Chicago Press, 2004.
———. *How "Natives" Think: About Captain Cook, For Example*. Chicago: University of Chicago Press, 1995.
———. *The Use and Abuse of Biology: An Anthropological Critique of Sociobiology*. Ann Arbor: University of Michigan Press, 1976.
Salguero, C. Pierce. "'On Eliminating Disease': Translations of the Medical Chapter from the Chinese Versions of the *Sutra of Golden Light*." *eJournal of Indian Medicine* 6 (2013): 21–43.
Sanders, Graham. "A New Note on *Shishuo xinyu*." *Early Medieval China* 20 (2014): 9–22.
Sanft, Charles. "Edict of Monthly Ordinances for the Four Seasons in Fifty Articles from 5 CE: Introduction to the Wall Inscription Discovered at Xuanquanzhi, with Annotated Translation." *Early China* 32 (2008–09): 125–208.
Saussy, Haun. *Great Walls of Discourse and Other Adventures in Cultural China*. Cambridge, MA: Harvard University Asia Center, 2001.
———. *The Problem of a Chinese Aesthetic*. Stanford: Stanford University Press, 1993.
———. *Translation as Citation: Zhuangzi Inside Out*. Oxford: Oxford University Press, 2017.
Schaberg, David. *A Patterned Past: Form and Thought in Early Chinese Historiography*. Cambridge, MA: Harvard University Press, 2001.
———. "The *Zhouli* as Constitutional Text." In *Statecraft and Classical Learning: The Rituals of Zhou in East Asian History*, edited by Benjamin A. Elman and Martin Kern, 33–63. Leiden: E. J. Brill, 2010.
Schafer, Edward H. *Pacing the Void: T'ang Approaches to the Stars*. Berkeley: University of California Press, 1977.

Scharff, David E. "Psychoanalysis in China: An Essay on the Recent Literature in English." *The Psychoanalytic Quarterly* 85.4 (2016): 1037–67.
Schilling, Dennis. *Spruch und Zahl: Die chinesischen Oraklbücher "Kanon der Höchsten Geheimen" (Taixuanjing) und "Wald der Wandlungen" (Yilin) aus der Han-Zeit*. Aalen: Scientia Verlag, 1998.
Schipper, Kristofer M., and Franciscus Verellen, eds. *The Taoist Canon: A Historical Companion to the Daozang*. Chicago: University of Chicago Press, 2004.
Schmitt, Jean-Claude. "The Liminality and Centrality of Dreams in the Medieval West." In *Dream Cultures: Explorations in the Comparative History of Dreaming*, edited by David Shulman and Guy G. Stroumsa, 274–87. New York: Oxford University Press, 1999.
Schnepel, Burkhard. "'In Sleep a King…': The Politics of Dreaming in a Cross-Cultural Perspective." *Paideuma: Mitteilungen zur Kulturkunde* 51 (2005): 209–20.
Schredl, Michael. "Frequency of Precognitive Dreams: Association with Dream Recall and Personality Variables." *Journal of the Society for Psychical Research* 73.2 (2009): 83–91.
———. "Positive and Negative Attitudes towards Dreaming: A Representative Study." *Dreaming* 23.3 (2013): 194–201.
———. "Reading Books about Dream Interpretation: Gender Differences." *Dreaming* 20.4 (2010): 248–53.
———. "Theorizing about the Continuity between Waking and Dreaming." *Dreaming* 27 (2017): 351–59.
Schredl, Michael, and Anja S. Göritz. "Dream Recall Frequency, Attitude toward Dreams, and the Big Five Personality Factors." *Dreaming* 27.1 (2017): 49–58.
Schredl, Michael, and Edgar Piel. "Interest in Dream Interpretation: A Gender Difference." *Dreaming* 18.1 (2008): 11–15.
Schultz, Celia E. "Argument and Anecdote in Cicero's *De divinatione*." In *Maxima Debetur Magistro Reverentia: Essays on Rome and the Roman Tradition in Honor of Russell T. Scott*, edited by P. B. Harvey, Jr., and C. Conybeare, 193–206. Como: New Press Edizioni, 2009.
———. *Commentary on Cicero De Divinatione I*. Ann Arbor: University of Michigan Press, 2014.
Schwartz, Sophie. "A Historical Loop of One Hundred Years: Similarities between 19th Century and Contemporary Dream Research." *Dreaming* 10 (2000): 55–66.
Schweitzer, Robert. "A Phenomenological Study of Dream Interpretation among the Xhosa-Speaking People in Rural South Africa." *Journal of Phenomenological Psychology* 27.1 (1996): 72–96.
Schwitzgebel, Eric. "Zhuangzi's Attitude Toward Language and His Skepticism." In *Essays on Skepticism, Relativism, and Ethics in the "Zhuangzi,"* edited by Paul Kjellberg and Philip J. Ivanhoe, 68–96. Albany: State University of New York Press, 1996.
Scioli, Emma, and Christine Walde. "Introduction." In *Sub Imagine Somni: Nighttime Phenomena in Greco-Roman Culture*, edited by Emma Scioli and Christine Walde, vii–xvii. Pisa: Edizioni ETS, 2010.
Seligman, Adam B., Robert P. Weller, Michael J. Puett, and Bennett Simon. *Ritual and Its Consequences: An Essay on the Limits of Sincerity*. New York: Oxford University Press, 2008.
Seligman, Martin E. P., Peter Railton, Roy F. Baumeister, and Chandra Sripada. *Homo Prospectus*. New York: Oxford University Press, 2016.

Selove, Emily, and Kyle Wanberg. "Authorizing the Authorless: A Classical Arabic Dream Interpretation Forgery." In *Mundus vult decipi: Estudios interdisciplinares sobre falsificación textual y literaria*, edited by Javier Martínez, 365–76. Madrid: Ediciones Clásicas, 2012.

Sen, Tansen. "Yijing and the Buddhist Cosmopolis of the Seventh Century." In *Texts and Transformations: Essays in Honor of the 75th Birthday of Victor H. Mair*, edited by Haun Saussy, 345–68. Amherst, NY: Cambria Press, 2018.

Sharf, Robert H. *Coming to Terms with Chinese Buddhism: A Reading of the Treasure Store Treatise*. Honolulu: University of Hawai'i Press, 2002.

Shaughnessy, Edward L. *I Ching: The Classic of Changes*. New York: Ballantine, 1996.

———. *Rewriting Early Chinese Texts*. Albany: State University of New York Press, 2006.

———. "Of Trees, a Son, and Kingship: Recovering an Ancient Chinese Dream." *Journal of Asian Studies* 77.3 (2018): 593–610.

———. *Unearthing the Changes: Recently Discovered Manuscripts of the Yi jing (I Ching) and Related Texts*. New York: Columbia University Press, 2014.

———. "The Wangjiatai *Gui cang*: An Alternative to *Yi Jing* Divination." In *Facets of Tibetan Religious Tradition and Contacts with Neighbouring Cultural Areas*, edited by A. Cadonna and E. Bianchi, 95–126. Orientalia Venetiana 12. Florence: Olschki, 2002.

Sherman, Jeremy. *Neither Ghost nor Machine: The Emergence and Nature of Selves*. New York: Columbia University Press, 2017.

Shima Kunio 島邦男. *Inkyo bokuji sōrui* 殷墟卜辭綜類. Tokyo: Kyuko shoin, 1967.

Shirakawa Shizuka 白川靜. *Kōkotsu kimbungaku ronshū* 甲骨金文学論集. Kyoto: Hōyū shoten, 1974.

Shulman, David, and Guy G. Stroumsa. "Introduction." In *Dream Cultures: Explorations in the Comparative History of Dreaming*, edited by David Shulman and Guy G. Stroumsa, 3–13. New York: Oxford University Press, 1999.

Slingerland, Edward. *Mind and Body in Early China: Beyond Orientalism and the Myth of Holism*. New York: Oxford University Press, 2019.

Smail, Daniel Lord. *On Deep History and the Brain*. Berkeley: University of California Press, 2008.

Smith, Jonathan Z. *Drudgery Divine: On the Comparison of Early Christianities and the Religions of Late Antiquity*. Chicago: University of Chicago Press, 1990.

———. *Imagining Religion: From Babylon to Jonestown*. Chicago: University of Chicago Press, 1982.

———. *Map Is Not Territory: Studies in the History of Religions*. Leiden: E. J. Brill, 1978.

———. *Relating Religion: Essays in the Study of Religion*. Chicago: University of Chicago Press, 2004.

Smith, Richard J. *Fathoming the Cosmos and Ordering the World: The* Yijing *(*I-Ching, *or* Classic of Changes*) and Its Evolution in China*. Charlottesville: University of Virginia Press, 2008.

———. *Fortune-Tellers and Philosophers: Divination in Traditional Chinese Society*. Boulder: Westview Press, 1991.

Smith, Thomas E. "Ritual and the Shaping of Narrative: The Legend of Han Emperor Wu." PhD diss., University of Michigan, 1992.

Sosa, Ernest. "Dreams and Philosophy." *Proceedings and Addresses of the American Philosophical Association* 79 (2005): 7–18.

Soymié, Michel. "Les songes et leur interprétation en Chine." In *Sources orientales II: Les songes et leur interprétation*, 275–305. Paris: Le Seuil, 1959.

Spaeth, Barbette Stanley. "'The Terror That Comes in the Night': The Night Hag and Supernatural Assault in Latin Literature." In *Sub Imagine Somni: Nighttime Phenomena*

in Greco-Roman Culture, edited by Emma Scioli and Christine Walde, 231–58. Pisa: Edizioni ETS, 2010.
States, Bert O. *Dreaming and Storytelling*. Ithaca: Cornell University Press, 1993.
———. *Seeing in the Dark: Reflections on Dreams and Dreaming*. New Haven: Yale University Press, 1997.
Stephen, Michele. *A'aisa's Gifts: A Study of Magic and the Self*. Berkeley: University of California Press, 1995.
———. "Dreams of Change: The Innovative Role of Altered States of Consciousness in Traditional Melanesian Religion." *Oceania* 50.3 (1979): 3–22.
———. "Memory, Emotion, and the Imaginal Mind." In *Dreaming and the Self: New Perspectives on Subjectivity, Identity, and Emotion*, edited by Jeannette Marie Mageo, 97–129. Albany: State University of New York Press, 2003.
Stephens, John. "The Dreams of Aelius Aristides: A Psychological Interpretation." *International Journal of Dream Research* 5 (2012): 76–86.
Sterckx, Roel. *The Animal and the Daemon in Early China*. Albany: State University of New York Press, 2002.
———. *Food, Sacrifice, and Sagehood in Early China*. Cambridge: Cambridge University Press, 2011.
———. "Le pouvoir des sens: Sagesse et perception sensorielle en Chine ancienne." *Cahiers d'Institut Marcel Granet* 1: 71–92.
———. "Searching for Spirit: Shen and Sacrifice in Warring States and Han Philosophy and Ritual." *Extrême-Orient, Extrême-Occident* 29 (2007): 23–54.
Stewart, Charles. *Dreaming and Historical Consciousness in Island Greece*. Chicago: University of Chicago Press, 2017.
———. "Fields in Dreams: Anxiety, Experience, and the Limits of Social Constructionism in Modern Greek Dream Narratives." *American Ethnologist* 24.4 (1997): 877–94.
Stewart, Pamela J., and Andrew J. Strathern. "Dreaming and Ghosts among the Hagen and Duna of the Southern Highlands, Papua New Guinea." In *Dream Travelers: Sleep Experiences and Culture in the Western Pacific*, edited by Roger Ivar Lohmann, 43–59. New York: Palgrave Macmillan, 2003.
Stocking, George W., Jr. *Delimiting Anthropology: Occasional Inquiries and Reflections*. Madison: University of Wisconsin Press, 2001.
———. *Victorian Anthropology*. New York: Free Press, 1987.
Strassberg, Richard E. "Glyphomantic Dream Anecdotes." In *Idle Talk: Gossip and Anecdote in Traditional China*, edited by Jack W. Chen and David Schaberg, 178–93. Berkeley: University of California Press, 2014.
———. *Wandering Spirits: Chen Shiyuan's Encyclopedia of Dreams*. Berkeley: University of California Press, 2008.
Strickmann, Michel. *Chinese Poetry and Prophecy: The Written Oracle in East Asia*. Edited by Bernard Faure. Stanford: Stanford University Press, 2005.
———. "The *Consecration Sūtra*: A Buddhist Book of Spells." In *Chinese Buddhist Apocrypha*, edited by Robert E. Buswell, Jr., 75–118. Honolulu: University of Hawai'i Press, 1990.
———. "Dreamwork of Psycho-Sinologists: Doctors, Taoists, Monks." In *Psycho-Sinology: The Universe of Dreams in Chinese Culture*, edited by Carolyn T. Brown, 25–46. Washington, D.C.: Woodrow Wilson International Center for Scholars, 1988.
———. *Mantras et mandarins: Le bouddhisme tantrique en Chine*. Paris: Gallimard, 1996.
———. "Saintly Fools and Taoist Masters (Holy Fools)." *Asia Major* 3rd series 7.1 (1994): 35–57.
Strong, Pauline Turner. "A. Irving Hallowell and the Ontological Turn." *Hau: Journal of Ethnographic Theory* 7.1 (2017): 468–72.

Stroumsa, Guy G. "Dreams and Visions in Early Christian Discourse." In *Dream Cultures: Explorations in the Comparative History of Dreaming,* edited by David Shulman and Guy G. Stroumsa, 189–212. New York: Oxford University Press, 1999.

Struve, Lynn A. "Dreaming and Self-search during the Ming Collapse: The *Xue xiemeng biji*, 1642–1646." *T'oung Pao* 93 (2007): 159–92.

———. *The Dreaming Mind and the End of the Ming World*. Honolulu: University of Hawai'i Press, 2019.

Svenbro, Jesper. *Phrasikleia: An Anthropology of Reading in Ancient Greece*. Translated by Janet Lloyd. Ithaca: Cornell University Press, 1993.

Sviri, Sara. "Dreaming Analyzed and Recorded: Dreams in the World of Medieval Islam." In *Dream Cultures: Explorations in the Comparative History of Dreaming,* edited by David Shulman and Guy G. Stroumsa, 252–73. New York: Oxford University Press, 1999.

Swain, Simon, ed. *Seeing the Face, Seeing the Soul: Polemon's "Physiognomy" from Classical Antiquity to Medieval Islam*. Oxford: Oxford University Press, 2007.

Swanson, Paul L. *Clear Serenity, Quiet Insight: T'ien-t'ai Chih-i's Mo-ho chih-kuan*. 3 vols., continuously paginated. Honolulu: University of Hawai'i Press, 2018.

Swartz, Wendy. *Reading Philosophy, Writing Poetry: Intertextual Modes of Making Meaning in Early Medieval China*. Cambridge, MA: Harvard University Asia Center, 2018.

Swartz, Wendy, Robert Ford Campany, Yang Lu, and Jessey J. C. Choo, eds. *Early Medieval China: A Sourcebook*. New York: Columbia University Press, 2014.

Szpakowska, Kasia. "Dream Interpretation in the Ramesside Age." In *Ramesside Studies in Honour of K. A. Kitchen*, edited by Mark Collier and Steven Snape, 509–17. Bolton: Rutherford Press, 2011.

Takashima Ken-ichi 高嶋謙一. "Negatives in the King Wu-ting Bone Inscriptions." PhD diss., University of Washington, 1973.

Taves, Ann. "The Fragmentation of Consciousness and *The Varieties of Religious Experience*: William James's Contribution to a Theory of Religion." In *William James and a Science of Religions*, edited by Wayne Proudfoot, 48–72. New York: Columbia University Press, 2004.

———. *Religious Experience Reconsidered: A Building-Block Approach to the Study of Religion and Other Special Things*. Princeton: Princeton University Press, 2009.

Taylor, Charles. "Western Secularity." In *Rethinking Secularism*, edited by Craig Calhoun, Mark Juergensmeyer, and Jonathan VanAntwerpen, 31–53. New York: Oxford University Press, 2011.

Tedlock, Barbara, ed. *Dreaming: Anthropological and Psychological Interpretations*. 2nd edition. Santa Fe: School of American Research Press, 1992.

———. "Dreaming and Dream Research." In *Dreaming: Anthropological and Psychological Interpretations*, edited by Barbara Tedlock, 1–30. 2nd edition. Santa Fe: School of American Research Press, 1992.

———. "A New Anthropology of Dreaming." In *Dreams: A Reader on the Religious, Cultural, and Psychological Dimensions of Dreaming*, edited by Kelly Bulkeley, 249–64. New York: Palgrave Macmillan, 2001.

———. "Sharing and Interpreting Dreams in Amerindian Nations." In *Dream Cultures: Explorations in the Comparative History of Dreaming,* edited by David Shulman and Guy G. Stroumsa, 87–103. New York: Oxford University Press, 1999.

———. "Zuni and Quiché Dream Sharing and Interpreting." In *Dreaming: Anthropological and Psychological Interpretations*, edited by Barbara Tedlock, 105–31. 2nd edition. Santa Fe: School of American Research Press, 1992.

Tedlock, Dennis. "Mythic Dreams and Double Voicing." In *Dream Cultures: Explorations in the Comparative History of Dreaming*, edited by David Shulman and Guy G. Stroumsa, 104–18. New York: Oxford University Press, 1999.

Teng, Ssu-yu. *Family Instructions for the Yan Clan: Yen-shih Chia-hsun*. Leiden: E. J. Brill, 1966.

ter Haar, Barend. Review of Eggert, *Rede vom Traum*. *T'oung Pao* 85 (1999): 197–200.

Thompson, Evan. *Waking, Dreaming, Being: Self and Consciousness in Neuroscience, Meditation, and Philosophy*. New York: Columbia University Press, 2015.

Thompson, Laurence G. "Dream Divination and Chinese Popular Religion." *Journal of Chinese Religions* 16 (1988): 73–82.

Thote, Alain. "Shang and Zhou Funeral Practices: Interpretation of Material Vestiges." In *Early Chinese Religion, Part One: Shang through Han (1250 BC–220 AD)*, edited by John Lagerwey and Marc Kalinowski, 103–42. Leiden: E. J. Brill, 2009.

Tian, Xiaofei. *Beacon Fire and Shooting Star: The Literary Culture of the Liang (502–557)*. Cambridge, MA: Harvard University Press, 2007.

Tonkinson, Robert. "Ambrymese Dreams and the Mardu Dreaming." In *Dream Travelers: Sleep Experiences and Culture in the Western Pacific*, edited by Roger Ivar Lohmann, 87–105. New York: Palgrave Macmillan, 2003.

Tsukamoto Zenryū 塚本善隆. *A History of Early Chinese Buddhism*. Translated by Leon Hurvitz. 2 vols. Tokyo: Kodansha, 1985.

Turner, Edith. *Experiencing Ritual: A New Interpretation of African Healing*. Philadelphia: University of Pennsylvania Press, 1992.

Tuzin, Donald. "The Breath of a Ghost: Dreams and the Fear of the Dead." *Ethos* 3.4 (1975): 555–78.

Twitchett, Denis. *The Writing of Official History under the T'ang*. Cambridge: Cambridge University Press, 1992.

Tylor, Edward Burnett. *The Origins of Culture*. With an introduction by Paul Radin. Gloucester: Peter Smith, 1970. First published as Chapters I–X of *Primitive Culture* in 1871 by John Murray.

———. *Religion in Primitive Culture*. With an introduction by Paul Radin. Gloucester: Peter Smith, 1970. First published as Chapters XI–XIX of *Primitive Culture* in 1871 by John Murray.

Tzohar, Roy. "Imagine Being a Preta: Early Indian Yogācāra Approaches to Intersubjectivity." *Sophia* 56 (2017): 337–54.

———. *A Yogācāra Buddhist Theory of Metaphor*. Oxford: Oxford University Press, 2018.

Uexküll, Jakob von. *A Foray into the Worlds of Animals and Humans, with A Theory of Meaning*. Translated by Joseph D. O'Neil. Minneapolis: University of Minnesota Press, 2010.

Ullman, Montague. *Appreciating Dreams: A Group Approach*. New York: Cosimo, 2006.

Unger, Ulrich. "Die Fragmente des *So-Yü*." In *Studia Sino-Mongolica: Festschrift für Herbert Franke*, edited by Wolfgang Bauer, 373–400. Wiesbaden: Franz Steiner, 1979.

Unschuld, Paul U. *Huang Di Nei Jing Ling Shu: The Ancient Classic on Needle Therapy*. Berkeley: University of California Press, 2016.

van Els, Paul, and Sarah A. Queen, eds. *Between History and Philosophy: Anecdotes in Early China*. Albany: State University of New York Press, 2017.

van Zoeren, Steven. *Poetry and Personality: Reading, Exegesis, and Hermeneutics in Traditional China*. Stanford: Stanford University Press, 1991.

Vance, Brigid E. "Deciphering Dreams: How Glyphomancy Worked in Late Ming Dream Encyclopedic Divination." *Chinese Historical Review* 24 (2017): 5–20.

———. "Divining Political Legitimacy in a Late Ming Dream Encyclopedia: The Encyclopedia and Its Historical Context." *Extrême-Orient, Extrême-Occident* 42 (2018): 15–42.

———. "Exorcising Dreams and Nightmares in Late Ming China." In *Psychiatry and Chinese History*, edited by Howard Chiang, 17–36. London: Pickering & Chatto, 2014.

———. "Textualizing Dreams in a Late Ming Dream Encyclopedia." PhD diss., Princeton University, 2012.

Vann, Barbara, and Neil Alperstein. "Dream Sharing as Social Interaction." *Dreaming* 10.2 (2000): 111–19.

Verellen, Franciscus. "Evidential Miracles in Support of Taoism: The Inversion of a Buddhist Apologetic Tradition in Late Tang China." *T'oung Pao* 2nd series 78 (1992): 217–63.

Vogelsang, Kai. "The Shape of History: On Reading Li Wai-yee." *Early China* 37 (2014): 579–99.

Vovin, Alexander, Edward Vajda, and Étienne de la Vaissière. "Who Were the Kjet (羯) and What Language Did They Speak?" *Journal Asiatique* 304.1 (2016): 125–44.

Wagner, Rudolf G. "Imperial Dreams in China." In *Psycho-Sinology: The Universe of Dreams in Chinese Culture*, edited by Carolyn T. Brown, 11–24. Washington, D.C.: Woodrow Wilson International Center for Scholars, 1988.

Wakatsuki Toshihide 若槻 俊秀, Hasegawa Makoto 長谷川 慎, and Inagaki Akio 稲垣淳央, eds. *Hōon jurin no sōgōteki kenkyū: Omo to shite Hōon jurin shoroku Meishoki no honbun kōtei narabi ni senchū senyaku* 法苑珠林の總合的研究：主として 法苑珠林所錄 冥祥記 の本文校訂竝びに選注選譯. *Shinshū Sōgō Kenkyū Sho kenkyū kiyō* 眞宗総合研究所研究紀要 (*Annual Memoirs of the Otani Shin Buddhist Comprehensive Research Institute*) 25 (2007): 1–224.

Walde, Christine. "Dream Interpretation in a Prosperous Age? Artemidorous, the Greek Interpreter of Dreams." In *Dream Cultures: Explorations in the Comparative History of Dreaming*, edited by David Shulman and Guy G. Stroumsa, 121–42. New York: Oxford University Press, 1999.

Waley, Arthur. *The Book of Songs*. Edited with additional translations by Joseph R. Allen. Foreword by Stephen Owen. New York: Grove, 1996.

Walker, Matthew. *Why We Sleep: Unlocking the Power of Sleep and Dreams*. New York: Scribner, 2017.

Wang, Aihe. *Cosmology and Political Culture in Early China*. Cambridge: Cambridge University Press, 2000.

Wang Guoliang 王國良. *Han Wu Dongming ji yanjiu* 漢武洞冥記研究. Taipei: Wenshizhe chubanshe, 1989.

———. *Mingxiang ji yanjiu* 冥祥記研究. Taibei: Wenshizhe chubanshe, 1999.

———. *Wei Jin nanbeichao zhiguai xiaoshuo yanjiu* 魏晋南北朝志怪小説研究. Taipei: Wenshizhe chubanshe, 1984.

Wang Li 王力. *Wang Li Gu Hanyu zidian* 王力古漢語字典. Beijing: Zhonghua shuju, 2000.

Wang Qing 王青. *Zhongguo shenhua yanjiu* 中国神话研究. Beijing: Zhonghua shuju, 2010.

Wang Zijin 王子今. *Changsha jiandu yanjiu* 长沙简牍研究. Beijing: Zhongguo shehui kexue chubanshe, 2017.

Wansbrough, John. *Quranic Studies: Sources and Methods of Scriptural Interpretation*. New York: Prometheus, 2004.

Watson, Burton. *The Complete Works of Chuang Tzu*. New York: Columbia University Press, 1968.

Wechsler, Howard. *Offerings of Jade and Silk: Ritual and Symbol in the Legitimation of the T'ang Dynasty*. New Haven: Yale University Press, 1985.

Weinstein, Stanley. *Buddhism under the T'ang*. Cambridge: Cambridge University Press, 1987.

Wheeler, Wendy. *The Whole Creature: Complexity, Biosemiotics and the Evolution of Culture*. London: Lawrence & Wishart, 2006.

White, Jonathan W. *Midnight in America: Darkness, Sleep, and Dreams during the Civil War*. Chapel Hill: University of North Carolina Press, 2017.

Wilkinson, Endymion. *Chinese History: A New Manual*. 4th edition. Cambridge, MA: Harvard University Press, 2015.

Williams, Paul. *Mahāyāna Buddhism: The Doctrinal Foundations*. 2nd edition. London: Routledge, 2009.

Wilson, Thomas. "Spirits and the Soul in Confucian Ritual Discourse." *Journal of Chinese Religions* 42 (2014): 185–212.

Windt, Jennifer M. *Dreaming: A Conceptual Framework for Philosophy of Mind and Empirical Research*. Cambridge, MA: MIT Press, 2015.

Windt, Jennifer M., and Thomas Metzinger. "The Philosophy of Dreaming and Self-Consciousness: What Happens to the Experiential Subject during the Dream State?" In *The New Science of Dreaming*, Volume 3: *Cultural and Theoretical Perspectives*, edited by Deirdre Barrett and Patrick McNamara, 193–247. Westport, CT: Praeger, 2007.

Wright, Arthur F. *Studies in Chinese Buddhism*. Edited by Robert M. Somers. New Haven: Yale University Press, 1990.

Xiao Ai 蕭艾. *Zhongguo gudai xiangshu yanjiu yu pipan* 中國古代相術研究與批判. Changsha: Yuelu shushe, 1996.

Xu Zhongshu 徐中舒. *Jiaguwen zidian* 甲骨文字典. Chengdu: Sichuan cishu chubanshe, 1988.

Yang Jianmin 楊健民. *Zhongguo gudai meng wenhua shi* 中國古代夢文化史. Beijing: Shehui kexue wenxian chubanshe, 2015.

Yelle, Robert. "The Peircean Icon and the Study of Religion: A Brief Overview." *Material Religion* 12.2 (2016): 241–45. DOI: 10.1080/17432200.2016.1172771.

Yifa. *The Origins of Buddhist Monastic Codes in China: An Annotated Translation and Study of the "Chanyuan qingqui."* Honolulu: University of Hawai'i Press, 2002.

Yoshikawa Tadao 吉川忠夫. *Liuchao jingshenshi yanjiu* 六朝精神史研究. Translated from *Rikuchō seishinshi kenkyū* (Kyoto: Dōhōsha, 1984) by Wang Qifa 王启发. Nanjing: Jiangsu renmin chubanshe, 2010.

Yu, Calvin Kai-Ching. "Typical Dreams Experienced by Chinese People." *Dreaming* 18.1 (2008): 1–10.

———. "We Dream Typical Themes Every Single Night." *Dreaming* 26.4 (2016): 319–29.

Yuan Ke 袁珂. *Zhongguo gudai shenhua* 中國古代神話. Beijing: Zhonghua shuju, 1960.

Zhan Shichuang 詹石窗, ed. *Meng yu dao: Zhonghua chuantong meng wenhua yanjiu* 夢與道：中華傳統夢文化研究. 2 vols. Beijing: Dongfang chubanshe, 2009.

Zhang Hanmo. *Authorship and Text-Making in Early China*. Boston and Berlin: Walter de Gruyter, 2018.

Zhang Jiefu 張捷夫. *Zhongguo sangzang shi* 中國喪葬史. Taibei: Wenjin, 1995.
Zhang Longxi. *Mighty Opposites: From Dichotomies to Differences in the Comparative Study of China*. Stanford: Stanford University Press, 1998.
Zhang Zhenjun. *Hidden and Visible Realms: Early Medieval Chinese Tales of the Supernatural and the Fantastic*. New York: Columbia University Press, 2018.
———. "Observations on the Life and Works of Liu Yiqing." *Early Medieval China* 20 (2014): 83–104.
Zheng Binglin 鄭炳林. *Dunhuang xieben jiemeng shu jiaolu yanjiu* 敦煌寫本解夢書校錄研究. Beijing: Minzu chubanshe, 2005.
Zheng Binglin 鄭炳林 and Yang Ping 羊萍. *Dunhuang ben mengshu* 敦煌本夢書. Lanzhou: Gansu wenhua chubanshe, 1995.
Zhu Hanmin 朱漢民 and Chen Songchang 陳松長. *Yuelu shuyuan cang Qin jian* 嶽麓書院藏秦簡. 2 vols. Shanghai: Shanghai cishu chubanshe, 2010.
Zhu Pingyi 祝平一. *Han dai de xiangren shu* 漢代的相人術. Taibei: Xuesheng shuju, 1990.
Zufferey, Nicolas. *Discussions critiques par Wang Chong*. Paris: Gallimard, 1997.
Zürcher, Erik. *The Buddhist Conquest of China: The Spread and Adaptation of Buddhism in Early Medieval China*. 3rd edition. Leiden: E. J. Brill, 2007.
Zysk, Kenneth G. *The Indian System of Human Marks*. Leiden: E. J. Brill, 2016.

Index

Italic page numbers refer to tables.

Harvard-Yenching Institute Monograph Series (titles now in print)

24. *Population, Disease, and Land in Early Japan, 645–900*, by William Wayne Farris
25. *Shikitei Sanba and the Comic Tradition in Edo Fiction*, by Robert W. Leutner
26. *Washing Silk: The Life and Selected Poetry of Wei Chuang (834?–910)*, by Robin D. S. Yates
28. *Tang Transformation Texts: A Study of the Buddhist Contribution to the Rise of Vernacular Fiction and Drama in China*, by Victor H. Mair
30. *Readings in Chinese Literary Thought*, by Stephen Owen
31. *Remembering Paradise: Nativism and Nostalgia in Eighteenth-Century Japan*, by Peter Nosco
33. *Escape from the Wasteland: Romanticism and Realism in the Fiction of Mishima Yukio and Oe Kenzaburo*, by Susan Jolliffe Napier
34. *Inside a Service Trade: Studies in Contemporary Chinese Prose*, by Rudolf G. Wagner
35. *The Willow in Autumn: Ryutei Tanehiko, 1783–1842*, by Andrew Lawrence Markus
36. *The Confucian Transformation of Korea: A Study of Society and Ideology*, by Martina Deuchler
37. *The Korean Singer of Tales*, by Marshall R. Pihl
38. *Praying for Power: Buddhism and the Formation of Gentry Society in Late-Ming China*, by Timothy Brook
39. *Word, Image, and Deed in the Life of Su Shi*, by Ronald C. Egan
41. *Studies in the Comic Spirit in Modern Japanese Fiction*, by Joel R. Cohn
42. *Wind Against the Mountain: The Crisis of Politics and Culture in Thirteenth-Century China*, by Richard L. Davis
43. *Powerful Relations: Kinship, Status, and the State in Sung China (960–1279)*, by Beverly Bossler
44. *Limited Views: Essays on Ideas and Letters*, by Qian Zhongshu; selected and translated by Ronald Egan
45. *Sugar and Society in China: Peasants, Technology, and the World Market*, by Sucheta Mazumdar
49. *Precious Volumes: An Introduction to Chinese Sectarian Scriptures from the Sixteenth and Seventeenth Centuries*, by Daniel L. Overmyer
50. *Poetry and Painting in Song China: The Subtle Art of Dissent*, by Alfreda Murck
51. *Evil and/or/as the Good: Omnicentrism, Intersubjectivity, and Value Paradox in Tiantai Buddhist Thought*, by Brook Ziporyn

53. *Articulated Ladies: Gender and the Male Community in Early Chinese Texts*, by Paul Rouzer
55. *Allegories of Desire: Esoteric Literary Commentaries of Medieval Japan*, by Susan Blakeley Klein
56. *Printing for Profit: The Commercial Publishers of Jianyang, Fujian (11th-17th Centuries)*, by Lucille Chia
57. *To Become a God: Cosmology, Sacrifice, and Self-Divinization in Early China*, by Michael J. Puett
58. *Writing and Materiality in China: Essays in Honor of Patrick Hanan*, edited by Judith T. Zeitlin and Lydia H. Liu
59. Rulin waishi *and Cultural Transformation in Late Imperial China*, by Shang Wei
60. *Words Well Put: Visions of Poetic Competence in the Chinese Tradition*, by Graham Sanders
61. *Householders: The Reizei Family in Japanese History*, by Steven D. Carter
62. *The Divine Nature of Power: Chinese Ritual Architecture at the Sacred Site of Jinci*, by Tracy Miller
63. *Beacon Fire and Shooting Star: The Literary Culture of the Liang (502–557)*, by Xiaofei Tian
64. *Lost Soul: "Confucianism" in Contemporary Chinese Academic Discourse*, by John Makeham
65. *The Sage Learning of Liu Zhi: Islamic Thought in Confucian Terms*, by Sachiko Murata, William C. Chittick, and Tu Weiming
66. *Through a Forest of Chancellors: Fugitive Histories in Liu Yuan's* Lingyan ge, *an Illustrated Book from Seventeenth-Century Suzhou*, by Anne Burkus-Chasson
67. *Empire of Texts in Motion: Chinese, Korean, and Taiwanese Transculturations of Japanese Literature*, by Karen Laura Thornber
68. *Empire's Twilight: Northeast Asia Under the Mongols*, by David M. Robinson
69. *Ancestors, Virgins, and Friars: Christianity as a Local Religion in Late Imperial China*, by Eugenio Menegon
70. *Manifest in Words, Written on Paper: Producing and Circulating Poetry in Tang Dynasty China*, by Christopher M. B. Nugent
71. *The Poetics of Sovereignty: On Emperor Taizong of the Tang Dynasty*, by Jack W. Chen
72. *Ancestral Memory in Early China*, by K. E. Brashier
73. *'Dividing the Realm in Order to Govern': The Spatial Organization of the Song State*, by Ruth Mostern
74. *The Dynamics of Masters Literature: Early Chinese Thought from Confucius to Han Feizi*, by Wiebke Denecke
75. *Songs of Contentment and Transgression: Discharged Officials and Literati Communities in Sixteenth-Century North China*, by Tian Yuan Tan
76. *Ten Thousand Scrolls: Reading and Writing in the Poetics of Huang Tingjian and the Late Northern Song*, by Yugen Wang
77. *A Northern Alternative: Xue Xuan (1389-1464) and the Hedong School*, by Khee Heong Koh
78. *Visionary Journeys: Travel Writings from Early Medieval and Nineteenth-Century China*, by Xiaofei Tian

79. *Making Personas: Transnational Film Stardom in Modern Japan*, by Hideaki Fujiki
80. *Strange Eventful Histories: Identity, Performance, and Xu Wei's* Four Cries of a Gibbon, by Shiamin Kwa
81. *Critics and Commentators: The* Book of Poems *as Classic and Literature*, by Bruce Rusk
82. *Home and the World: Editing the Glorious Ming in Woodblock-Printed Books of the Sixteenth and Seventeenth Centuries*, by Yuming He
83. *Courtesans, Concubines, and the Cult of Female Fidelity*, by Beverly Bossler
84. *Chinese History: A New Manual, Third Edition*, by Endymion Wilkinson
85. *A Comprehensive Manchu-English Dictionary*, by Jerry Norman
86. *Drifting among Rivers and Lakes: Southern Song Dynasty Poetry and the Problem of Literary History*, by Michael Fuller
87. *Martial Spectacles of the Ming Court*, by David M. Robinson
88. *Modern Archaics: Continuity and Innovation in the Chinese Lyric Tradition, 1900-1937*, by Shengqing Wu
89. *Cherishing Antiquity: The Cultural Construction of an Ancient Chinese Kingdom*, by Olivia Milburn
90. *The Burden of Female Talent: The Poet Li Qingzhao and Her History in China*, by Ronald Egan
91. *Public Memory in Early China*, by K. E. Brashier
92. *Women and National Trauma in Late Imperial Chinese Literature*, by Wai-yee Li
93. *The Destruction of the Medieval Chinese Aristocracy*, by Nicolas Tackett
94. *Savage Exchange: Han Imperialism, Chinese Literary Style, and the Economic Imagination*, by Tamara T. Chin
95. *Shifting Stories: History, Gossip, and Lore in Narratives from Tang Dynasty China*, by Sarah M. Allen
96. *One Who Knows Me: Friendship and Literary Culture in Mid-Tang China*, by Anna Shields
97. *Materializing Magic Power: Chinese Popular Religion in Villages and Cities*, by Wei-Ping Lin
98. *Traces of Grand Peace: Classics and State Activism in Imperial China*, by Jaeyoon Song
99. *Fiction's Family: Zhan Xi, Zhan Kai, and the Business of Women in Late-Qing China*, by Ellen Widmer
100. *Chinese History: A New Manual, Fourth Edition*, by Endymion Wilkinson
101. *After the Prosperous Age: State and Elites in Early Nineteenth-Century Suzhou*, by Seunghyun Han
102. *Celestial Masters: History and Ritual in Early Daoist Communities*, by Terry F. Kleeman
103. *Transgressive Typologies: Constructions of Gender and Power in Early Tang China*, by Rebecca Doran
104. *Li Mengyang, the North-South Divide, and Literati Learning in Ming China*, by Chang Woei Ong
105. *Bannermen Tales (Zidishu): Manchu Storytelling and Cultural Hybridity in the Qing Dynasty*, by Elena Suet-Ying Chiu

106. *Upriver Journeys: Diaspora and Empire in Southern China, 1570–1850*, by Steven B. Miles
107. *Ancestors, Kings, and the Dao*, by Constance A. Cook
108. *The Halberd at Red Cliff: Jian'an and the Three Kingdoms*, by Xiaofei Tian
109. *Speaking of Profit: Bao Shichen and Reform in Nineteenth-Century China,* by William T. Rowe
110. *Building for Oil: Daqing and the Formation of the Chinese Socialist State,* by Hou Li
111. *Reading Philosophy, Writing Poetry: Intertextual Modes of Making Meaning in Early Medieval China,* by Wendy Swartz
112. *Writing for Print: Publishing and the Making of Textual Authority in Late Imperial China,* by Suyoung Son
113. *Shen Gua's Empiricism,* by Ya Zuo
114. *Just a Song: Chinese Lyrics from the Eleventh and Early Twelfth Centuries,* by Stephen Owen
115. *Shrines to Living Men in the Ming Political Cosmos,* by Sarah Schneewind
116. *In the Wake of the Mongols: The Making of a New Social Order in North China, 1200–1600,* by Jinping Wang
117. *Opera, Society, and Politics in Modern China,* by Hsiao-t'i Li
118. *Imperiled Destinies: The Daoist Quest for Deliverance in Medieval China,* by Franciscus Verellen
119. *Ethnic Chrysalis: China's Orochen People and the Legacy of Qing Borderland Administration,* by Loretta Kim
120. *The Paradox of Being: Truth, Identity, and Images in Daoism*, by Poul Andersen
121. *Feeling the Past in Seventeenth-Century China*, by Xiaoqiao Ling
122. *The Chinese Dreamscape, 300 BCE–800 CE*, by Robert Ford Campany
123. *Structures of the Earth: Metageographies of Early Medieval China*, by D. Jonathan Felt